Shojo Beat

il Moon

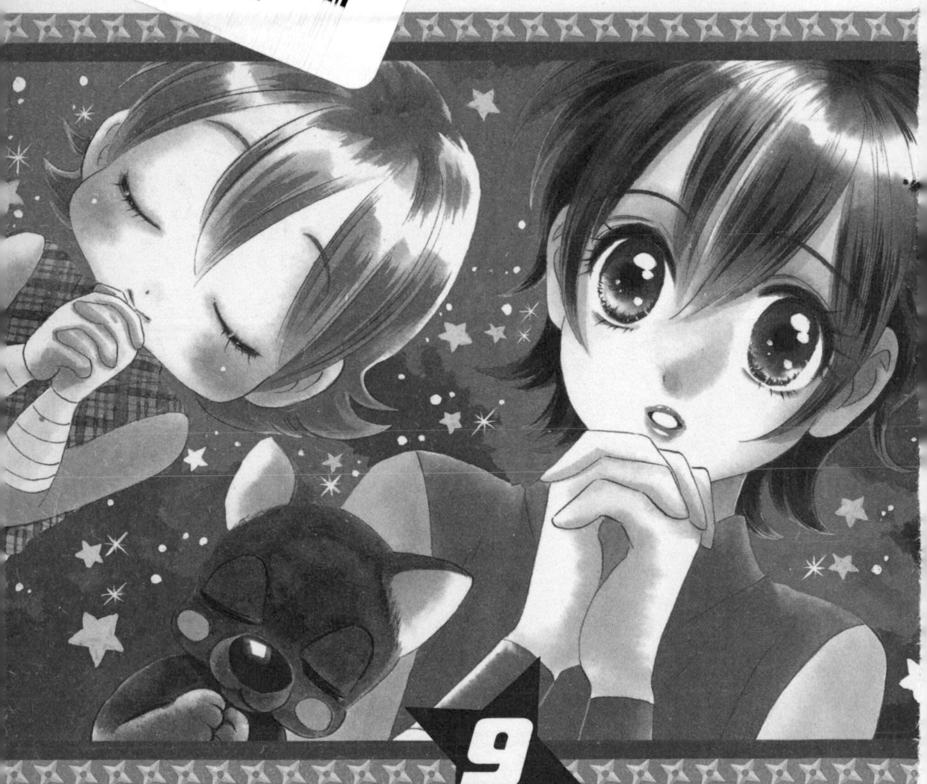

9

Story & Art by

Rinko Ueda

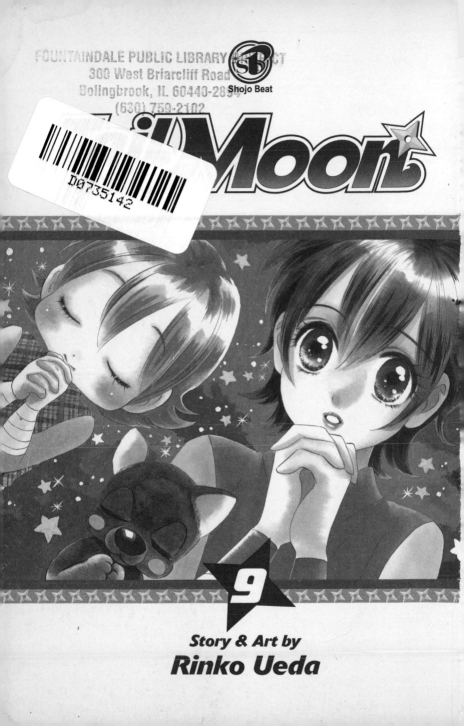

Volume 9

CONTENTS

Story Thus Far...

It is the Era of the Warring States. Usagi is a failure as a ninja, but she is a skilled herbalist. She is working hard to qualify as a ninja so she can be the bride of Hattori Hanzo (aka "Shimo no Hanzo")!

Usagi's feelings for Hanzo are finally mutual, and she can't wait to marry him once they return to Iga. Unfortunately, they're forced to go to Okazaki instead because they can't reveal their true identities to Ranmaru, Oda Nobunaga's page. On the way, Usagi learns that Nobunaga plans to attack Iga!

Hanzo heads out to Azuchi to find out more about Nobunaga's strategy. Meanwhile, Usagi and Goemon are ordered to gather information at the capital, posing as a husband and wife who run a dumpling shop. When Usagi hears that Nobunaga is at Honnoji, she goes there alone to investigate.

Usagi succeeds in getting information about the attack, but Ranmaru finds out she's a ninja! At a tea ceremony, Usagi uses a sleeping potion on the attendees in an attempt to escape, but Ranmaru discovers the tea's effects and orders Usagi's capture. Suddenly, Hanzo appears!

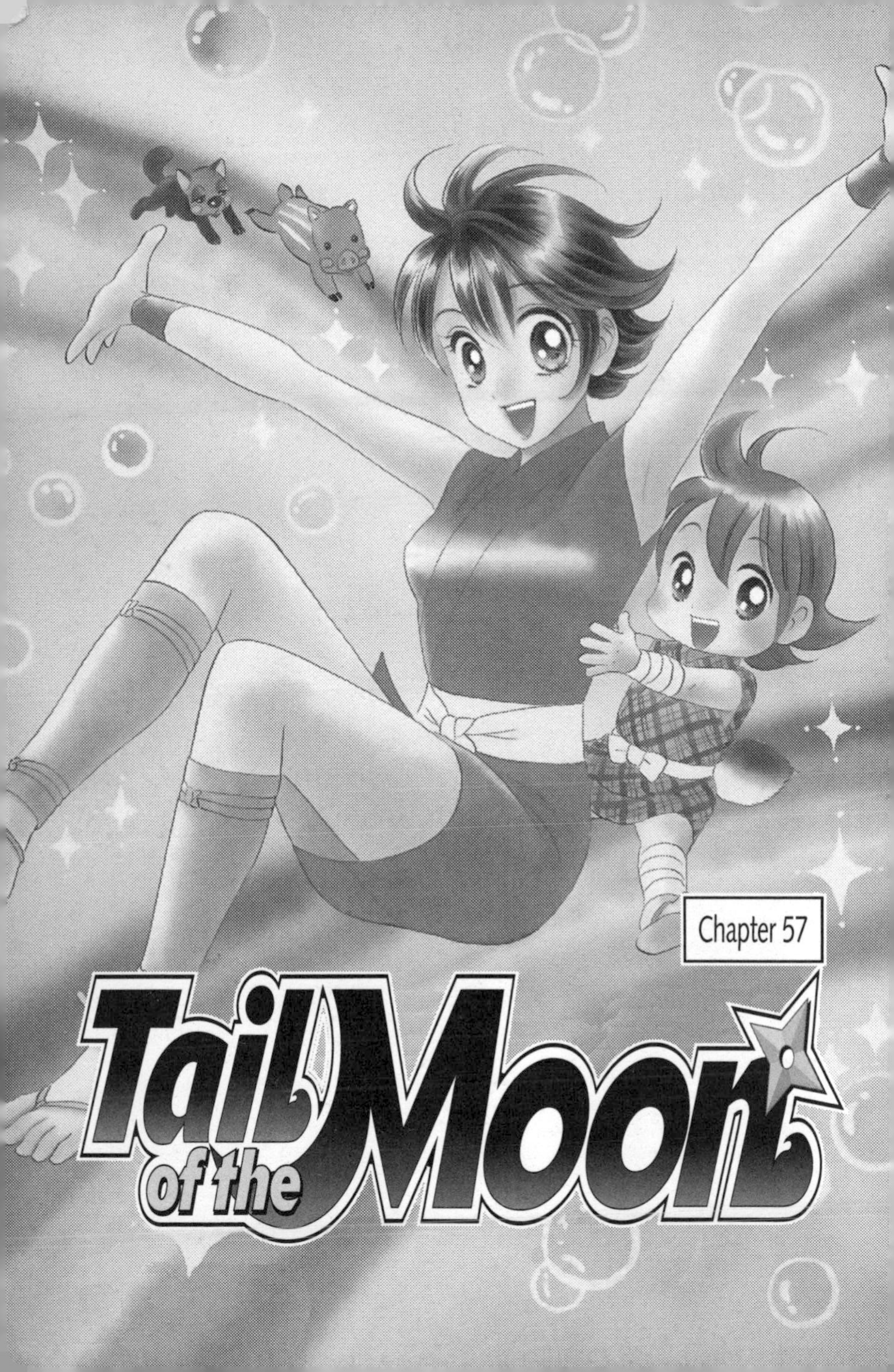
Chapter 57
Tail of the Moon

TAIL OF THE MOON EXTRA: TODAY'S MISSION

"I WANT TO SEE USAGI AND YURI WEARING CHINESE DRESSES!"

-MIINA KONDO, GUNMA PREFECTURE

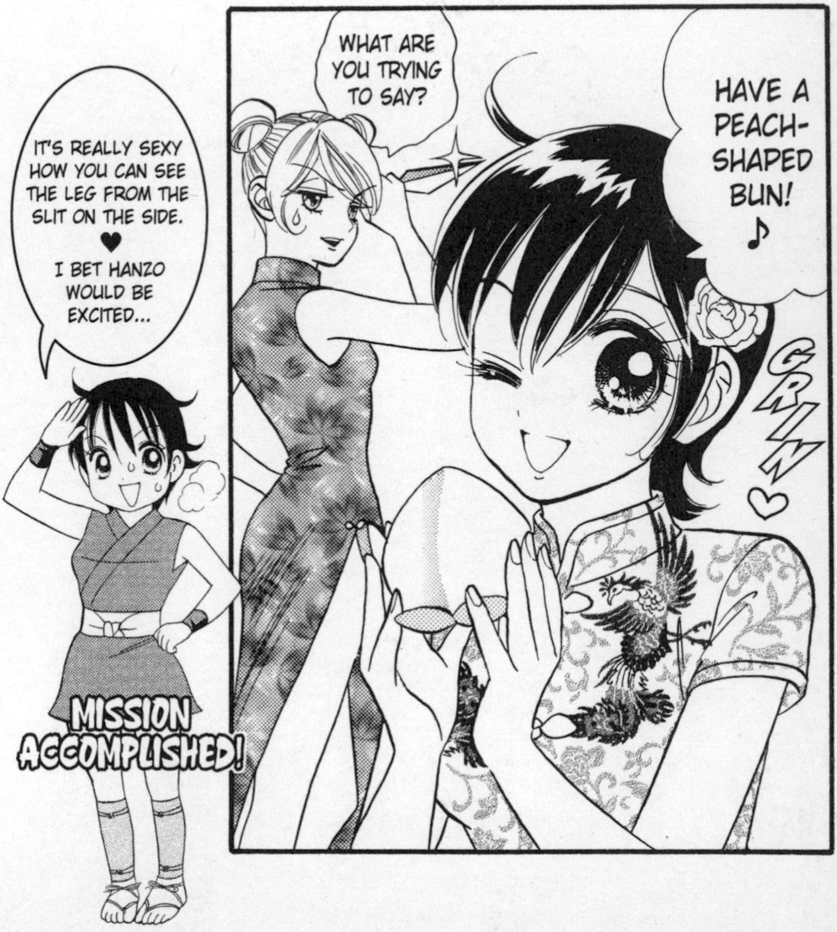
HAVE A PEACH-SHAPED BUN! ♪
GRIN ♥
WHAT ARE YOU TRYING TO SAY?
IT'S REALLY SEXY HOW YOU CAN SEE THE LEG FROM THE SLIT ON THE SIDE. ♥ I BET HANZO WOULD BE EXCITED...
MISSION ACCOMPLISHED!

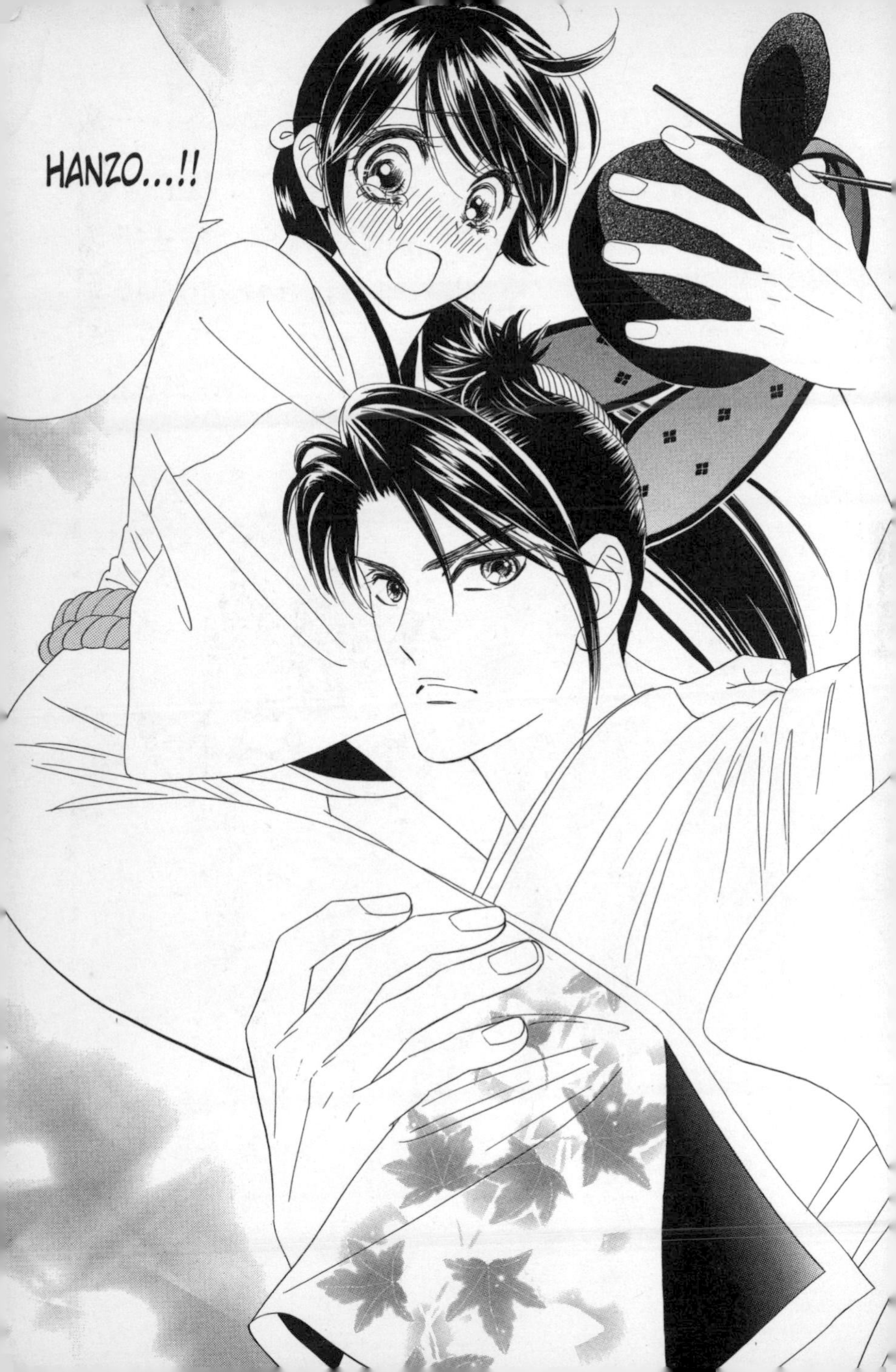
HANZO...!!

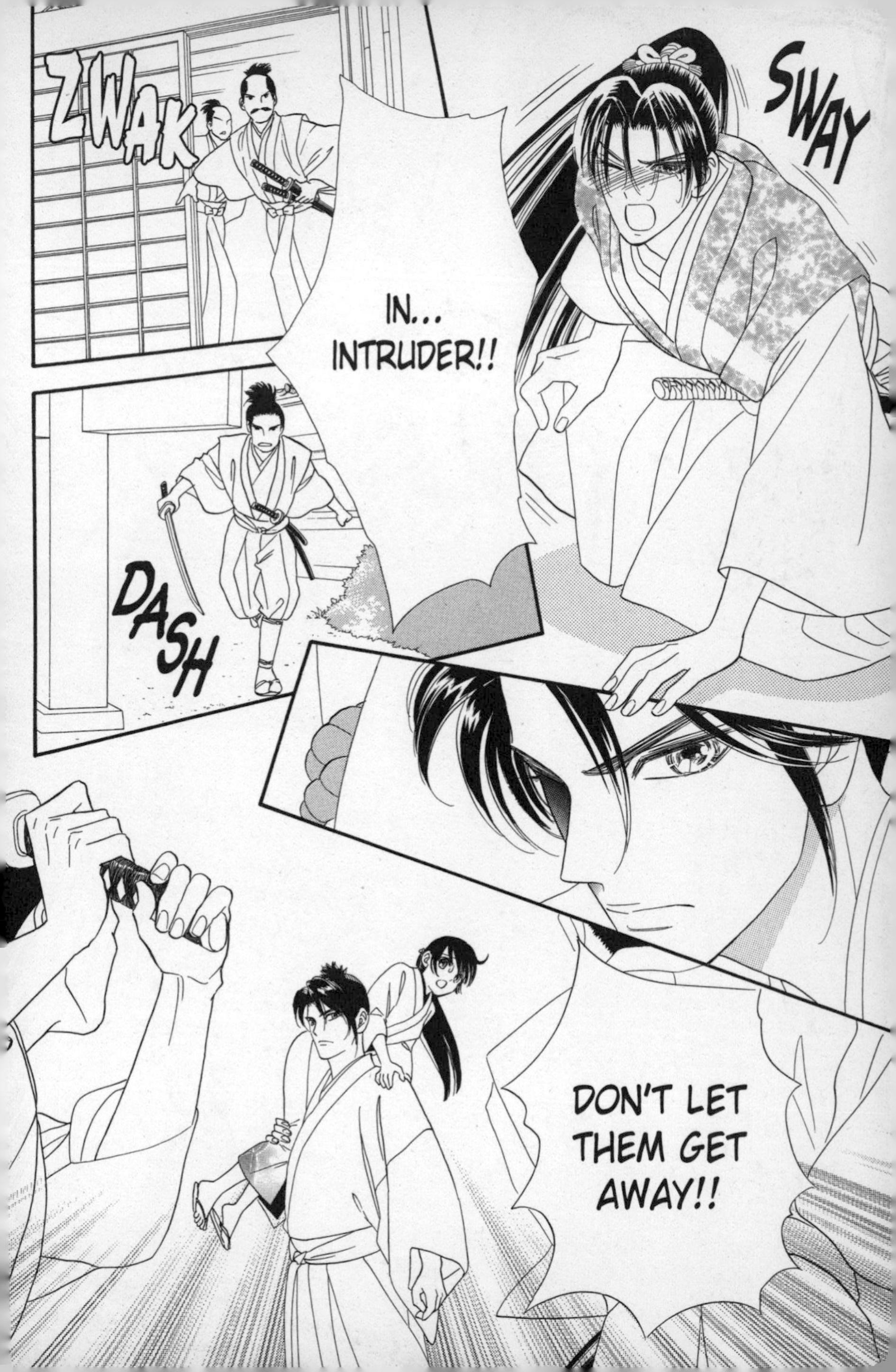
SWAY
IN... INTRUDER!!
ZWAK
DASH
DON'T LET THEM GET AWAY!!

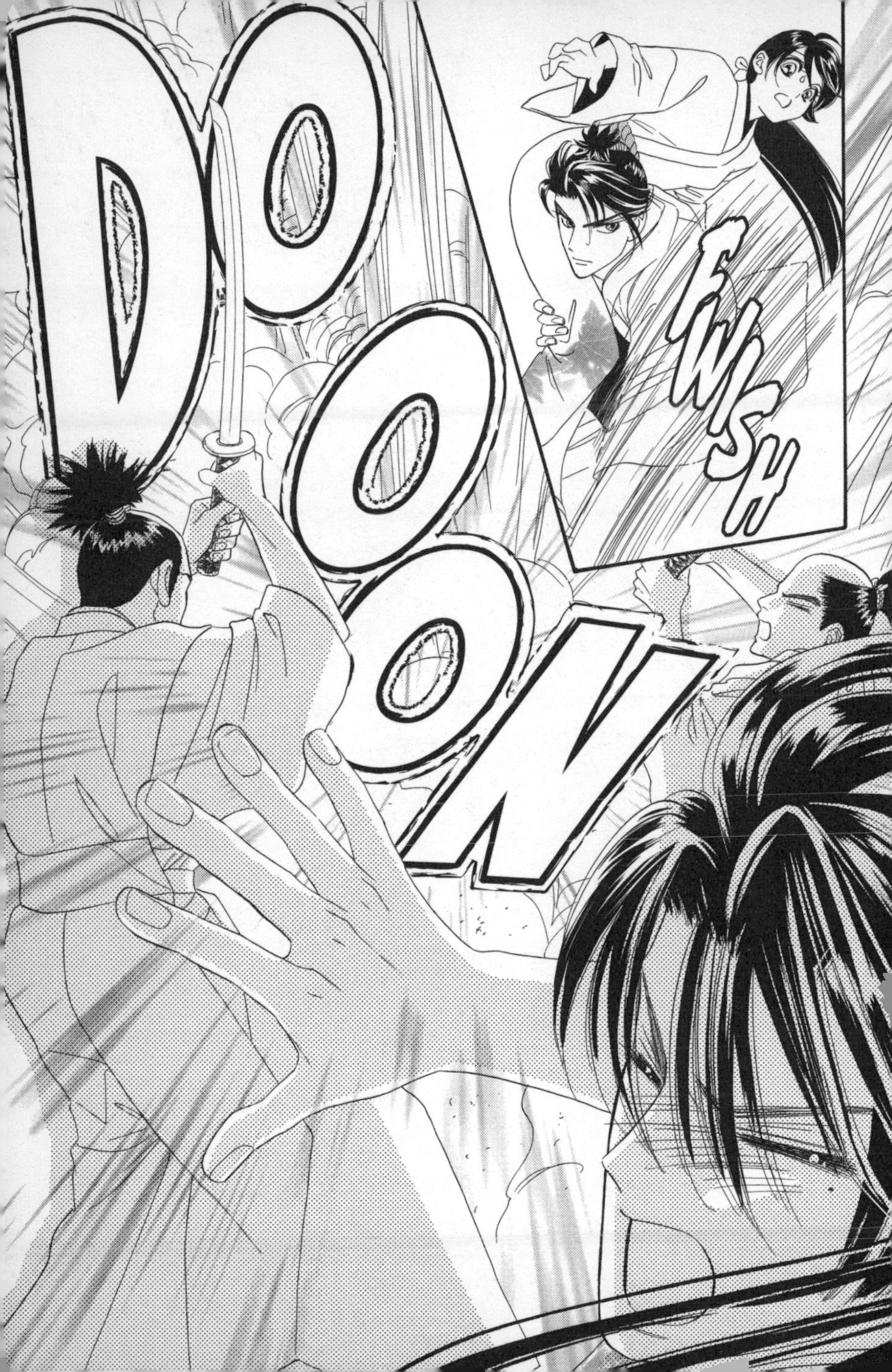
FWISH
DOOOON

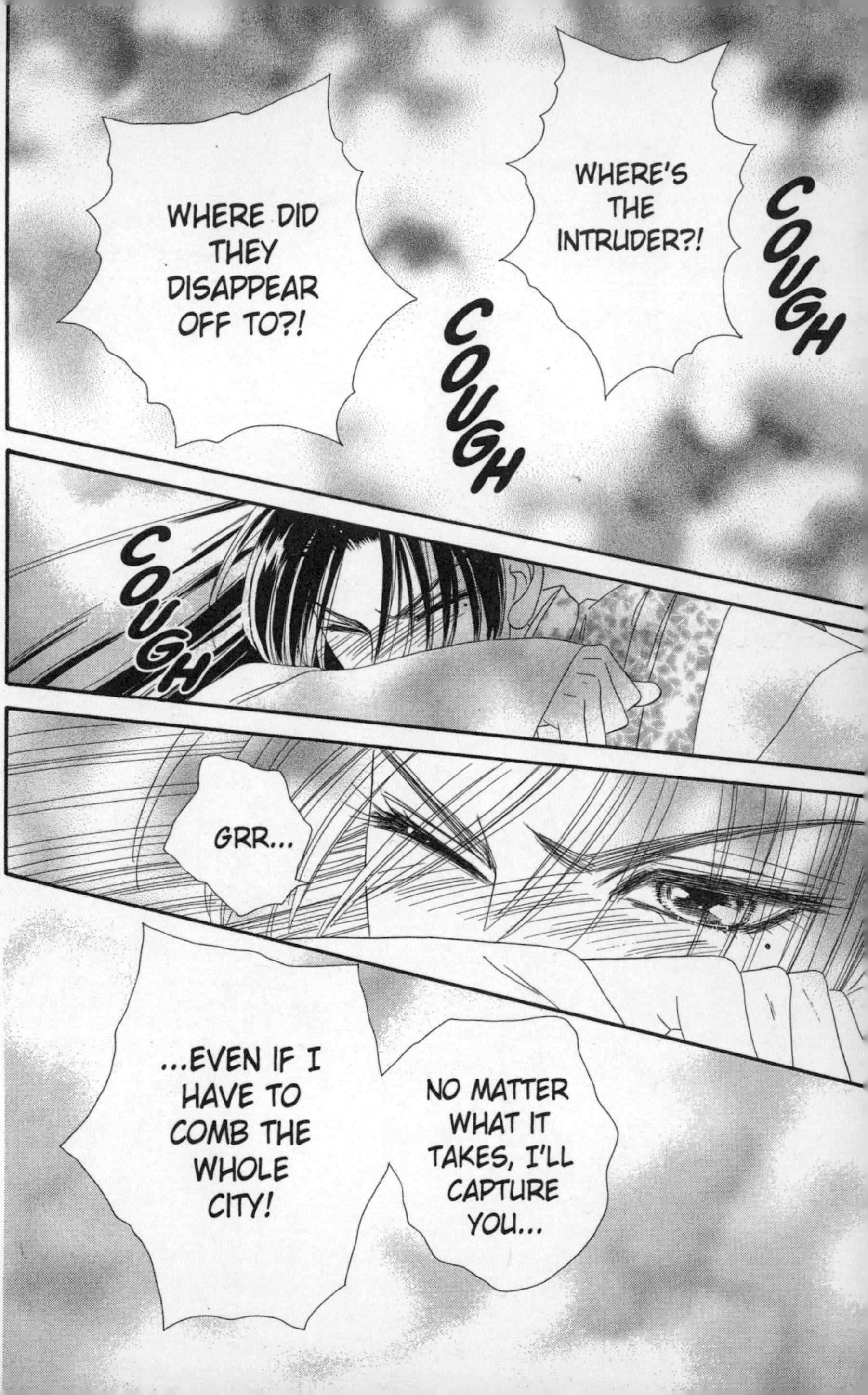
COUGH
WHERE'S THE INTRUDER?!
COUGH
WHERE DID THEY DISAPPEAR OFF TO?!
COUGH
GRR...
NO MATTER WHAT IT TAKES, I'LL CAPTURE YOU...
...EVEN IF I HAVE TO COMB THE WHOLE CITY!

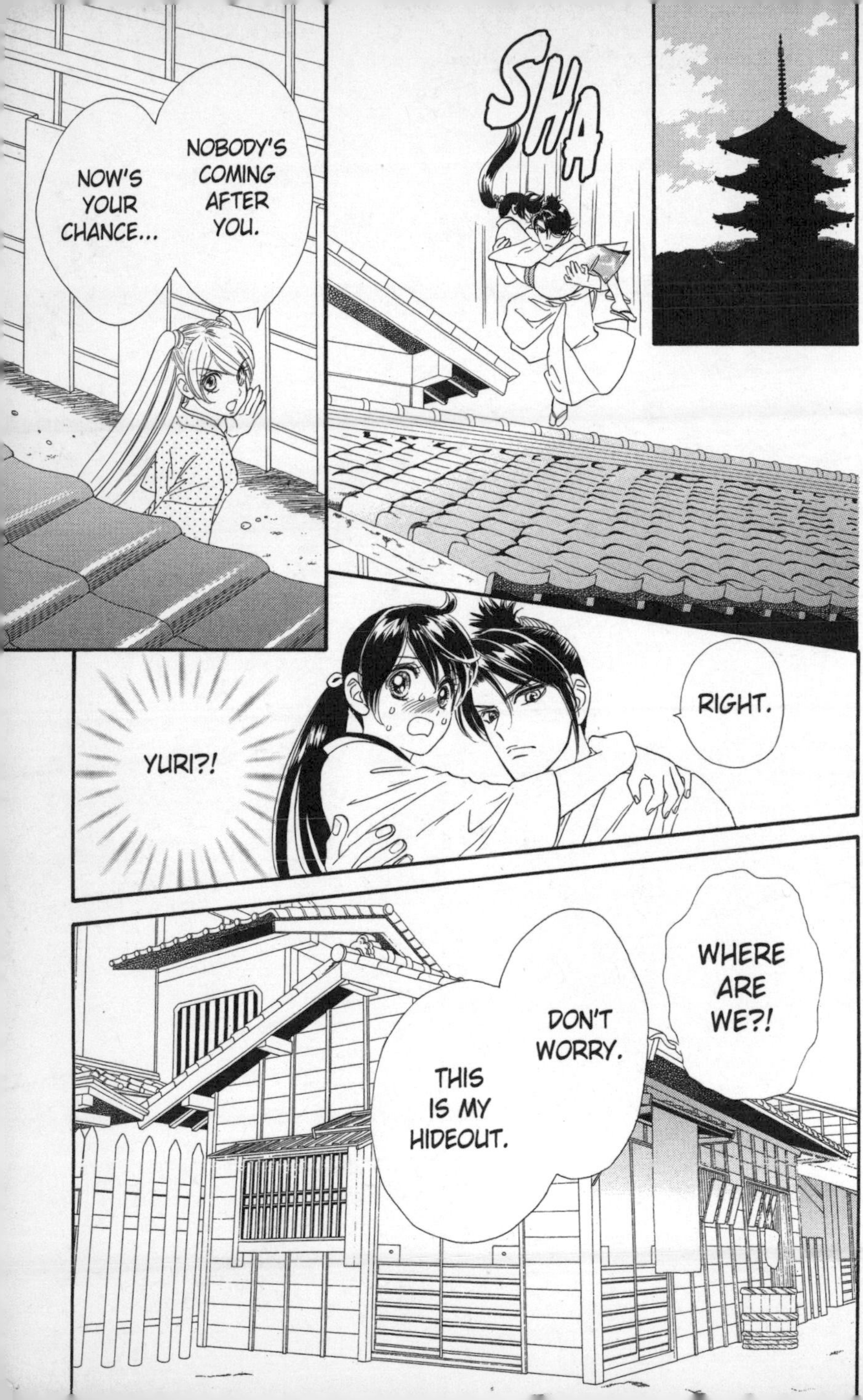
SHA
NOBODY'S COMING AFTER YOU.
NOW'S YOUR CHANCE...
RIGHT.
YURI?!
WHERE ARE WE?!
DON'T WORRY.
THIS IS MY HIDEOUT.

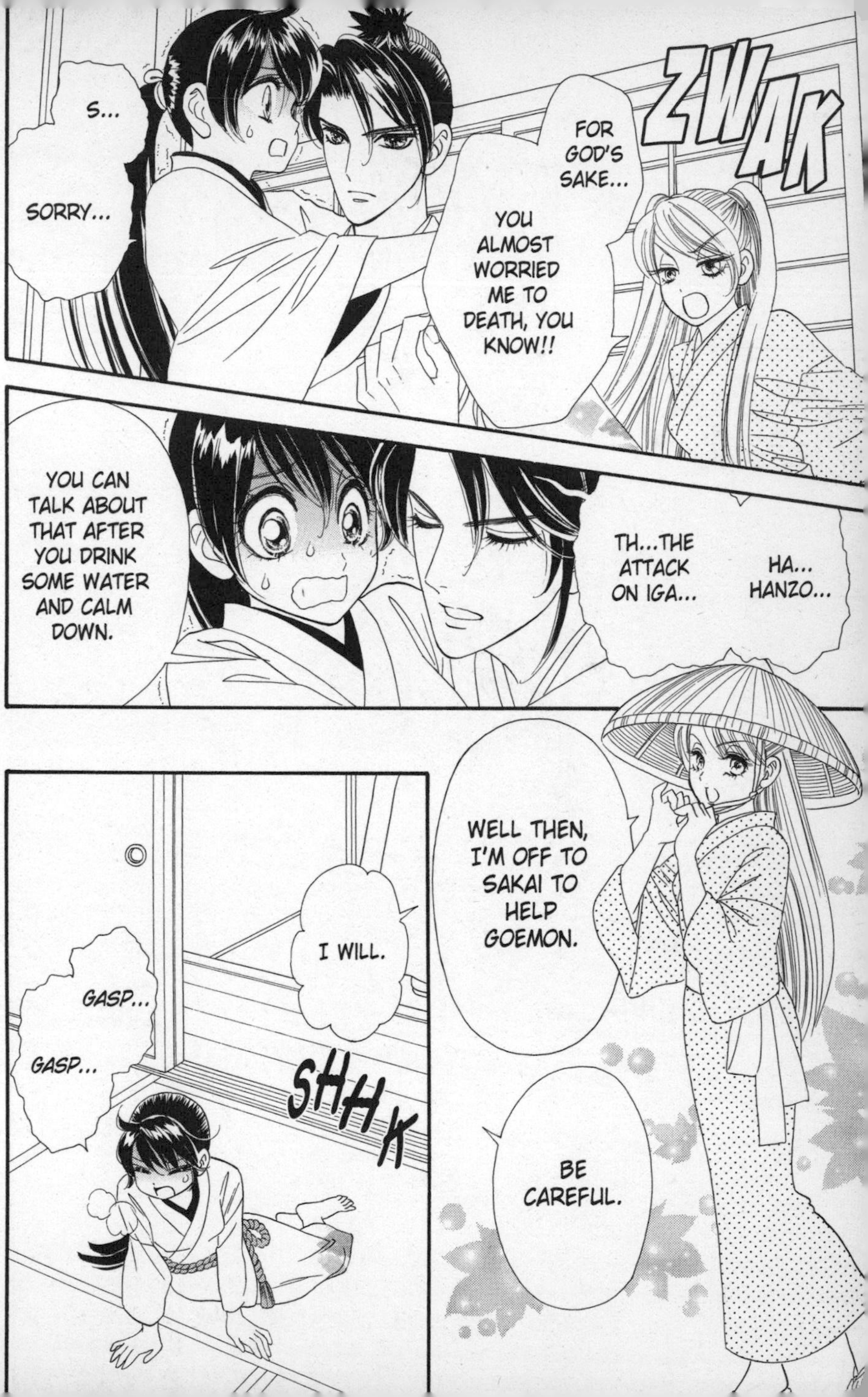
ZWAK
FOR GOD'S SAKE...
YOU ALMOST WORRIED ME TO DEATH, YOU KNOW!!
S...
SORRY...
HA... HANZO...
TH...THE ATTACK ON IGA...
YOU CAN TALK ABOUT THAT AFTER YOU DRINK SOME WATER AND CALM DOWN.
WELL THEN, I'M OFF TO SAKAI TO HELP GOEMON.
BE CAREFUL.
I WILL.
SHHK
GASP...
GASP...

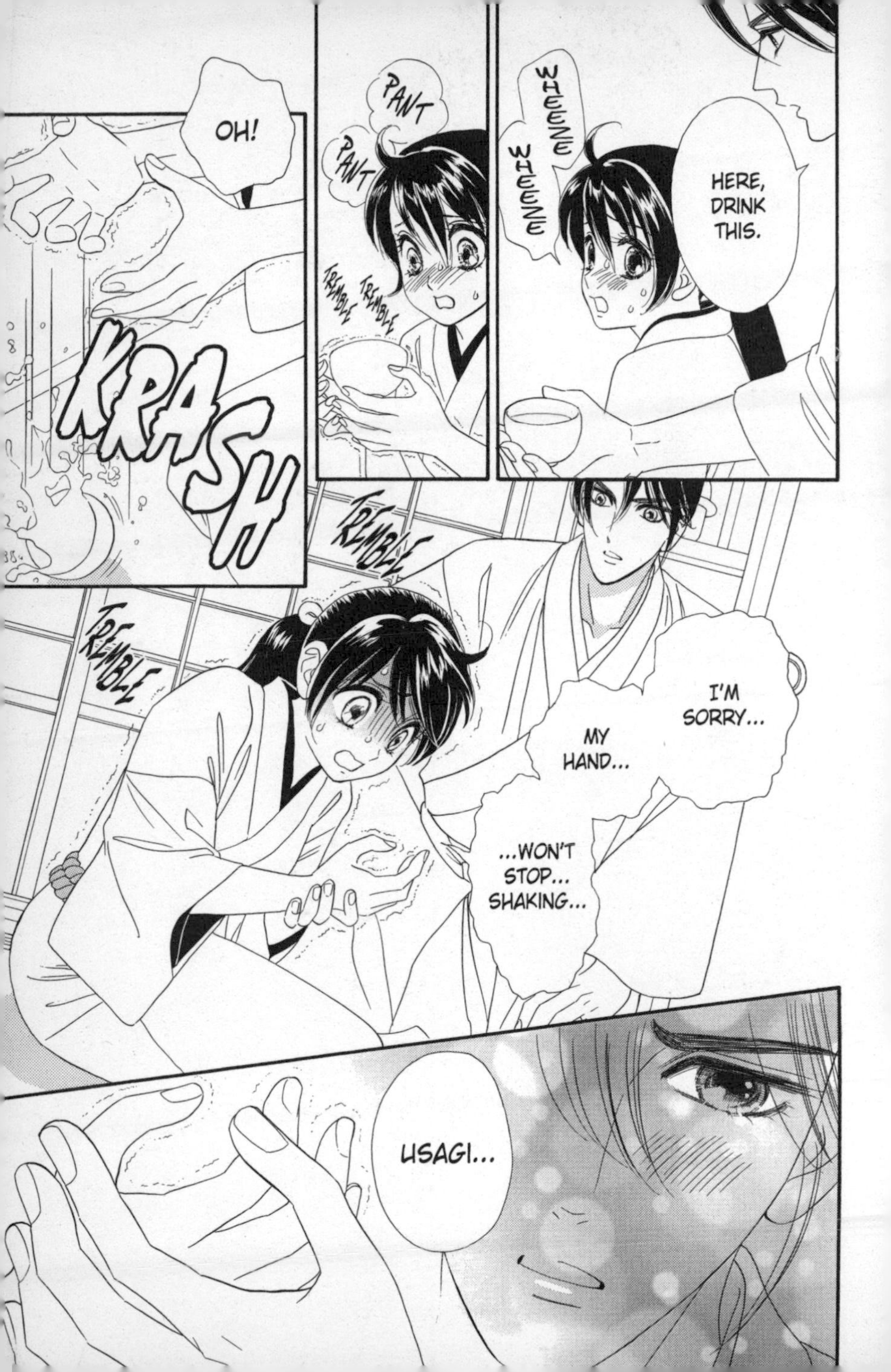
HERE, DRINK THIS.
WHEEZE
WHEEZE
PANT
PANT
TREMBLE
TREMBLE
OH!
KRASH
TREMBLE
TREMBLE
I'M SORRY...
MY HAND...
...WON'T STOP... SHAKING...
USAGI...

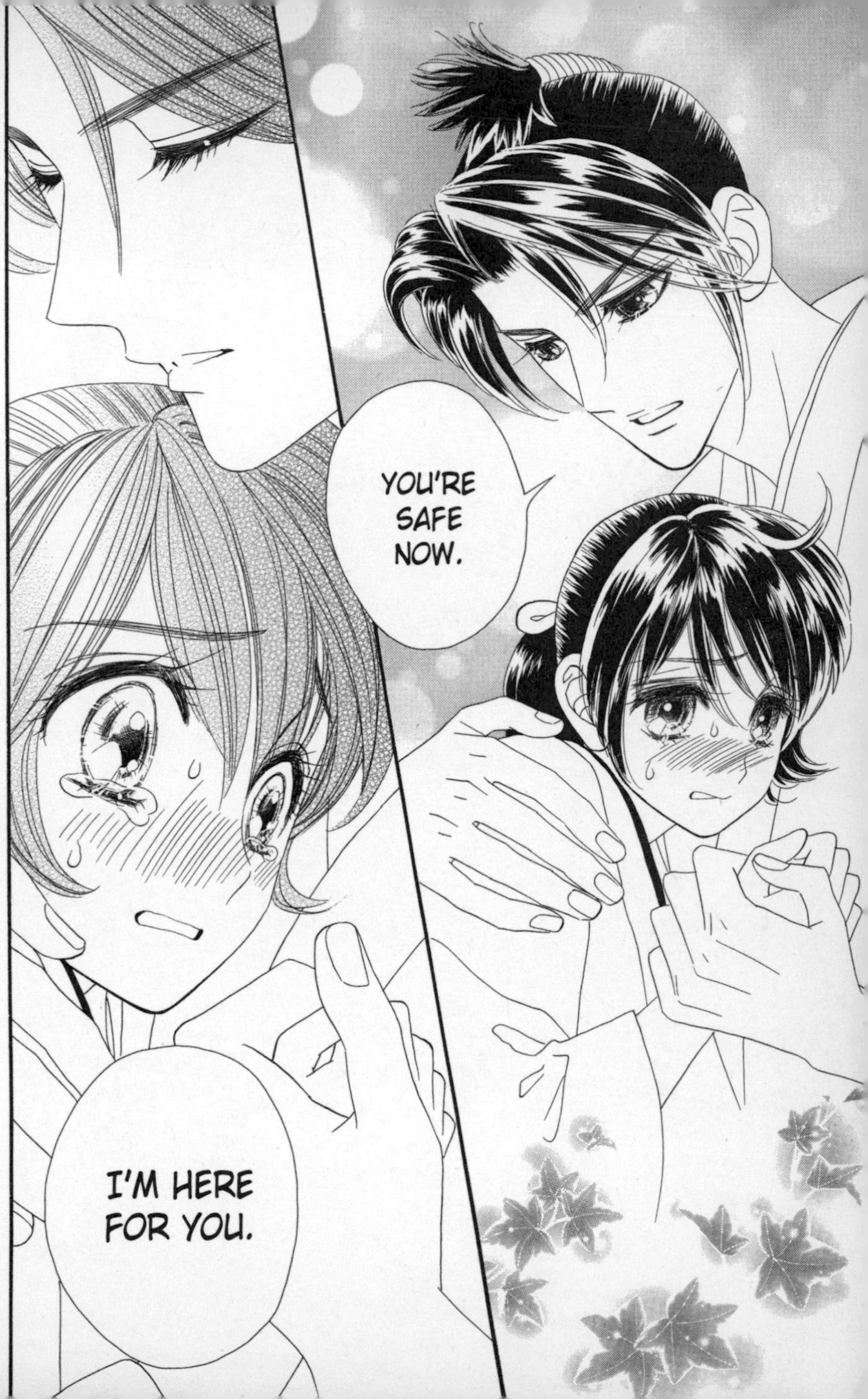

YOU'RE SAFE NOW.
I'M HERE FOR YOU.

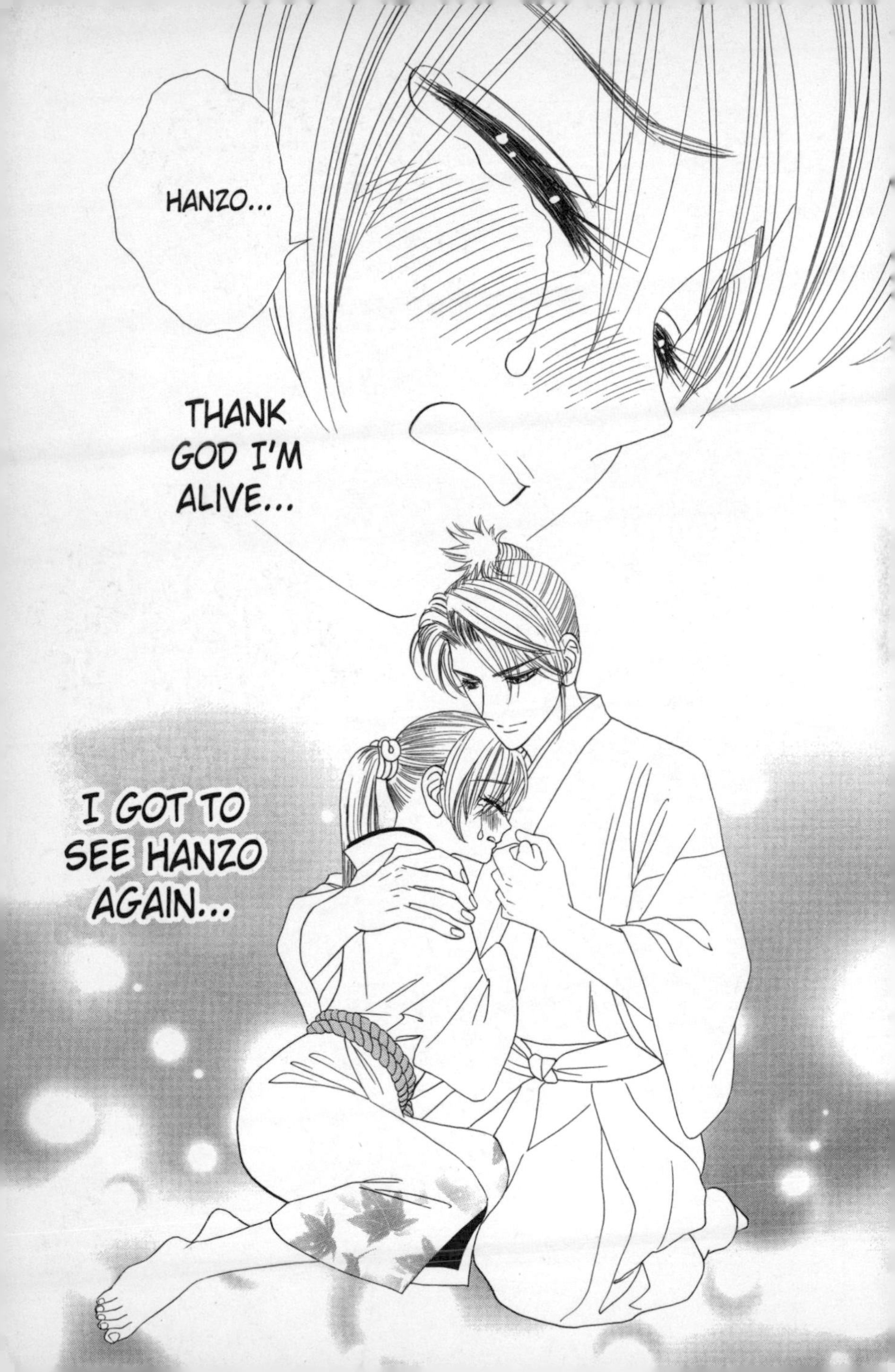
HANZO...
THANK GOD I'M ALIVE...
I GOT TO SEE HANZO AGAIN...

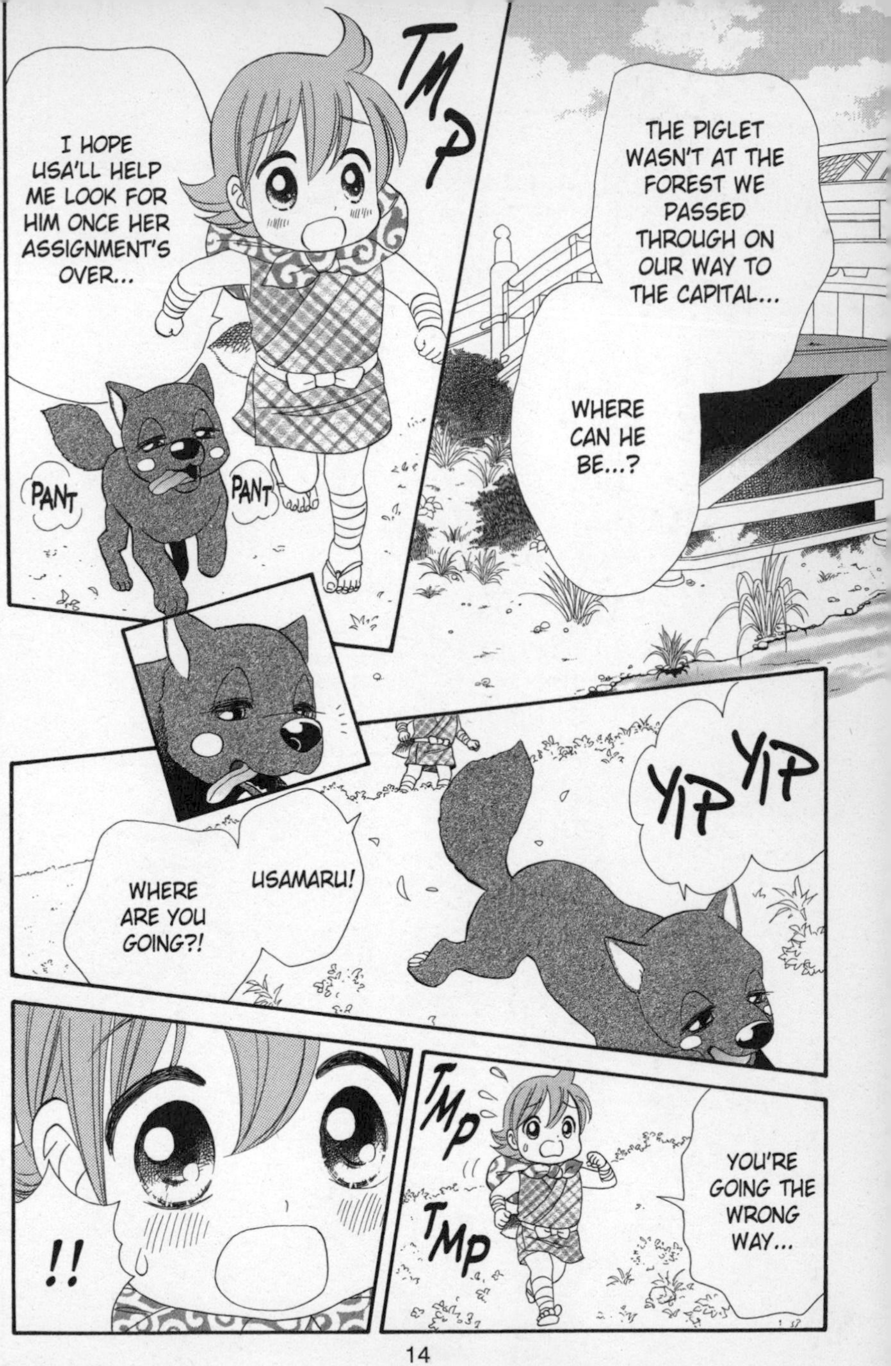
THE PIGLET WASN'T AT THE FOREST WE PASSED THROUGH ON OUR WAY TO THE CAPITAL...
WHERE CAN HE BE...?
TMP
I HOPE USA'LL HELP ME LOOK FOR HIM ONCE HER ASSIGNMENT'S OVER...
PANT
PANT
YIP YIP
USAMARU!
WHERE ARE YOU GOING?!
TMP
TMP
YOU'RE GOING THE WRONG WAY...
!!

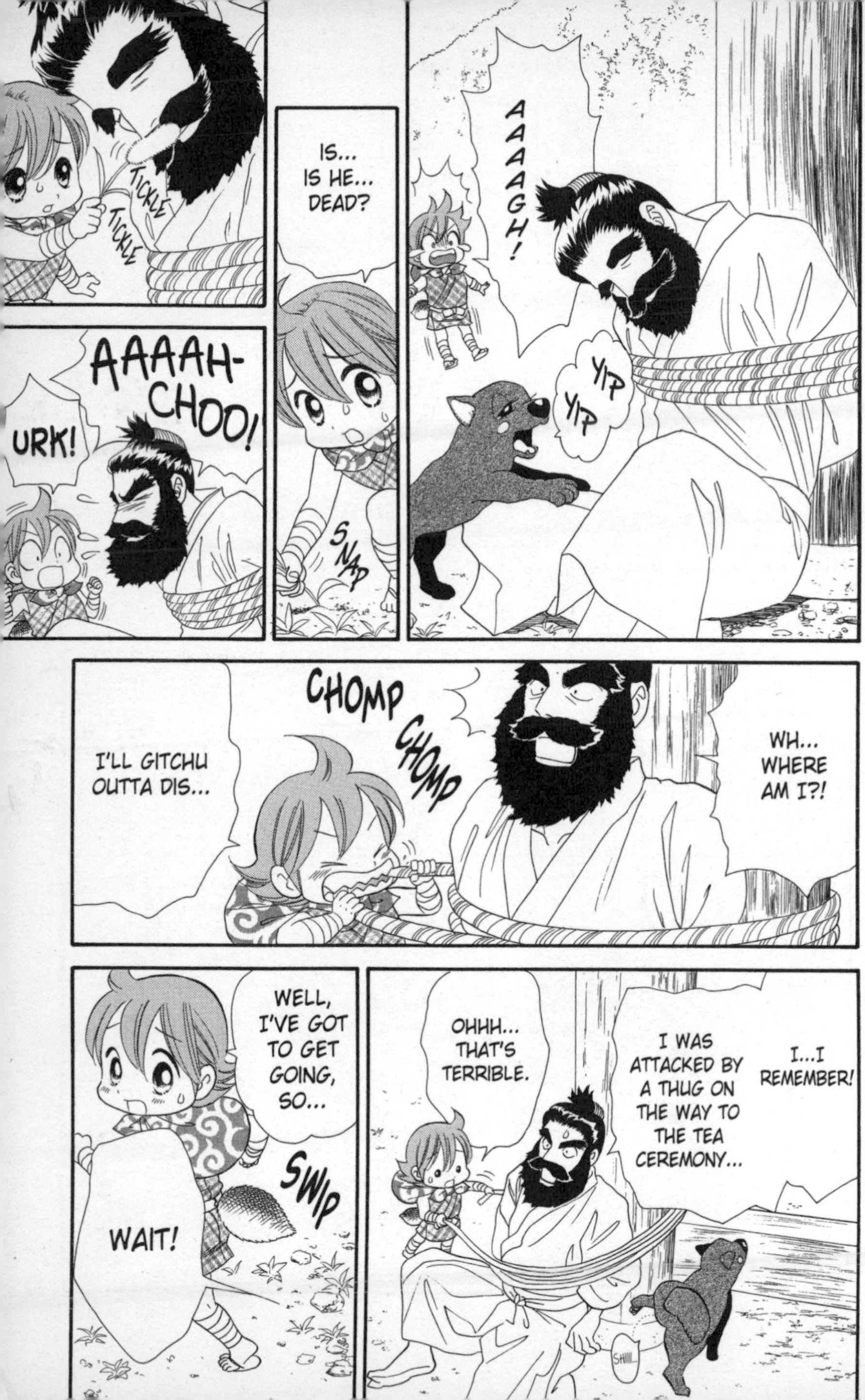

AAAAAGH!
YIP
YIP
IS... IS HE... DEAD?
SNAP
TICKLE
TICKLE
AAAAH-CHOO!
URK!
WH... WHERE AM I?!
CHOMP
CHOMP
I'LL GITCHU OUTTA DIS...
I...I REMEMBER!
I WAS ATTACKED BY A THUG ON THE WAY TO THE TEA CEREMONY...
OHHH... THAT'S TERRIBLE.
SHIIII...
WELL, I'VE GOT TO GET GOING, SO...
SWIP
WAIT!

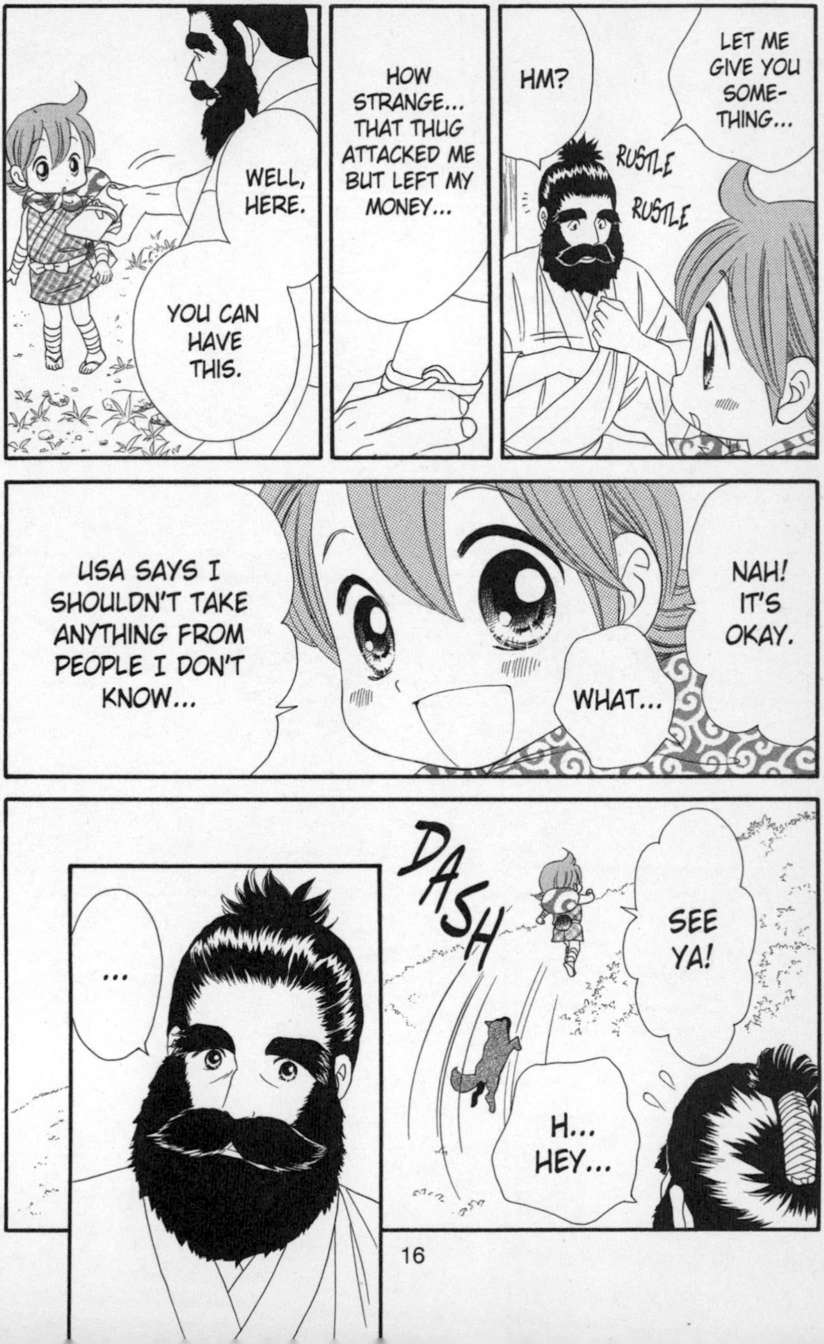
LET ME GIVE YOU SOME-THING...
HM?
RUSTLE
RUSTLE
HOW STRANGE... THAT THUG ATTACKED ME BUT LEFT MY MONEY...
WELL, HERE.
YOU CAN HAVE THIS.
NAH! IT'S OKAY.
WHAT...
USA SAYS I SHOULDN'T TAKE ANYTHING FROM PEOPLE I DON'T KNOW...
SEE YA!
DASH
H... HEY...
...

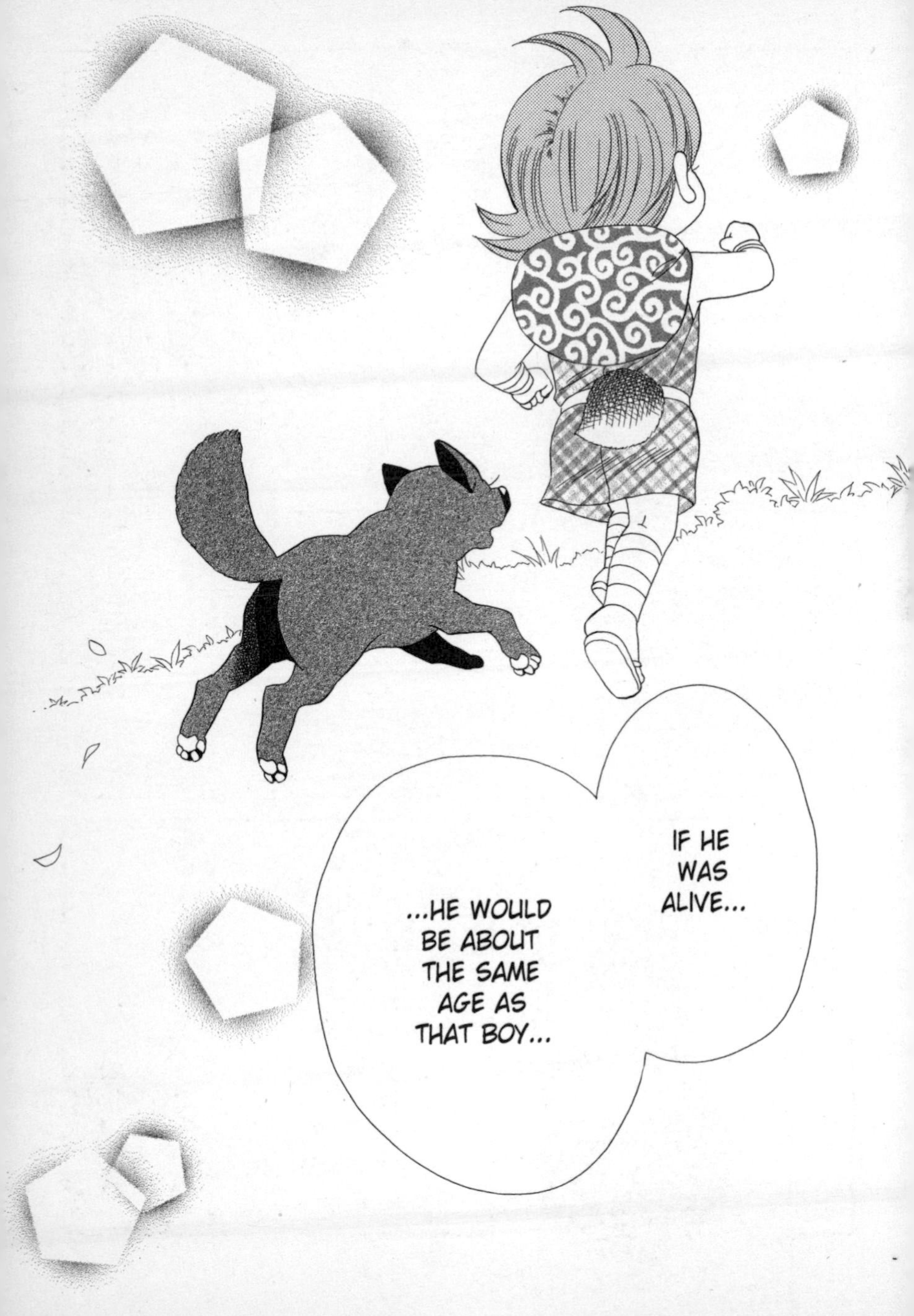
IF HE WAS ALIVE...
...HE WOULD BE ABOUT THE SAME AGE AS THAT BOY...

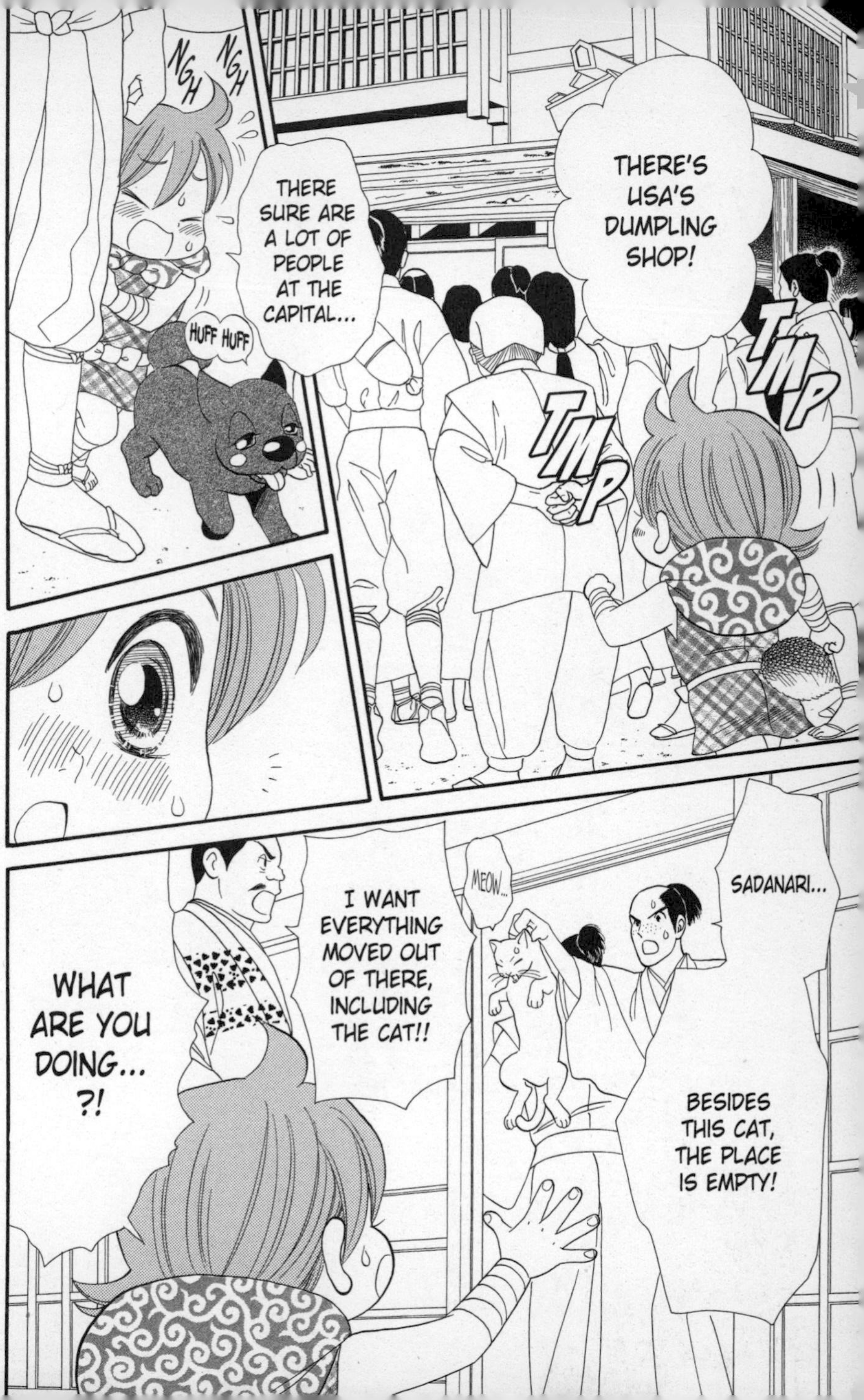

THERE'S USA'S DUMPLING SHOP!
TMP
TMP
NGH NGH
THERE SURE ARE A LOT OF PEOPLE AT THE CAPITAL...
HUFF HUFF
SADANARI...
BESIDES THIS CAT, THE PLACE IS EMPTY!
MEOW...
I WANT EVERYTHING MOVED OUT OF THERE, INCLUDING THE CAT!!
WHAT ARE YOU DOING...?!

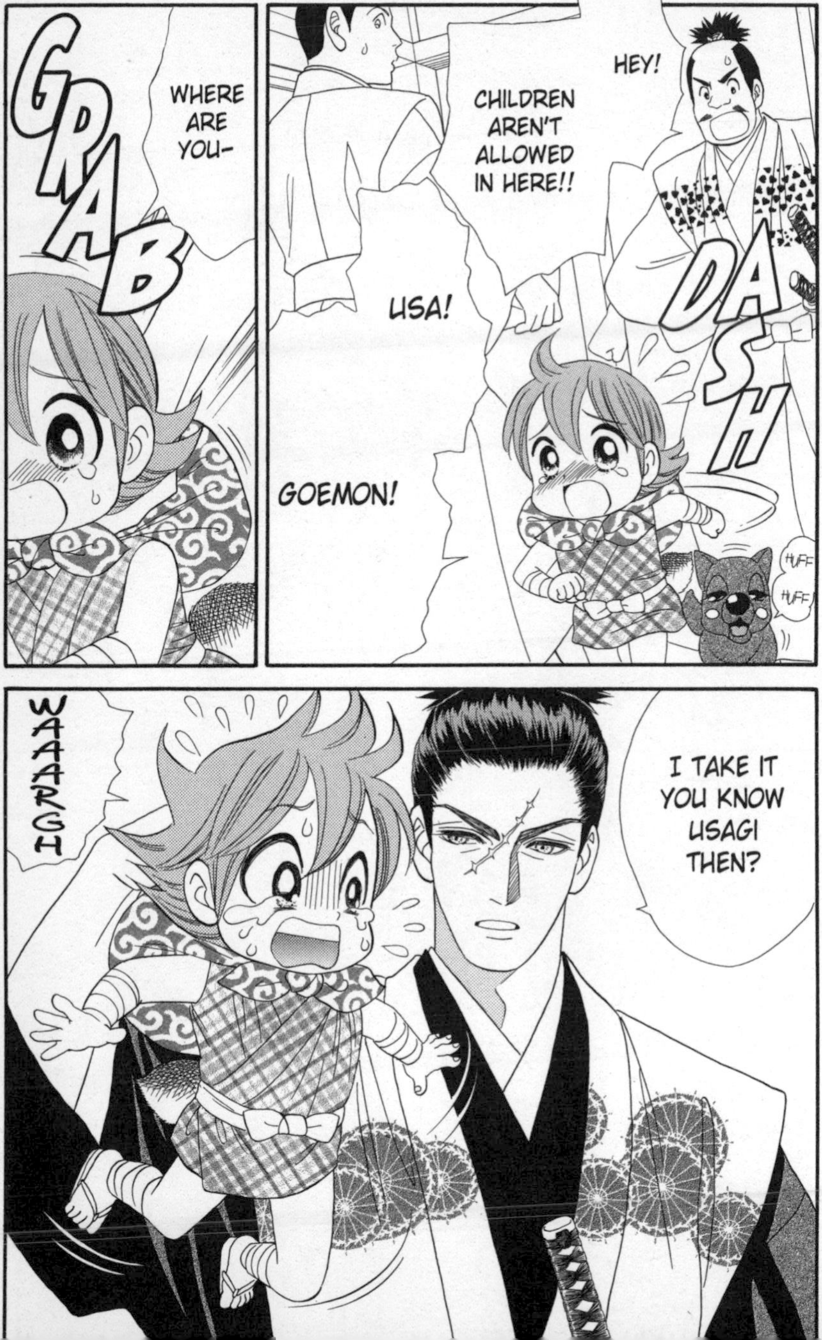
HEY!
CHILDREN AREN'T ALLOWED IN HERE!!
DASH
USA!
HUFF
HUFF
GOEMON!
WHERE ARE YOU-
GRAB
I TAKE IT YOU KNOW USAGI THEN?
WAAAARGH

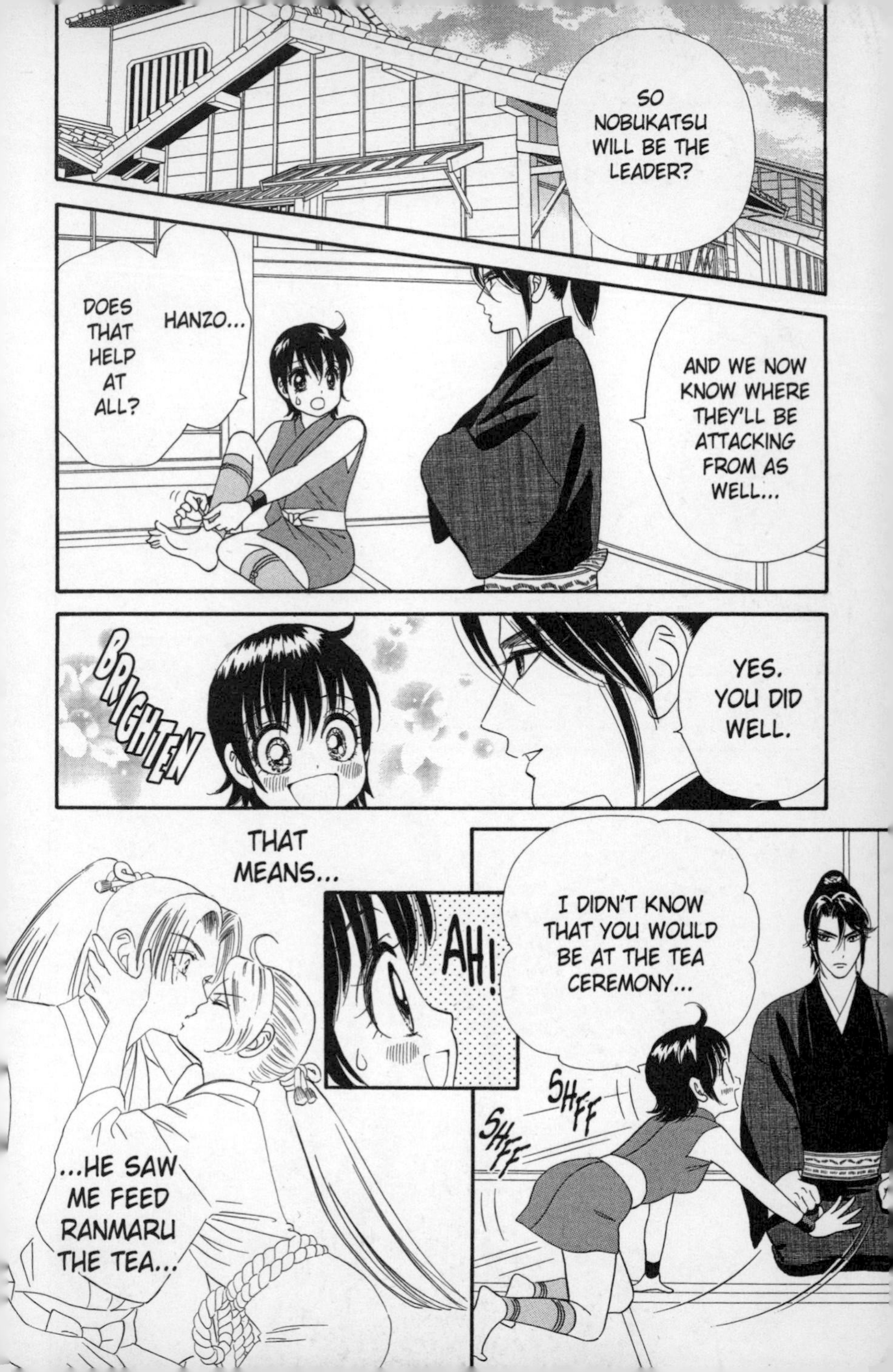
SO NOBUKATSU WILL BE THE LEADER?
AND WE NOW KNOW WHERE THEY'LL BE ATTACKING FROM AS WELL...
HANZO...
DOES THAT HELP AT ALL?
YES. YOU DID WELL.
BRIGHTEN
I DIDN'T KNOW THAT YOU WOULD BE AT THE TEA CEREMONY...
SHFF
SHFF
AH!
THAT MEANS...
...HE SAW ME FEED RANMARU THE TEA...

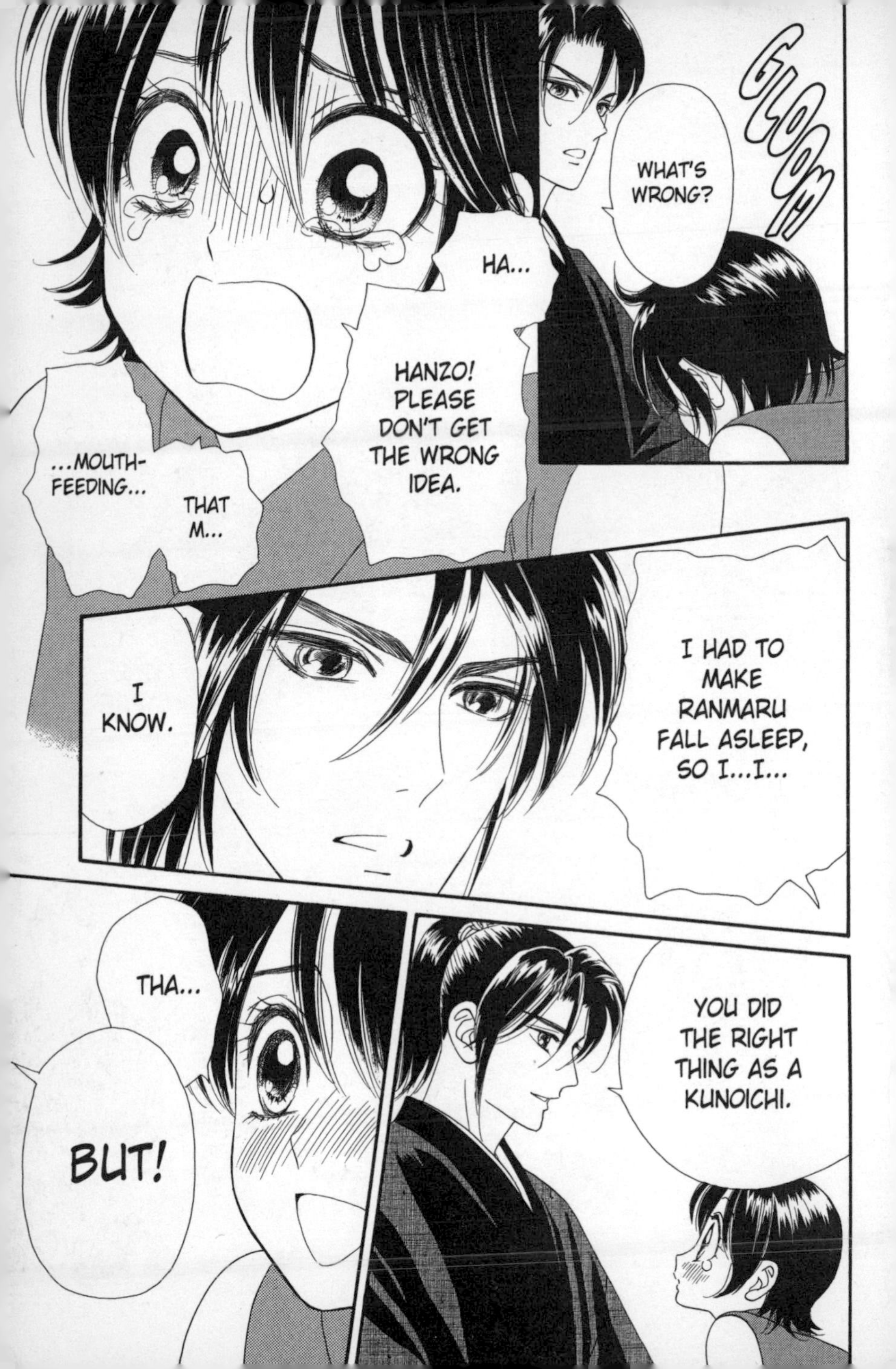
GLOOM
WHAT'S WRONG?
HA...
HANZO! PLEASE DON'T GET THE WRONG IDEA.
THAT M...
...MOUTH-FEEDING...
I HAD TO MAKE RANMARU FALL ASLEEP, SO I...I...
I KNOW.
YOU DID THE RIGHT THING AS A KUNOICHI.
THA...
BUT!

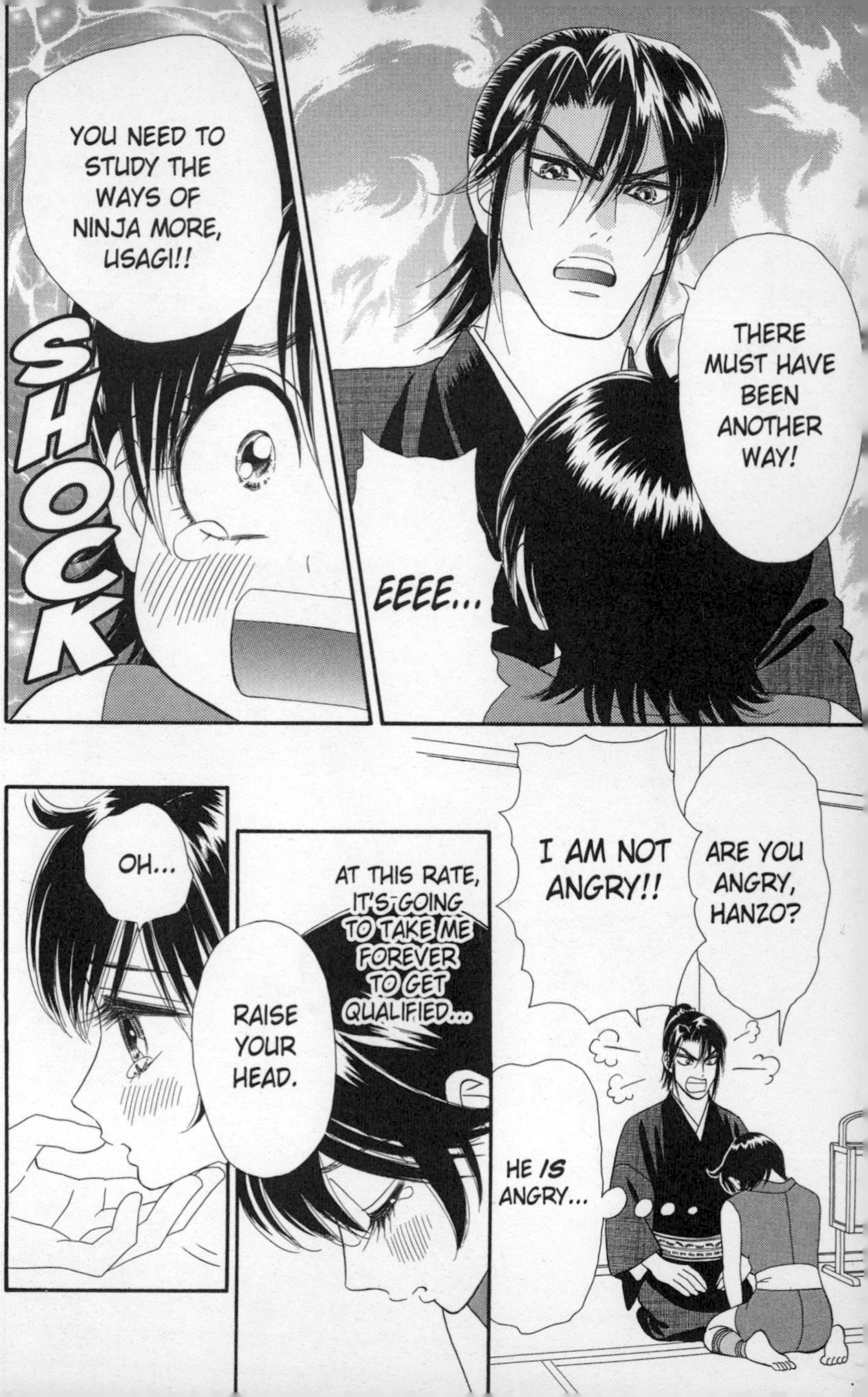
THERE MUST HAVE BEEN ANOTHER WAY!
EEEE...
YOU NEED TO STUDY THE WAYS OF NINJA MORE, USAGI!!
SHOCK
ARE YOU ANGRY, HANZO?
I AM NOT ANGRY!!
HE *IS* ANGRY...
AT THIS RATE, IT'S GOING TO TAKE ME FOREVER TO GET QUALIFIED...
RAISE YOUR HEAD.
OH...

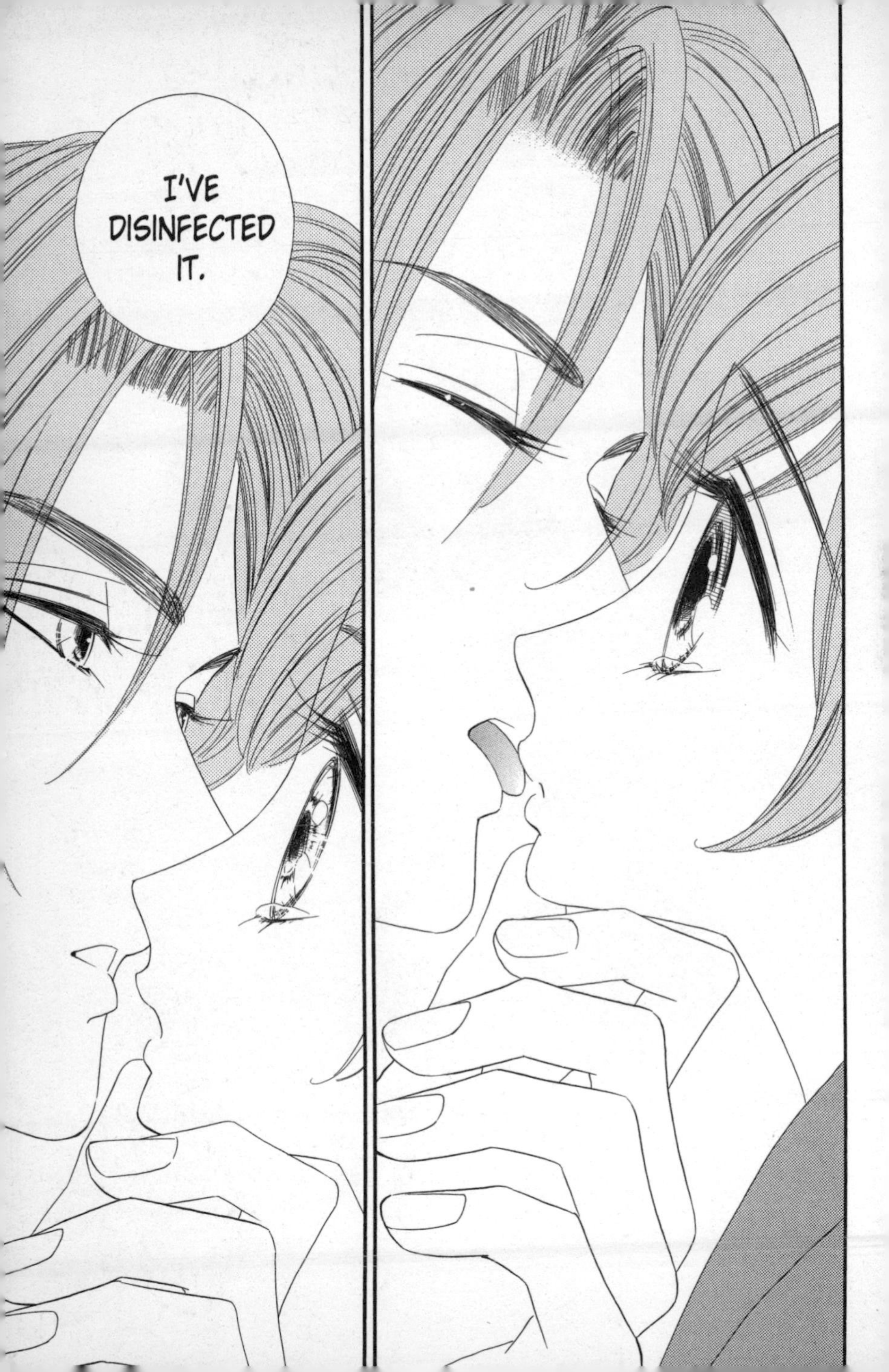
I'VE DISINFECTED IT.

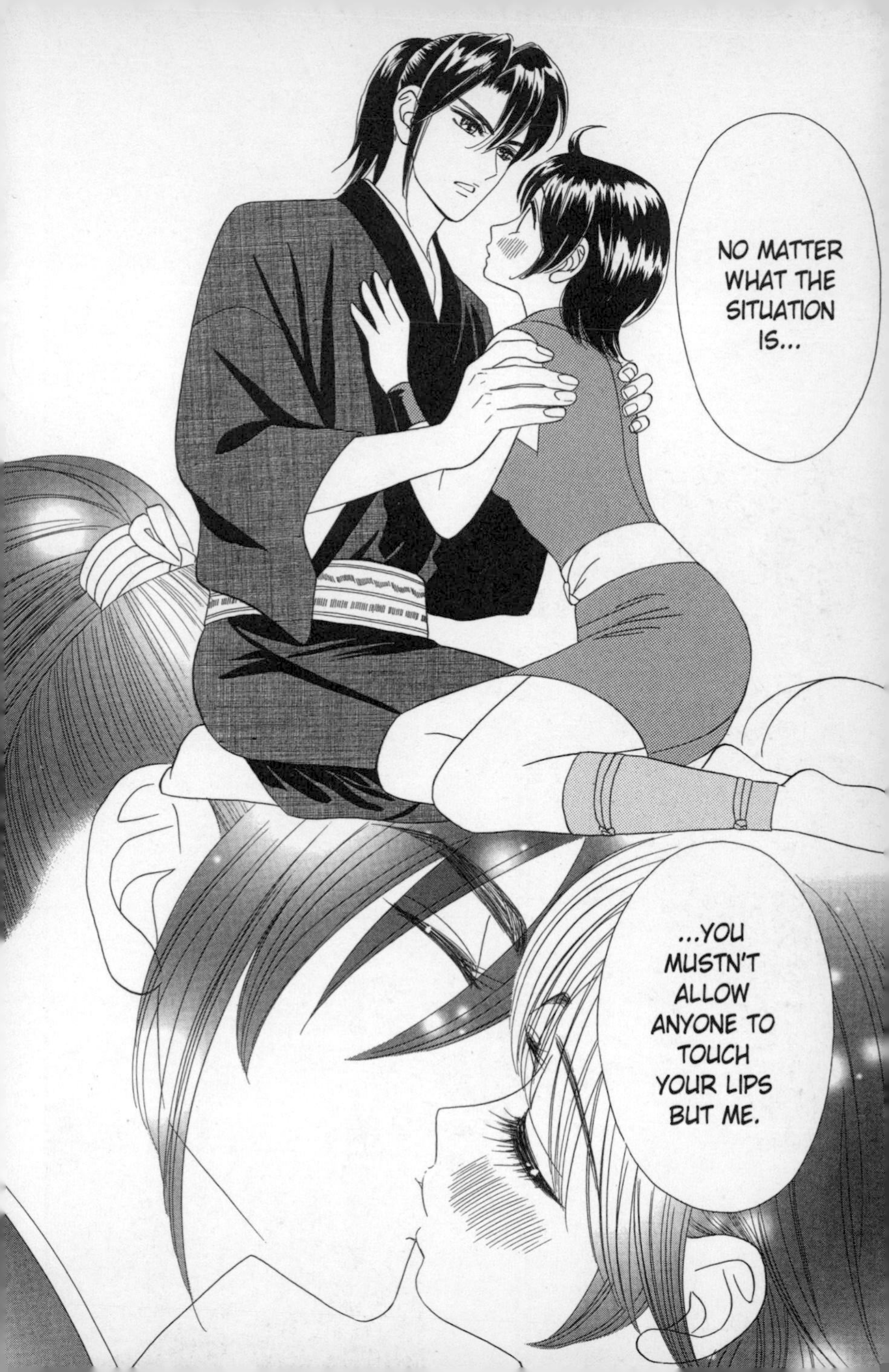
NO MATTER WHAT THE SITUATION IS...
...YOU MUSTN'T ALLOW ANYONE TO TOUCH YOUR LIPS BUT ME.

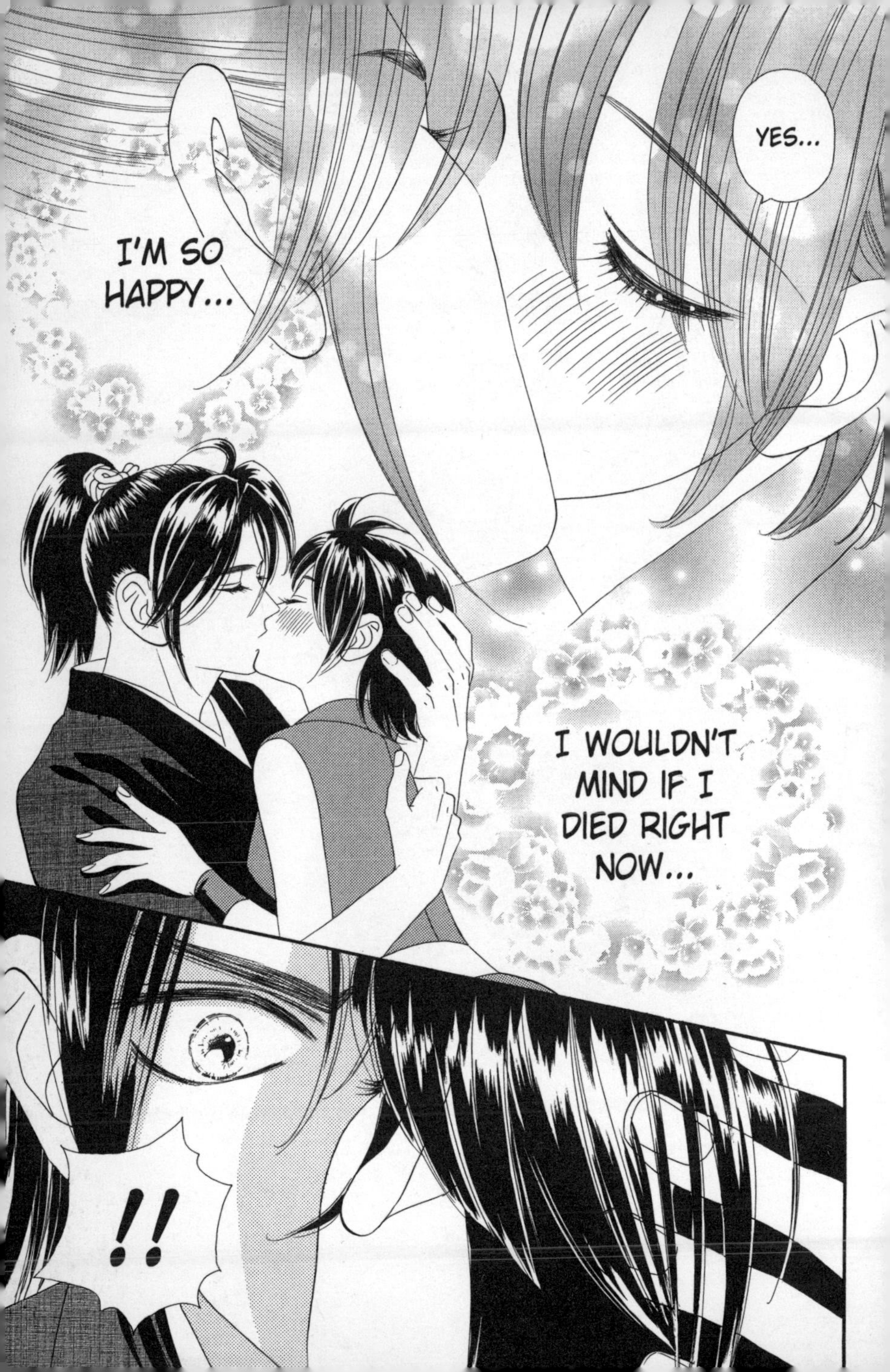
YES...
I'M SO HAPPY...
I WOULDN'T MIND IF I DIED RIGHT NOW...
!!

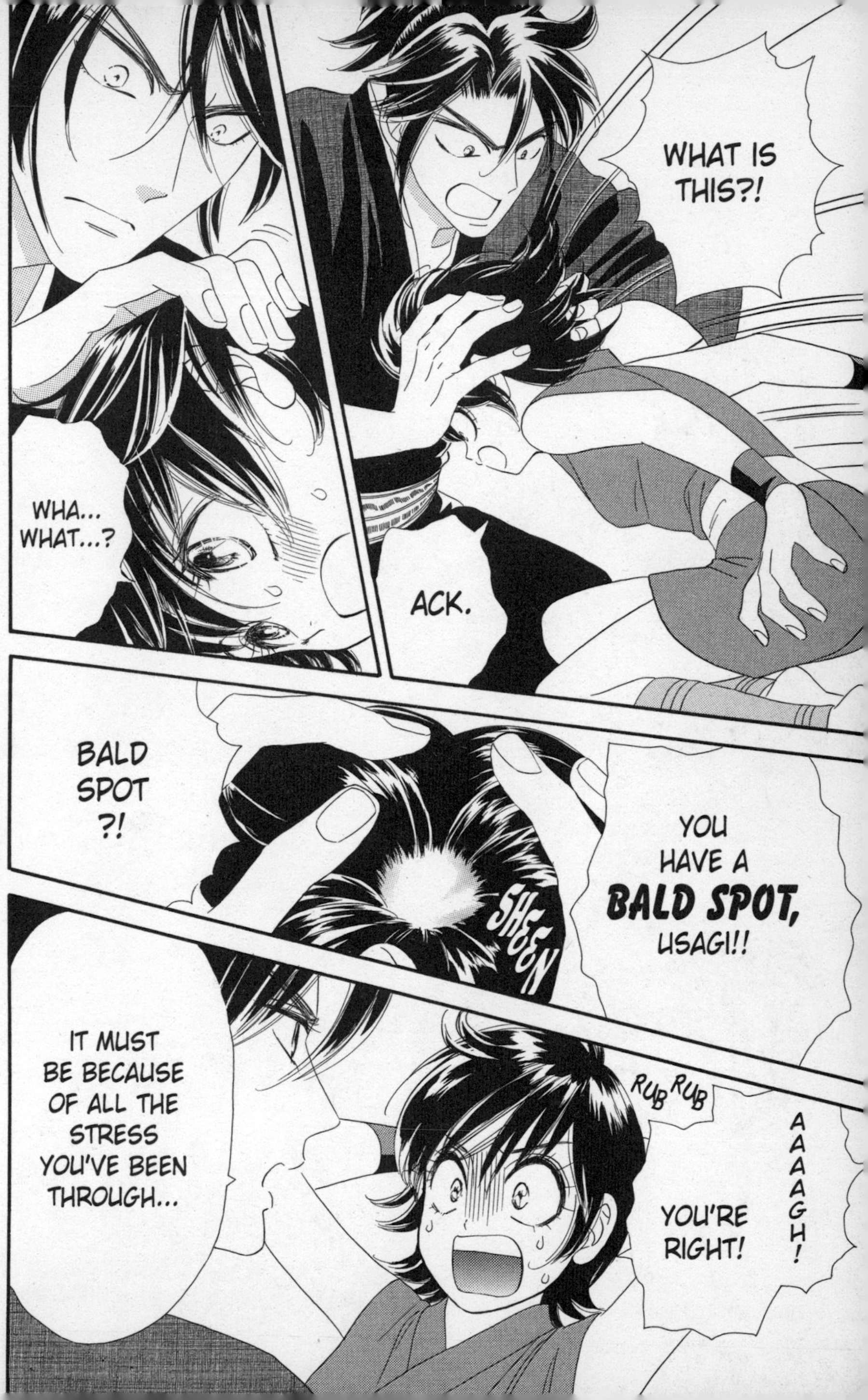
WHAT IS THIS?!
ACK.
WHA... WHAT...?
YOU HAVE A BALD SPOT, USAGI!!
SHEEN
BALD SPOT ?!
AAAAGH!
YOU'RE RIGHT!
RUB RUB
IT MUST BE BECAUSE OF ALL THE STRESS YOU'VE BEEN THROUGH...

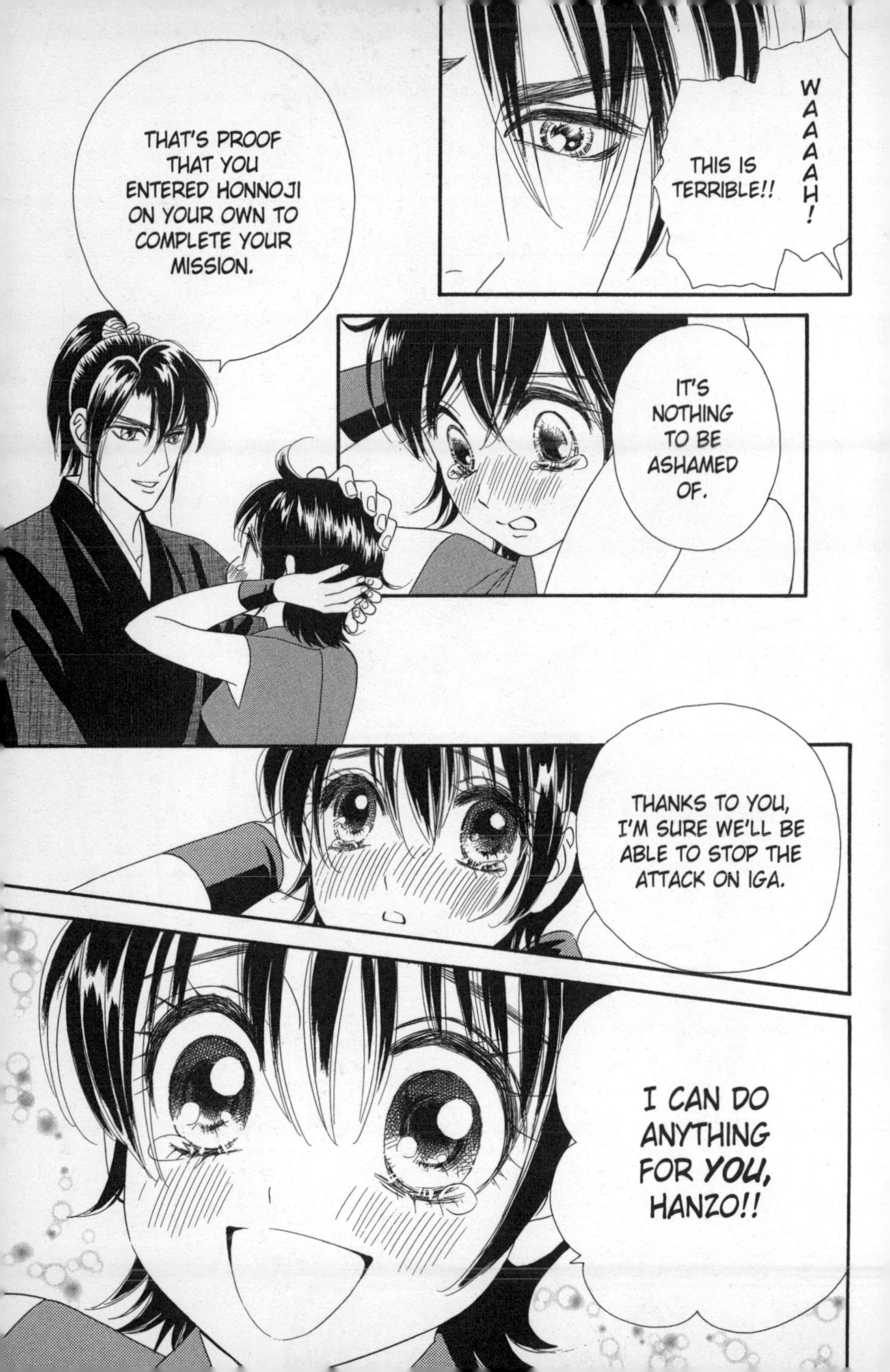
WAAAAH!
THIS IS TERRIBLE!!
IT'S NOTHING TO BE ASHAMED OF.
THAT'S PROOF THAT YOU ENTERED HONNOJI ON YOUR OWN TO COMPLETE YOUR MISSION.
THANKS TO YOU, I'M SURE WE'LL BE ABLE TO STOP THE ATTACK ON IGA.
I CAN DO ANYTHING FOR YOU, HANZO!!

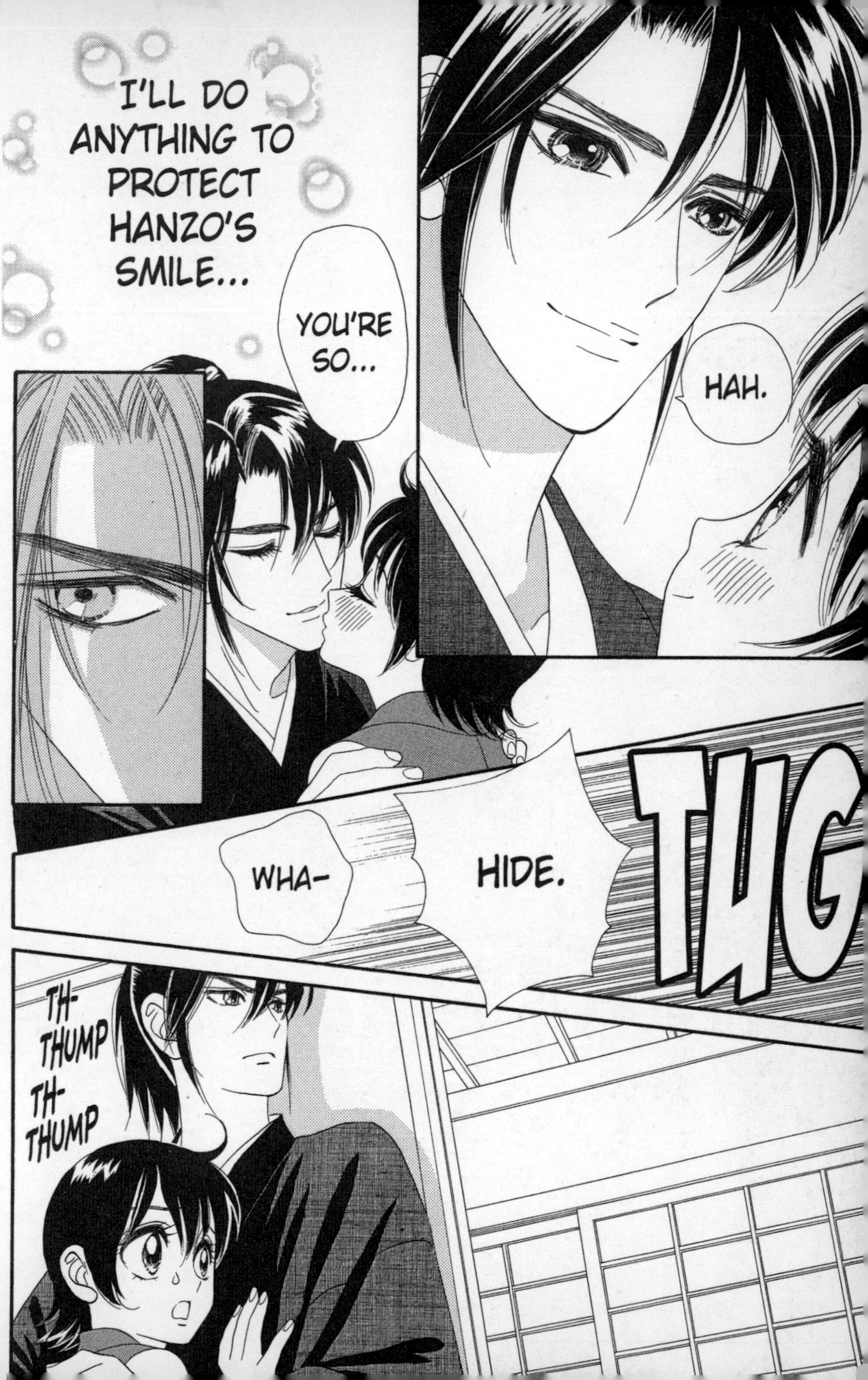
HAH.
I'LL DO ANYTHING TO PROTECT HANZO'S SMILE...
YOU'RE SO...
TUG
HIDE.
WHA-
TH-THUMP TH-THUMP

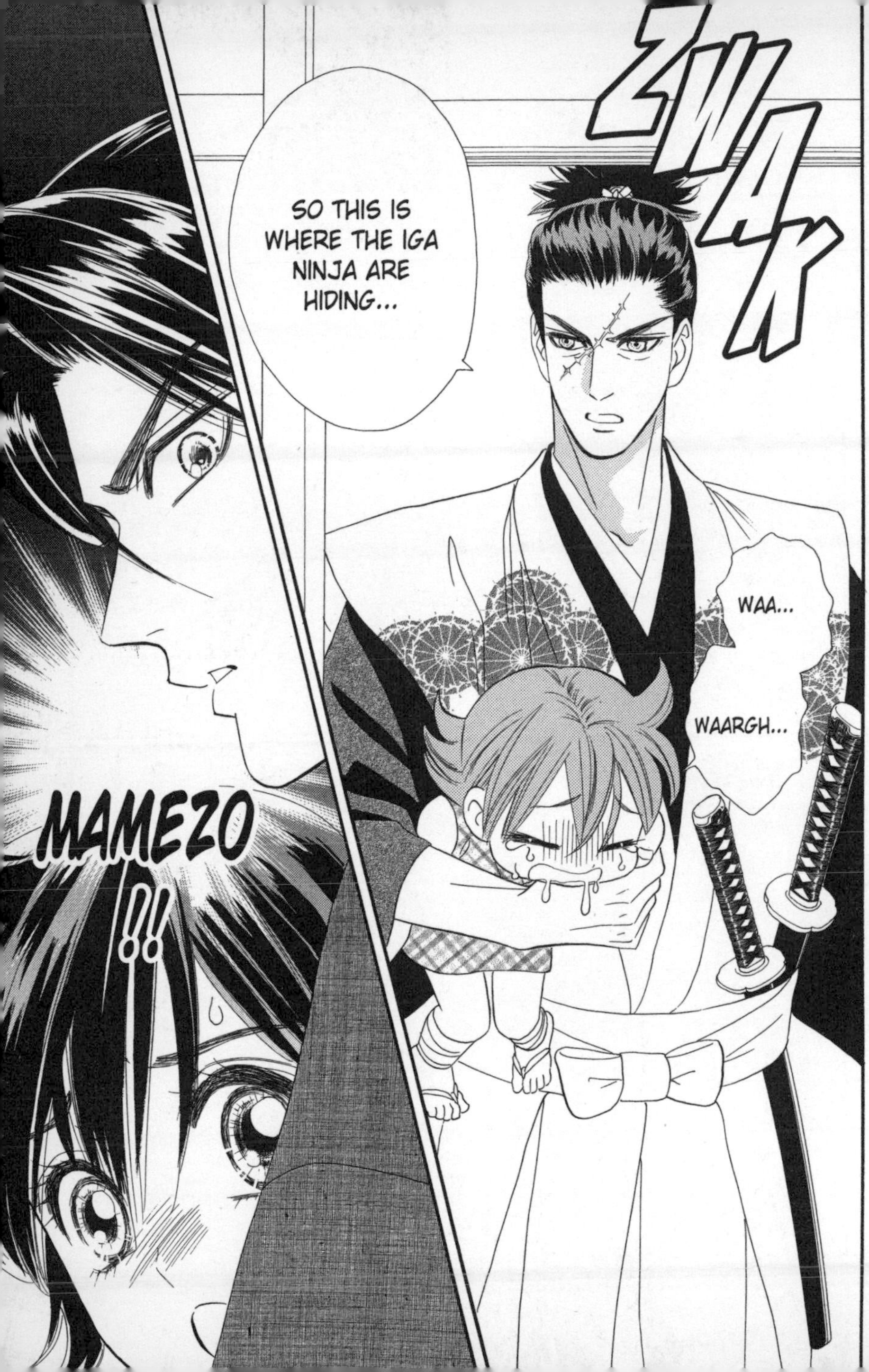
ZWAK
SO THIS IS WHERE THE IGA NINJA ARE HIDING...
WAA...
WAARGH...
MAMEZO !!

TAIL OF THE MOON EXTRA: TODAY'S MISSION

"I WANT TO SEE MAMEZO AS A HIGH SCHOOLER!"

-SHIIYAN, IBARAKI PREFECTURE

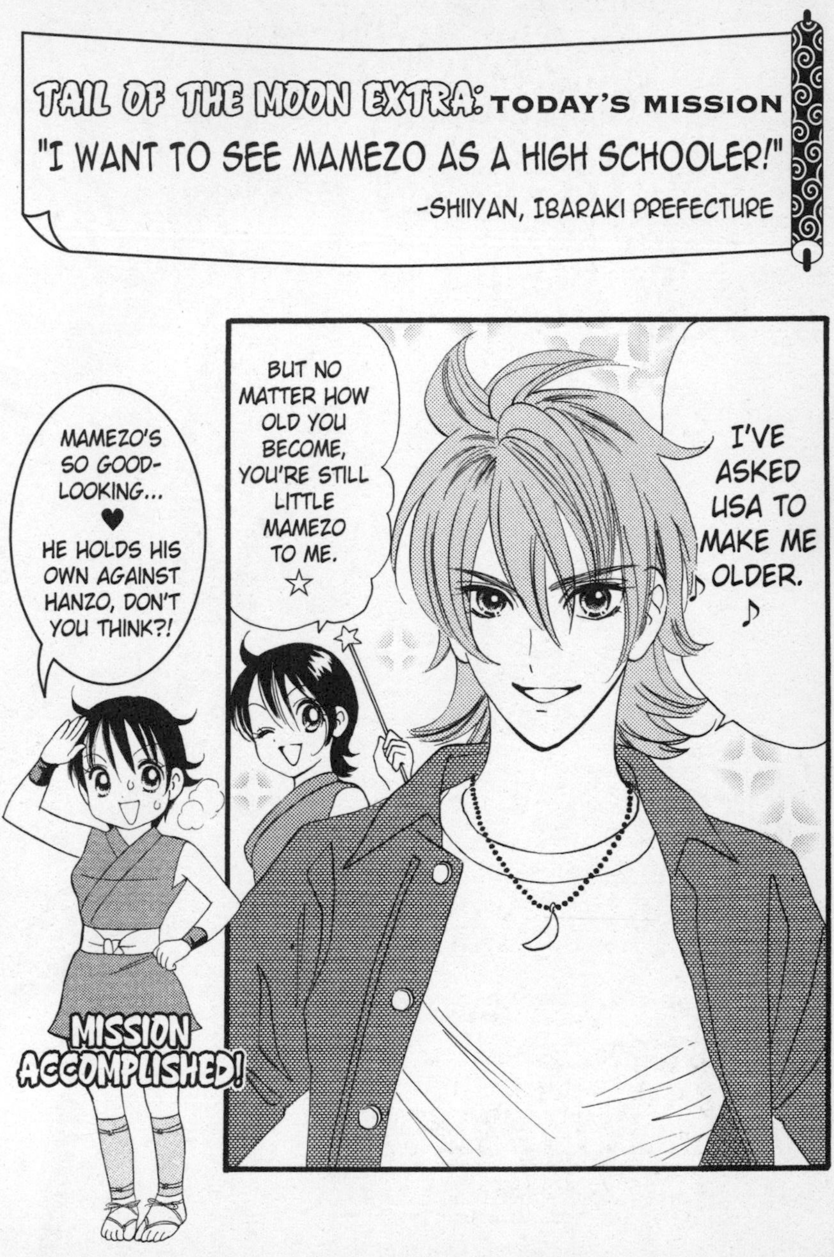
I'VE ASKED USA TO MAKE ME OLDER. ♪
BUT NO MATTER HOW OLD YOU BECOME, YOU'RE STILL LITTLE MAMEZO TO ME. ☆
MAMEZO'S SO GOOD-LOOKING... ♥ HE HOLDS HIS OWN AGAINST HANZO, DON'T YOU THINK?!
MISSION ACCOMPLISHED!

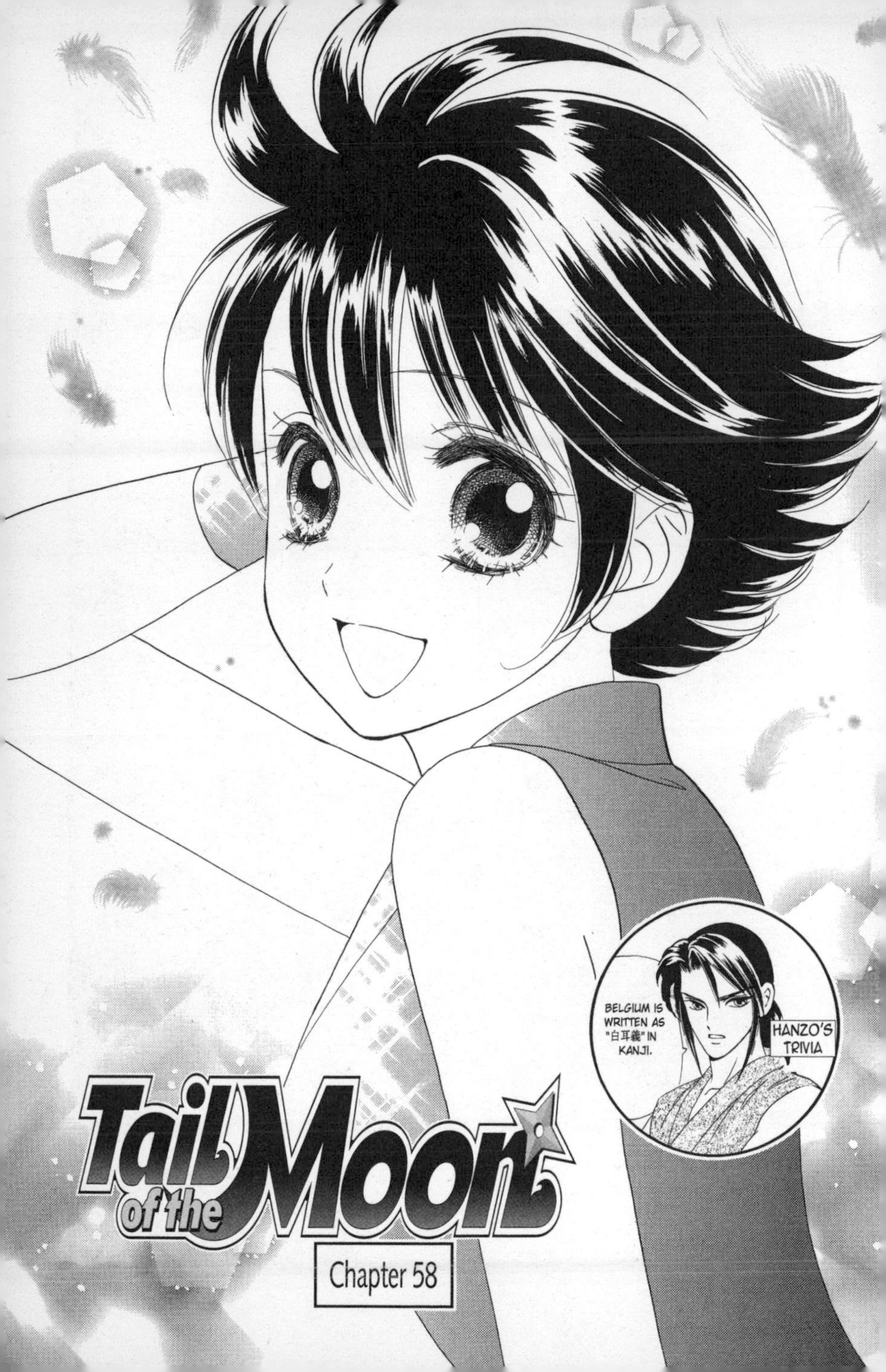
Tail of the Moon
Chapter 58
HANZO'S TRIVIA
BELGIUM IS WRITTEN AS "白耳義" IN KANJI.

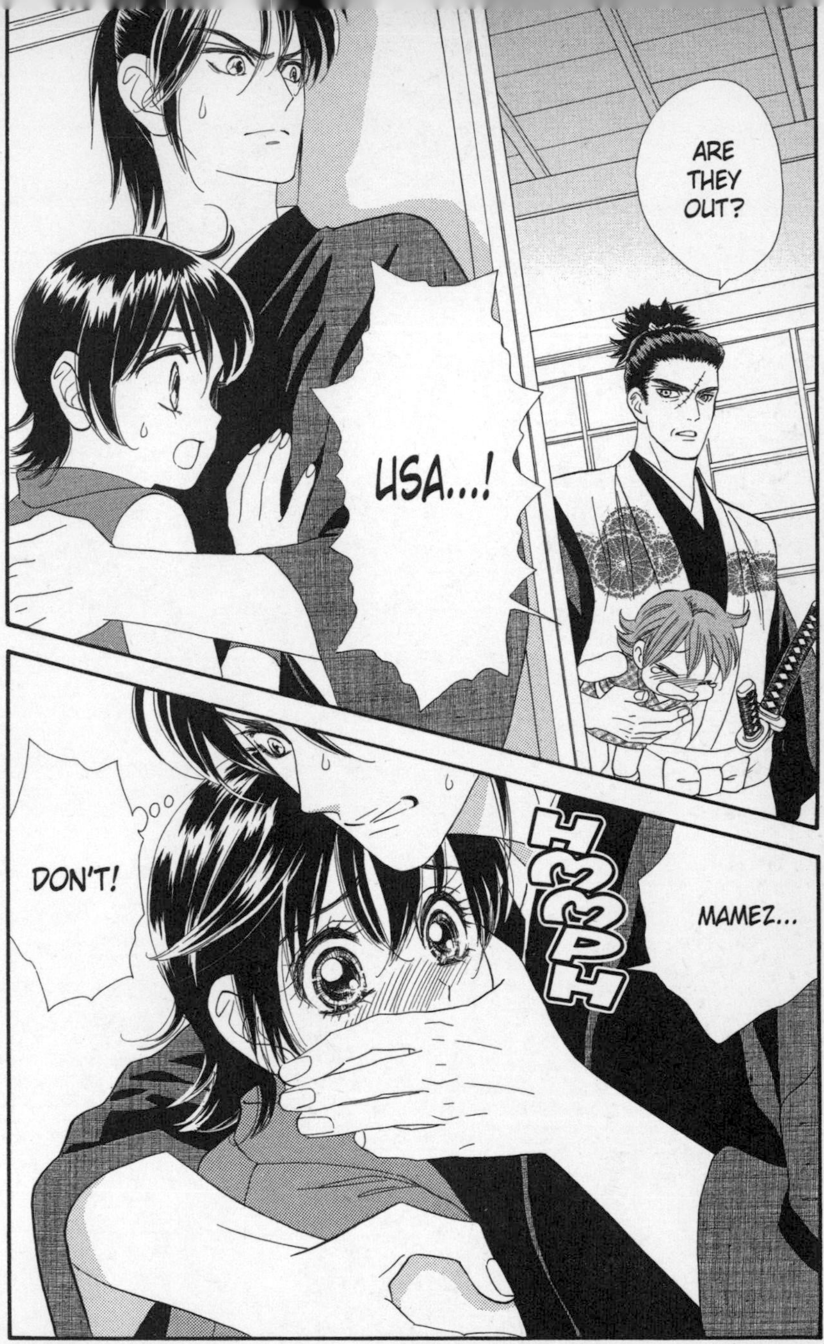
ARE THEY OUT?
USA...!
MAMEZ...
HMMPH
DON'T!

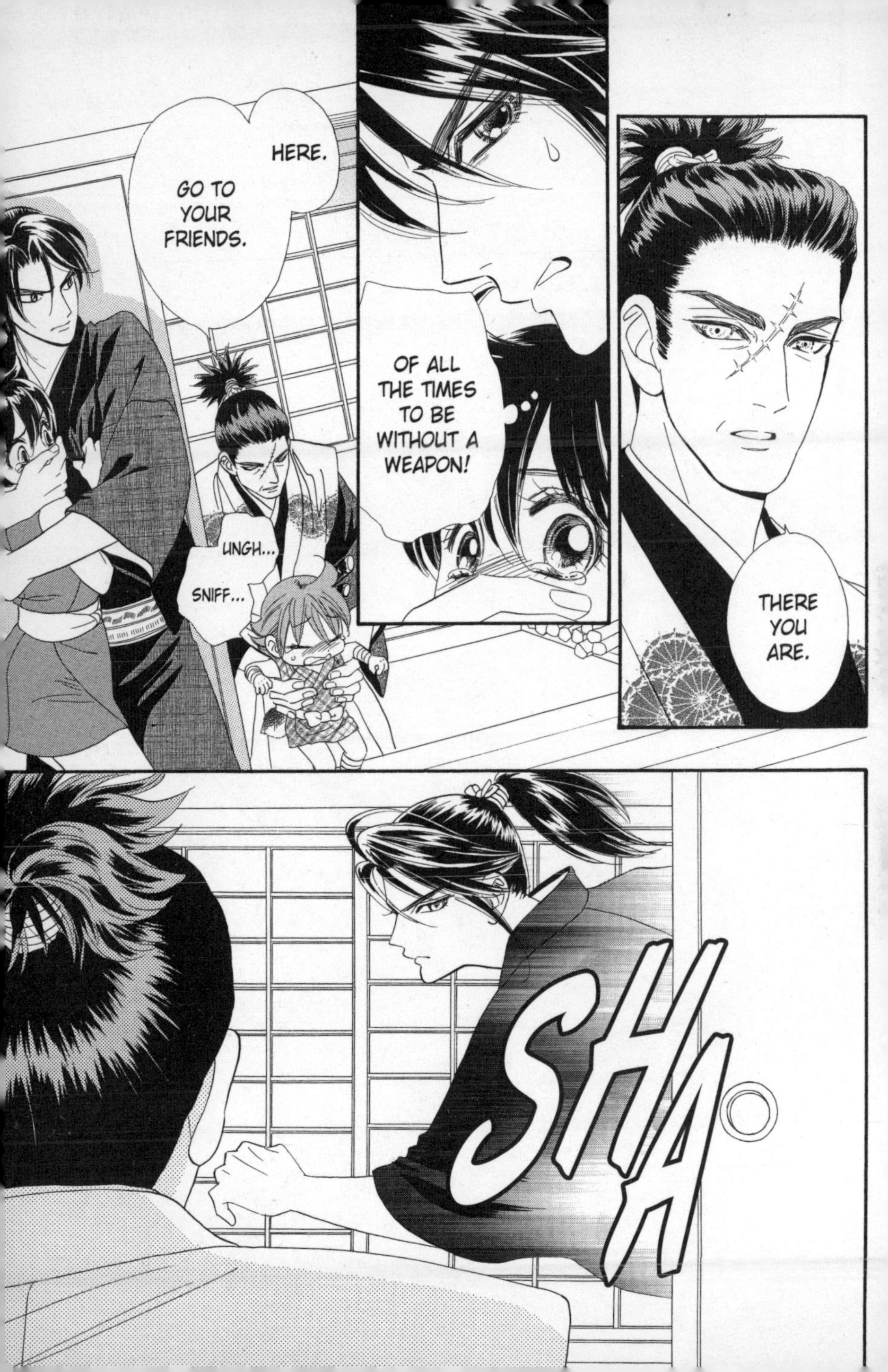
THERE YOU ARE.
OF ALL THE TIMES TO BE WITHOUT A WEAPON!
HERE. GO TO YOUR FRIENDS.
UNGH...
SNIFF...
SHA

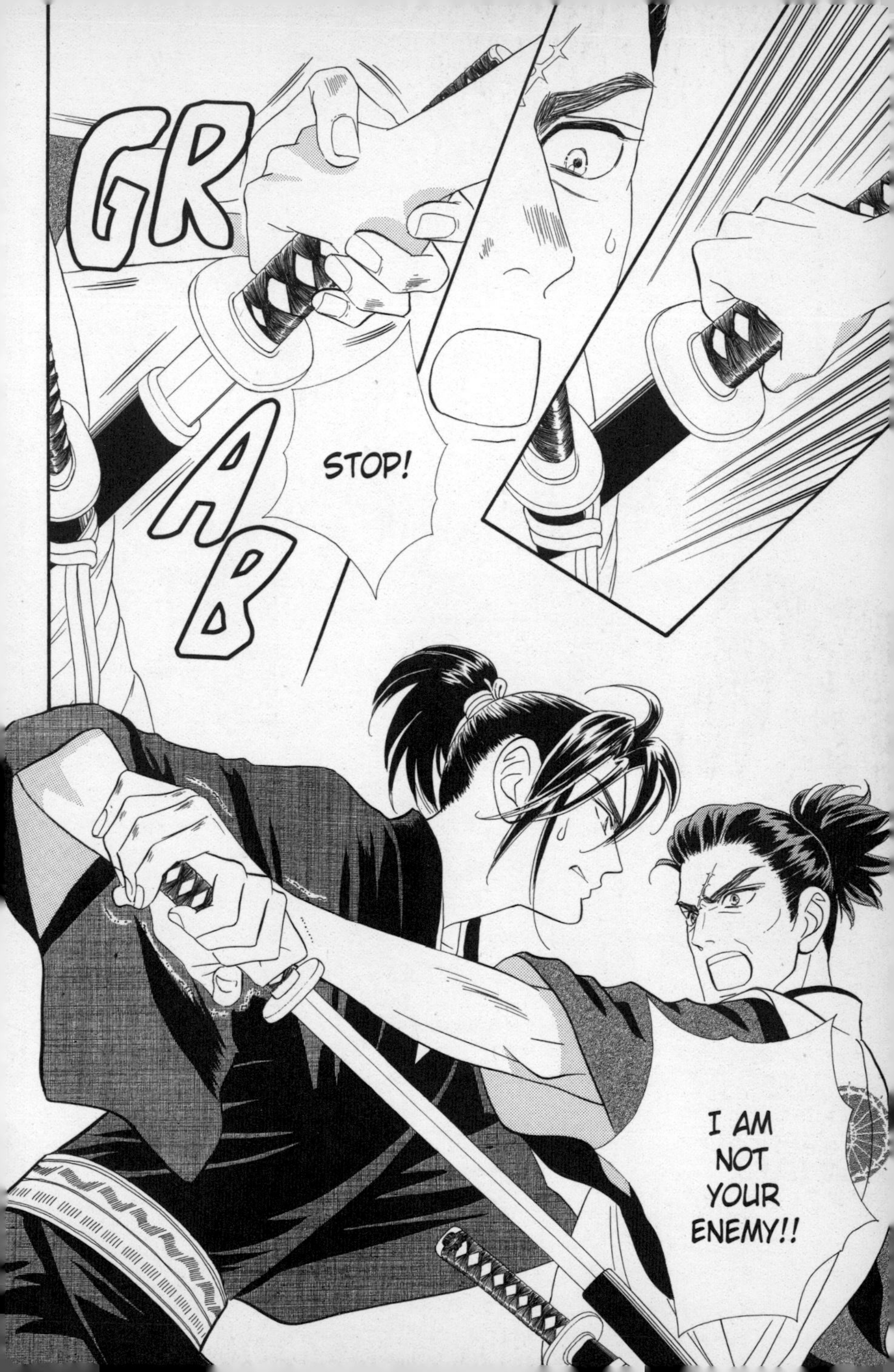
STOP!
GRAB
I AM NOT YOUR ENEMY!!

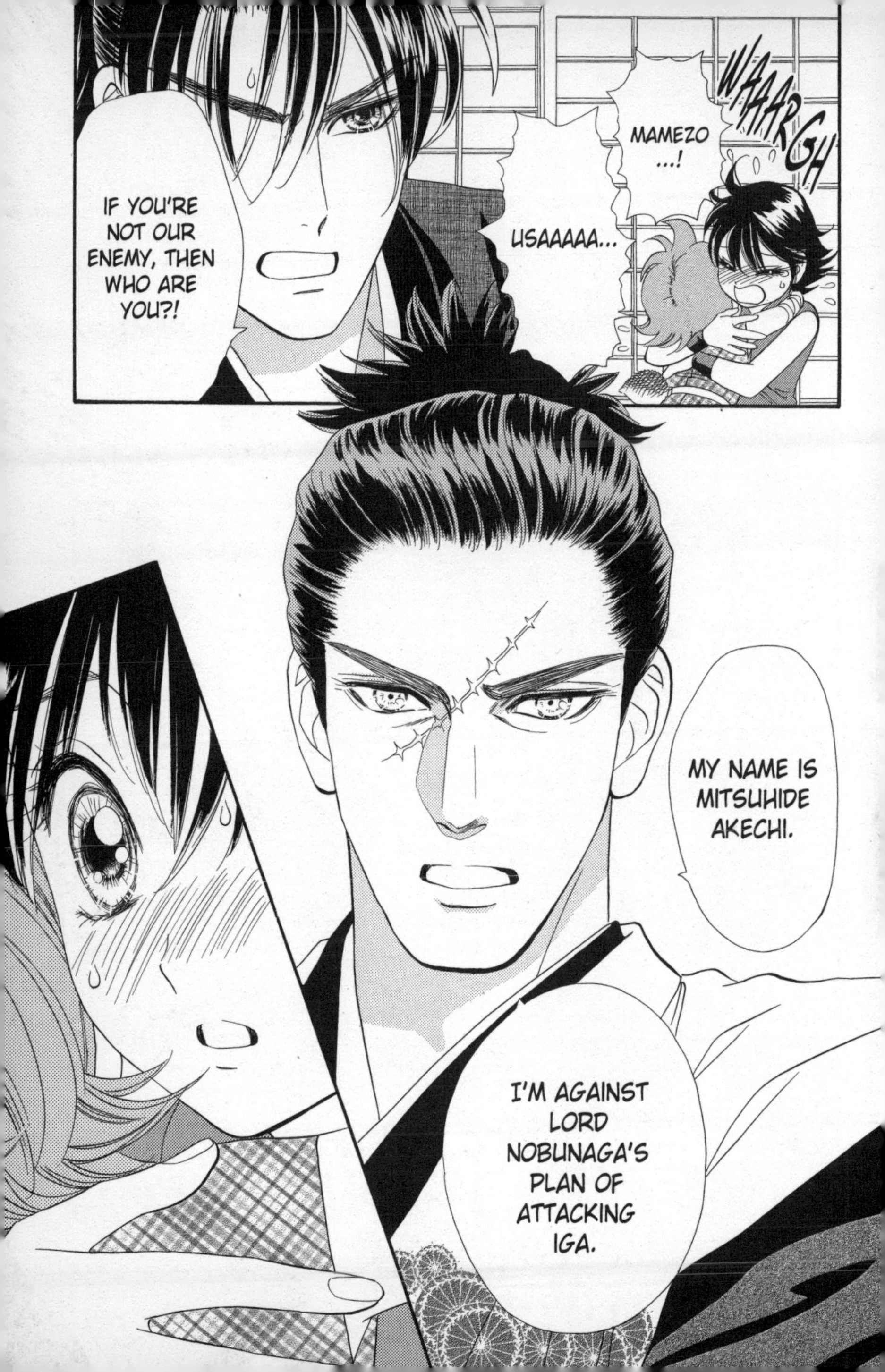
WAAARGH
MAMEZO ...!
USAAAAA...
IF YOU'RE NOT OUR ENEMY, THEN WHO ARE YOU?!
MY NAME IS MITSUHIDE AKECHI.
I'M AGAINST LORD NOBUNAGA'S PLAN OF ATTACKING IGA.

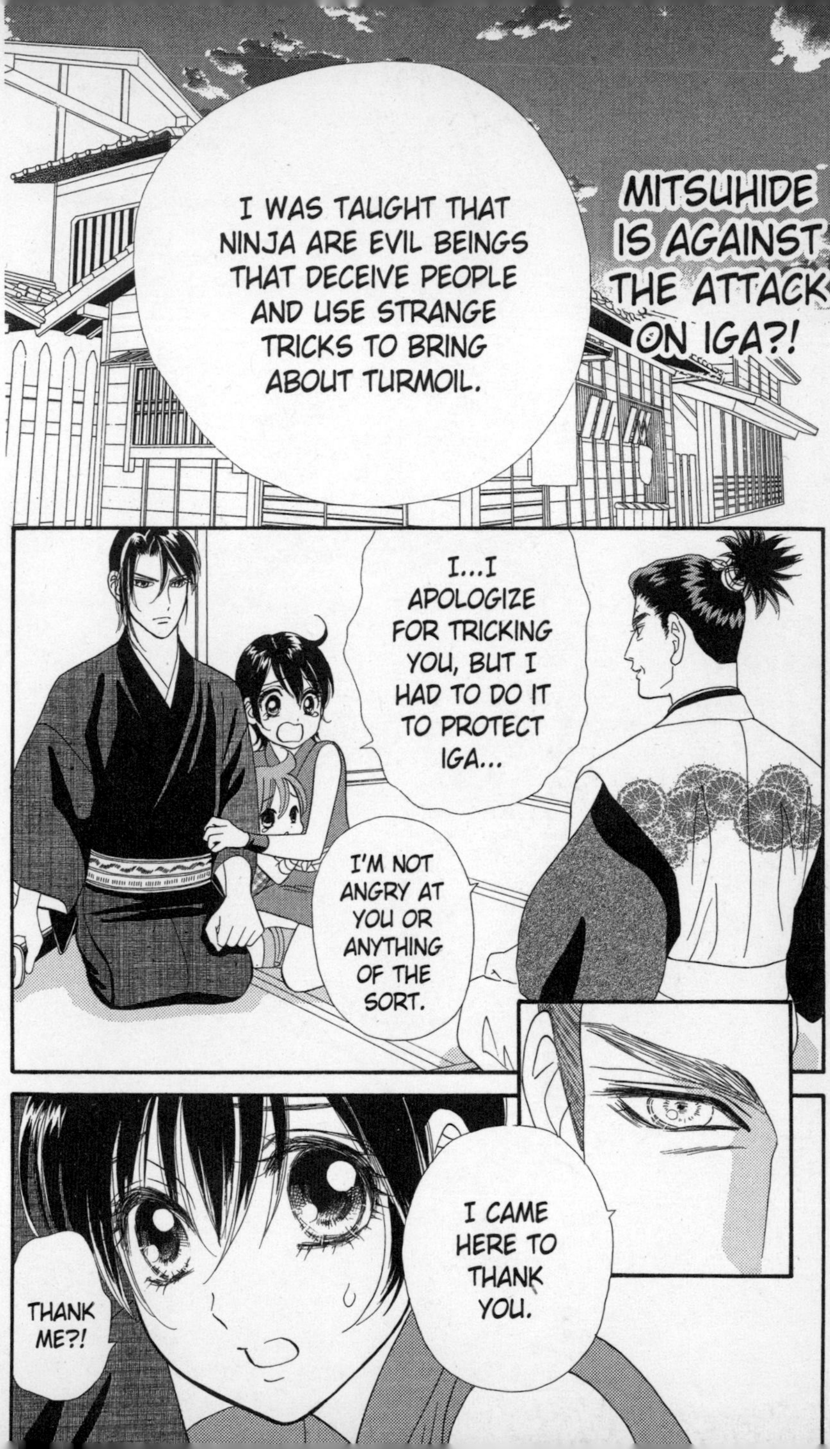
MITSUHIDE IS AGAINST THE ATTACK ON IGA?!
I WAS TAUGHT THAT NINJA ARE EVIL BEINGS THAT DECEIVE PEOPLE AND USE STRANGE TRICKS TO BRING ABOUT TURMOIL.
I...I APOLOGIZE FOR TRICKING YOU, BUT I HAD TO DO IT TO PROTECT IGA...
I'M NOT ANGRY AT YOU OR ANYTHING OF THE SORT.
I CAME HERE TO THANK YOU.
THANK ME?!

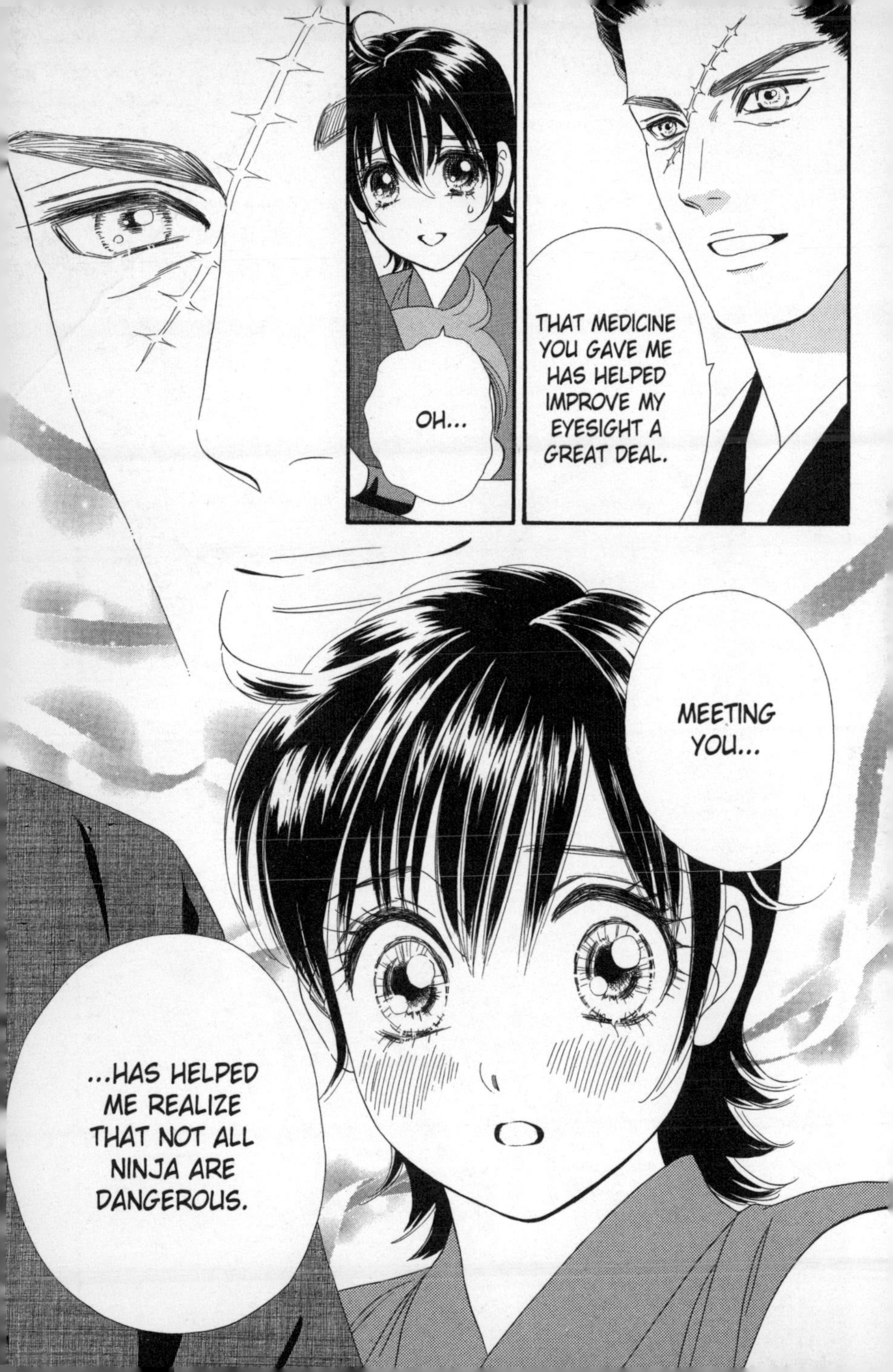
THAT MEDICINE YOU GAVE ME HAS HELPED IMPROVE MY EYESIGHT A GREAT DEAL.
OH...
MEETING YOU...
...HAS HELPED ME REALIZE THAT NOT ALL NINJA ARE DANGEROUS.

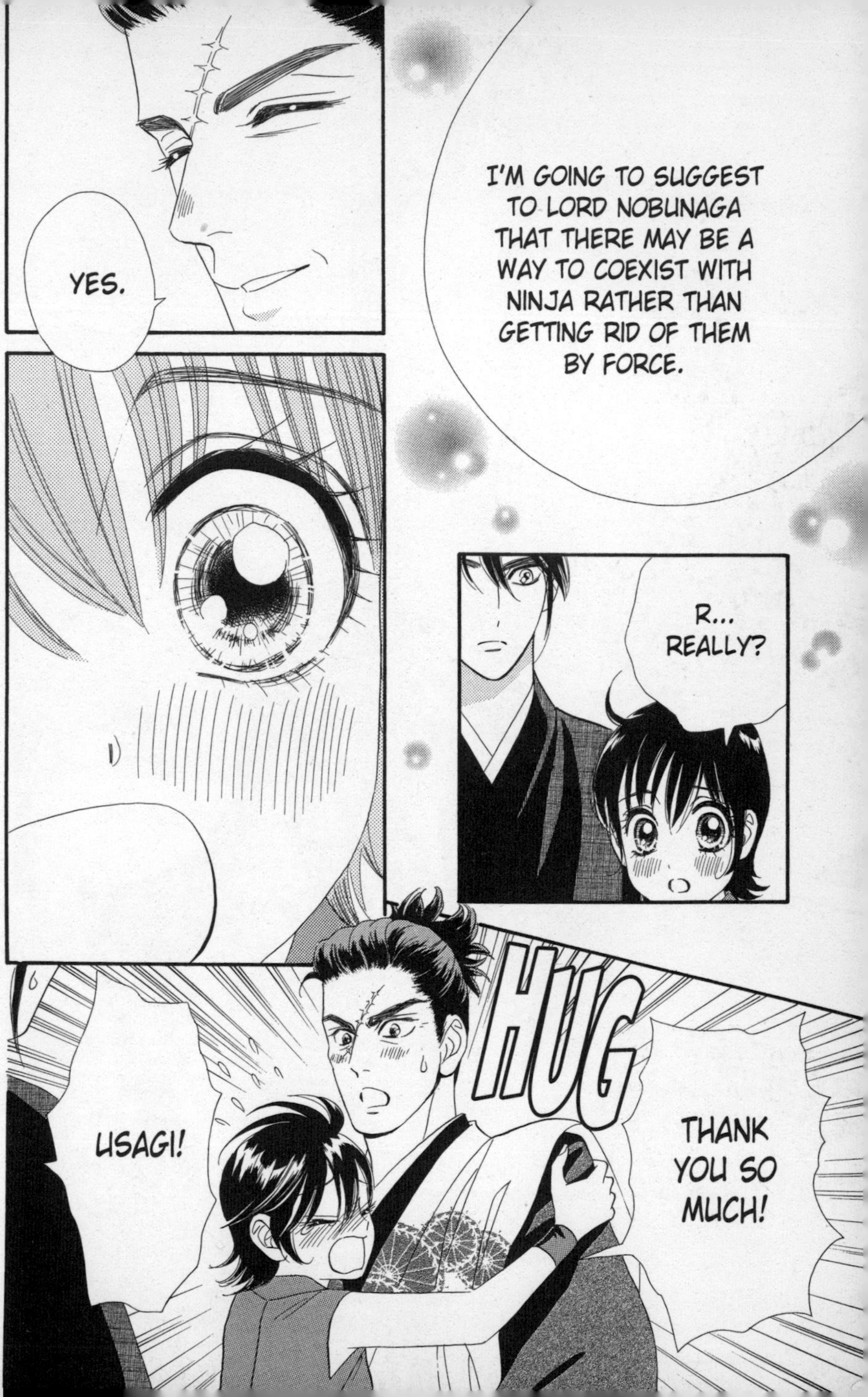
I'M GOING TO SUGGEST TO LORD NOBUNAGA THAT THERE MAY BE A WAY TO COEXIST WITH NINJA RATHER THAN GETTING RID OF THEM BY FORCE.
YES.
R... REALLY?
THANK YOU SO MUCH!
HUG
USAGI!

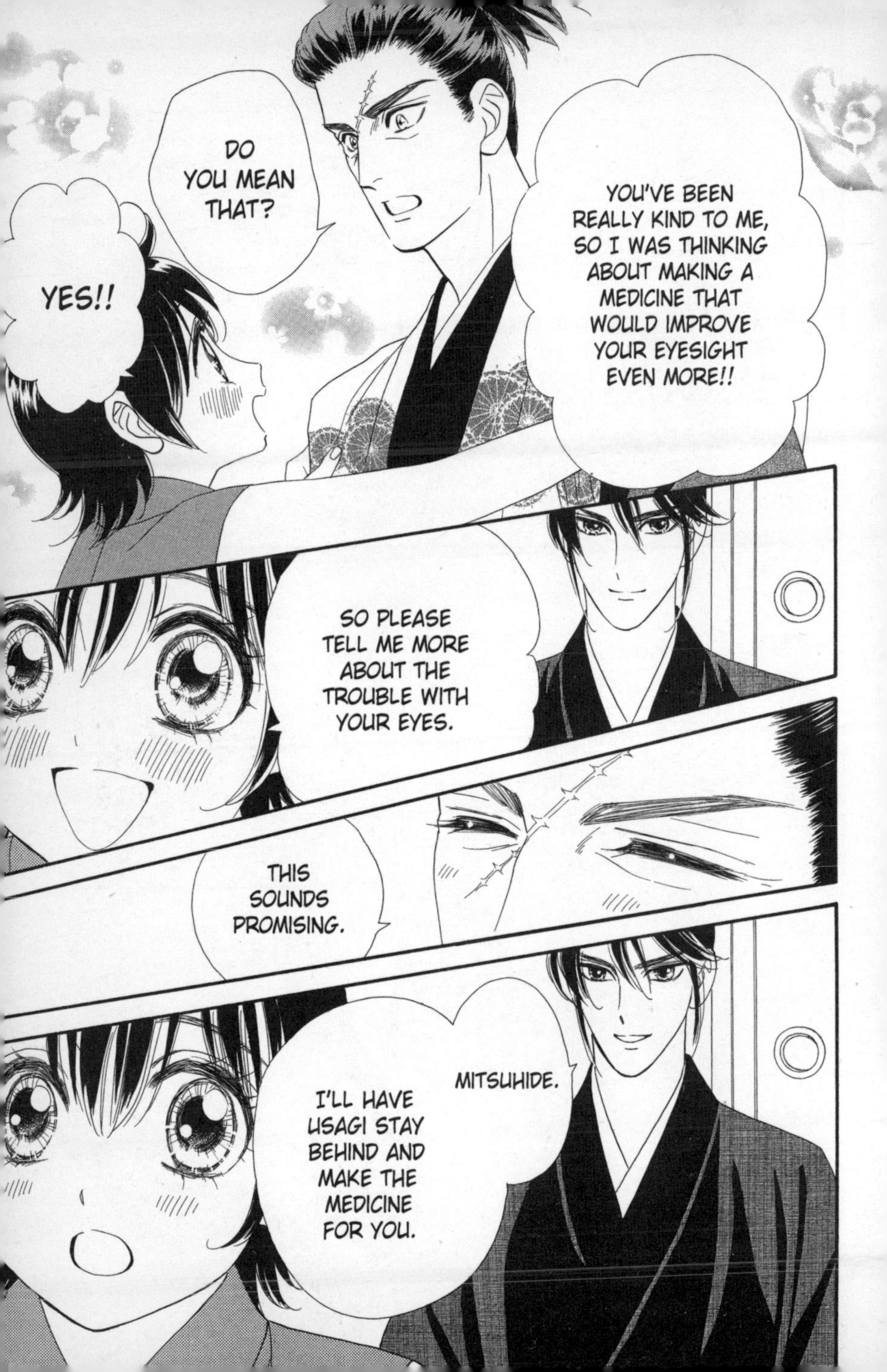
YOU'VE BEEN REALLY KIND TO ME, SO I WAS THINKING ABOUT MAKING A MEDICINE THAT WOULD IMPROVE YOUR EYESIGHT EVEN MORE!!
DO YOU MEAN THAT?
YES!!
SO PLEASE TELL ME MORE ABOUT THE TROUBLE WITH YOUR EYES.
THIS SOUNDS PROMISING.
MITSUHIDE.
I'LL HAVE USAGI STAY BEHIND AND MAKE THE MEDICINE FOR YOU.

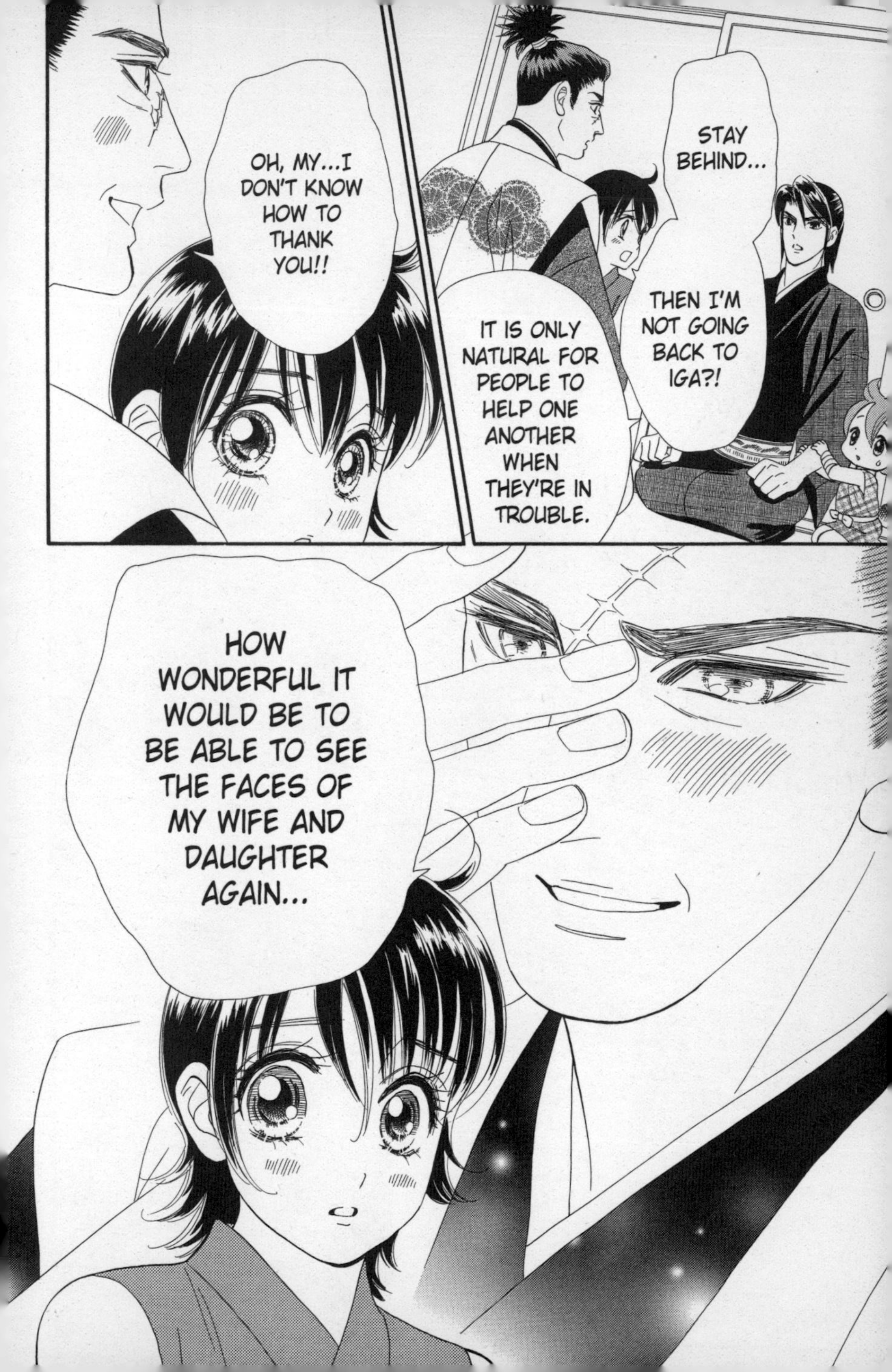
STAY BEHIND...
THEN I'M NOT GOING BACK TO IGA?!
IT IS ONLY NATURAL FOR PEOPLE TO HELP ONE ANOTHER WHEN THEY'RE IN TROUBLE.
OH, MY...I DON'T KNOW HOW TO THANK YOU!!
HOW WONDERFUL IT WOULD BE TO BE ABLE TO SEE THE FACES OF MY WIFE AND DAUGHTER AGAIN...

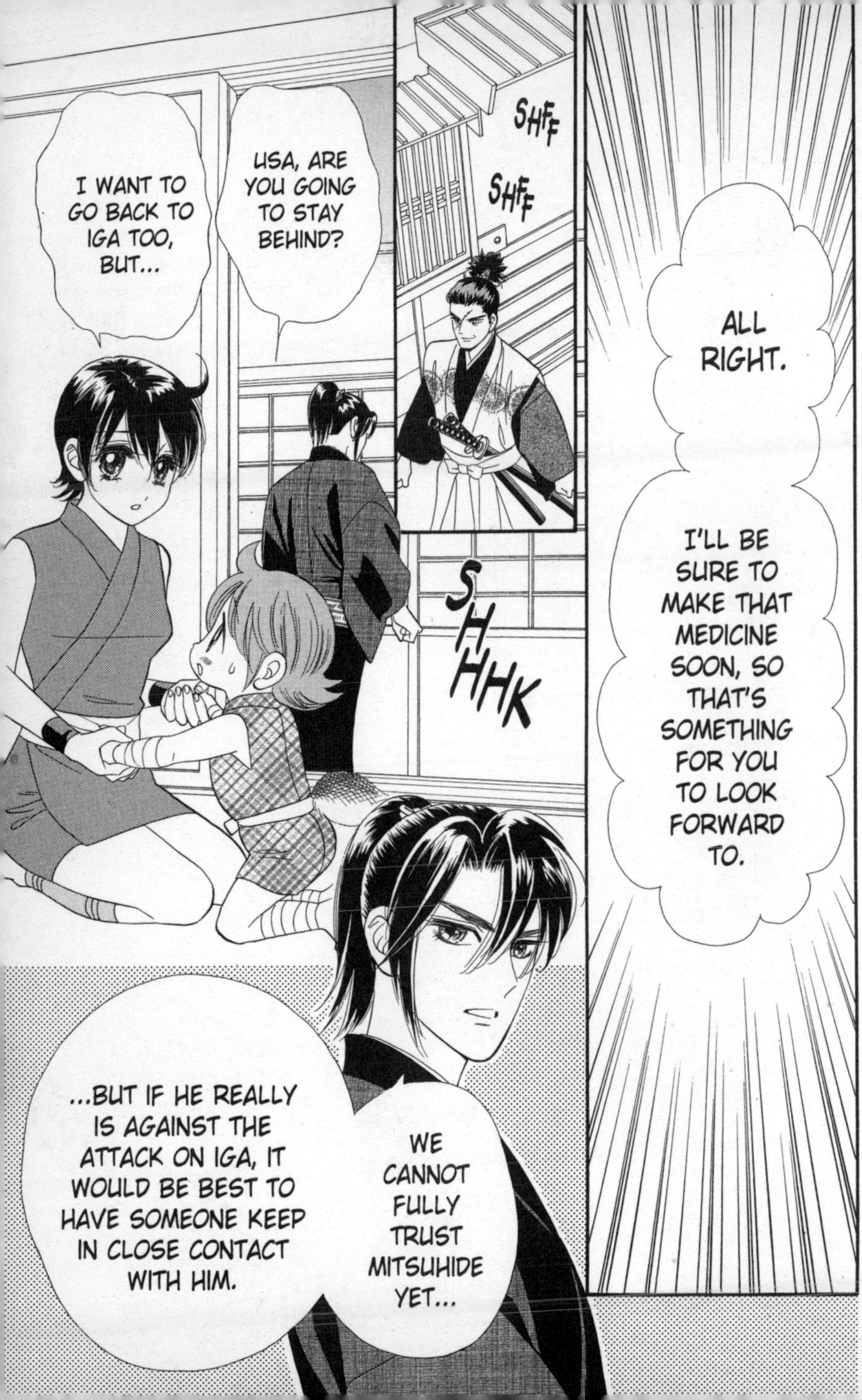
ALL RIGHT.
I'LL BE SURE TO MAKE THAT MEDICINE SOON, SO THAT'S SOMETHING FOR YOU TO LOOK FORWARD TO.
SHFF
SHFF
USA, ARE YOU GOING TO STAY BEHIND?
I WANT TO GO BACK TO IGA TOO, BUT...
SHHHK
WE CANNOT FULLY TRUST MITSUHIDE YET...
...BUT IF HE REALLY IS AGAINST THE ATTACK ON IGA, IT WOULD BE BEST TO HAVE SOMEONE KEEP IN CLOSE CONTACT WITH HIM.

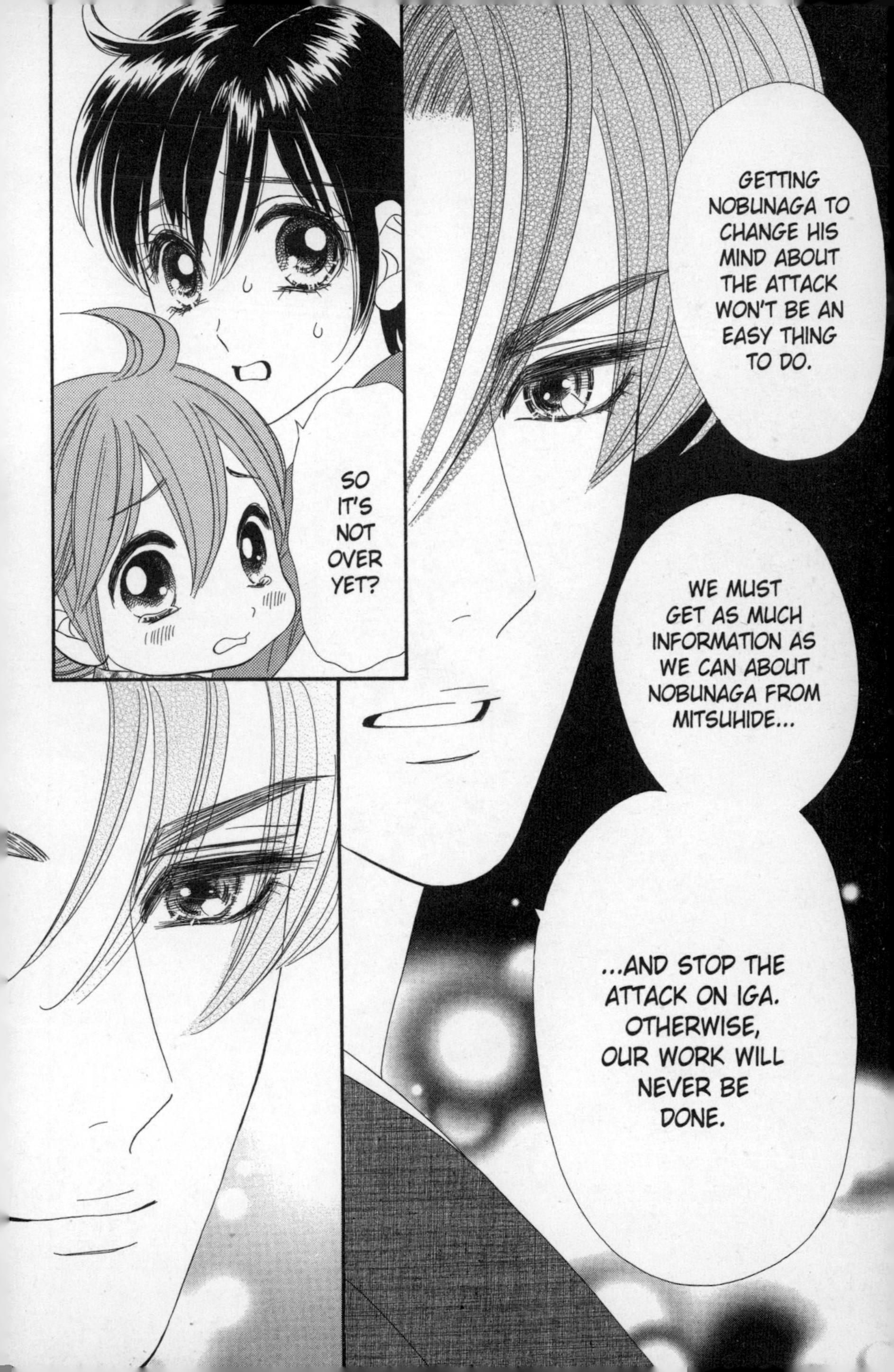
GETTING NOBUNAGA TO CHANGE HIS MIND ABOUT THE ATTACK WON'T BE AN EASY THING TO DO.
WE MUST GET AS MUCH INFORMATION AS WE CAN ABOUT NOBUNAGA FROM MITSUHIDE...
...AND STOP THE ATTACK ON IGA. OTHERWISE, OUR WORK WILL NEVER BE DONE.
SO IT'S NOT OVER YET?

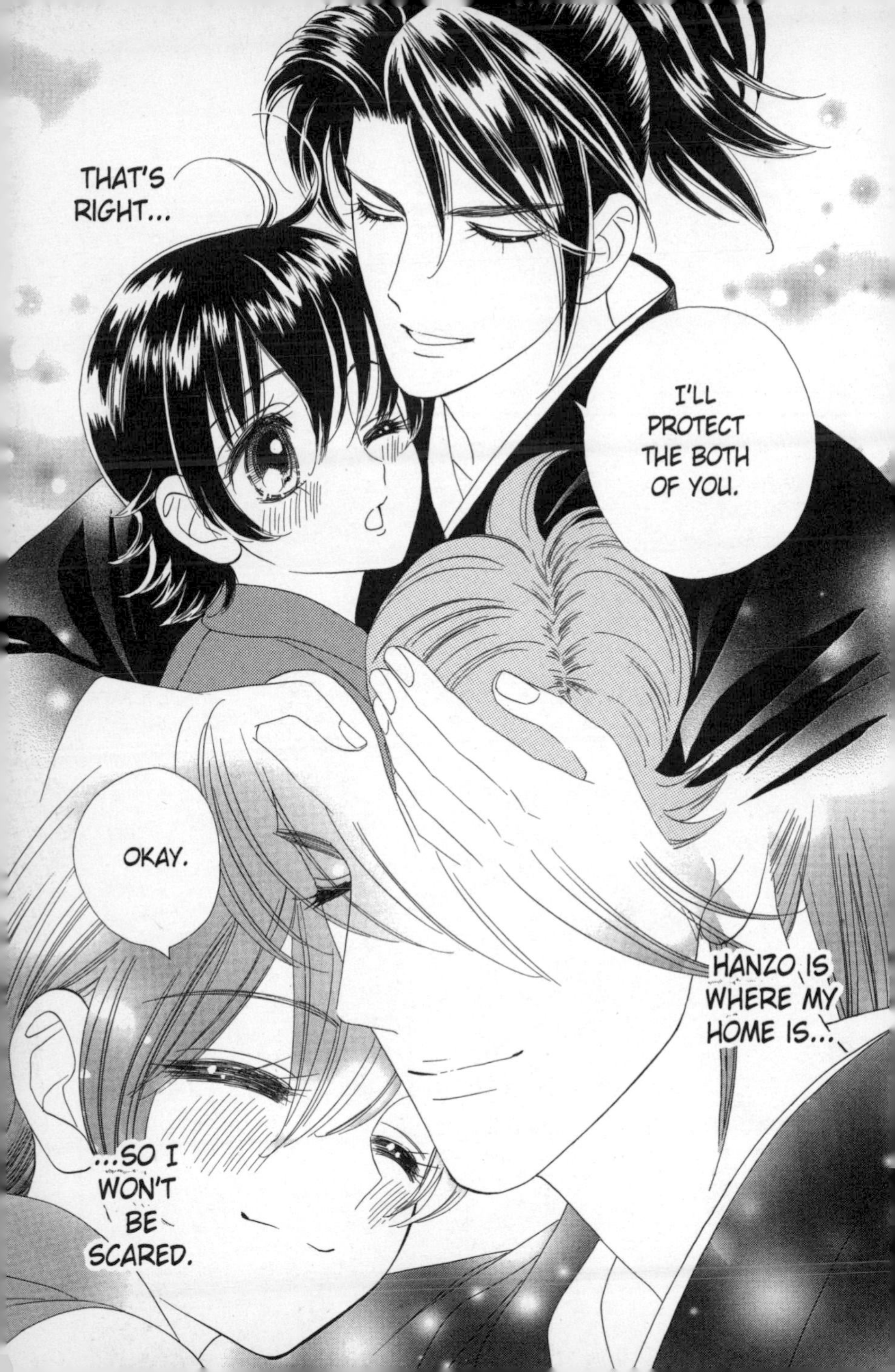
THAT'S RIGHT...
I'LL PROTECT THE BOTH OF YOU.
OKAY.
HANZO IS WHERE MY HOME IS...
...SO I WON'T BE SCARED.

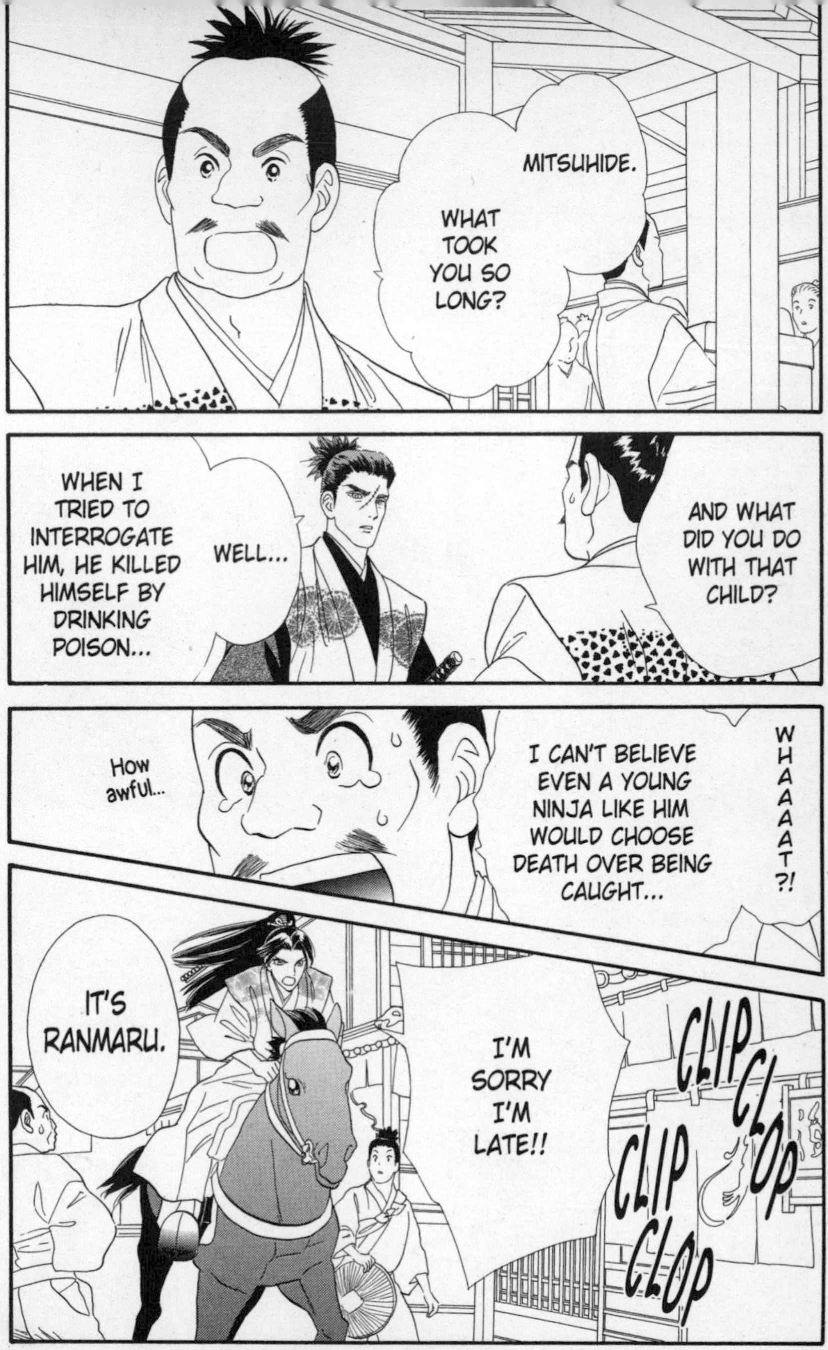
MITSUHIDE.
WHAT TOOK YOU SO LONG?
AND WHAT DID YOU DO WITH THAT CHILD?
WELL...
WHEN I TRIED TO INTERROGATE HIM, HE KILLED HIMSELF BY DRINKING POISON...
WHAAAAAT?!
I CAN'T BELIEVE EVEN A YOUNG NINJA LIKE HIM WOULD CHOOSE DEATH OVER BEING CAUGHT...
How awful...
CLIP CLOP
CLIP CLOP
I'M SORRY I'M LATE!!
IT'S RANMARU.

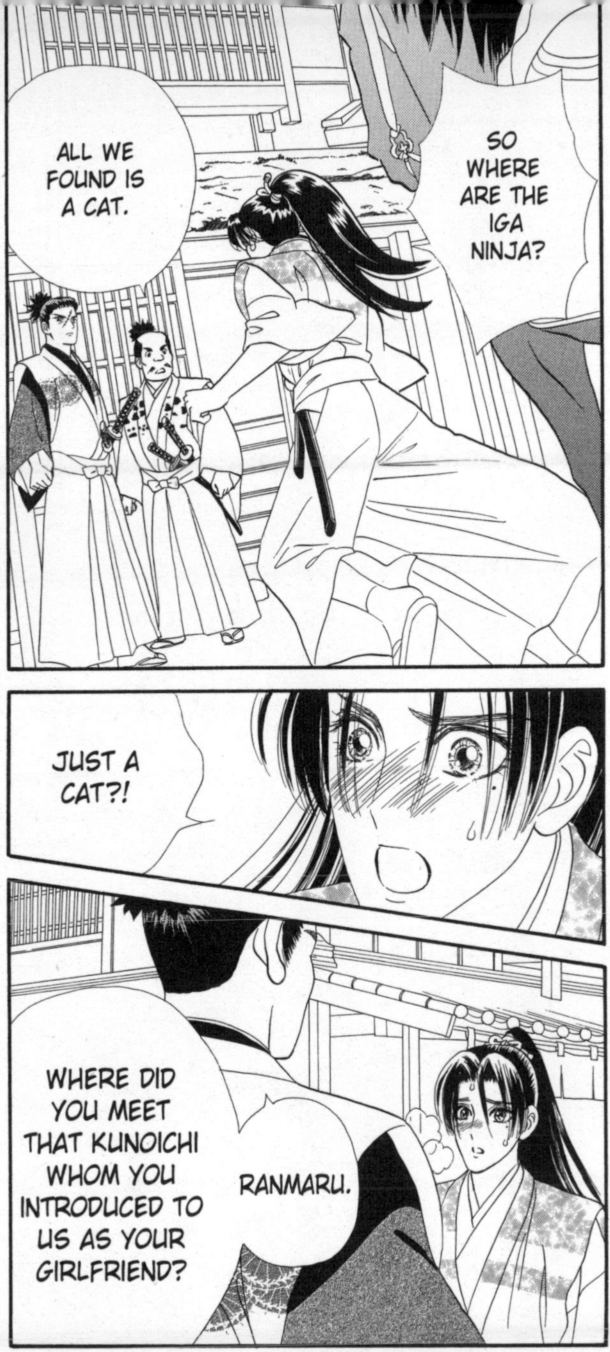
SO WHERE ARE THE IGA NINJA?
ALL WE FOUND IS A CAT.
JUST A CAT?!
RANMARU.
WHERE DID YOU MEET THAT KUNOICHI WHOM YOU INTRODUCED TO US AS YOUR GIRLFRIEND?

GREETINGS

Hello, it's Ue-Rin. I started writing the installments of "Ue-Rin's Manga School" from sheer momentum, so every time I continue writing it and read previous passages, I start feeling really embarrassed.

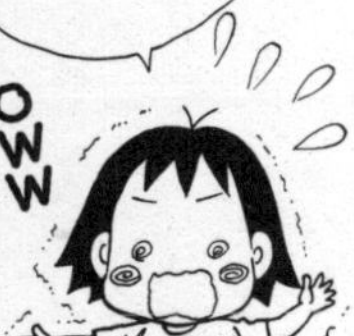
OWW
Rin

I've been rolling around every day on my balance ball, which I bought to lose weight.

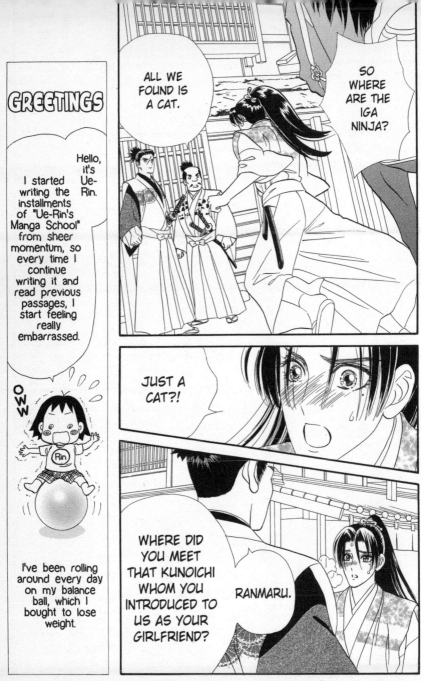

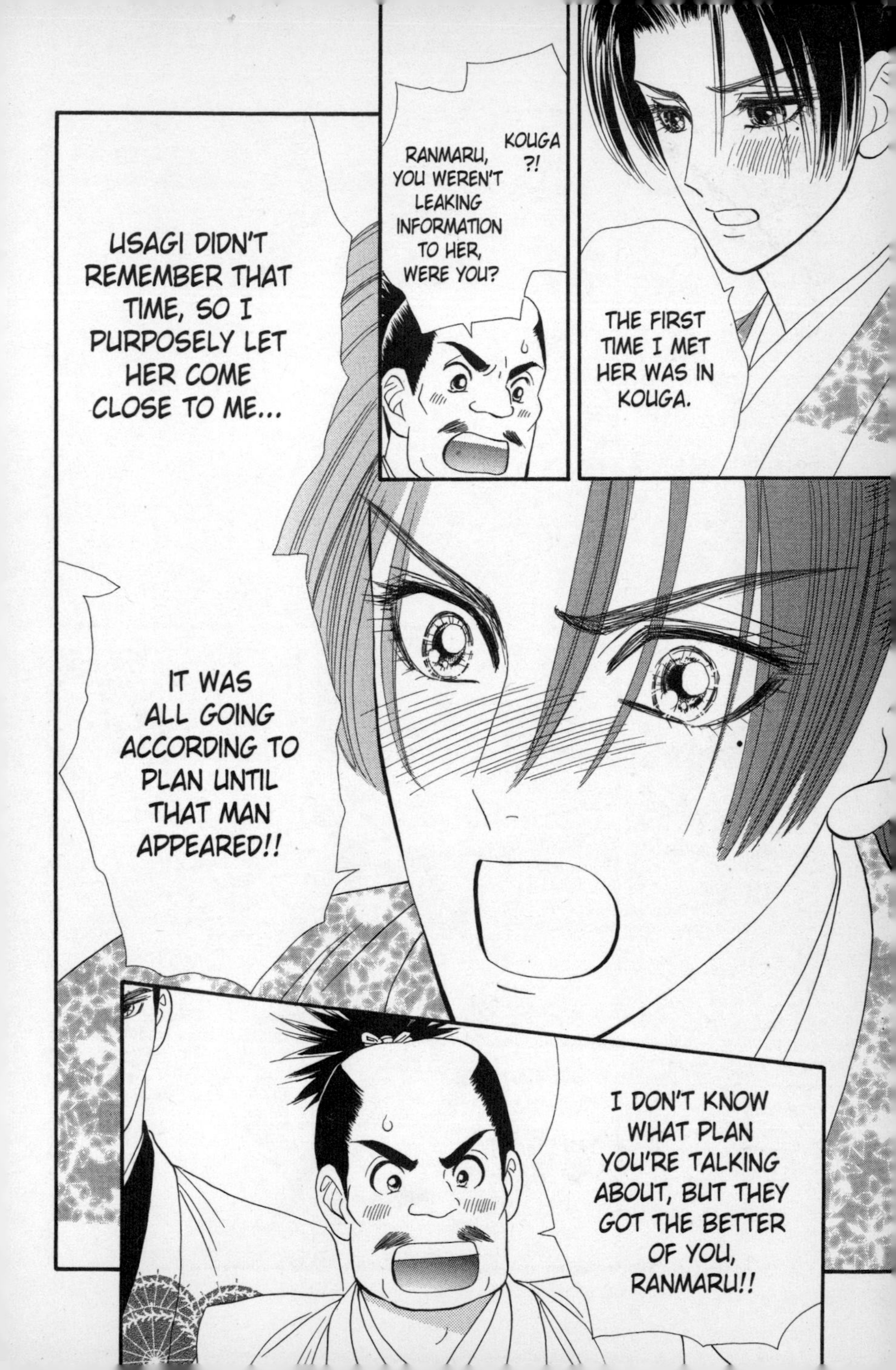
THE FIRST TIME I MET HER WAS IN KOUGA.
KOUGA ?!
RANMARU, YOU WEREN'T LEAKING INFORMATION TO HER, WERE YOU?
USAGI DIDN'T REMEMBER THAT TIME, SO I PURPOSELY LET HER COME CLOSE TO ME...
IT WAS ALL GOING ACCORDING TO PLAN UNTIL THAT MAN APPEARED!!
I DON'T KNOW WHAT PLAN YOU'RE TALKING ABOUT, BUT THEY GOT THE BETTER OF YOU, RANMARU!!

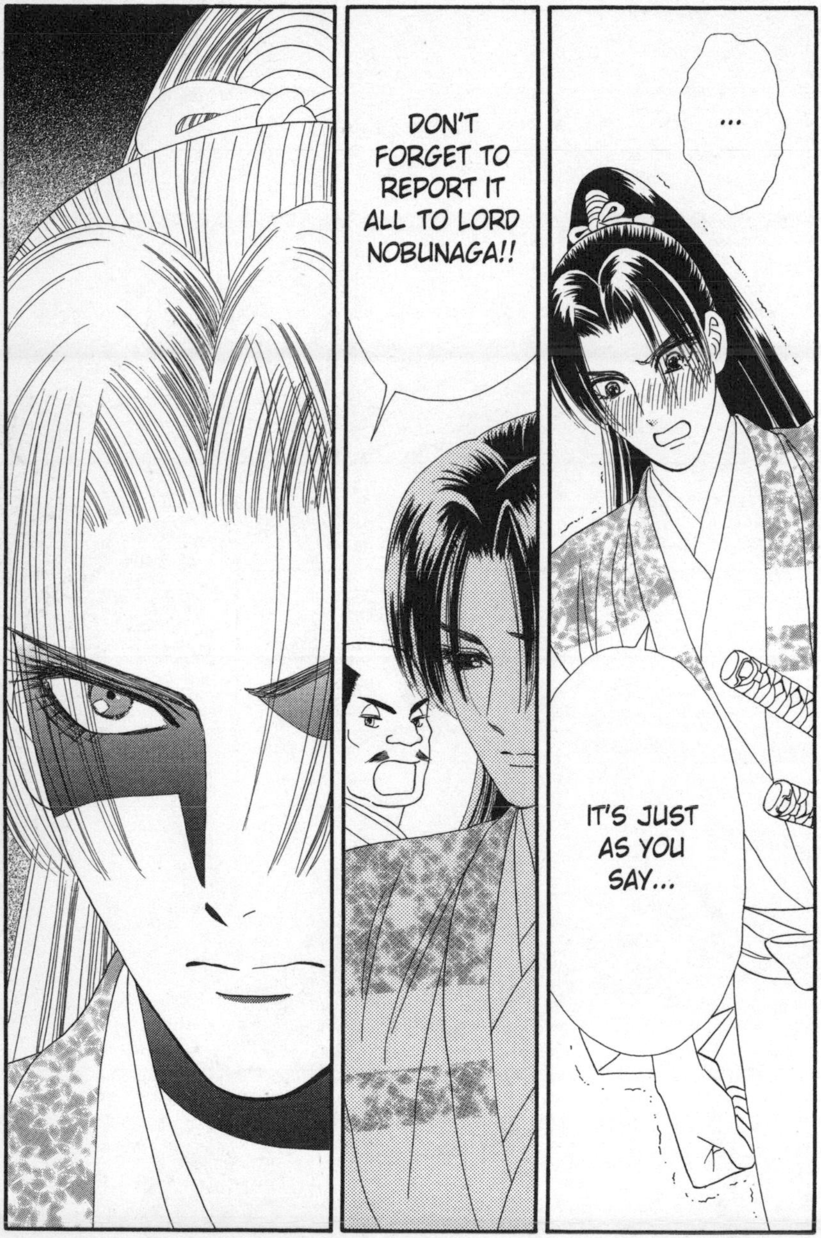
...
IT'S JUST AS YOU SAY...
DON'T FORGET TO REPORT IT ALL TO LORD NOBUNAGA!!

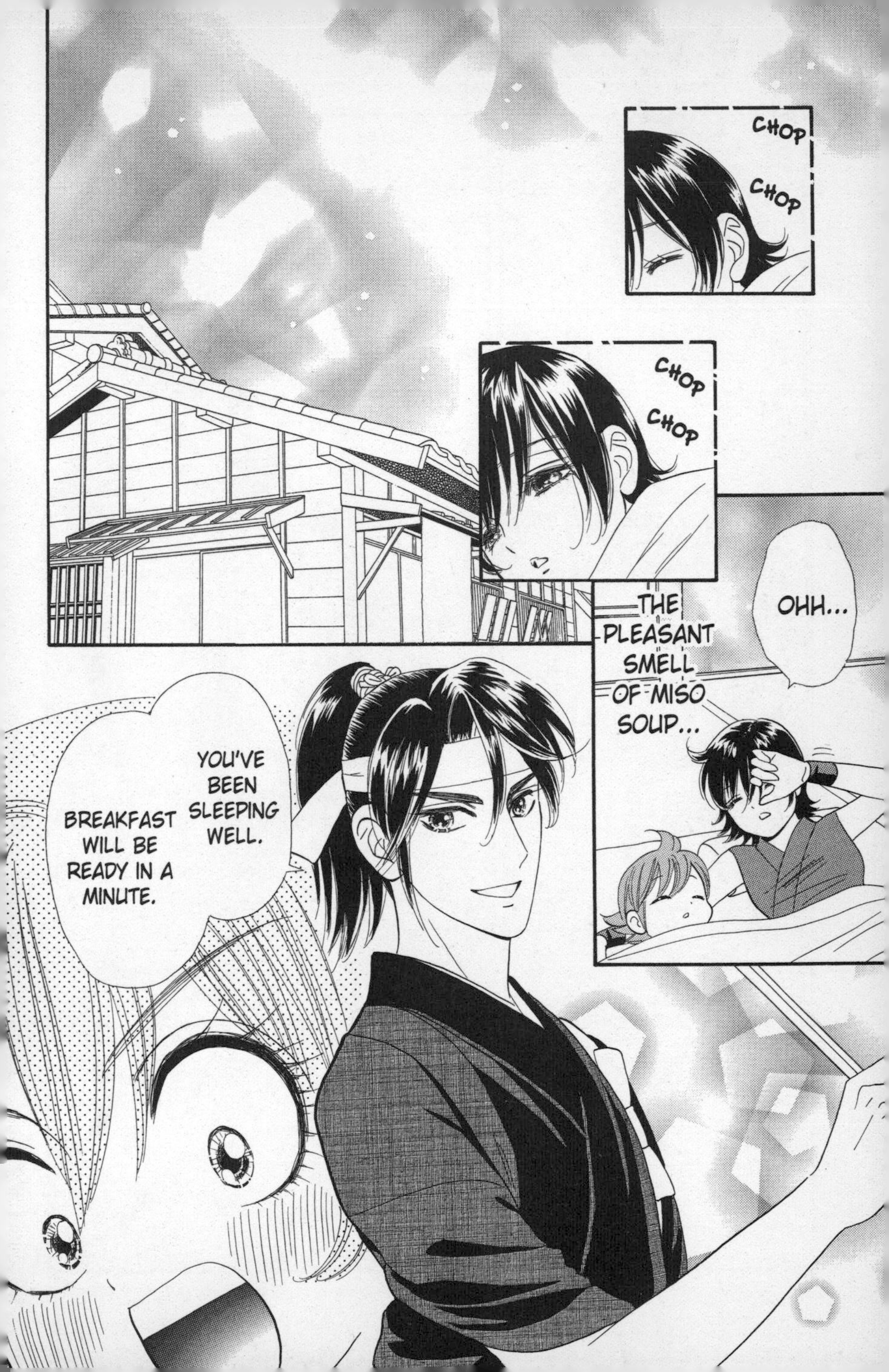
CHOP
CHOP
CHOP
CHOP
OHH...
THE PLEASANT SMELL OF MISO SOUP...
YOU'VE BEEN SLEEPING WELL.
BREAKFAST WILL BE READY IN A MINUTE.

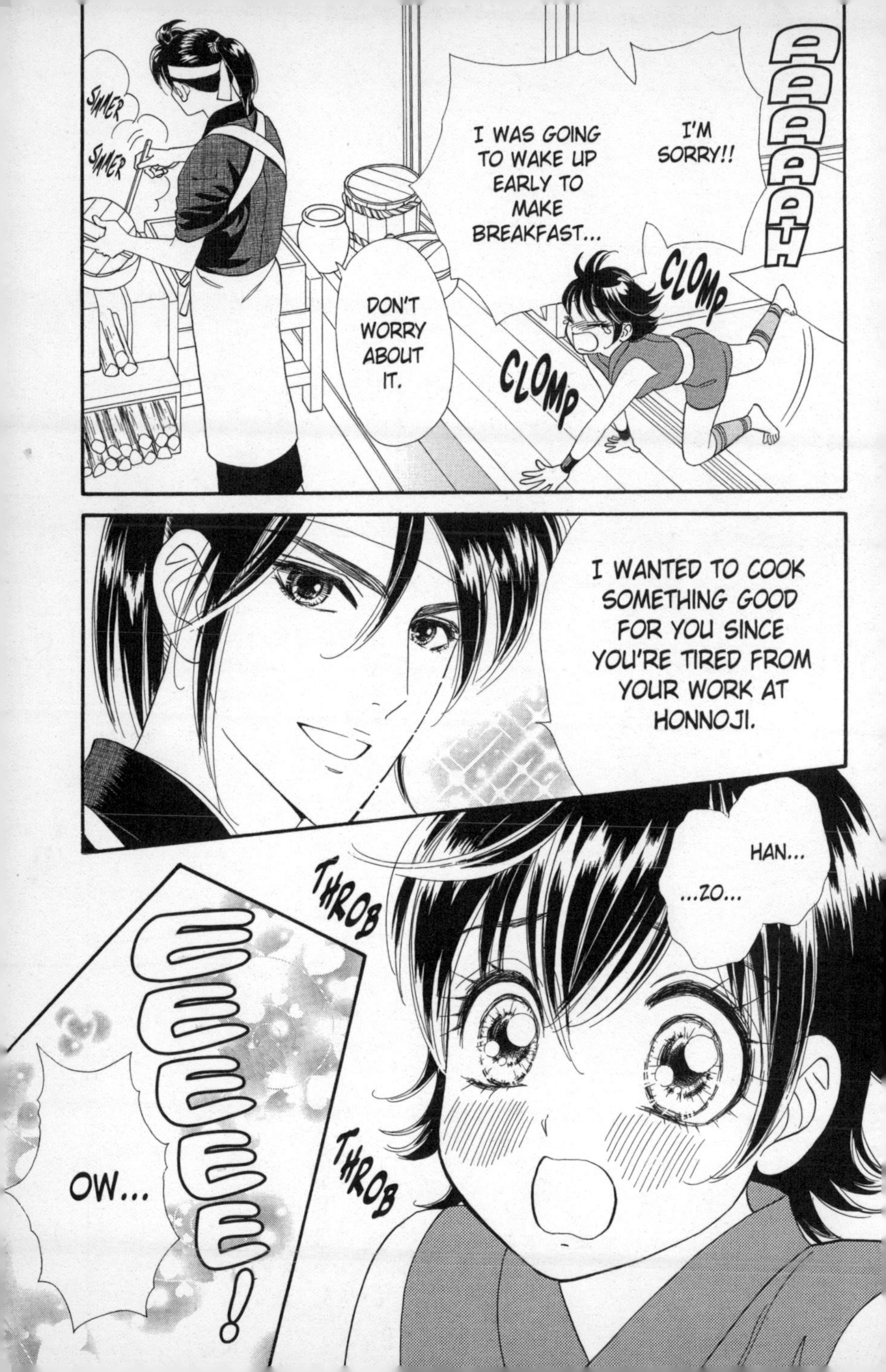
AAAAAH
I'M SORRY!!
I WAS GOING TO WAKE UP EARLY TO MAKE BREAKFAST...
CLOMP
CLOMP
DON'T WORRY ABOUT IT.
SIMMER
SIMMER
I WANTED TO COOK SOMETHING GOOD FOR YOU SINCE YOU'RE TIRED FROM YOUR WORK AT HONNOJI.
HAN...
...ZO...
THROB
THROB
EEEEE!
OW...

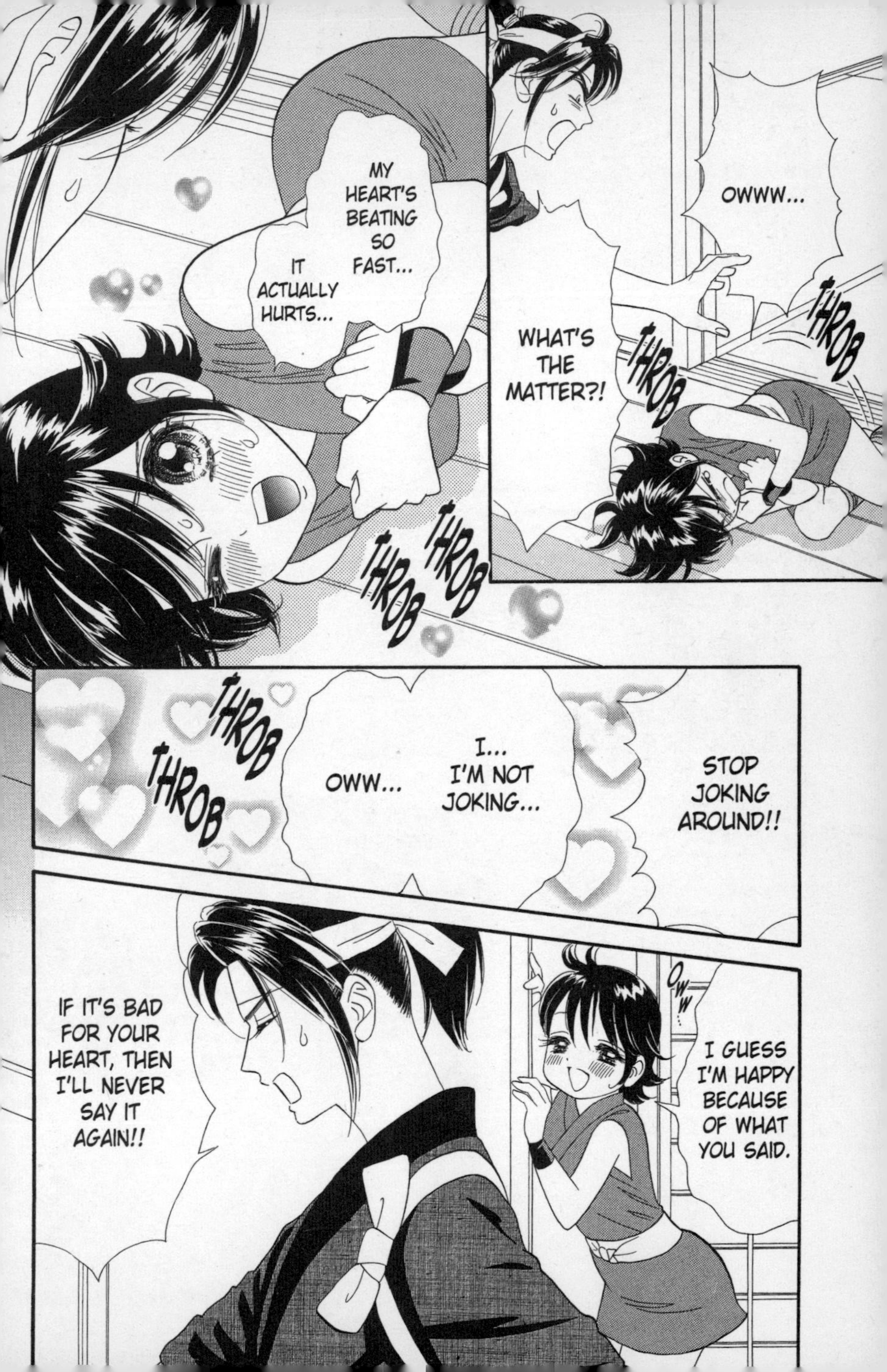
OWWW...
WHAT'S THE MATTER?!
THROB
THROB
MY HEART'S BEATING SO FAST...
IT ACTUALLY HURTS...
THROB
THROB
STOP JOKING AROUND!!
I... I'M NOT JOKING...
OWW...
THROB
THROB
I GUESS I'M HAPPY BECAUSE OF WHAT YOU SAID.
OWW...
IF IT'S BAD FOR YOUR HEART, THEN I'LL NEVER SAY IT AGAIN!!

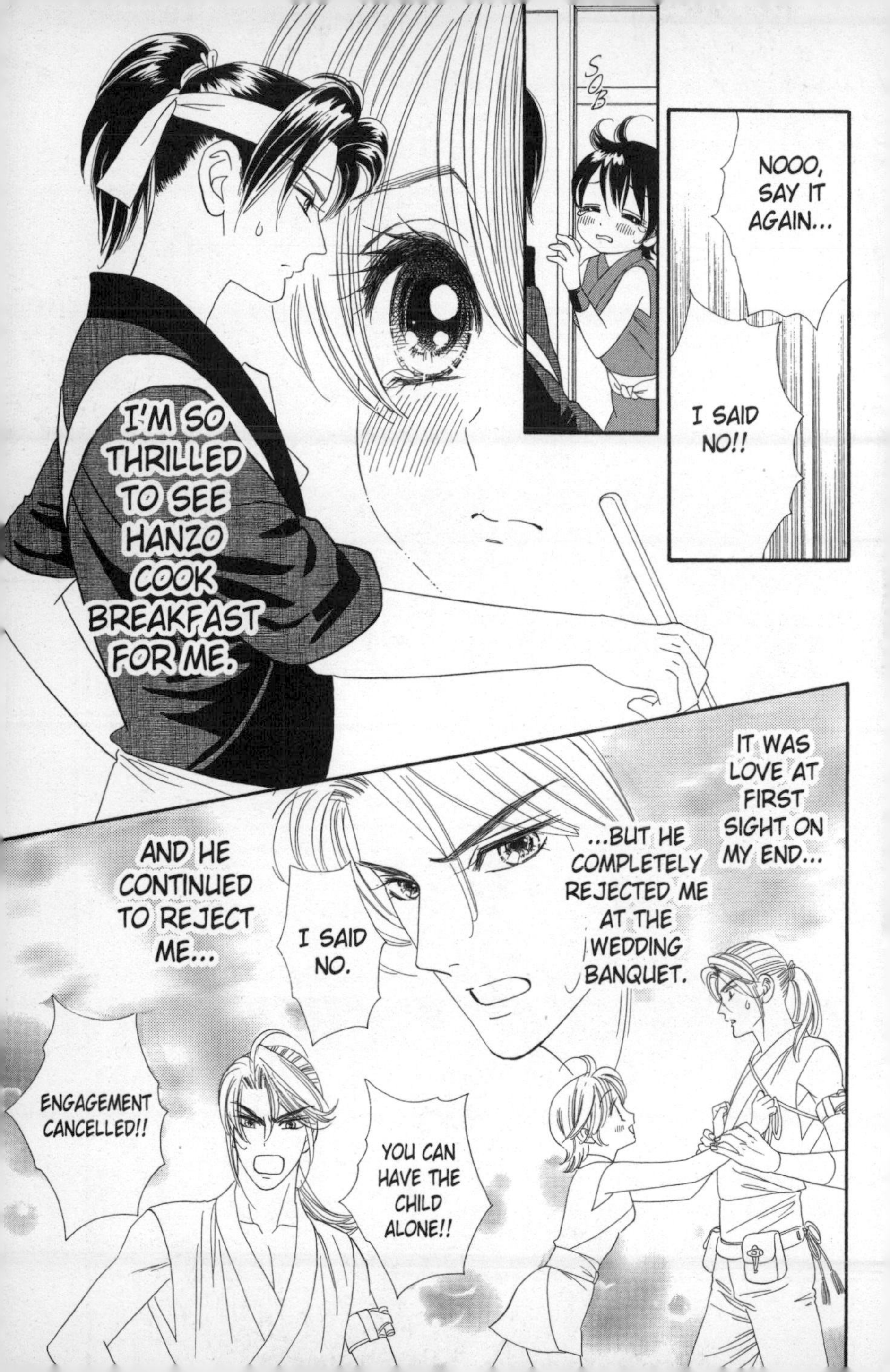
NOOO, SAY IT AGAIN...
I SAID NO!!
SOB
I'M SO THRILLED TO SEE HANZO COOK BREAKFAST FOR ME.
IT WAS LOVE AT FIRST SIGHT ON MY END...
...BUT HE COMPLETELY REJECTED ME AT THE WEDDING BANQUET.
I SAID NO.
AND HE CONTINUED TO REJECT ME...
YOU CAN HAVE THE CHILD ALONE!!
ENGAGEMENT CANCELLED!!

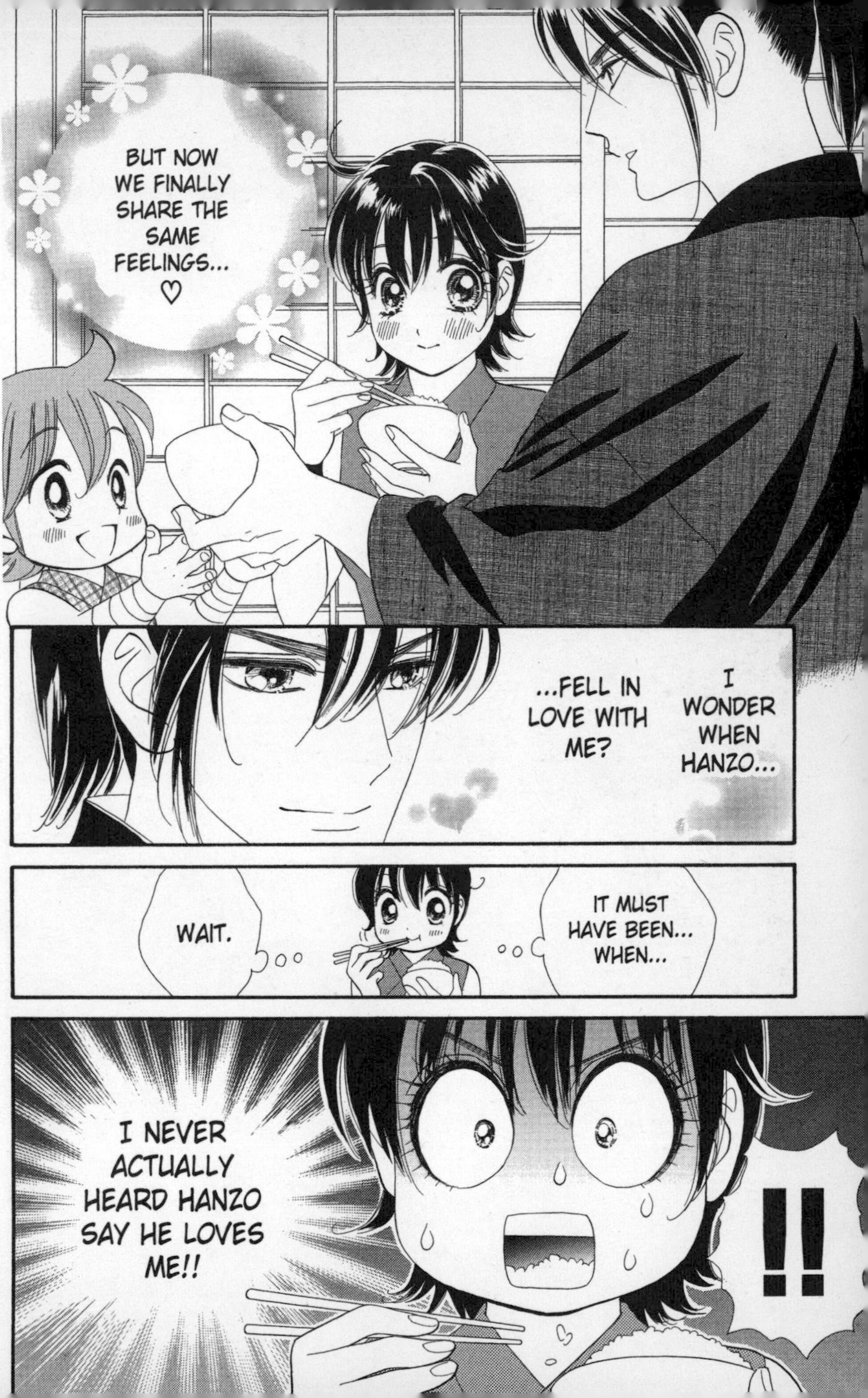
BUT NOW WE FINALLY SHARE THE SAME FEELINGS... ♡
I WONDER WHEN HANZO...
...FELL IN LOVE WITH ME?
IT MUST HAVE BEEN... WHEN...
WAIT.
I NEVER ACTUALLY HEARD HANZO SAY HE LOVES ME!!
!!

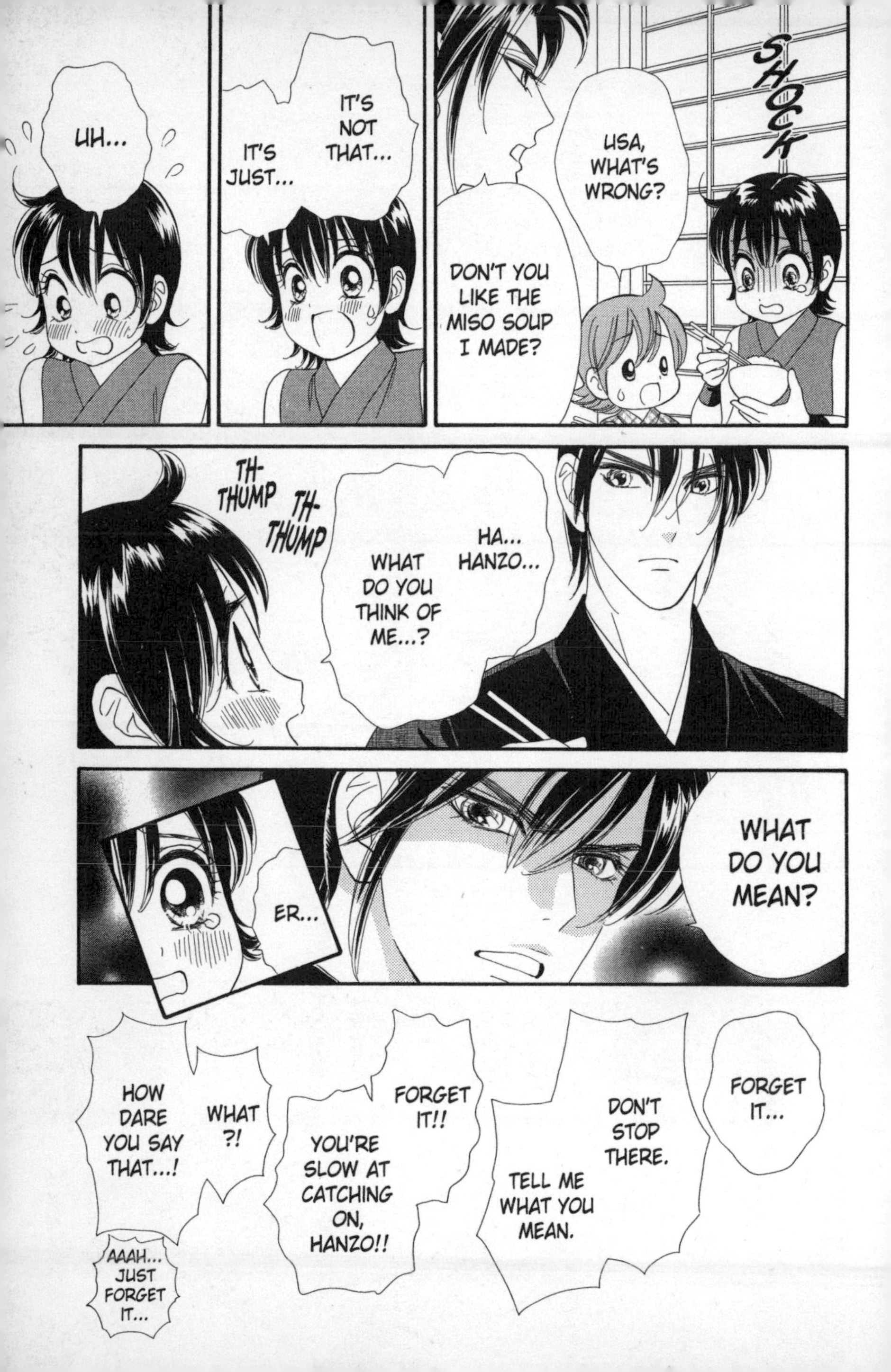
SHOCK
USA, WHAT'S WRONG?
DON'T YOU LIKE THE MISO SOUP I MADE?
IT'S NOT THAT...
IT'S JUST...
UH...
HA... HANZO...
WHAT DO YOU THINK OF ME...?
TH-THUMP TH-THUMP
WHAT DO YOU MEAN?
ER...
FORGET IT...
DON'T STOP THERE.
TELL ME WHAT YOU MEAN.
FORGET IT!!
YOU'RE SLOW AT CATCHING ON, HANZO!!
WHAT?!
HOW DARE YOU SAY THAT...!
AAAH... JUST FORGET IT...

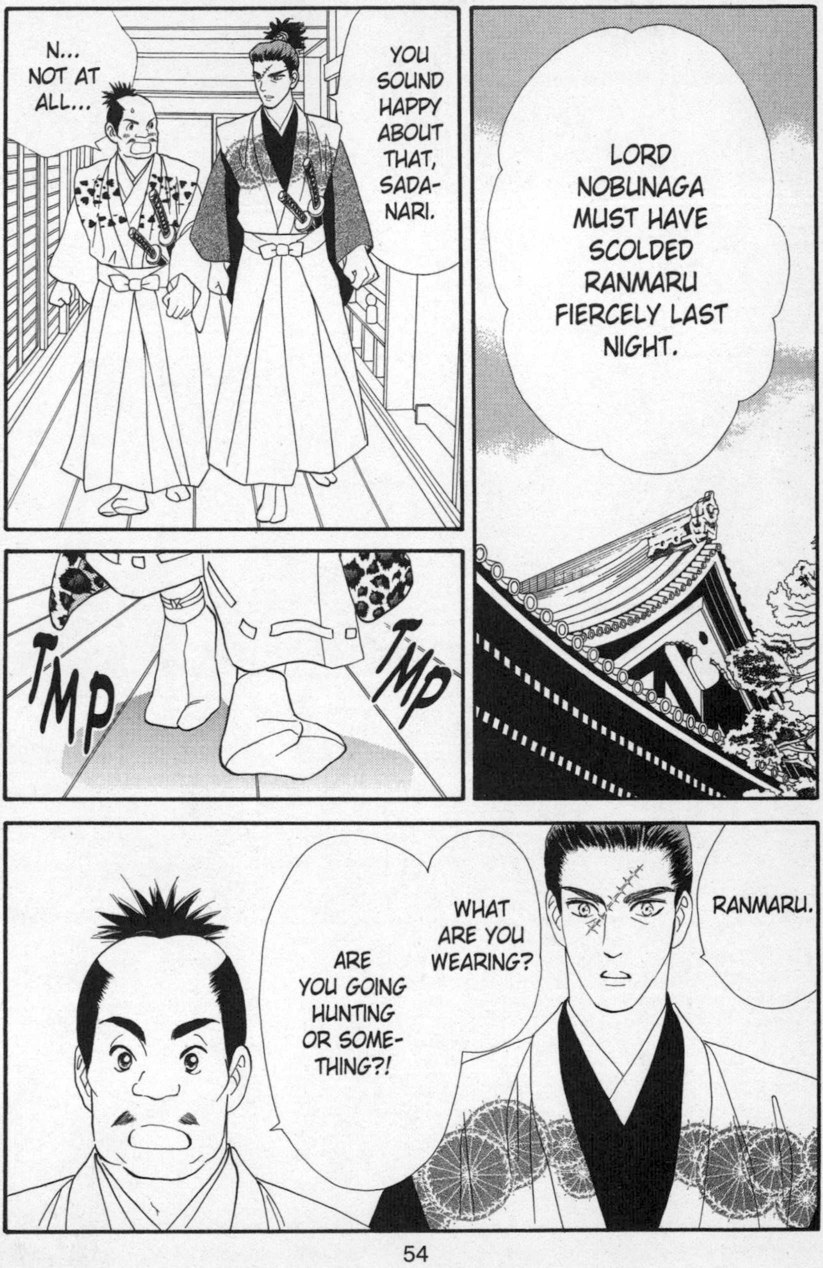
LORD NOBUNAGA MUST HAVE SCOLDED RANMARU FIERCELY LAST NIGHT.
YOU SOUND HAPPY ABOUT THAT, SADA-NARI.
N... NOT AT ALL...
TMP
TMP
RANMARU.
WHAT ARE YOU WEARING?
ARE YOU GOING HUNTING OR SOME-THING?!

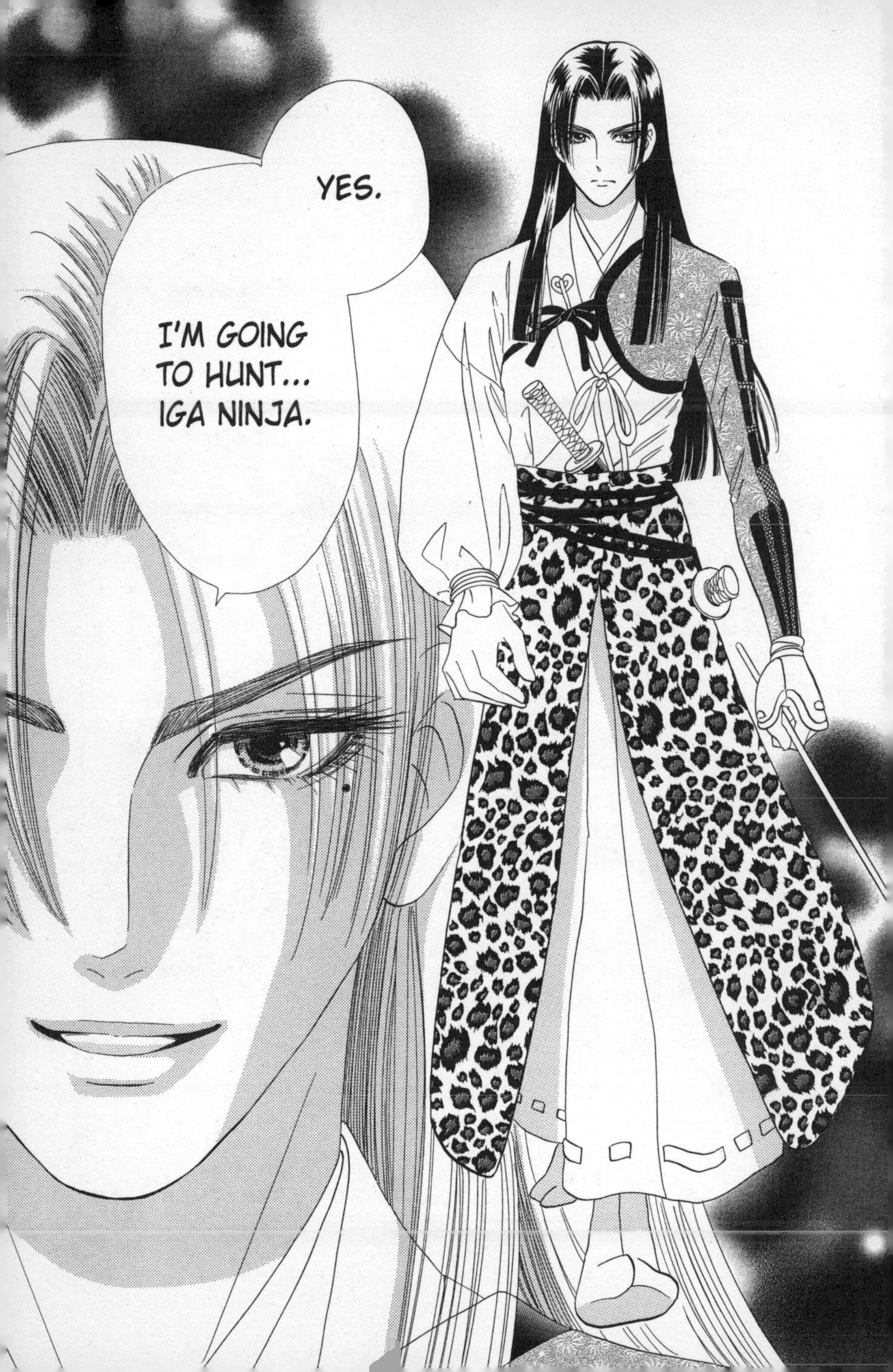
YES.
I'M GOING TO HUNT... IGA NINJA.

TAIL OF THE MOON EXTRA: TODAY'S MISSION

"I WANT TO SEE HANZO IN A SOCCER UNIFORM!"

-CM, NAGANO PREFECTURE

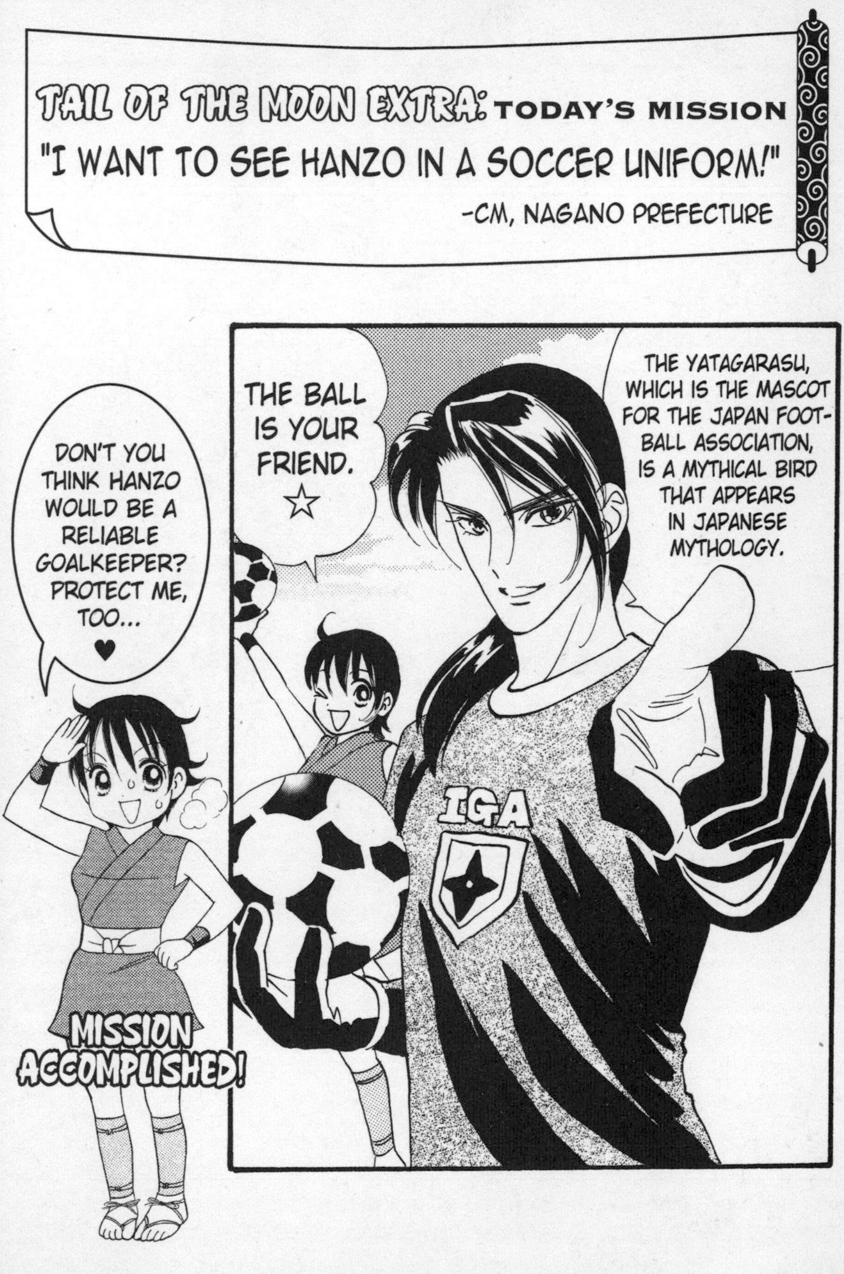
THE YATAGARASU, WHICH IS THE MASCOT FOR THE JAPAN FOOT-BALL ASSOCIATION, IS A MYTHICAL BIRD THAT APPEARS IN JAPANESE MYTHOLOGY.
THE BALL IS YOUR FRIEND. ☆
IGA
DON'T YOU THINK HANZO WOULD BE A RELIABLE GOALKEEPER? PROTECT ME, TOO... ♥
MISSION ACCOMPLISHED!

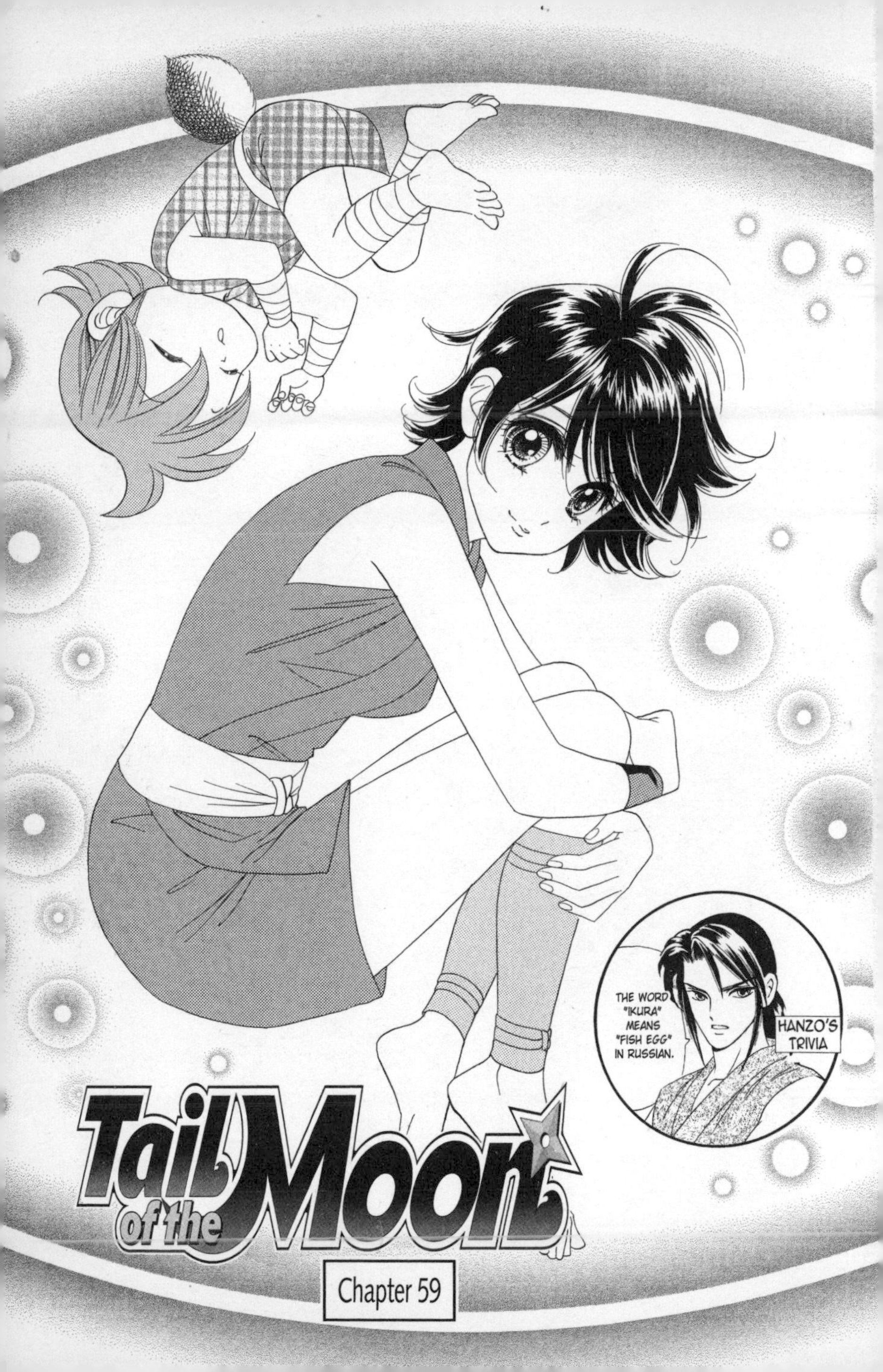
THE WORD "IKURA" MEANS "FISH EGG" IN RUSSIAN.
HANZO'S TRIVIA
Tail of the Moon
Chapter 59

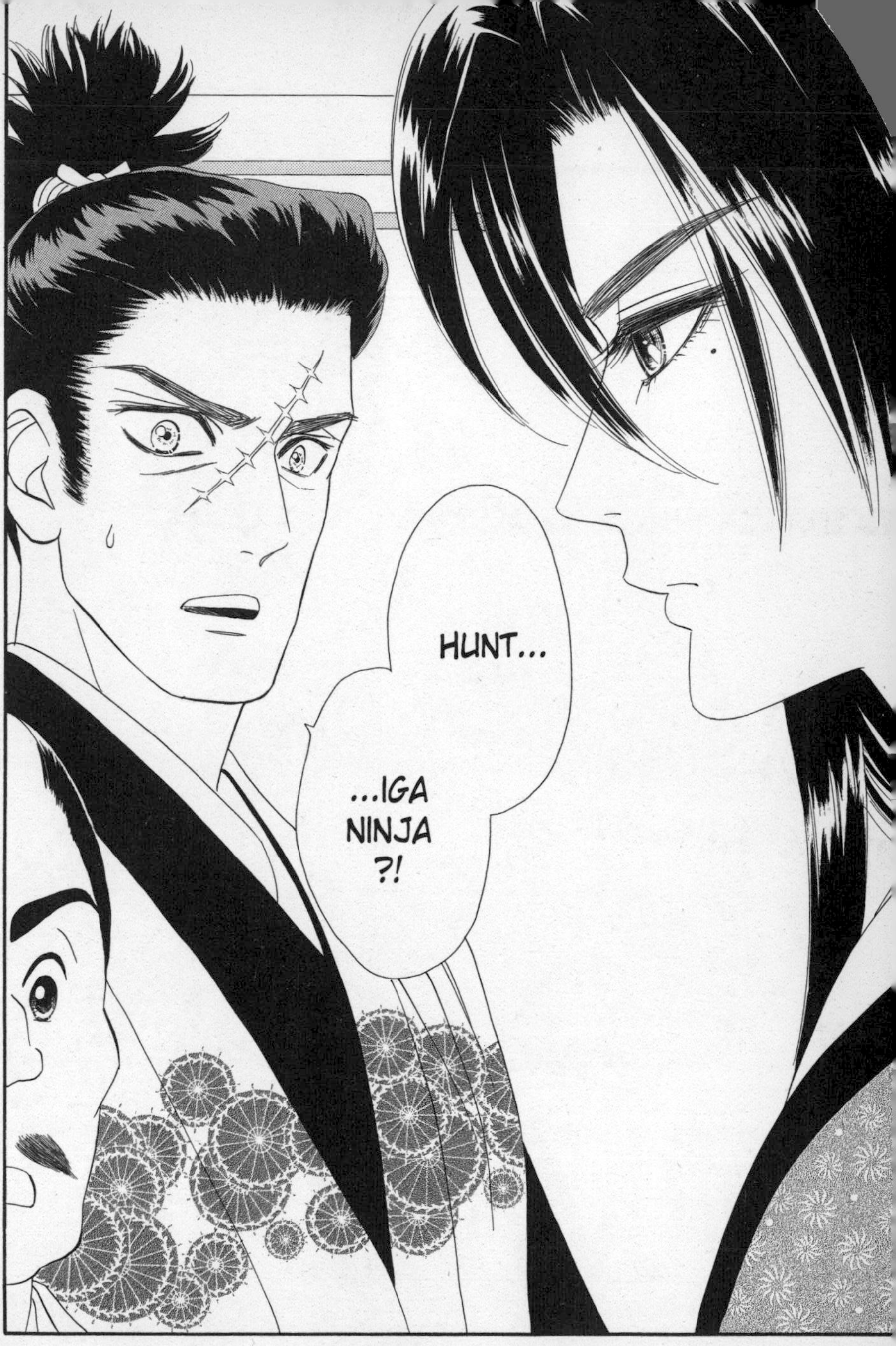
HUNT...
...IGA NINJA ?!

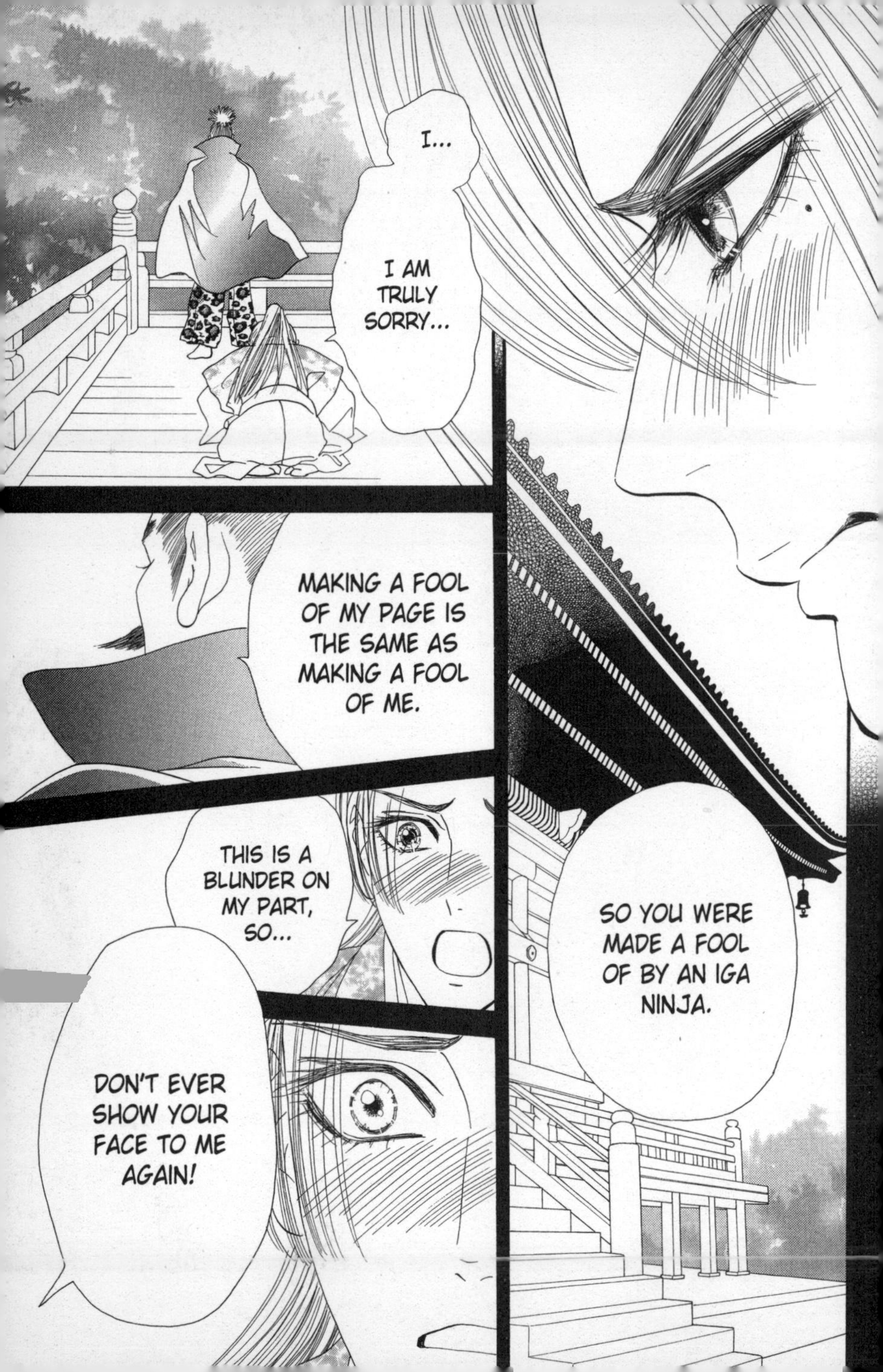
I...
I AM TRULY SORRY...
SO YOU WERE MADE A FOOL OF BY AN IGA NINJA.
MAKING A FOOL OF MY PAGE IS THE SAME AS MAKING A FOOL OF ME.
THIS IS A BLUNDER ON MY PART, SO...
DON'T EVER SHOW YOUR FACE TO ME AGAIN!

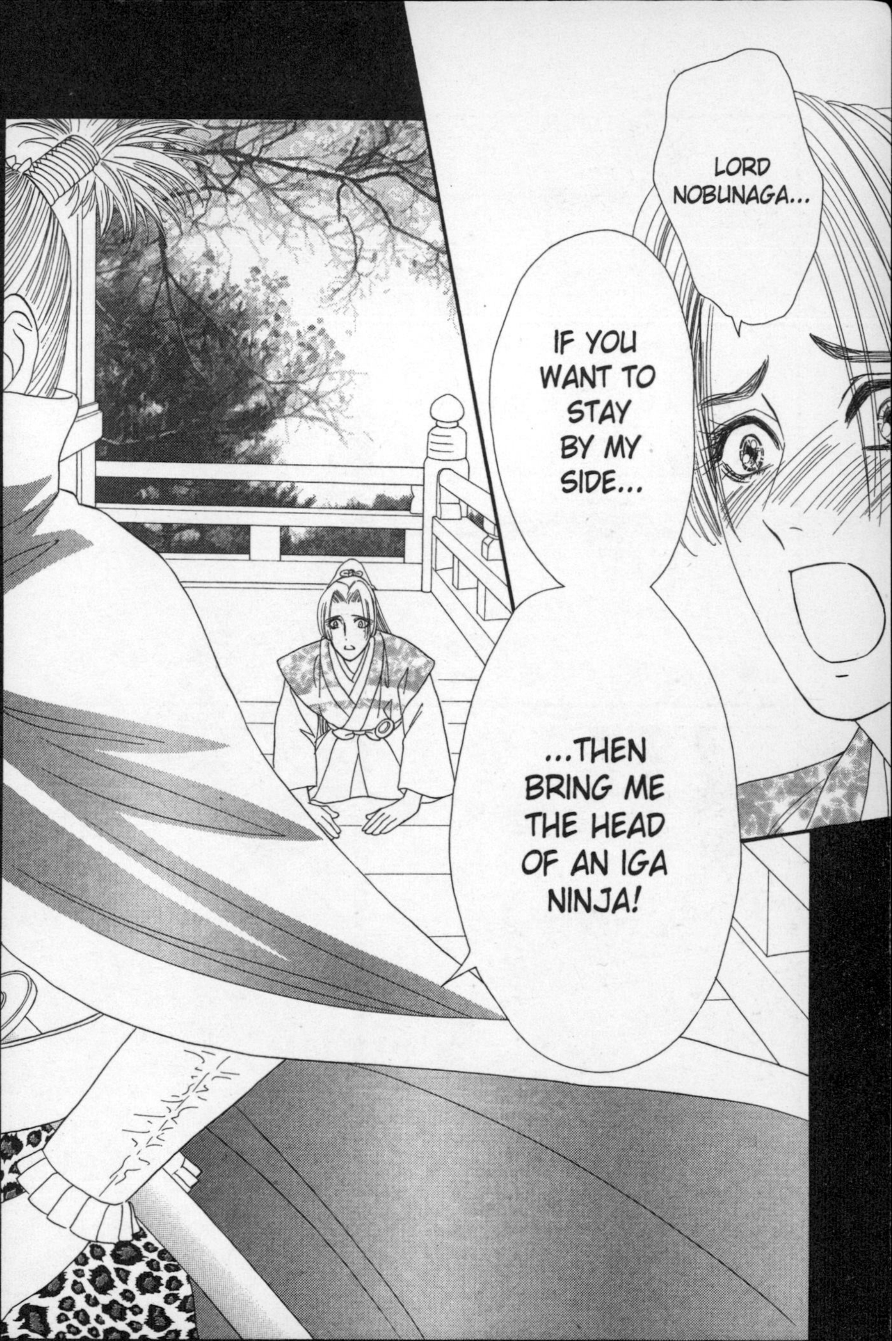
LORD NOBUNAGA...
IF YOU WANT TO STAY BY MY SIDE...
...THEN BRING ME THE HEAD OF AN IGA NINJA!

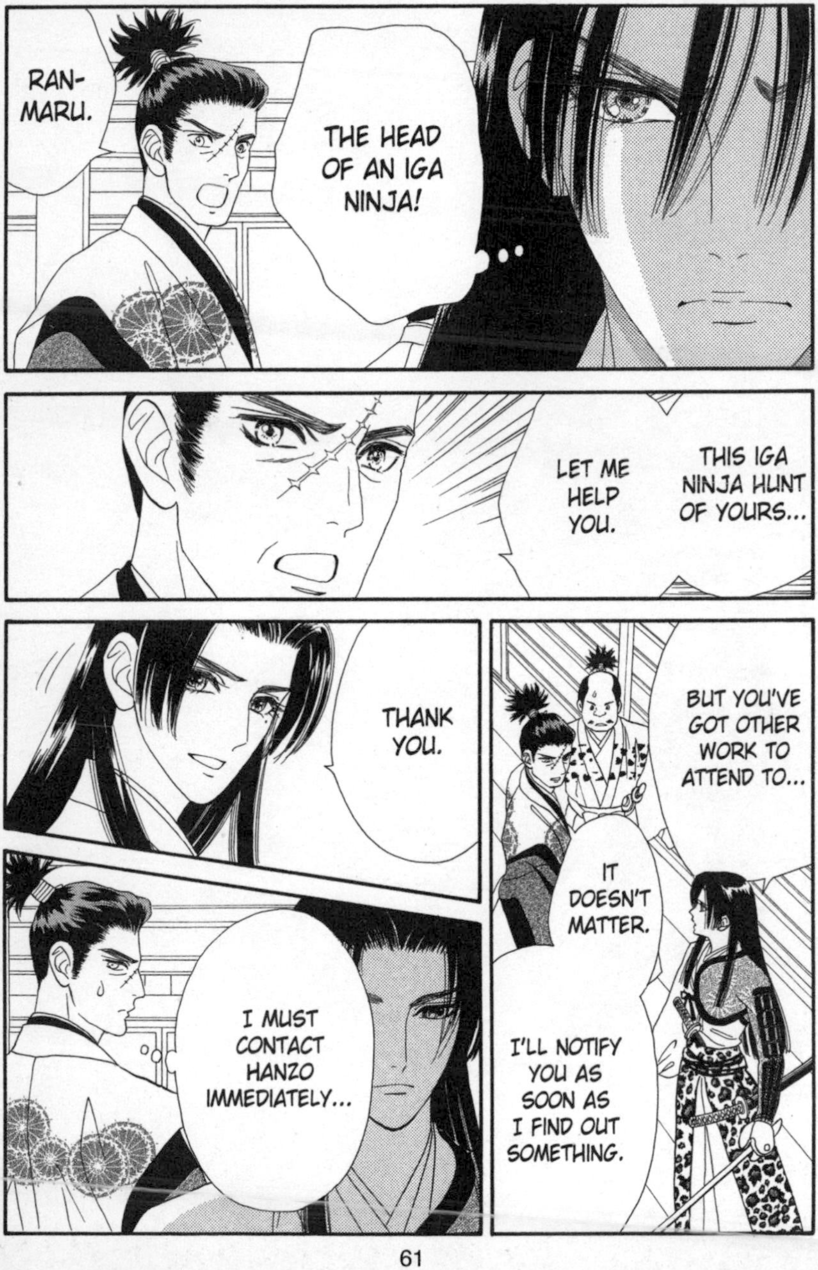
THE HEAD OF AN IGA NINJA!
RAN-MARU.
THIS IGA NINJA HUNT OF YOURS...
LET ME HELP YOU.
BUT YOU'VE GOT OTHER WORK TO ATTEND TO...
IT DOESN'T MATTER.
I'LL NOTIFY YOU AS SOON AS I FIND OUT SOMETHING.
THANK YOU.
I MUST CONTACT HANZO IMMEDIATELY...

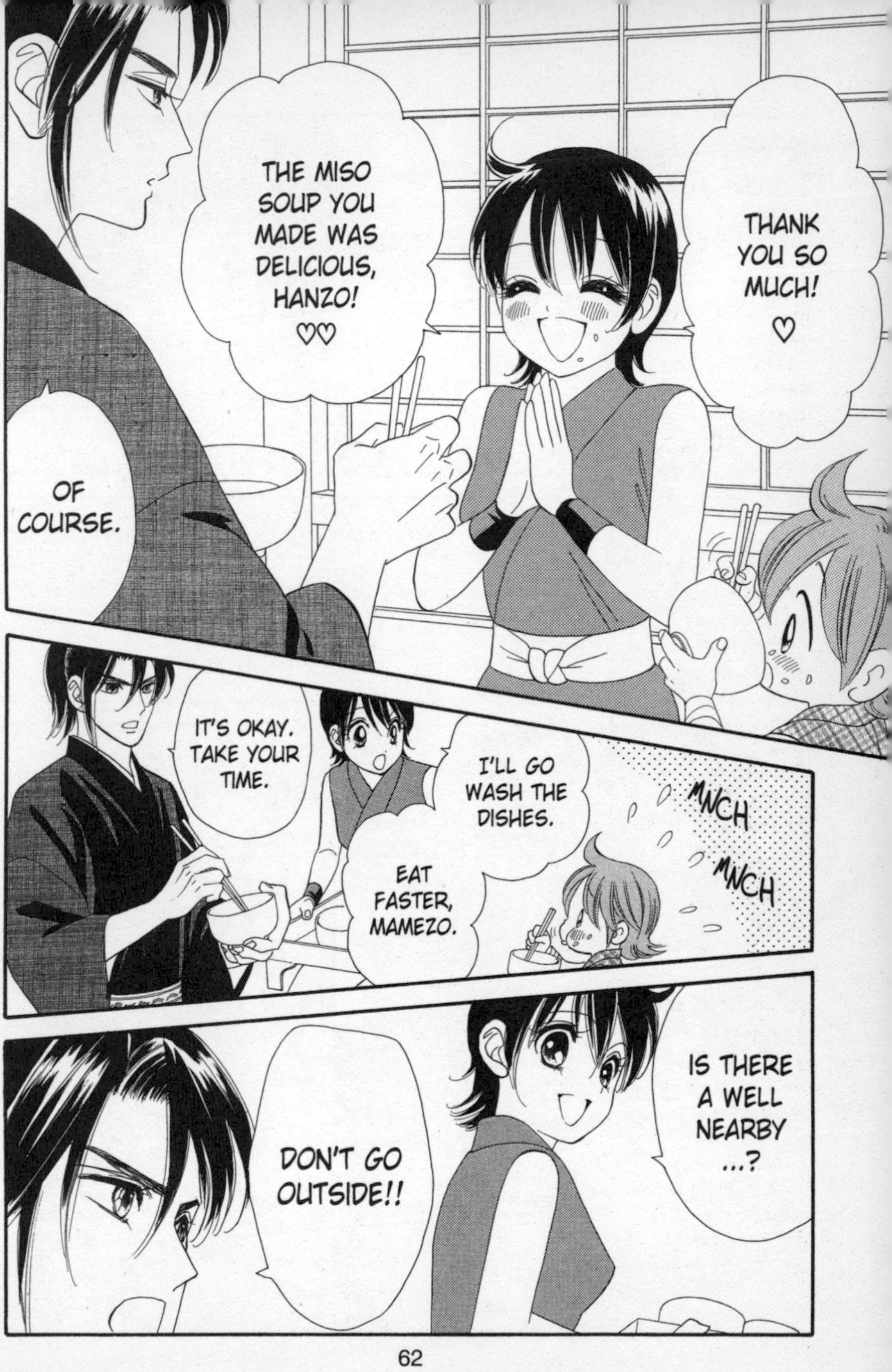
THE MISO SOUP YOU MADE WAS DELICIOUS, HANZO! ♡♡
THANK YOU SO MUCH! ♡
OF COURSE.
MNCH MNCH
I'LL GO WASH THE DISHES.
EAT FASTER, MAMEZO.
IT'S OKAY. TAKE YOUR TIME.
IS THERE A WELL NEARBY ...?
DON'T GO OUTSIDE!!

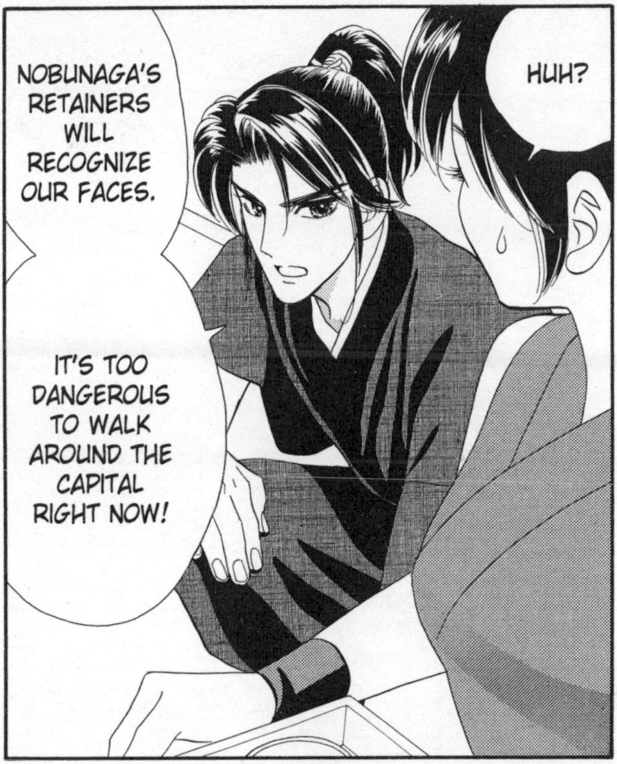
HUH?
NOBUNAGA'S RETAINERS WILL RECOGNIZE OUR FACES.
IT'S TOO DANGEROUS TO WALK AROUND THE CAPITAL RIGHT NOW!

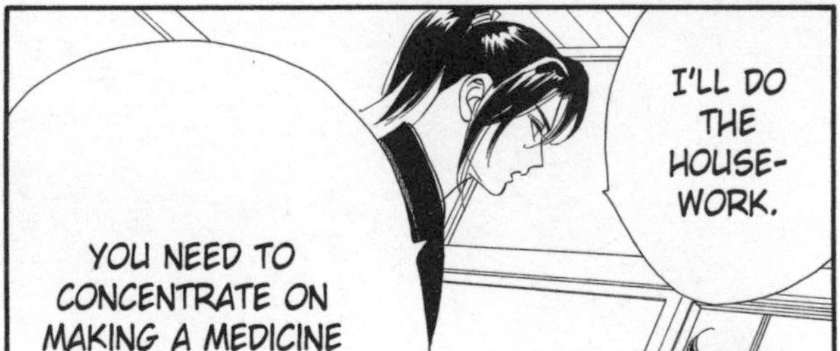
I'LL DO THE HOUSE-WORK.
YOU NEED TO CONCENTRATE ON MAKING A MEDICINE FOR MITSUHIDE'S EYES SO THAT WE GAIN HIS TRUST.

UE-RIN'S WAY OF THE MANGA 17

I felt stressed about the lateness of my editor's replies, so I began to draw a rough draft of a manga that I was going to send to a different publisher. Around that time, I finally received a reply from my editor telling me that the rough draft I'd sent them previously had been accepted, so I was able to start working on the final draft. That was around autumn of my third year in middle school, and my high school entrance exams were getting close. At first, I intended to apply to a normal local high school, but after I decided to become a manga artist, I became interested in going to a private high school with an art department.

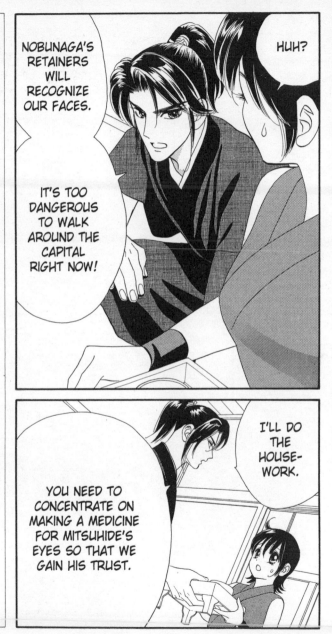

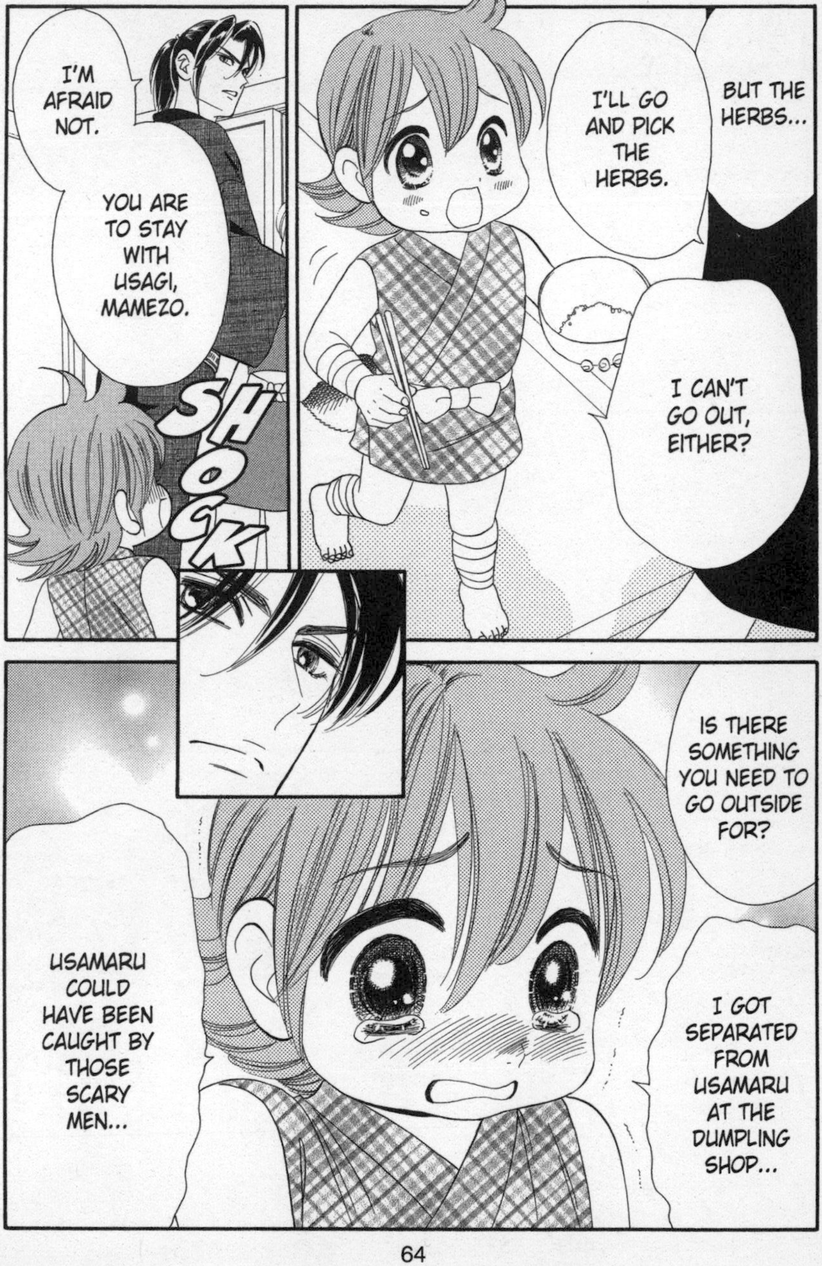

BUT THE HERBS...
I'LL GO AND PICK THE HERBS.
I CAN'T GO OUT, EITHER?
I'M AFRAID NOT.
YOU ARE TO STAY WITH USAGI, MAMEZO.
SHOCK
IS THERE SOMETHING YOU NEED TO GO OUTSIDE FOR?
I GOT SEPARATED FROM USAMARU AT THE DUMPLING SHOP...
USAMARU COULD HAVE BEEN CAUGHT BY THOSE SCARY MEN...

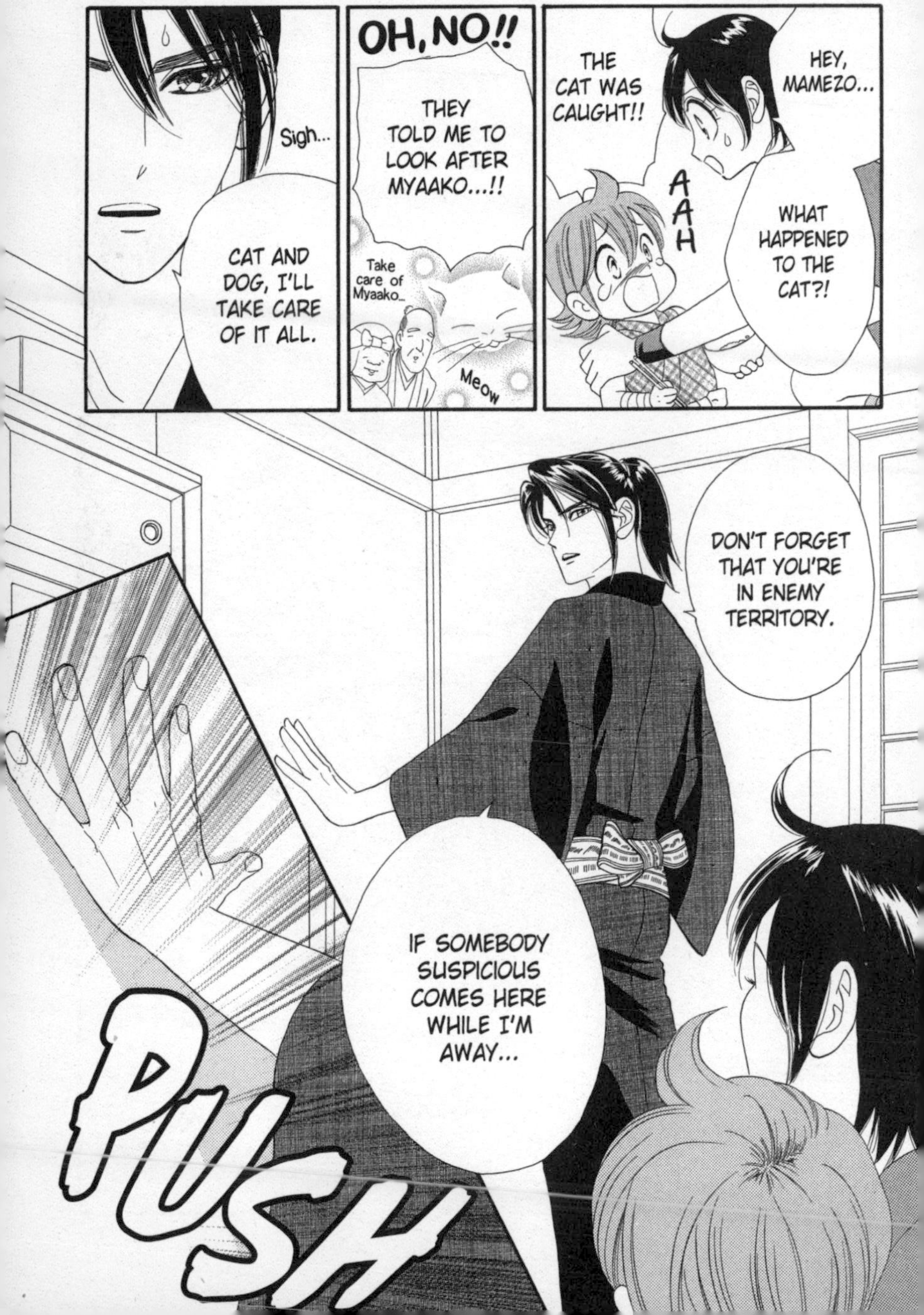
HEY, MAMEZO...
WHAT HAPPENED TO THE CAT?!
THE CAT WAS CAUGHT!!
AAH
OH, NO!!
THEY TOLD ME TO LOOK AFTER MYAAKO...!!
Take care of Myaako...
Meow
Sigh...
CAT AND DOG, I'LL TAKE CARE OF IT ALL.
DON'T FORGET THAT YOU'RE IN ENEMY TERRITORY.
IF SOMEBODY SUSPICIOUS COMES HERE WHILE I'M AWAY...
PUSH

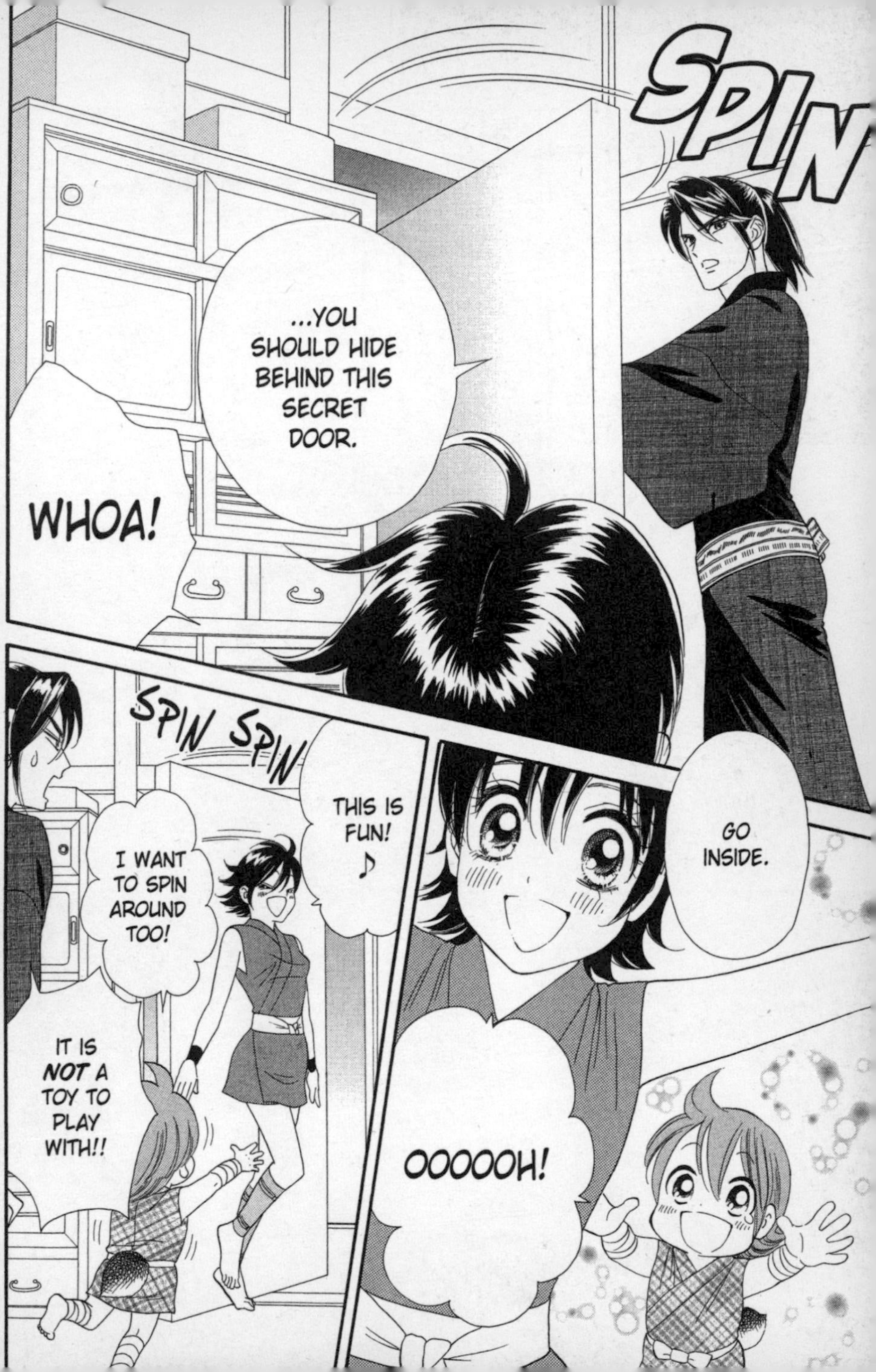
SPIN
...YOU SHOULD HIDE BEHIND THIS SECRET DOOR.
WHOA!
GO INSIDE.
OOOOOH!
SPIN SPIN
THIS IS FUN! ♪
I WANT TO SPIN AROUND TOO!
IT IS *NOT* A TOY TO PLAY WITH!!

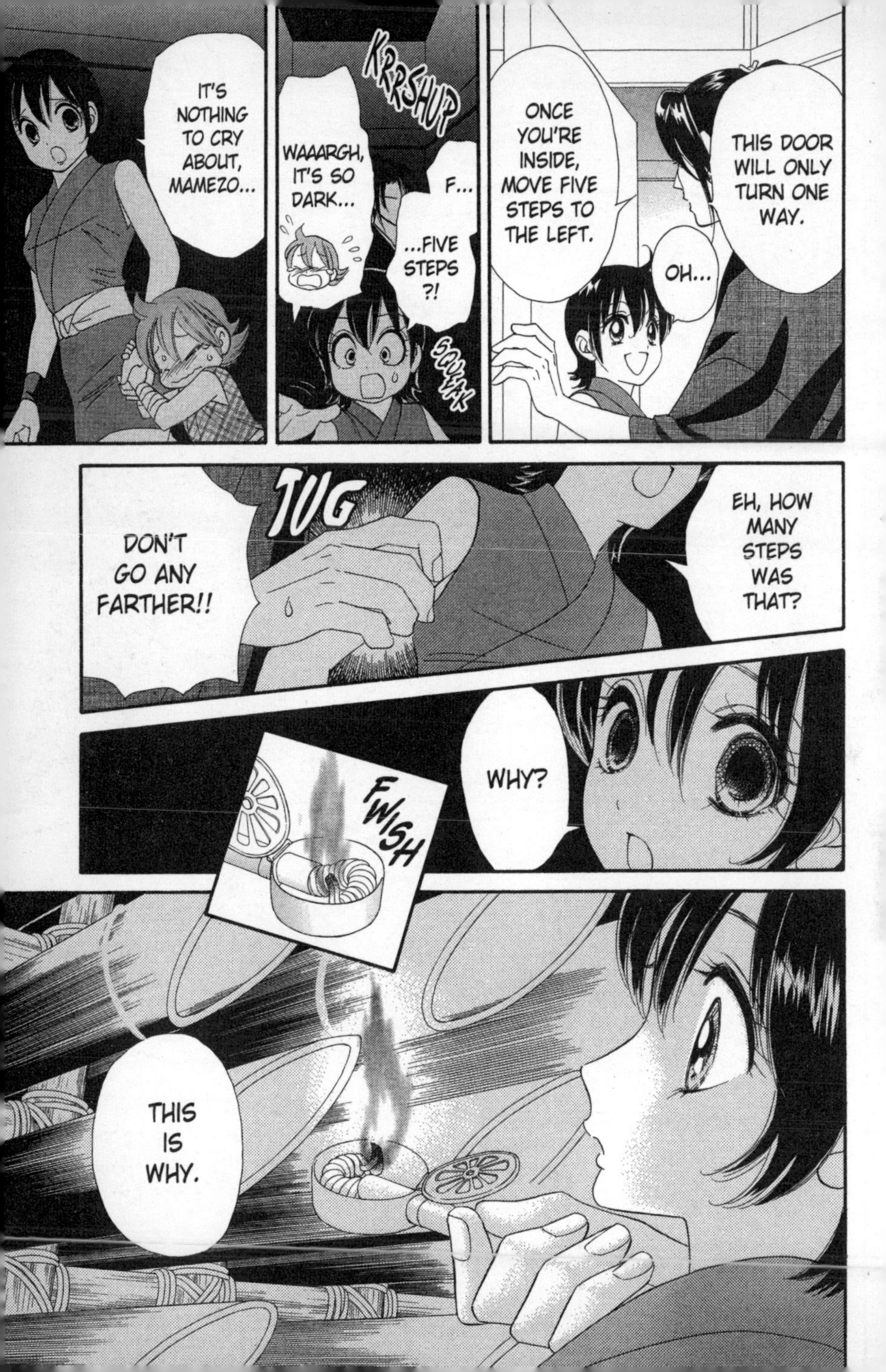
THIS DOOR WILL ONLY TURN ONE WAY.
ONCE YOU'RE INSIDE, MOVE FIVE STEPS TO THE LEFT.
OH...
KRRSHUP
F...
WAAARGH, IT'S SO DARK...
...FIVE STEPS ?!
SQUAWK
IT'S NOTHING TO CRY ABOUT, MAMEZO...
EH, HOW MANY STEPS WAS THAT?
TUG
DON'T GO ANY FARTHER!!
WHY?
FWISH
THIS IS WHY.

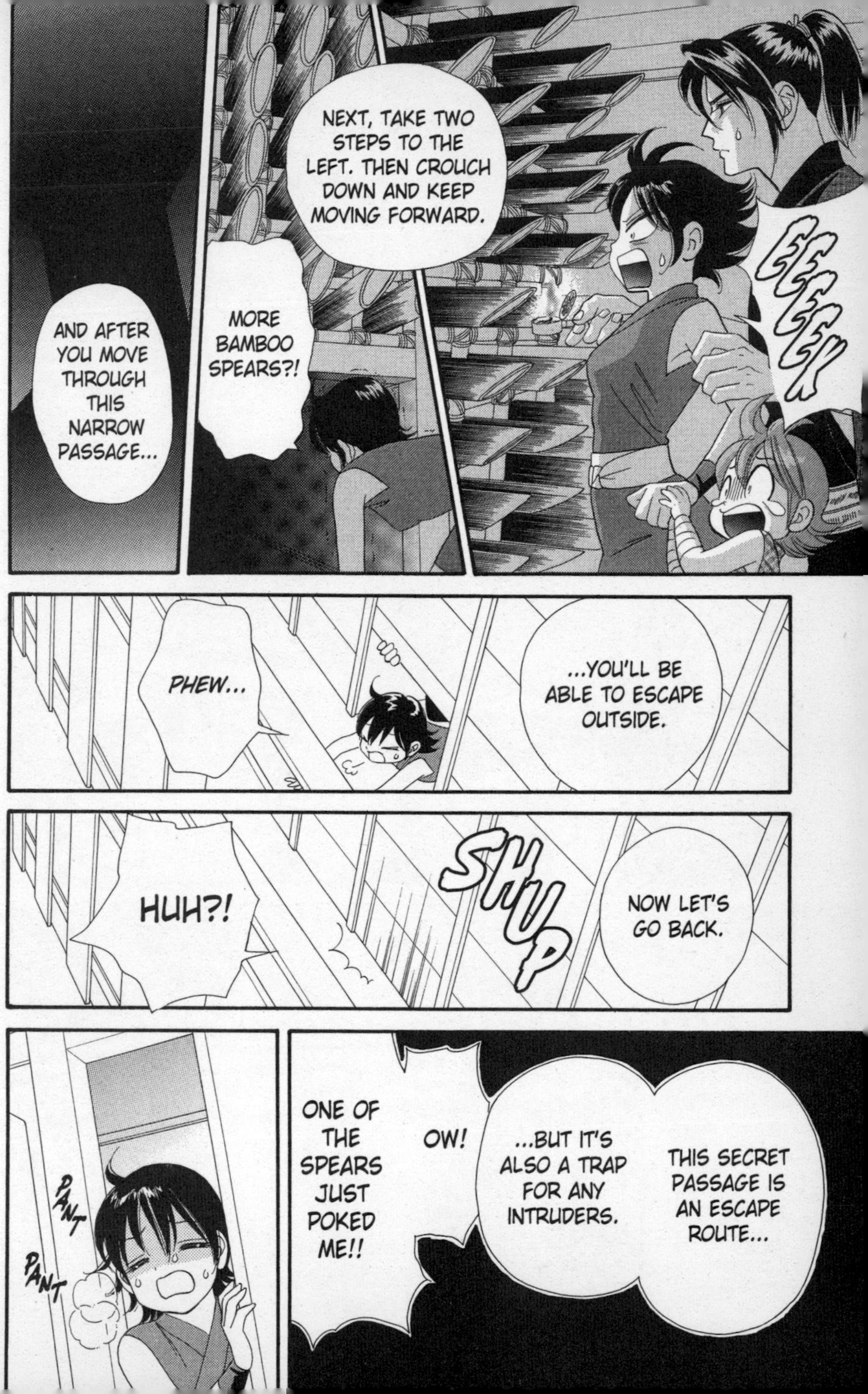
NEXT, TAKE TWO STEPS TO THE LEFT. THEN CROUCH DOWN AND KEEP MOVING FORWARD.
EEEEK
MORE BAMBOO SPEARS?!
AND AFTER YOU MOVE THROUGH THIS NARROW PASSAGE...
...YOU'LL BE ABLE TO ESCAPE OUTSIDE.
PHEW...
NOW LET'S GO BACK.
SHUP
HUH?!
THIS SECRET PASSAGE IS AN ESCAPE ROUTE...
...BUT IT'S ALSO A TRAP FOR ANY INTRUDERS.
OW!
ONE OF THE SPEARS JUST POKED ME!!
PANT
PANT

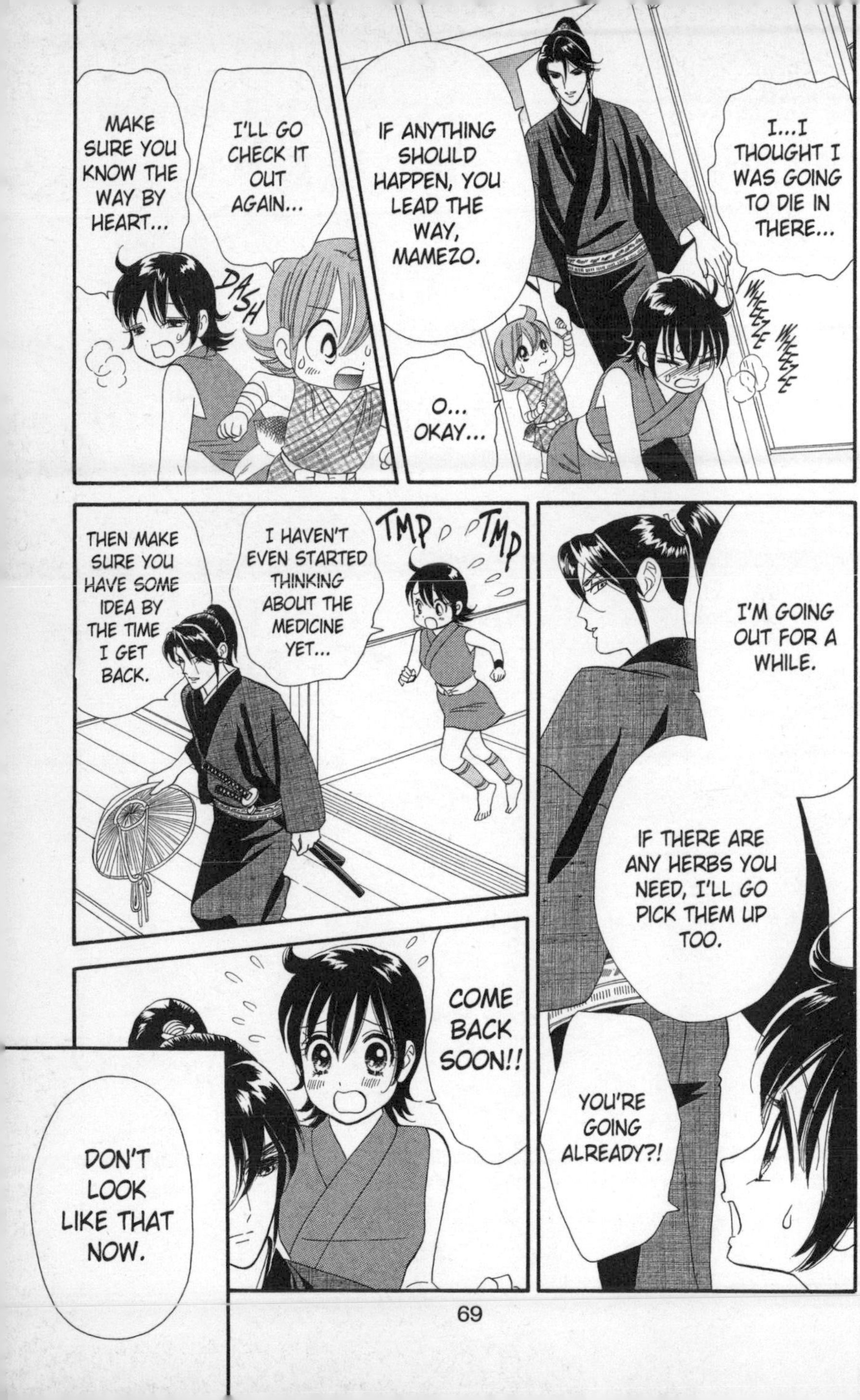
I...I THOUGHT I WAS GOING TO DIE IN THERE...
WHEEZE
WHEEZE
IF ANYTHING SHOULD HAPPEN, YOU LEAD THE WAY, MAMEZO.
O... OKAY...
I'LL GO CHECK IT OUT AGAIN...
DASH
MAKE SURE YOU KNOW THE WAY BY HEART...
I'M GOING OUT FOR A WHILE.
IF THERE ARE ANY HERBS YOU NEED, I'LL GO PICK THEM UP TOO.
YOU'RE GOING ALREADY?!
TMP
TMP
I HAVEN'T EVEN STARTED THINKING ABOUT THE MEDICINE YET...
THEN MAKE SURE YOU HAVE SOME IDEA BY THE TIME I GET BACK.
COME BACK SOON!!
DON'T LOOK LIKE THAT NOW.

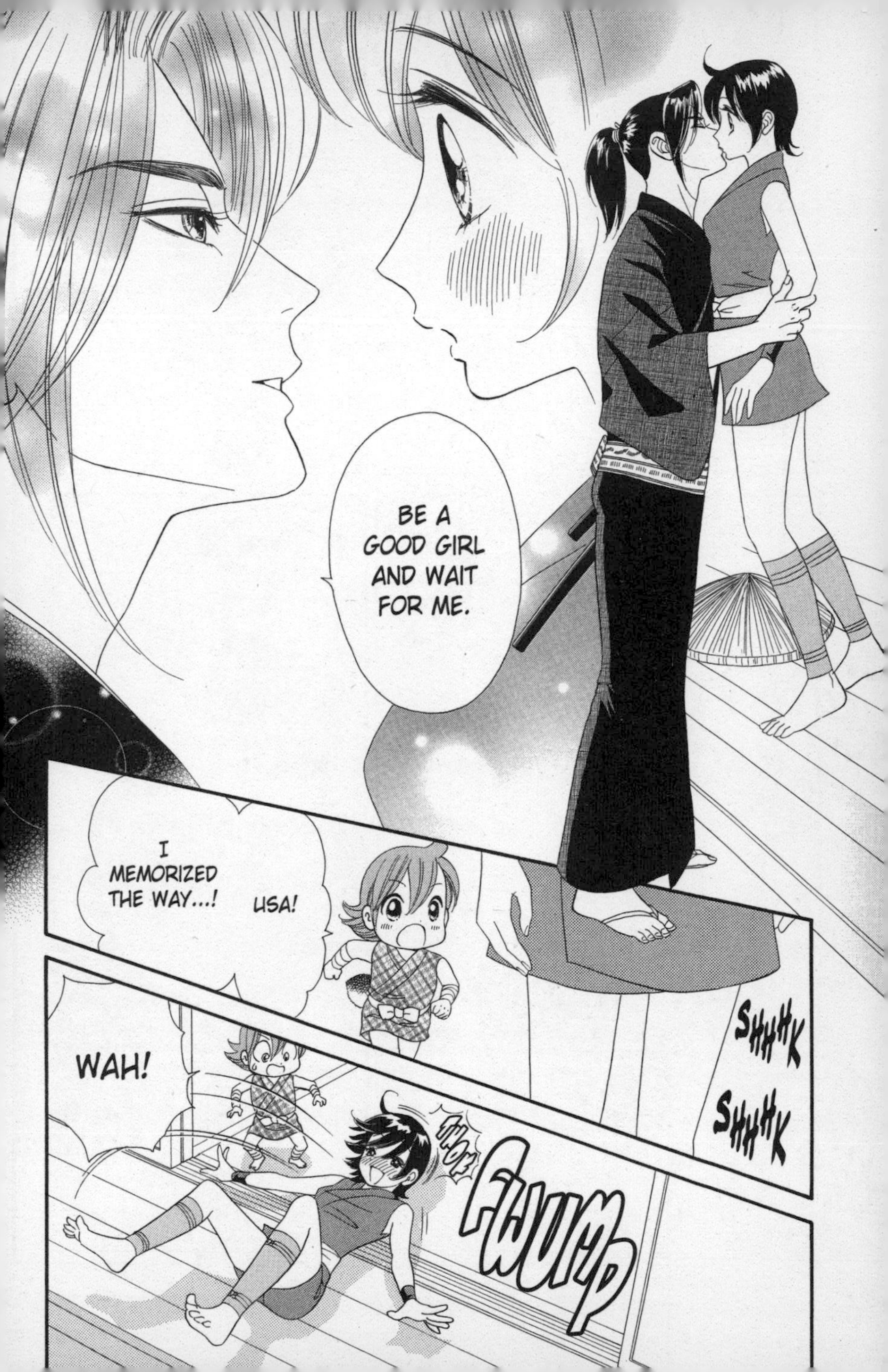
BE A GOOD GIRL AND WAIT FOR ME.
USA!
I MEMORIZED THE WAY...!
SHHHK
SHHHK
WAH!
THOK
FWUMP

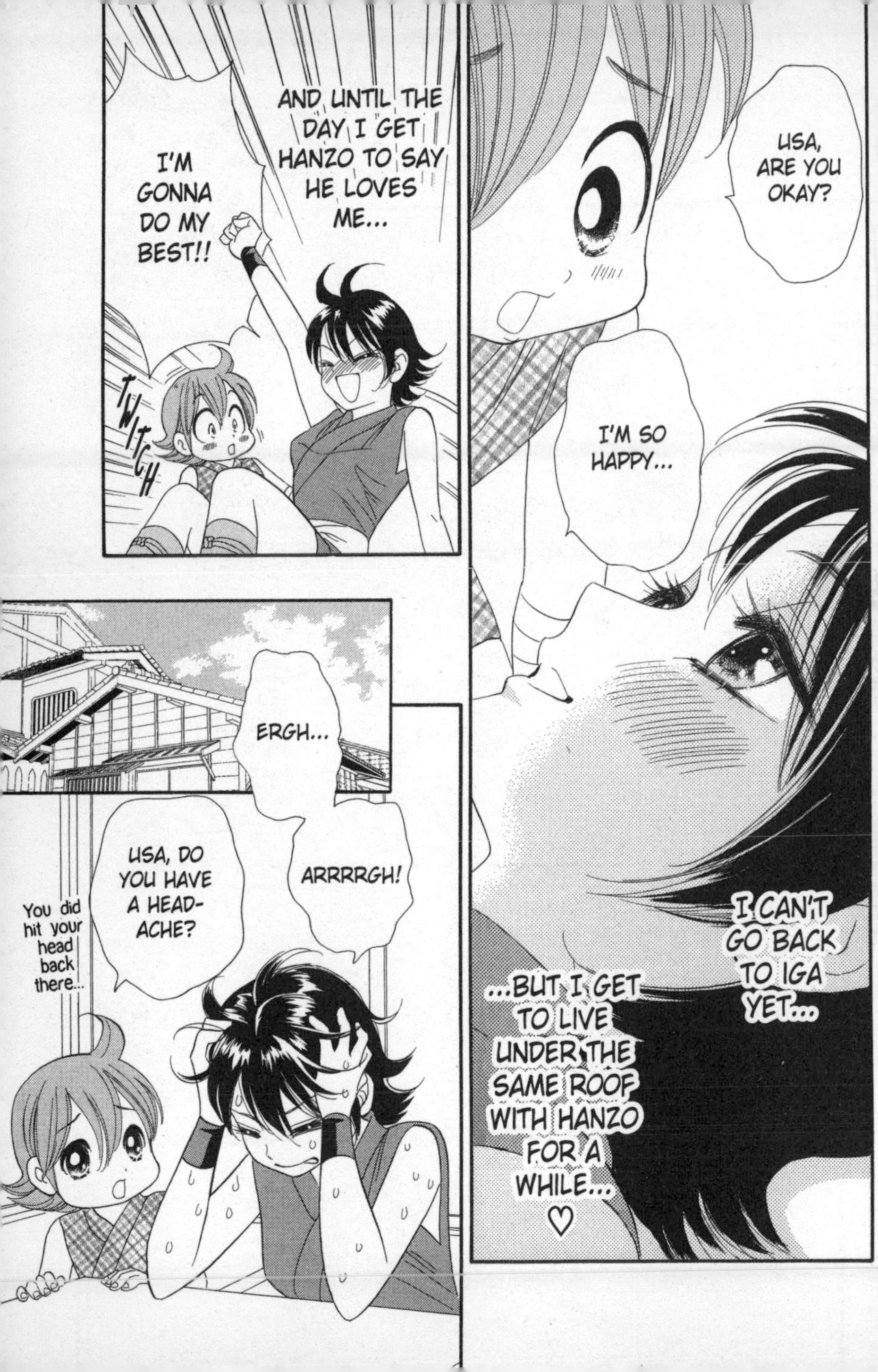
USA, ARE YOU OKAY?
I'M SO HAPPY...
I CAN'T GO BACK TO IGA YET...
...BUT I GET TO LIVE UNDER THE SAME ROOF WITH HANZO FOR A WHILE... ♡
AND UNTIL THE DAY I GET HANZO TO SAY HE LOVES ME...
I'M GONNA DO MY BEST!!
TWITCH
ERGH...
ARRRRGH!
USA, DO YOU HAVE A HEADACHE?
You did hit your head back there...

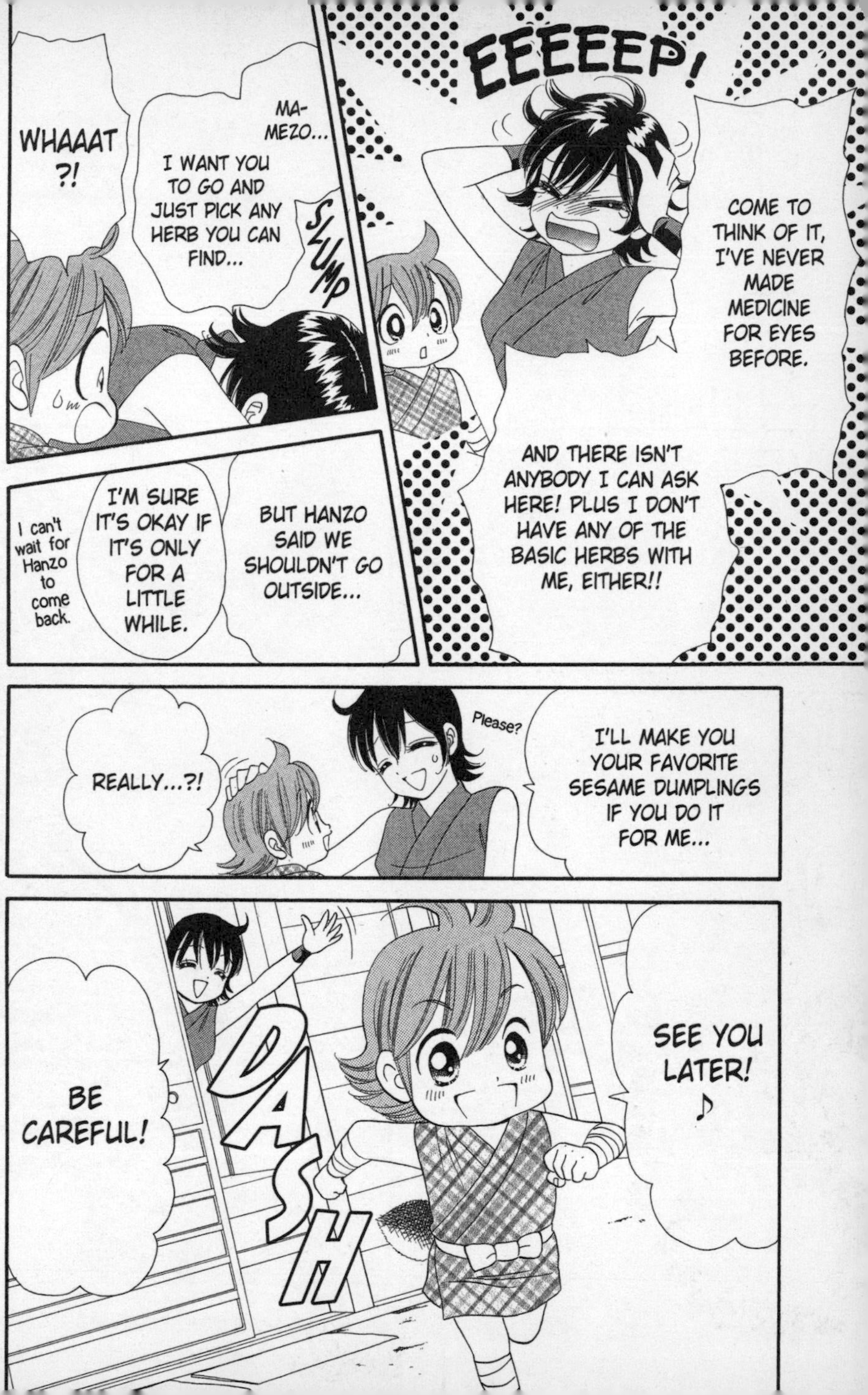
EEEEEP!
COME TO THINK OF IT, I'VE NEVER MADE MEDICINE FOR EYES BEFORE.
AND THERE ISN'T ANYBODY I CAN ASK HERE! PLUS I DON'T HAVE ANY OF THE BASIC HERBS WITH ME, EITHER!!
MA-MEZO... I WANT YOU TO GO AND JUST PICK ANY HERB YOU CAN FIND...
SLUMP
WHAAAT?!
BUT HANZO SAID WE SHOULDN'T GO OUTSIDE...
I'M SURE IT'S OKAY IF IT'S ONLY FOR A LITTLE WHILE.
I can't wait for Hanzo to come back.
I'LL MAKE YOU YOUR FAVORITE SESAME DUMPLINGS IF YOU DO IT FOR ME...
Please?
REALLY...?!
SEE YOU LATER! ♪
DASH
BE CAREFUL!

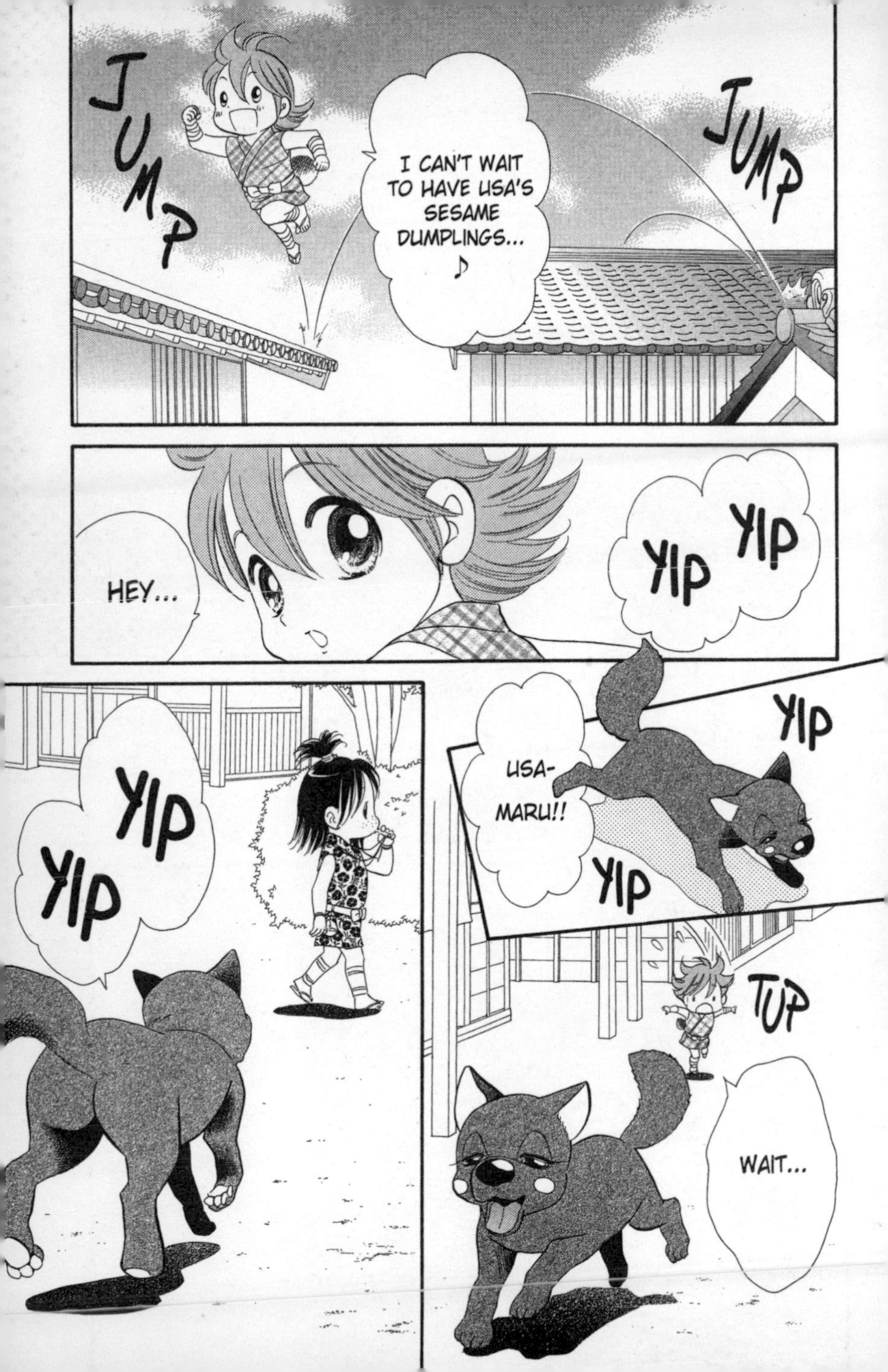
JUMP
I CAN'T WAIT TO HAVE USA'S SESAME DUMPLINGS... ♪
JUMP
YIP YIP
HEY...
YIP
USA-MARU!!
YIP
TUP
WAIT...
YIP YIP

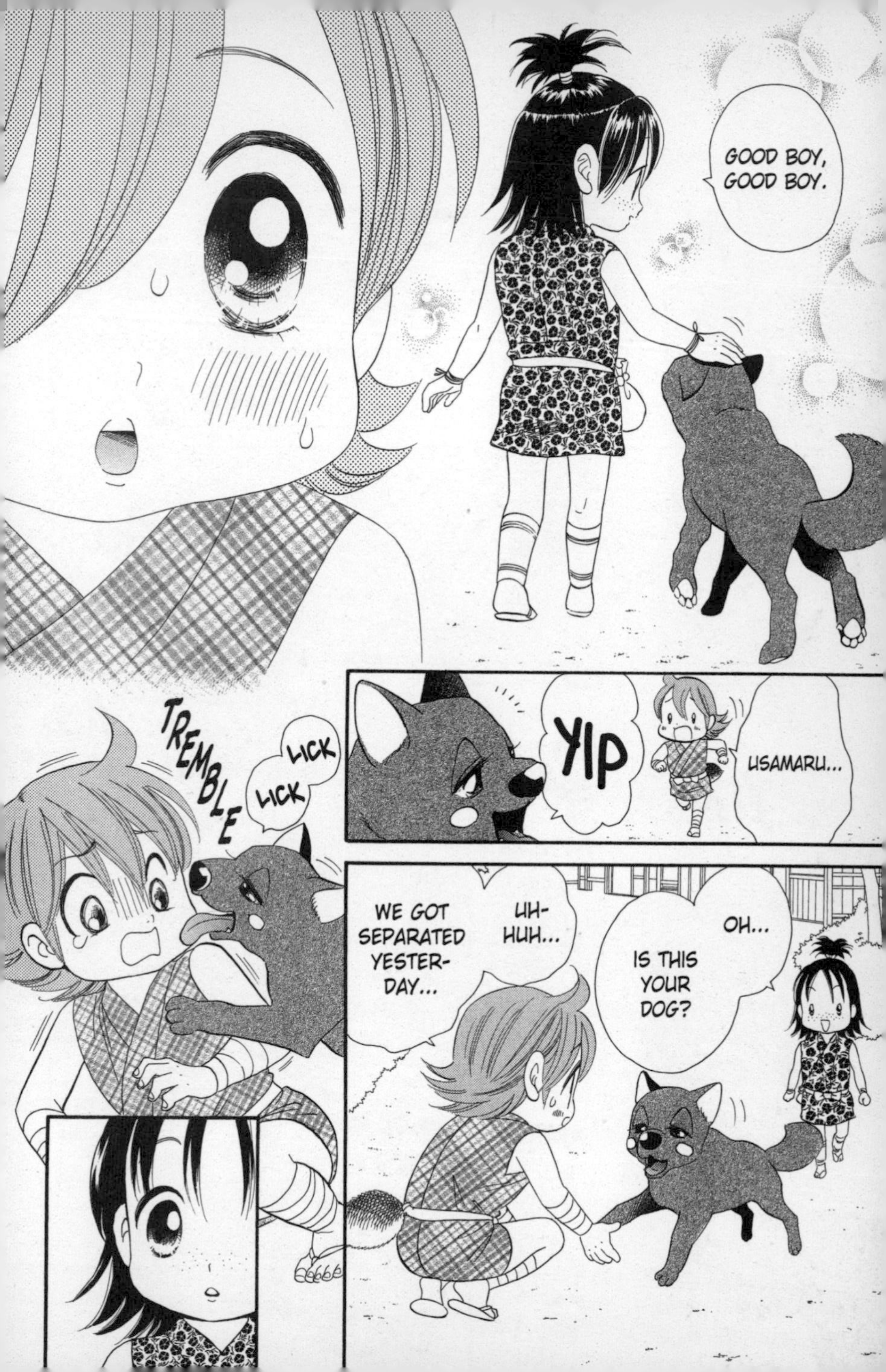
GOOD BOY, GOOD BOY.
USAMARU...
YIP
TREMBLE
LICK
LICK
OH...
IS THIS YOUR DOG?
UH-HUH...
WE GOT SEPARATED YESTER-DAY...

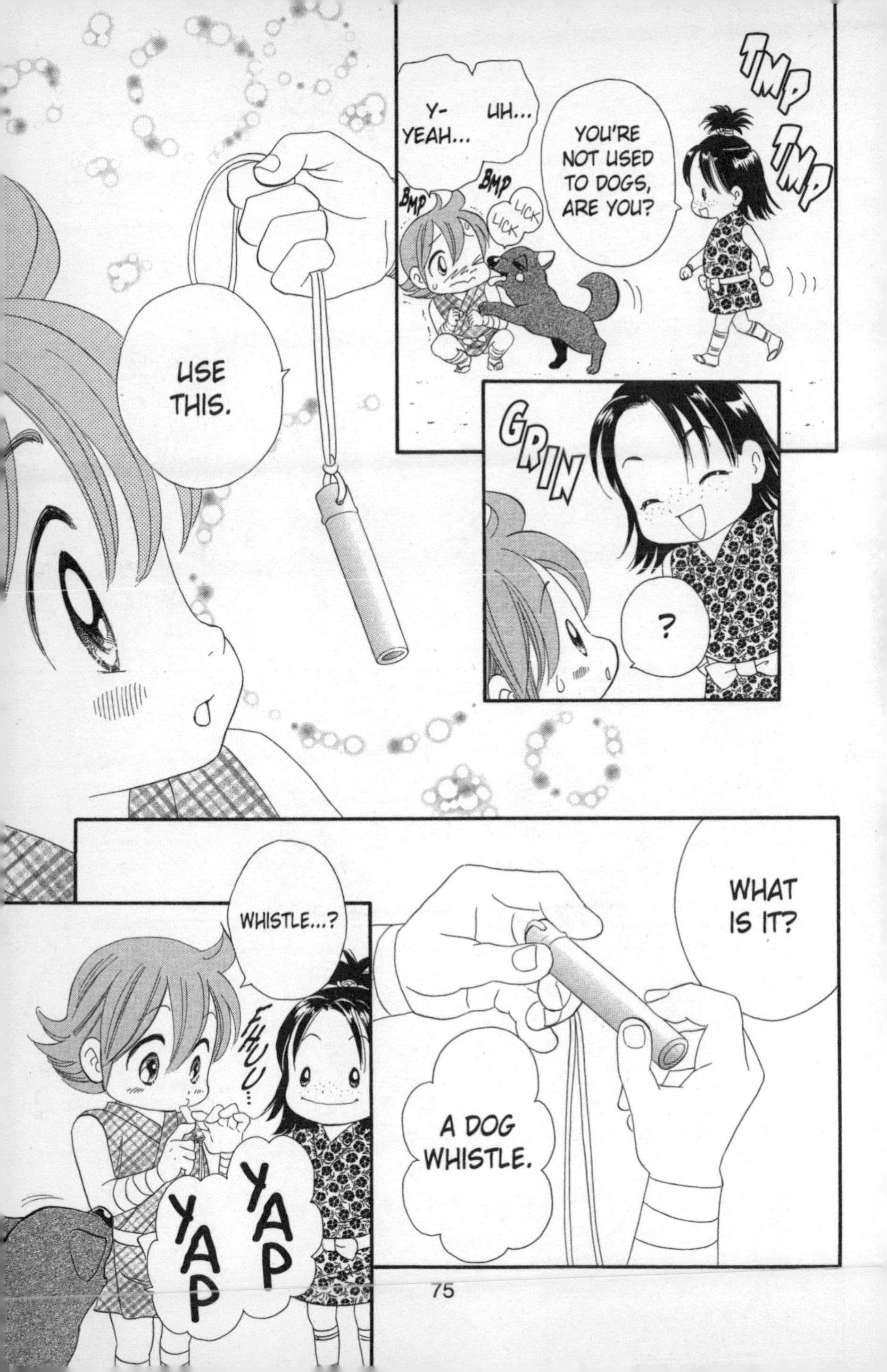

TMP TMP
YOU'RE NOT USED TO DOGS, ARE YOU?
Y- YEAH... UH...
BMP
BMP
LICK LICK
GRIN
?
USE THIS.
WHAT IS IT?
A DOG WHISTLE.
WHISTLE...?
FHUU...
YAP YAP YAP

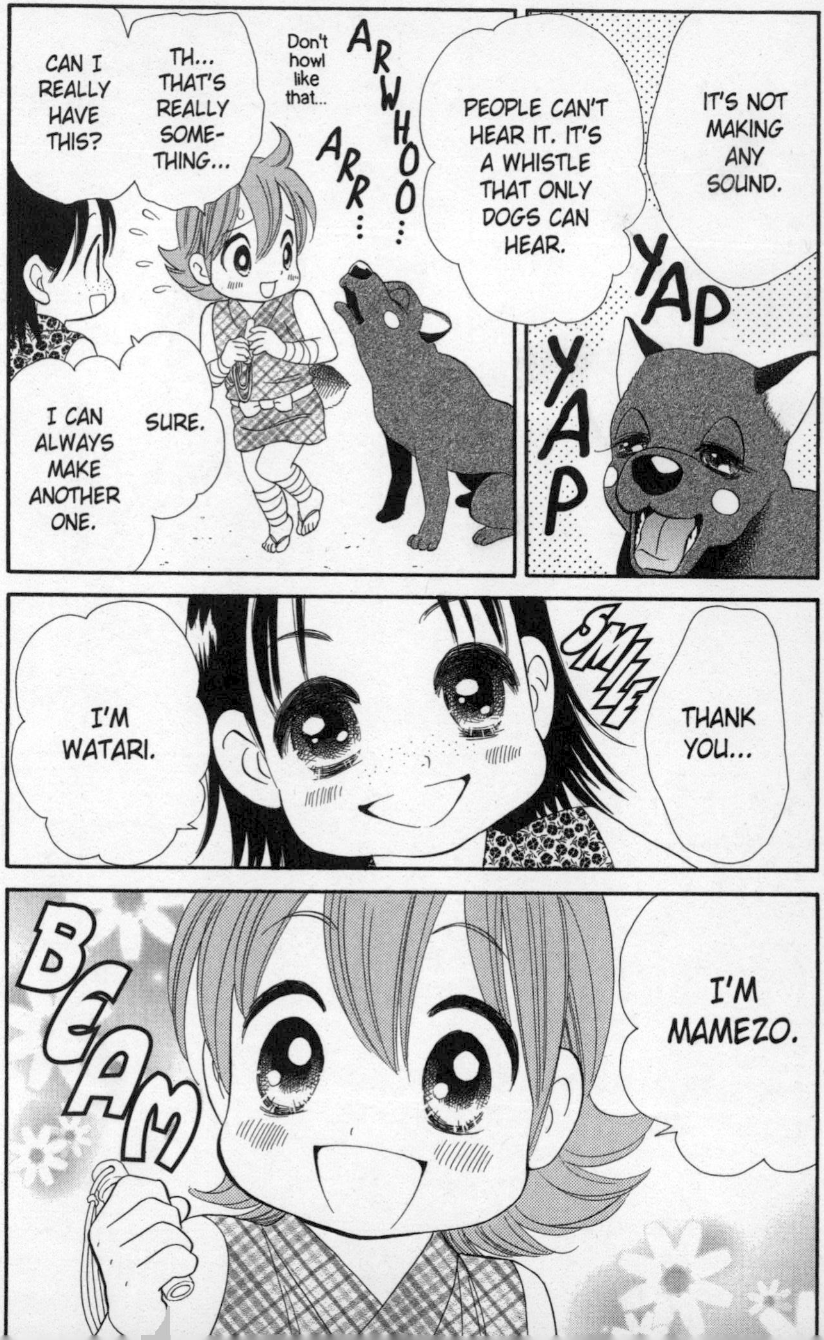
IT'S NOT MAKING ANY SOUND.
PEOPLE CAN'T HEAR IT. IT'S A WHISTLE THAT ONLY DOGS CAN HEAR.
YAP
YAP
YAP
ARWHOO...
ARR...
Don't howl like that...
TH... THAT'S REALLY SOME-THING...
CAN I REALLY HAVE THIS?
SURE.
I CAN ALWAYS MAKE ANOTHER ONE.
THANK YOU...
SMILE
I'M WATARI.
I'M MAMEZO.
BEAM

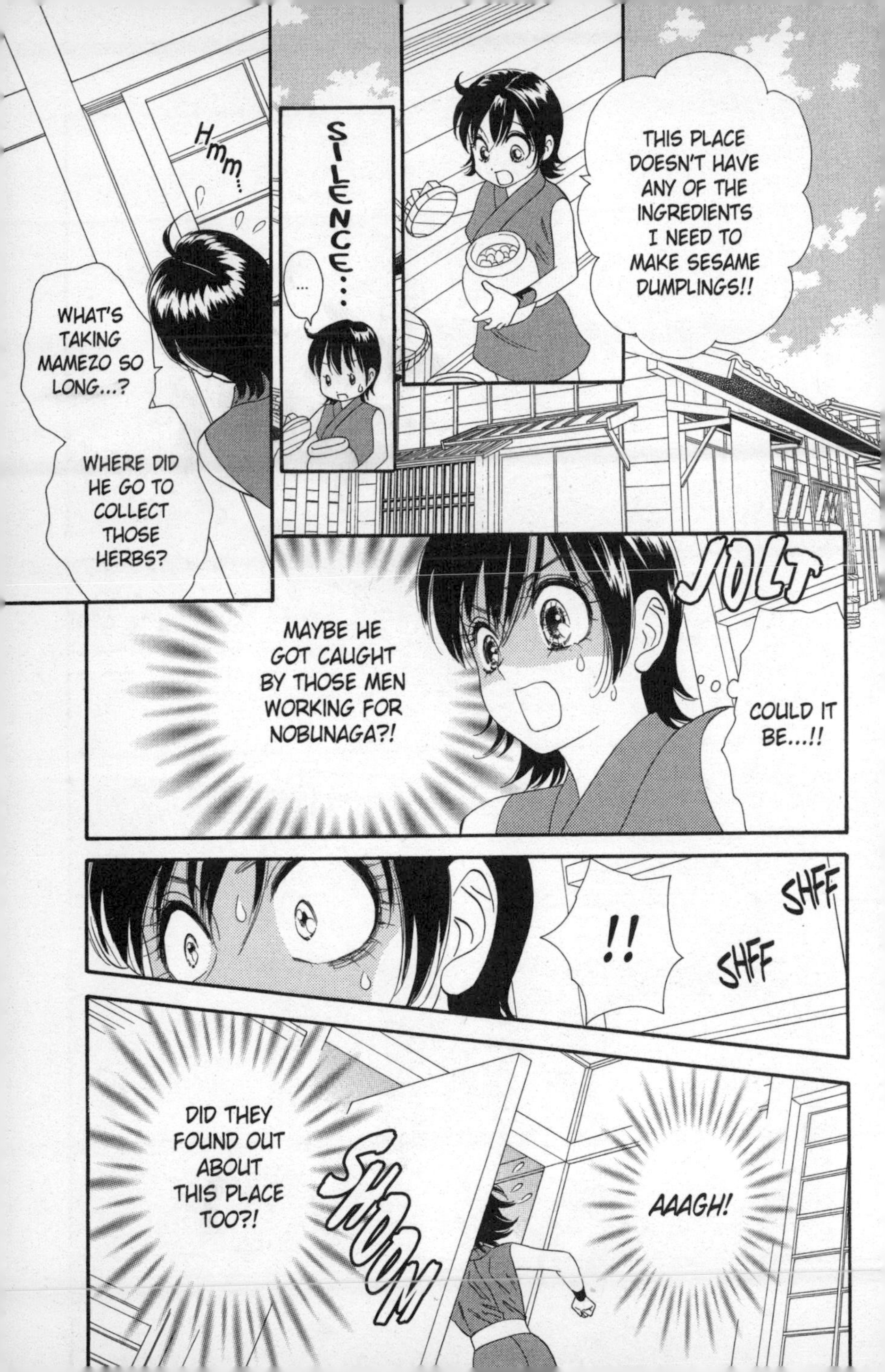
THIS PLACE DOESN'T HAVE ANY OF THE INGREDIENTS I NEED TO MAKE SESAME DUMPLINGS!!
SILENCE...
...
Hmm...
WHAT'S TAKING MAMEZO SO LONG...?
WHERE DID HE GO TO COLLECT THOSE HERBS?
JOLT
COULD IT BE...!!
MAYBE HE GOT CAUGHT BY THOSE MEN WORKING FOR NOBUNAGA?!
SHFF
SHFF
!!
AAAGH!
SHOOM
DID THEY FOUND OUT ABOUT THIS PLACE TOO?!

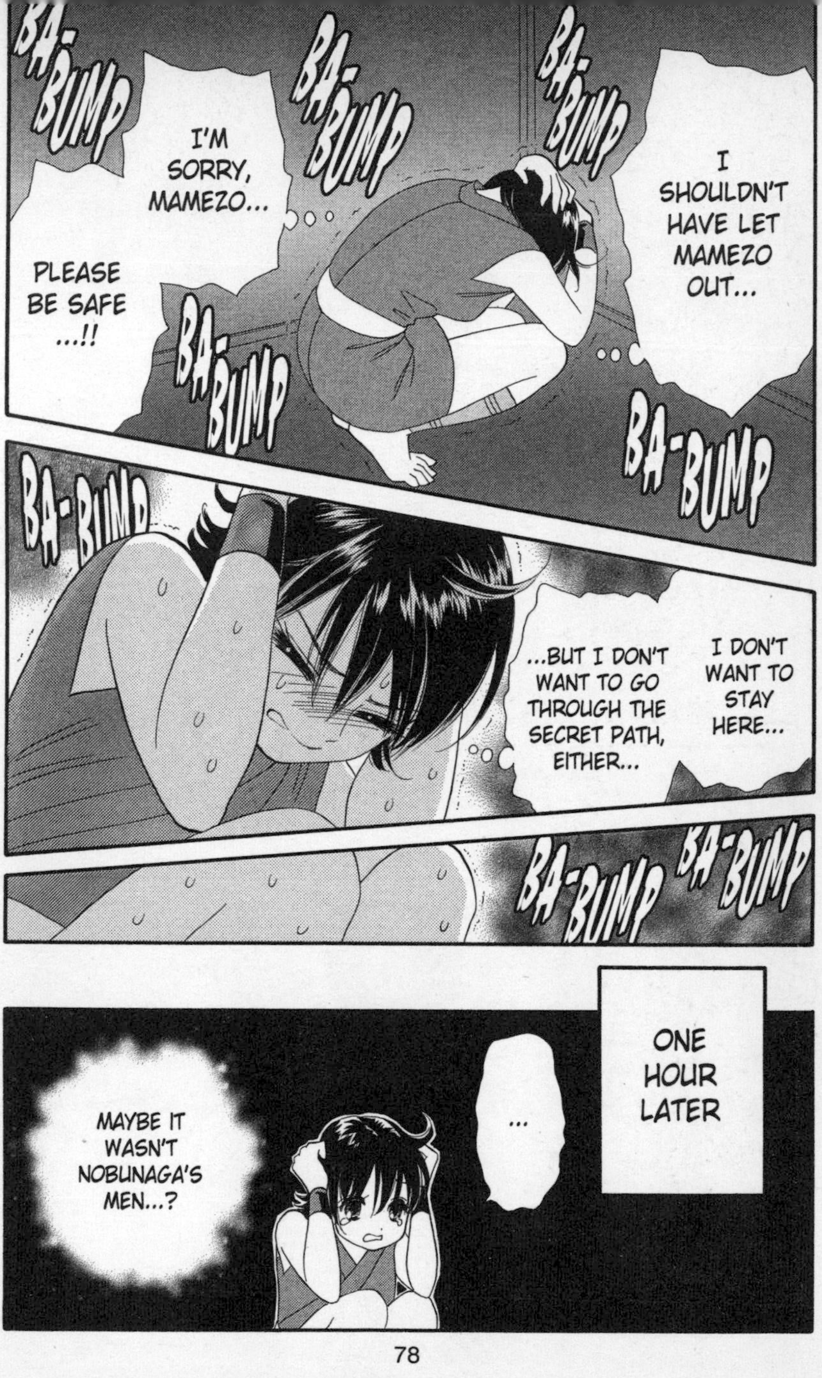

BA-BUMP
I SHOULDN'T HAVE LET MAMEZO OUT...
BA-BUMP
BA-BUMP
I'M SORRY, MAMEZO...
BA-BUMP
PLEASE BE SAFE ...!!
BA-BUMP
BA-BUMP
I DON'T WANT TO STAY HERE...
...BUT I DON'T WANT TO GO THROUGH THE SECRET PATH, EITHER...
BA-BUMP
BA-BUMP
BA-BUMP
ONE HOUR LATER
...
MAYBE IT WASN'T NOBUNAGA'S MEN...?

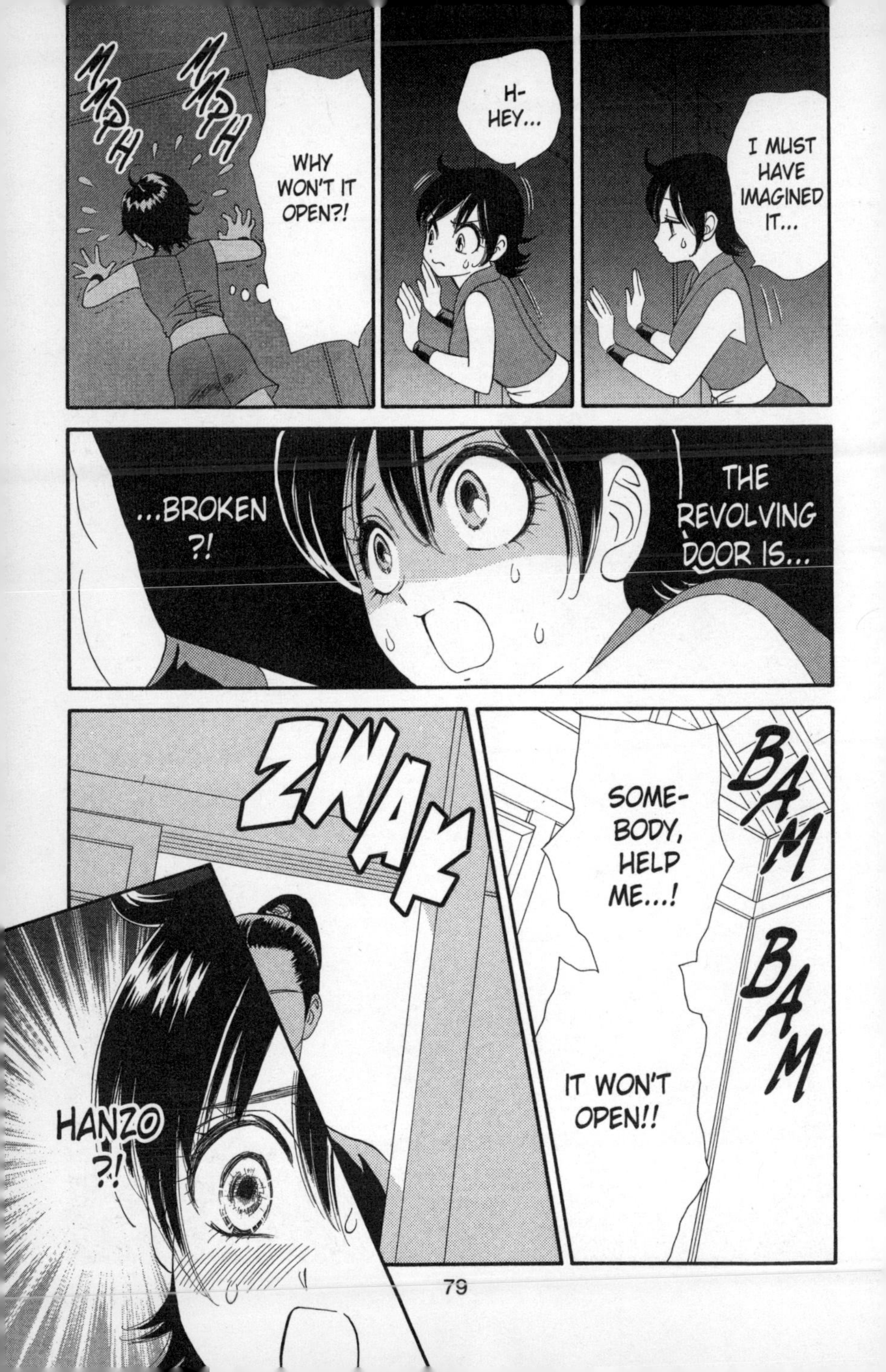
I MUST HAVE IMAGINED IT...
H- HEY...
WHY WON'T IT OPEN?!
MMPH MMPH
THE REVOLVING DOOR IS...
...BROKEN ?!
BAM BAM
SOMEBODY, HELP ME...!
IT WON'T OPEN!!
ZWAK
HANZO ?!

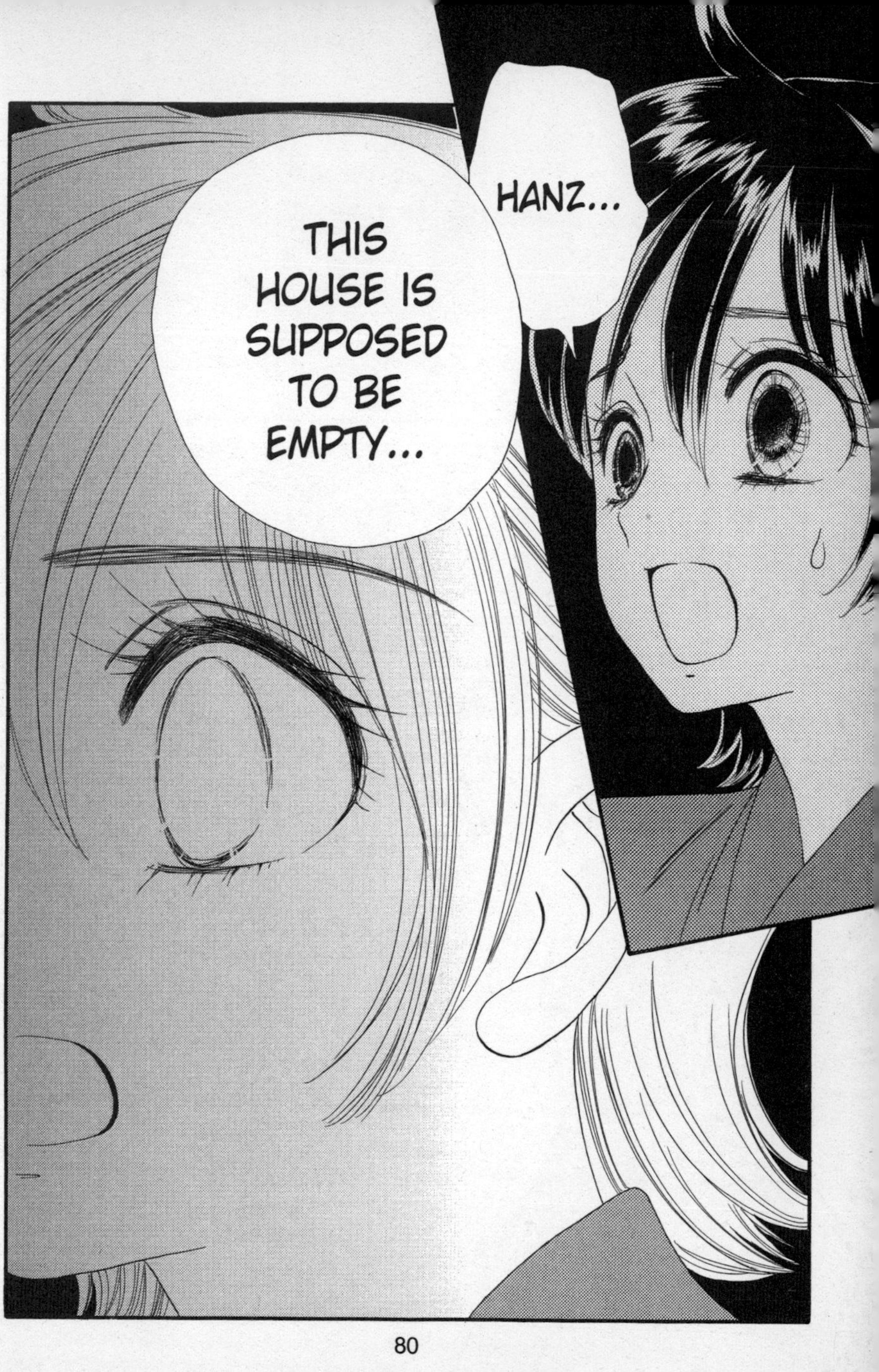
HANZ...
THIS HOUSE IS SUPPOSED TO BE EMPTY...

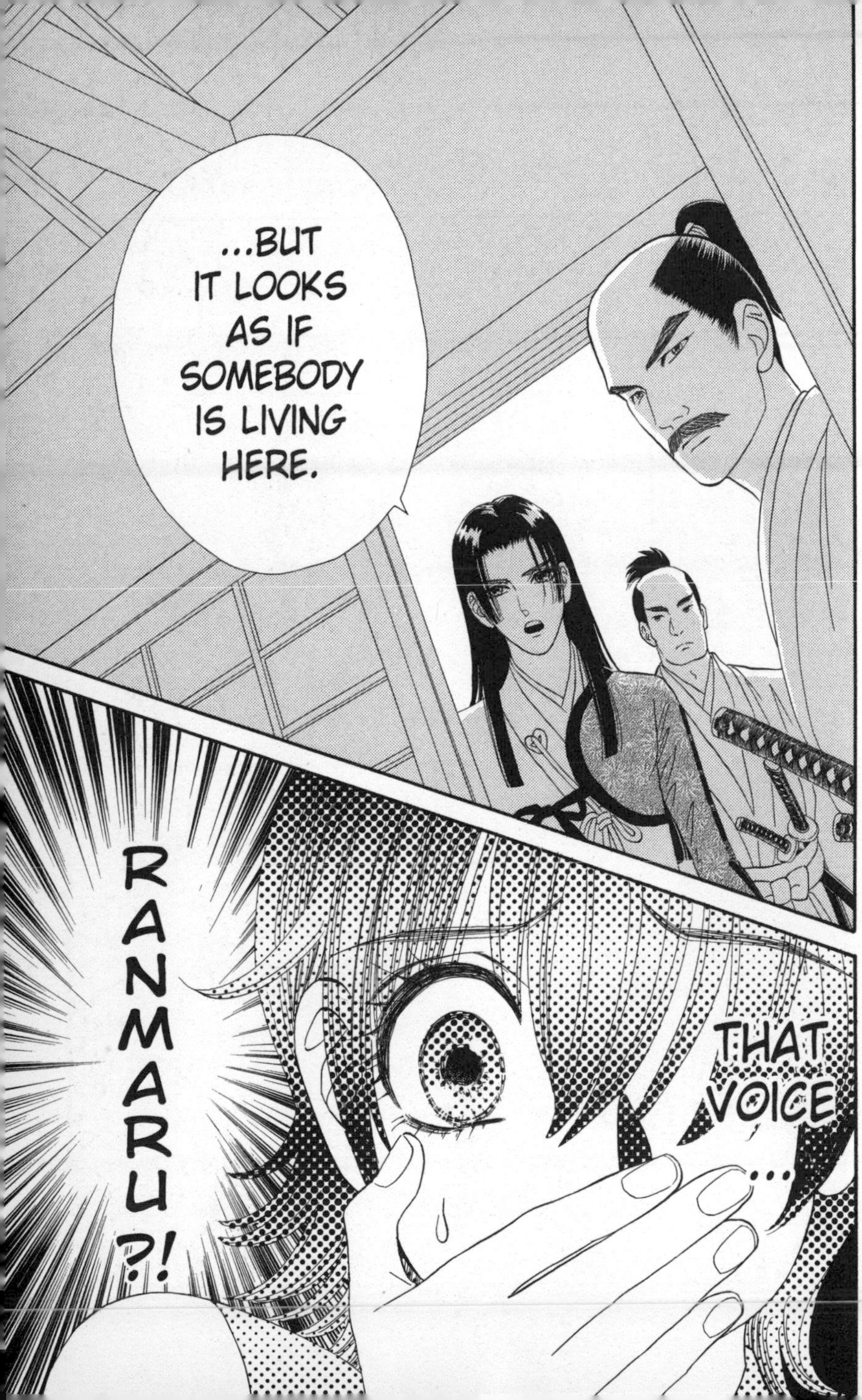
...BUT IT LOOKS AS IF SOMEBODY IS LIVING HERE.
THAT VOICE...
RANMARU?!

TAIL OF THE MOON EXTRA: TODAY'S MISSION

"I WANT TO SEE HANZO AS A RAKUGO STORYTELLER!"

-CHIE, TOCHIGI PREFECTURE

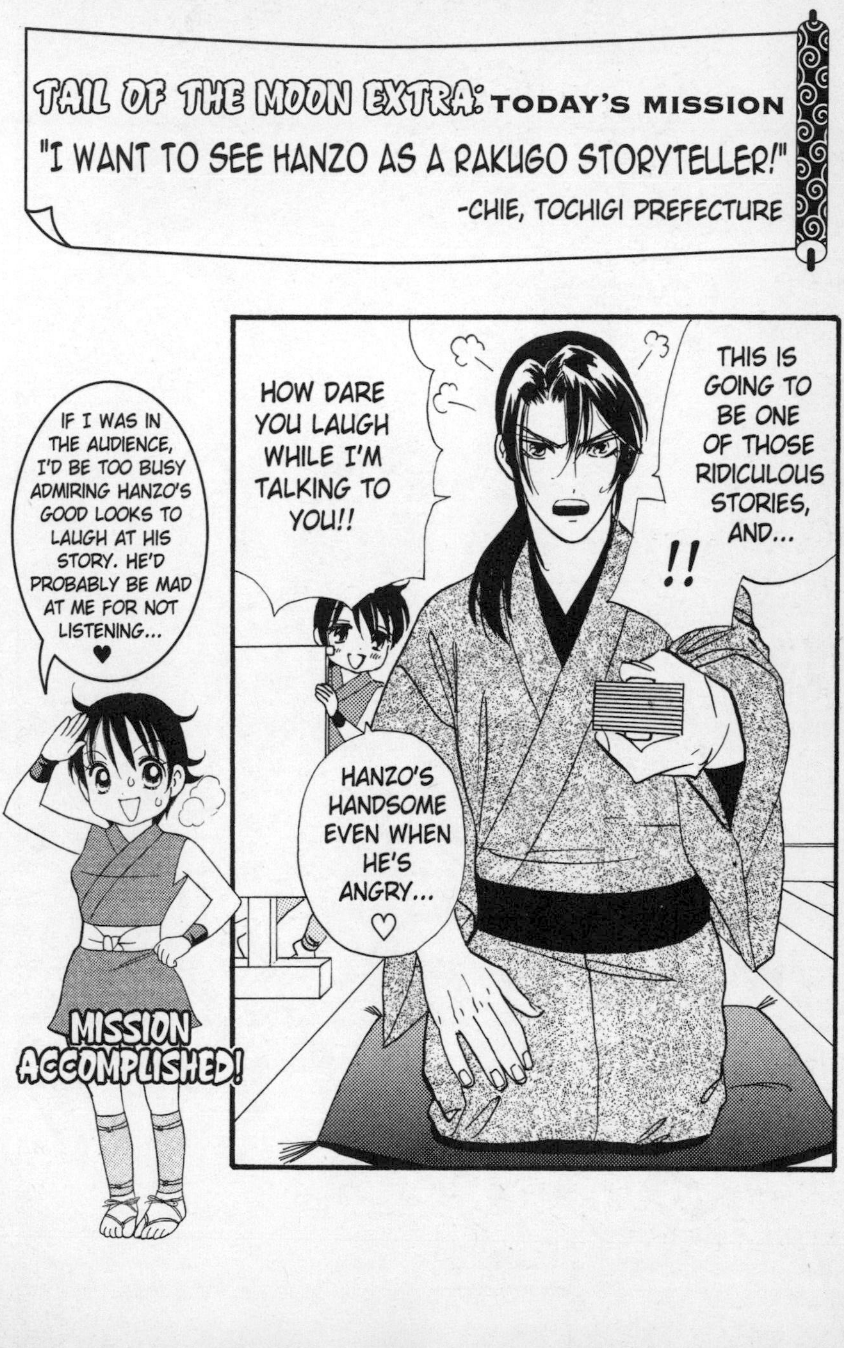
THIS IS GOING TO BE ONE OF THOSE RIDICULOUS STORIES, AND...
!!
HOW DARE YOU LAUGH WHILE I'M TALKING TO YOU!!
HANZO'S HANDSOME EVEN WHEN HE'S ANGRY... ♡
IF I WAS IN THE AUDIENCE, I'D BE TOO BUSY ADMIRING HANZO'S GOOD LOOKS TO LAUGH AT HIS STORY. HE'D PROBABLY BE MAD AT ME FOR NOT LISTENING... ♥
MISSION ACCOMPLISHED!

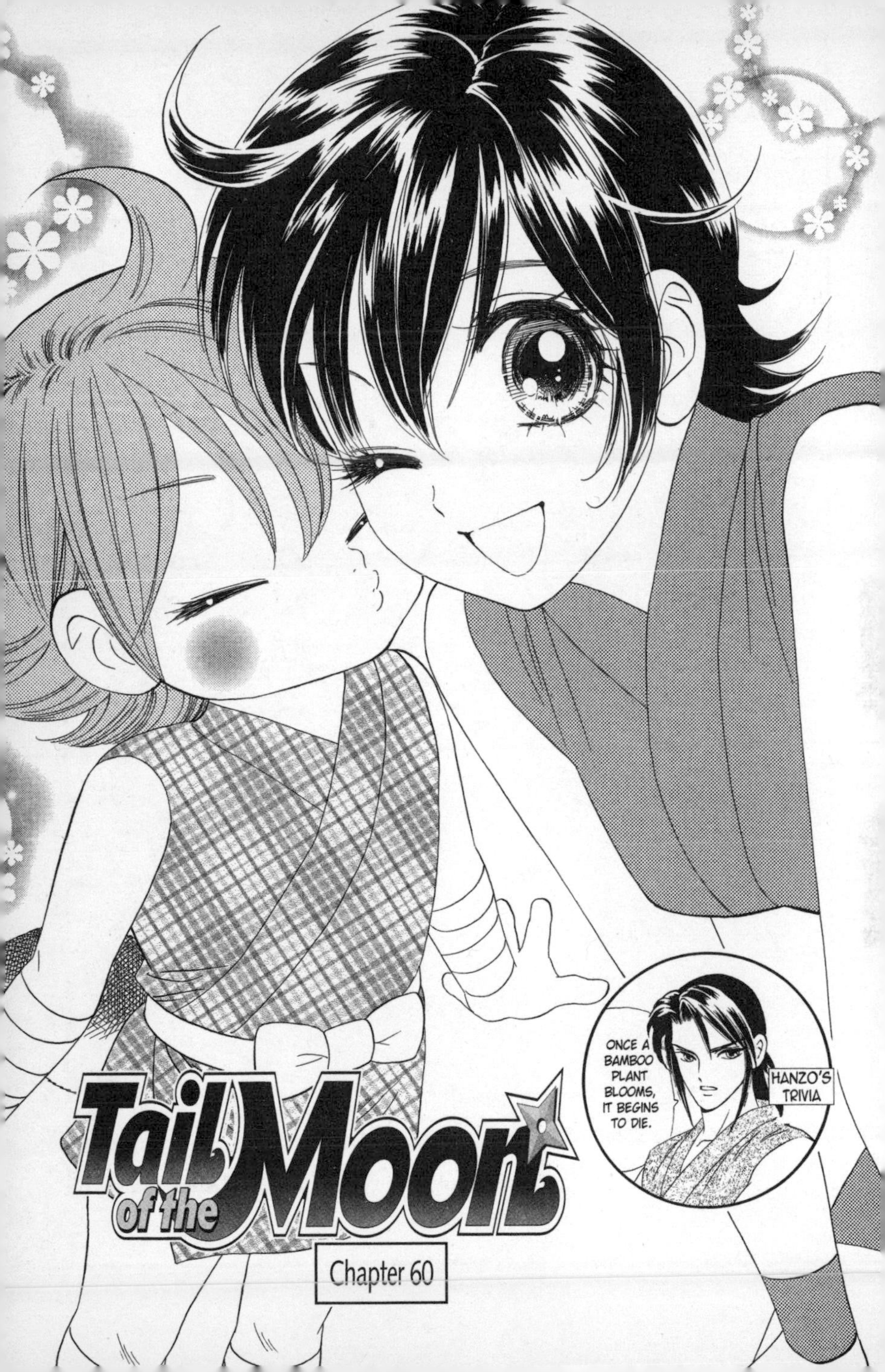
Tail of the Moon
Chapter 60
HANZO'S TRIVIA
ONCE A BAMBOO PLANT BLOOMS, IT BEGINS TO DIE.

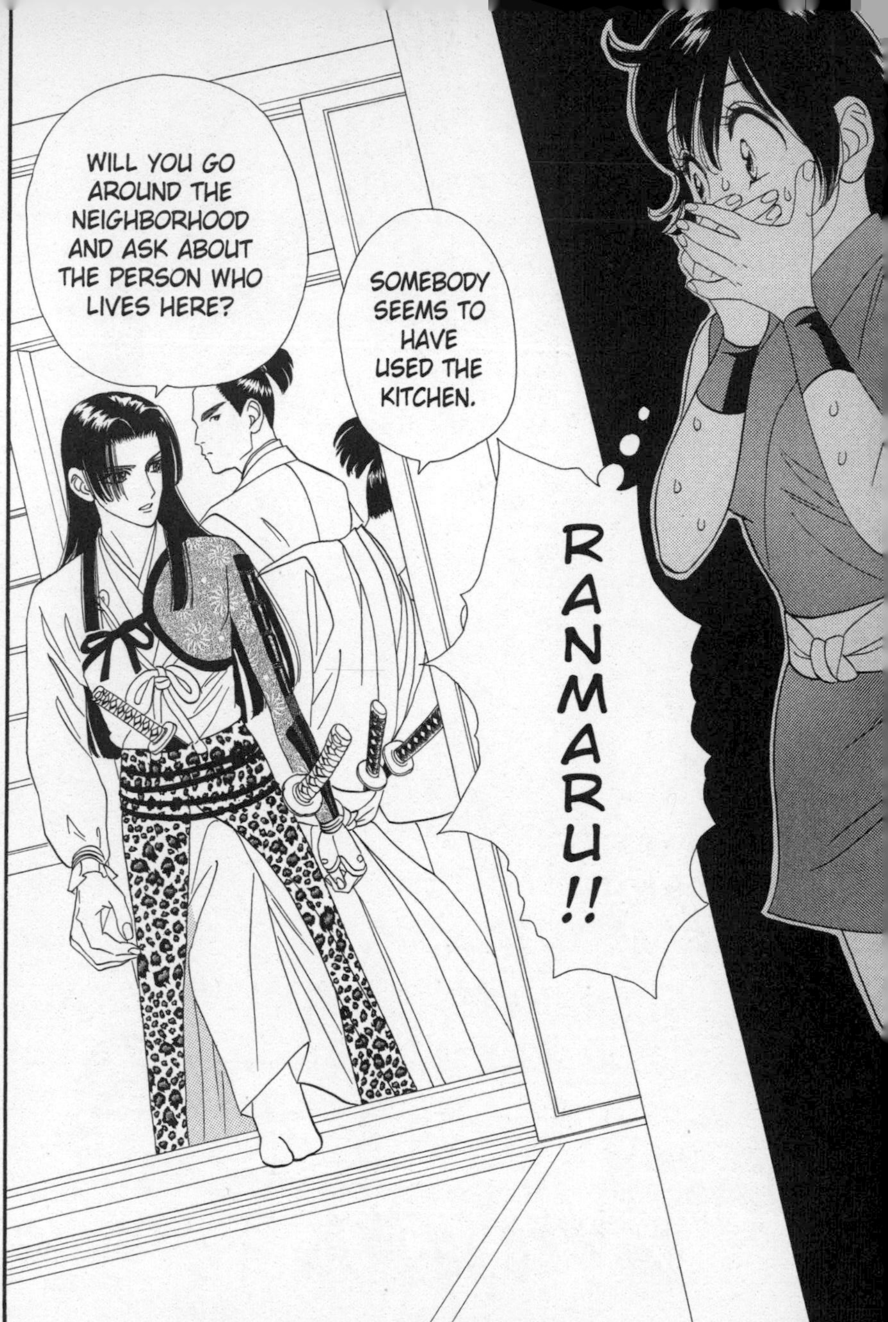
SOMEBODY SEEMS TO HAVE USED THE KITCHEN.
WILL YOU GO AROUND THE NEIGHBORHOOD AND ASK ABOUT THE PERSON WHO LIVES HERE?
RANMARU!!

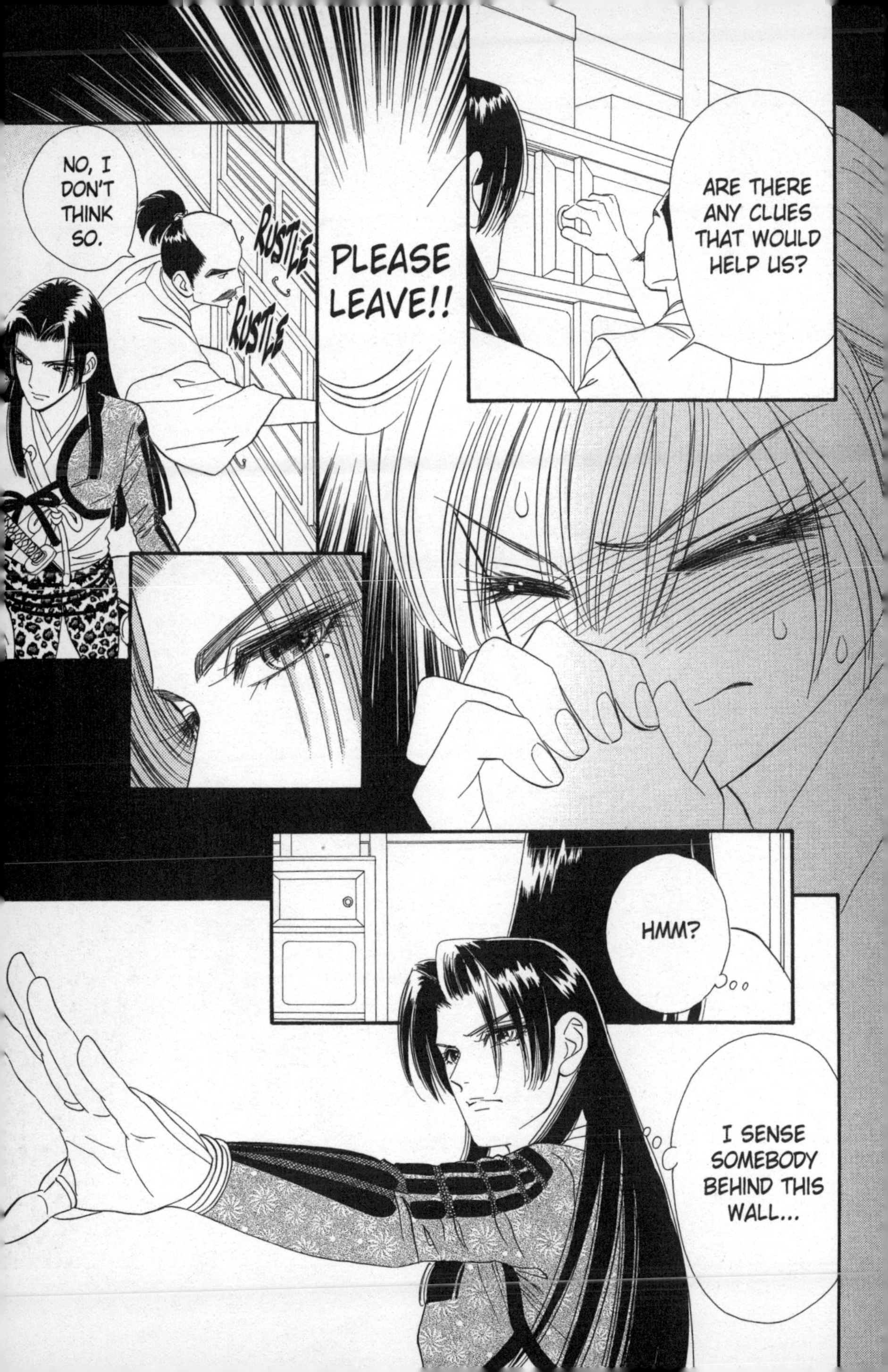
ARE THERE ANY CLUES THAT WOULD HELP US?
NO, I DON'T THINK SO.
RUSTLE
RUSTLE
PLEASE LEAVE!!
HMM?
I SENSE SOMEBODY BEHIND THIS WALL...

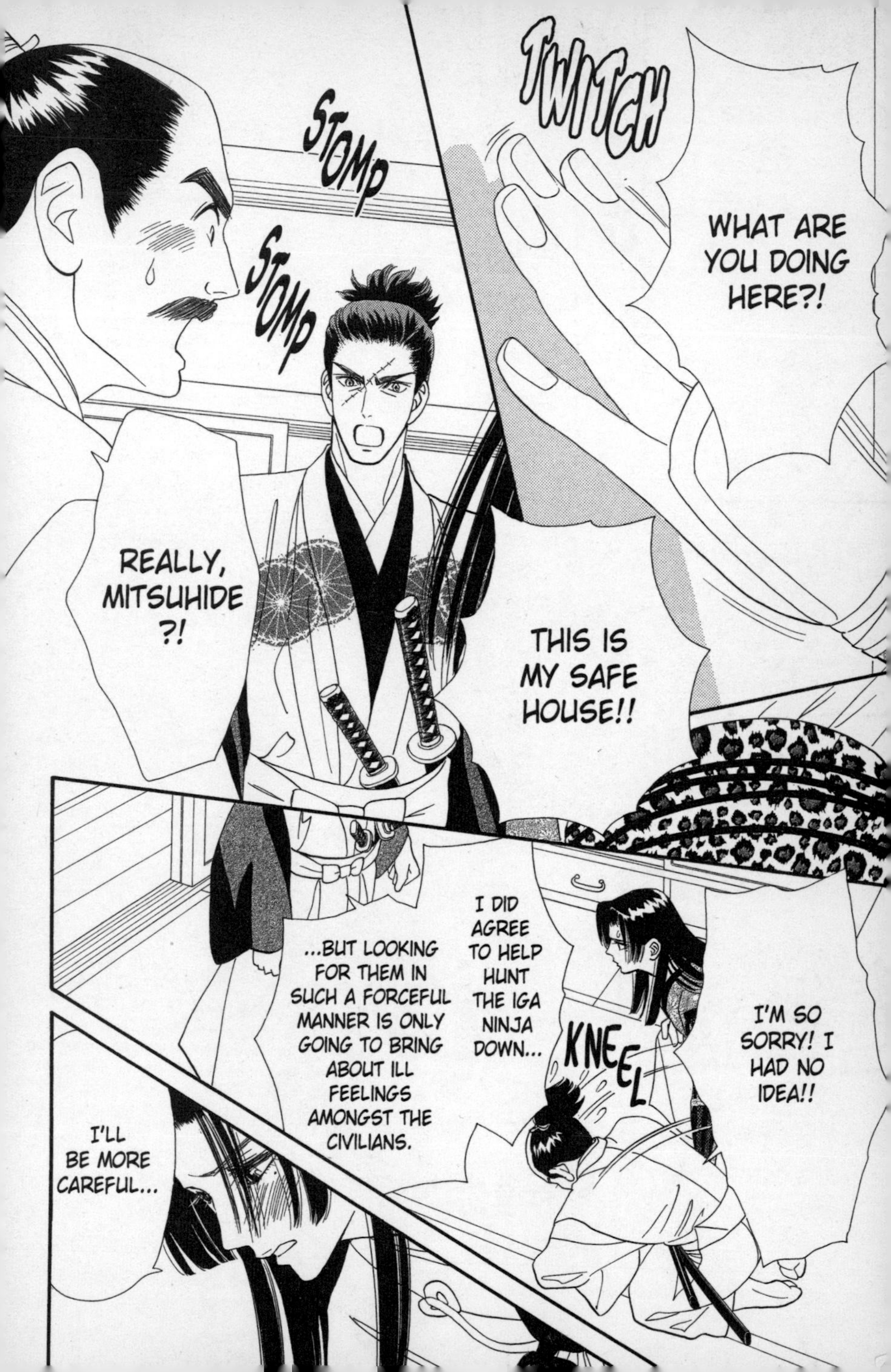
TWITCH
WHAT ARE YOU DOING HERE?!
THIS IS MY SAFE HOUSE!!
STOMP
STOMP
REALLY, MITSUHIDE?!
I'M SO SORRY! I HAD NO IDEA!!
KNEEL
I DID AGREE TO HELP HUNT THE IGA NINJA DOWN...
...BUT LOOKING FOR THEM IN SUCH A FORCEFUL MANNER IS ONLY GOING TO BRING ABOUT ILL FEELINGS AMONGST THE CIVILIANS.
I'LL BE MORE CAREFUL...

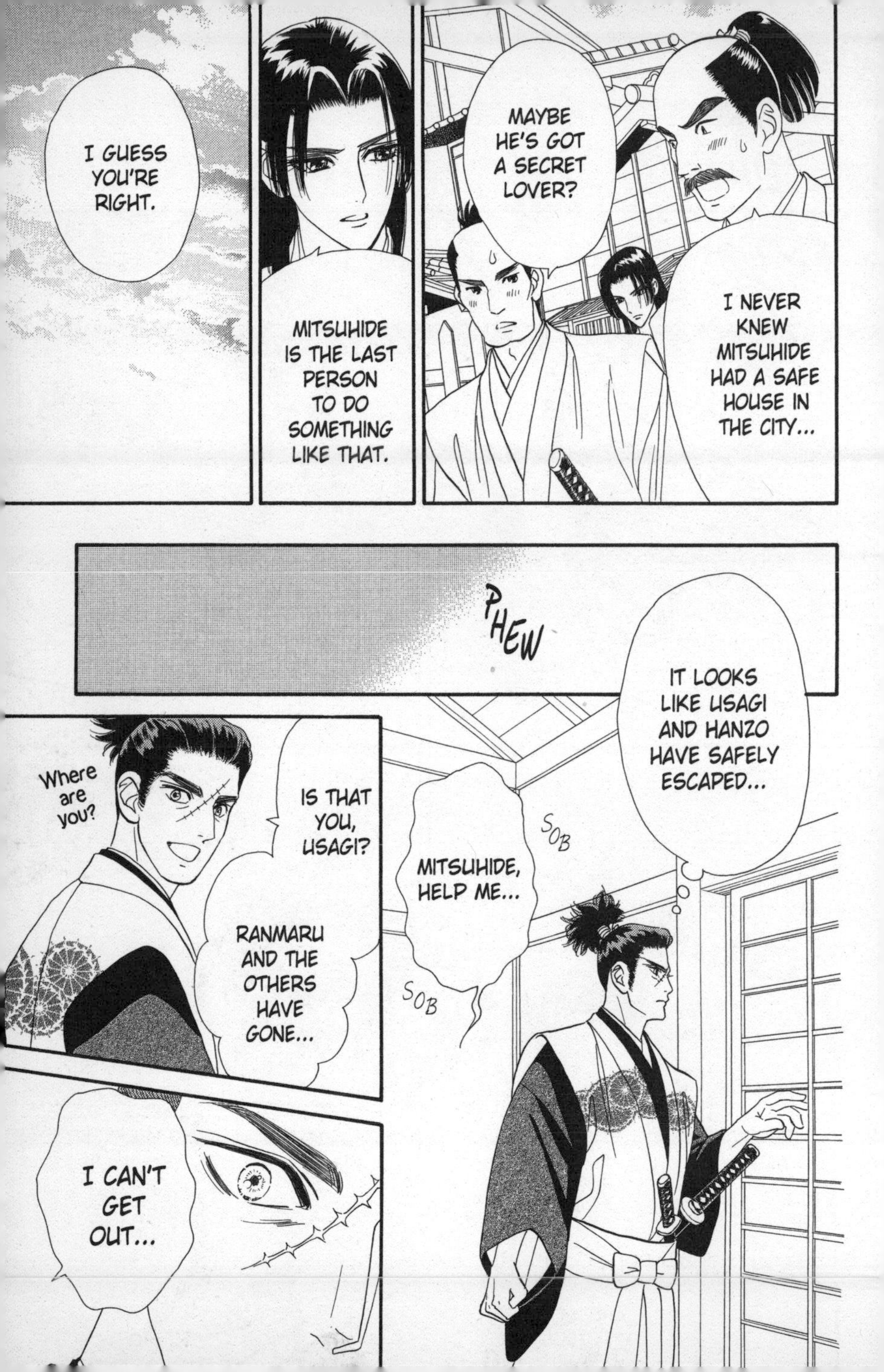
I NEVER KNEW MITSUHIDE HAD A SAFE HOUSE IN THE CITY...
MAYBE HE'S GOT A SECRET LOVER?
MITSUHIDE IS THE LAST PERSON TO DO SOMETHING LIKE THAT.
I GUESS YOU'RE RIGHT.
PHEW
IT LOOKS LIKE USAGI AND HANZO HAVE SAFELY ESCAPED...
SOB
MITSUHIDE, HELP ME...
SOB
IS THAT YOU, USAGI?
Where are you?
RANMARU AND THE OTHERS HAVE GONE...
I CAN'T GET OUT...

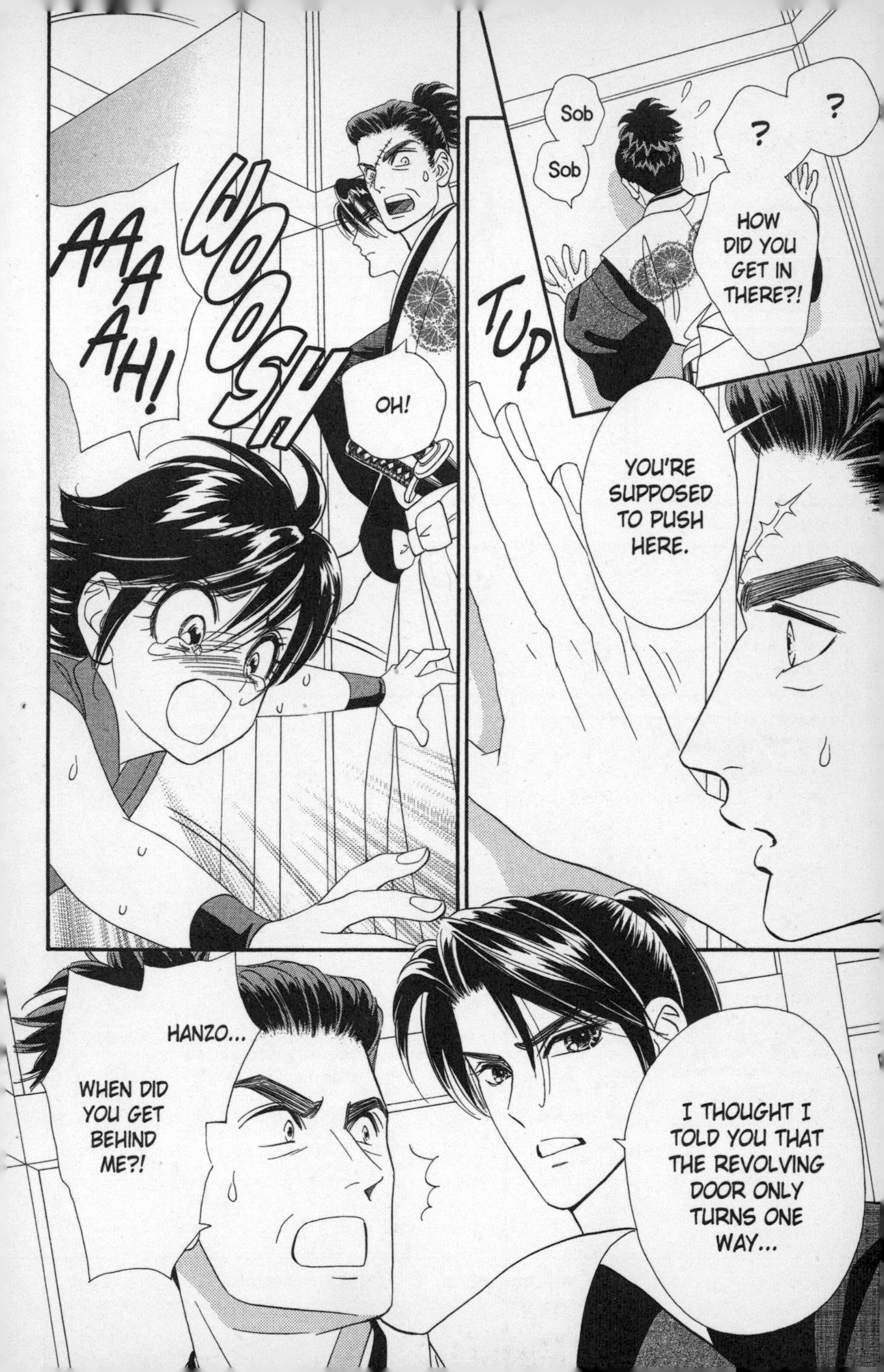
?
?
HOW DID YOU GET IN THERE?!
Sob
Sob
TUP
YOU'RE SUPPOSED TO PUSH HERE.
WOOOSH
AAAAH!
OH!
I THOUGHT I TOLD YOU THAT THE REVOLVING DOOR ONLY TURNS ONE WAY...
HANZO...
WHEN DID YOU GET BEHIND ME?!

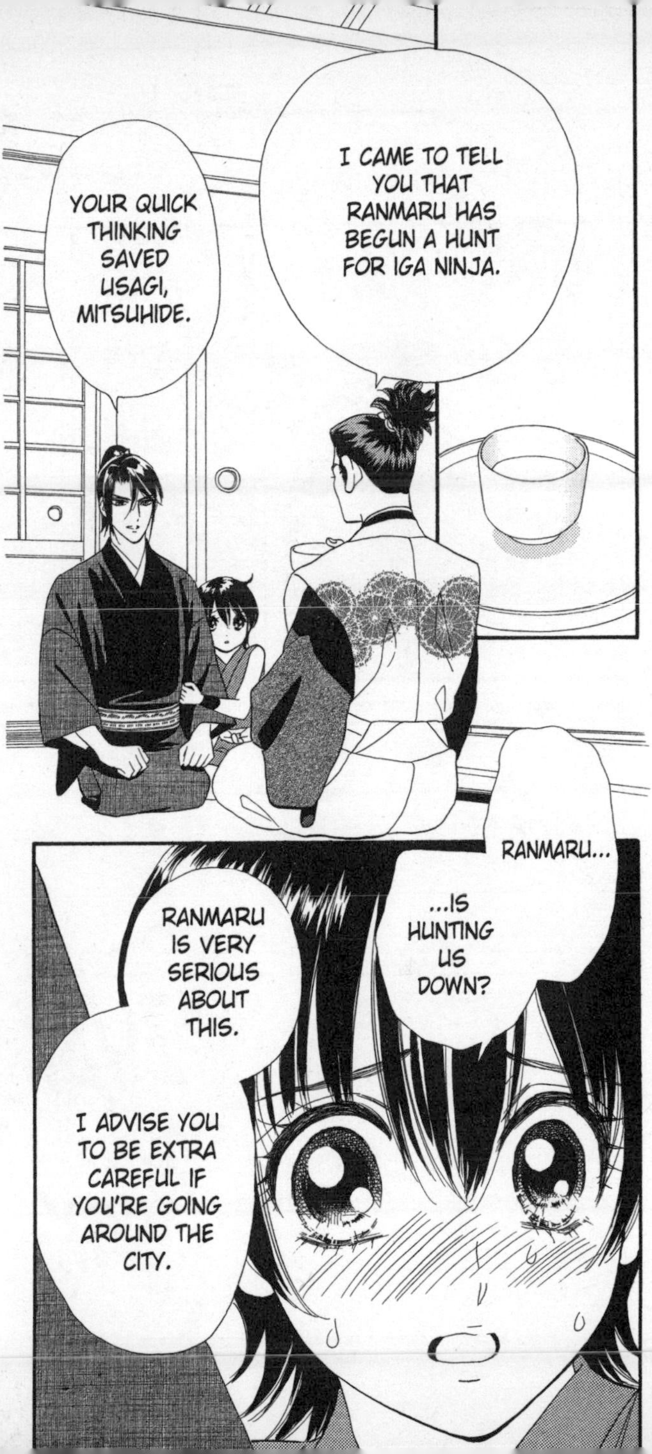
I CAME TO TELL YOU THAT RANMARU HAS BEGUN A HUNT FOR IGA NINJA.
YOUR QUICK THINKING SAVED USAGI, MITSUHIDE.
RANMARU...
...IS HUNTING US DOWN?
RANMARU IS VERY SERIOUS ABOUT THIS.
I ADVISE YOU TO BE EXTRA CAREFUL IF YOU'RE GOING AROUND THE CITY.

UE-RIN'S WAY OF THE MANGA (18)

I wasn't sure if going to a school with an art department was going to help me find a job in the future, but I had a passion for drawing ever since I was young. My desire to learn more techniques grew stronger, so I told my mother about my plan. Unfortunately, I got a straight "no" for an answer. The reason was that tuition fees for a private school were too expensive...

To be sure, going to a private school costs about 7-8 times more than going to a local high school, undoubtedly a big burden for a single-parent family like mine. But I still wanted to learn at an art department! That feeling just kept on growing...

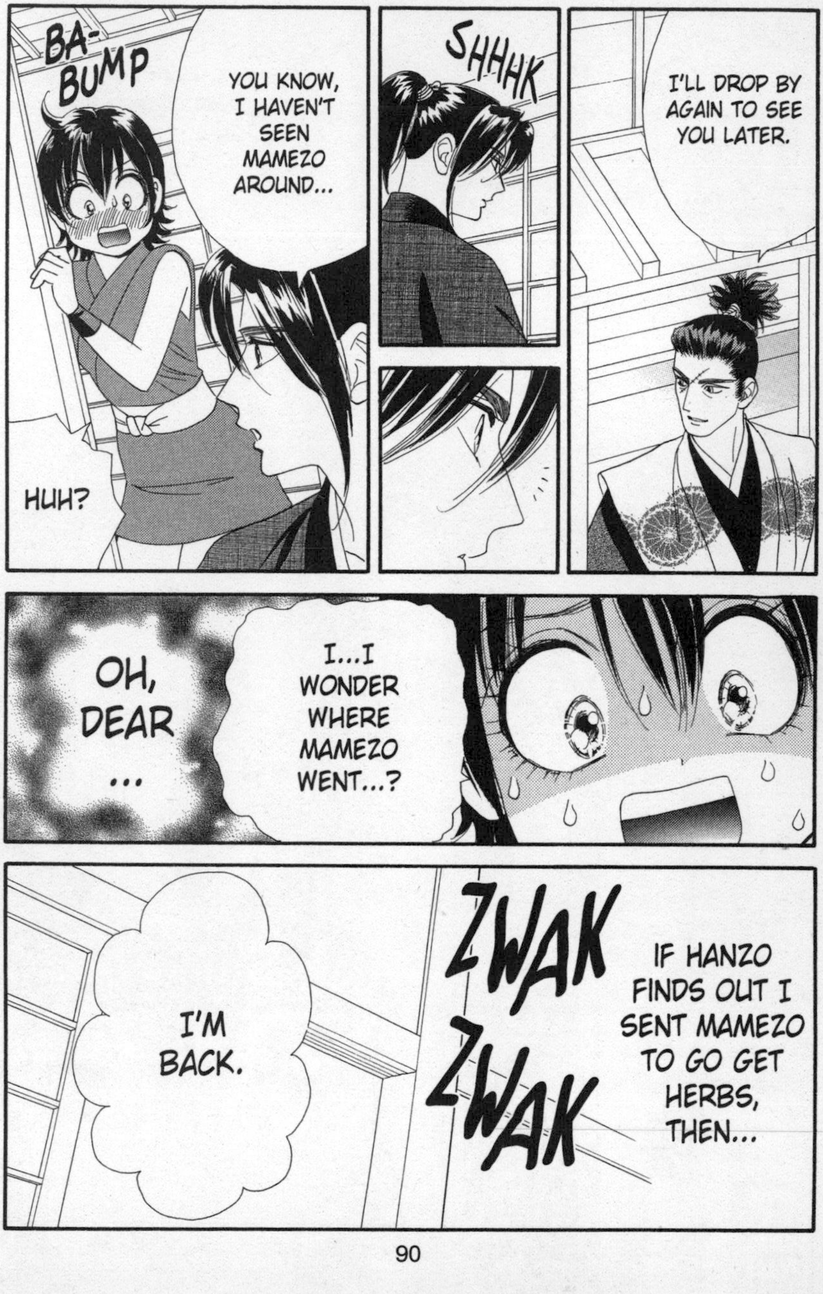
I'LL DROP BY AGAIN TO SEE YOU LATER.
SHHHK
YOU KNOW, I HAVEN'T SEEN MAMEZO AROUND...
BA-BUMP
HUH?
I...I WONDER WHERE MAMEZO WENT...?
OH, DEAR ...
IF HANZO FINDS OUT I SENT MAMEZO TO GO GET HERBS, THEN...
ZWAK ZWAK
I'M BACK.

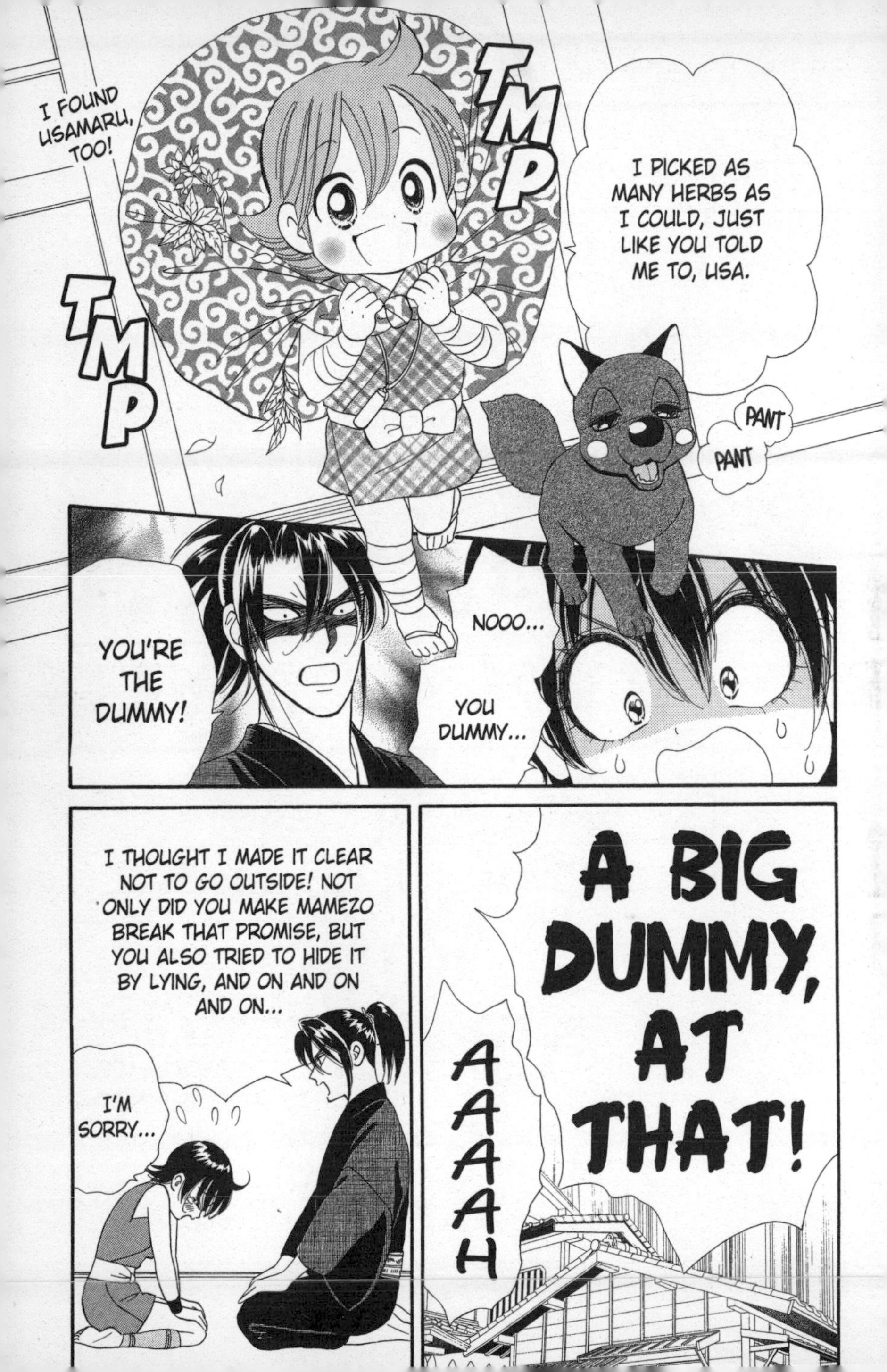
I PICKED AS MANY HERBS AS I COULD, JUST LIKE YOU TOLD ME TO, USA.
TMP
PANT
PANT
I FOUND USAMARU, TOO!
TMP
NOOO...
YOU DUMMY...
YOU'RE THE DUMMY!
A BIG DUMMY, AT THAT!
AAAAAH
I THOUGHT I MADE IT CLEAR NOT TO GO OUTSIDE! NOT ONLY DID YOU MAKE MAMEZO BREAK THAT PROMISE, BUT YOU ALSO TRIED TO HIDE IT BY LYING, AND ON AND ON AND ON...
I'M SORRY...

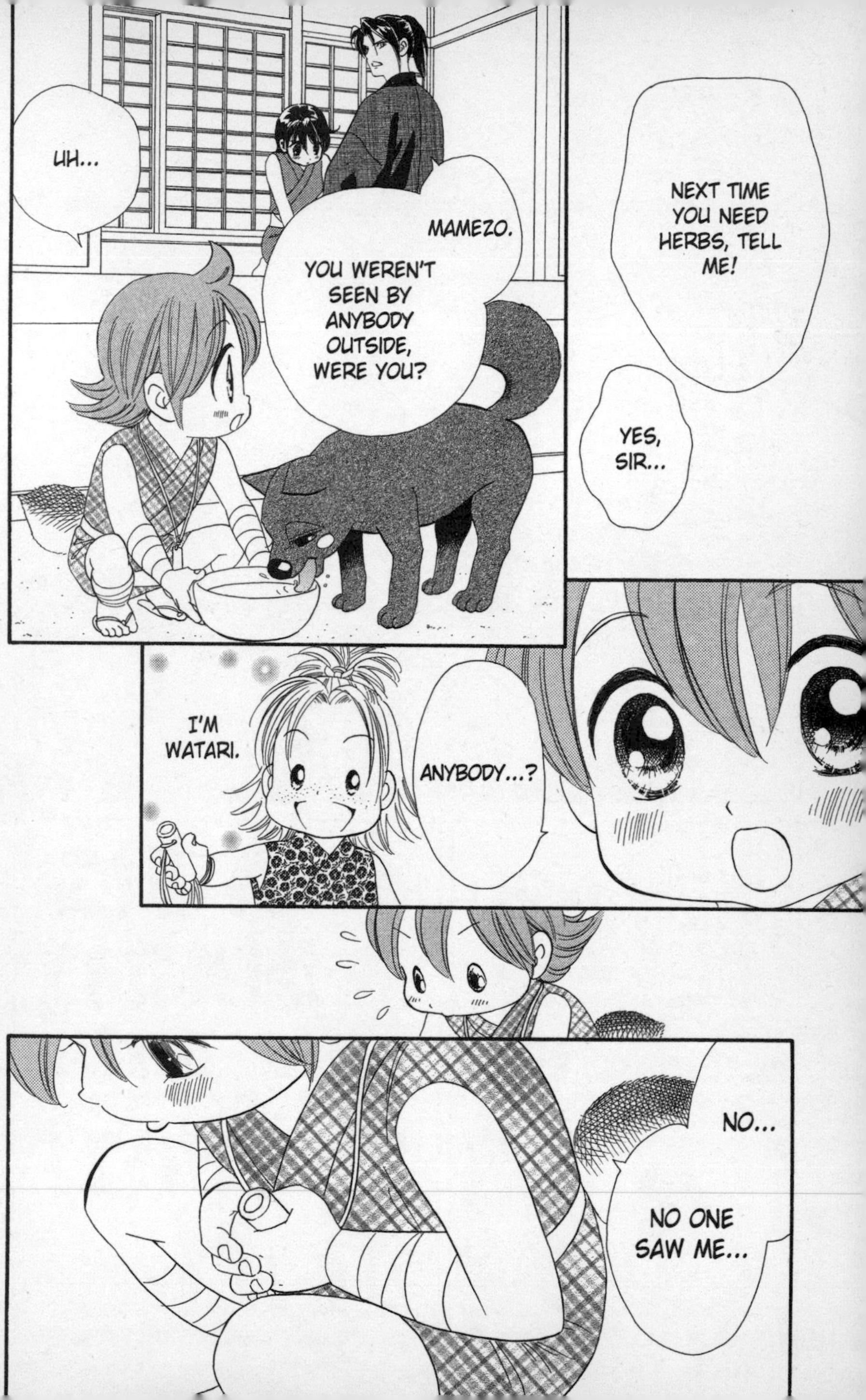
NEXT TIME YOU NEED HERBS, TELL ME!
YES, SIR...
MAMEZO.
YOU WEREN'T SEEN BY ANYBODY OUTSIDE, WERE YOU?
UH...
ANYBODY...?
I'M WATARI.
NO...
NO ONE SAW ME...

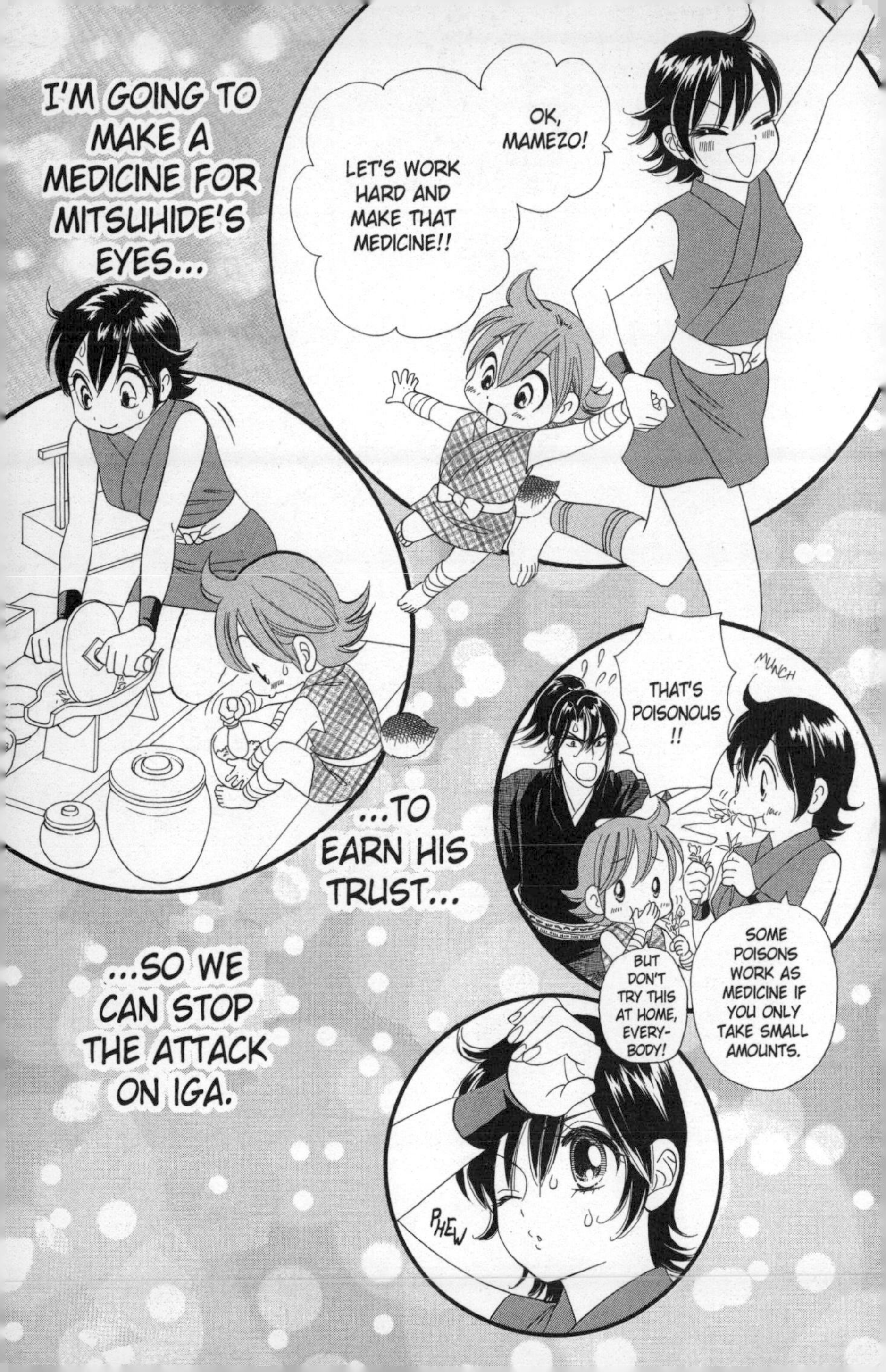
OK, MAMEZO!
LET'S WORK HARD AND MAKE THAT MEDICINE!!
I'M GOING TO MAKE A MEDICINE FOR MITSUHIDE'S EYES...
...TO EARN HIS TRUST...
MUNCH
THAT'S POISONOUS!!
SOME POISONS WORK AS MEDICINE IF YOU ONLY TAKE SMALL AMOUNTS.
BUT DON'T TRY THIS AT HOME, EVERY-BODY!
...SO WE CAN STOP THE ATTACK ON IGA.
PHEW

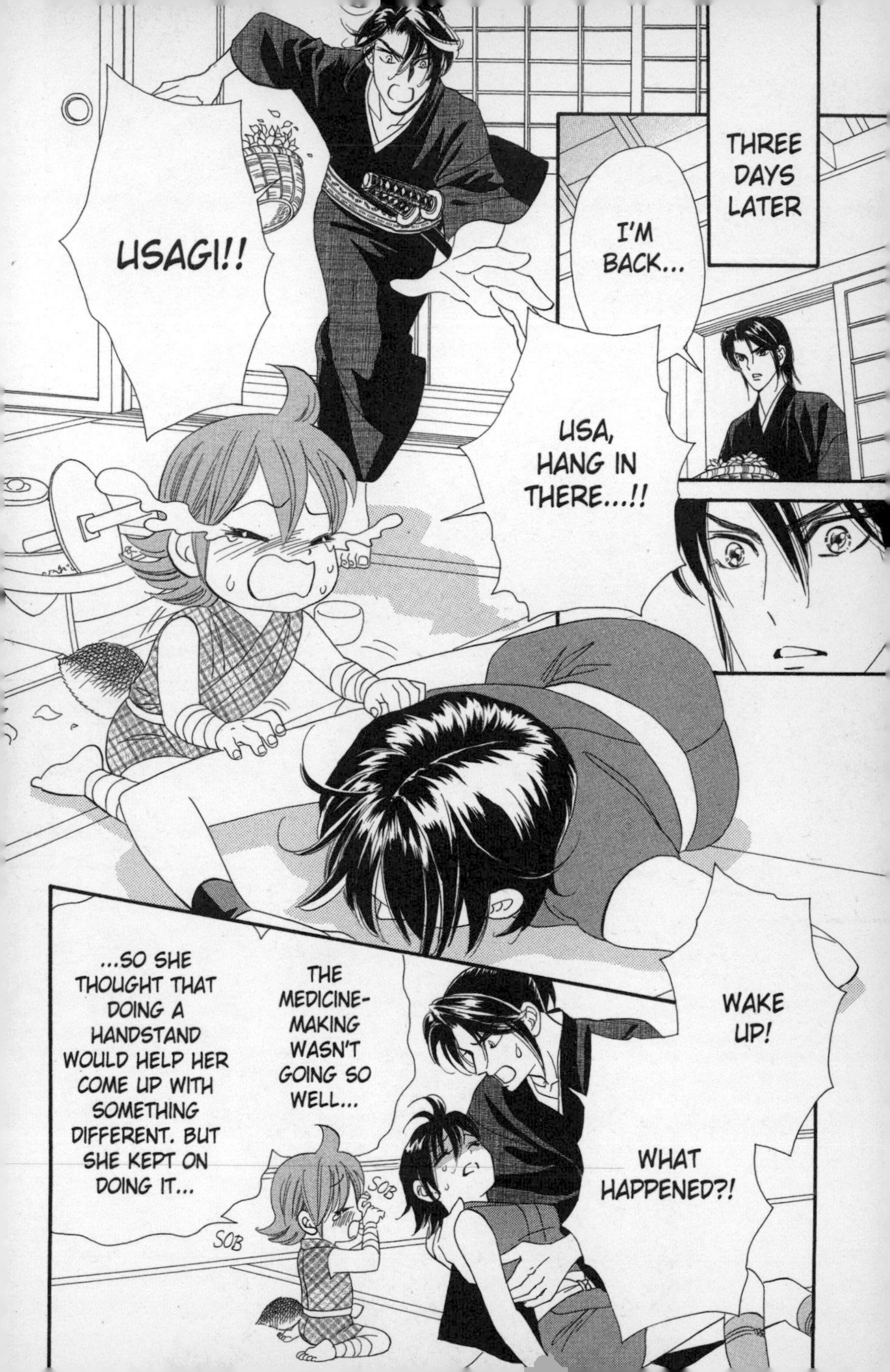
THREE DAYS LATER
I'M BACK...
USAGI!!
USA, HANG IN THERE...!!
WAKE UP!
WHAT HAPPENED?!
THE MEDICINE-MAKING WASN'T GOING SO WELL...
...SO SHE THOUGHT THAT DOING A HANDSTAND WOULD HELP HER COME UP WITH SOMETHING DIFFERENT. BUT SHE KEPT ON DOING IT...
SOB
SOB

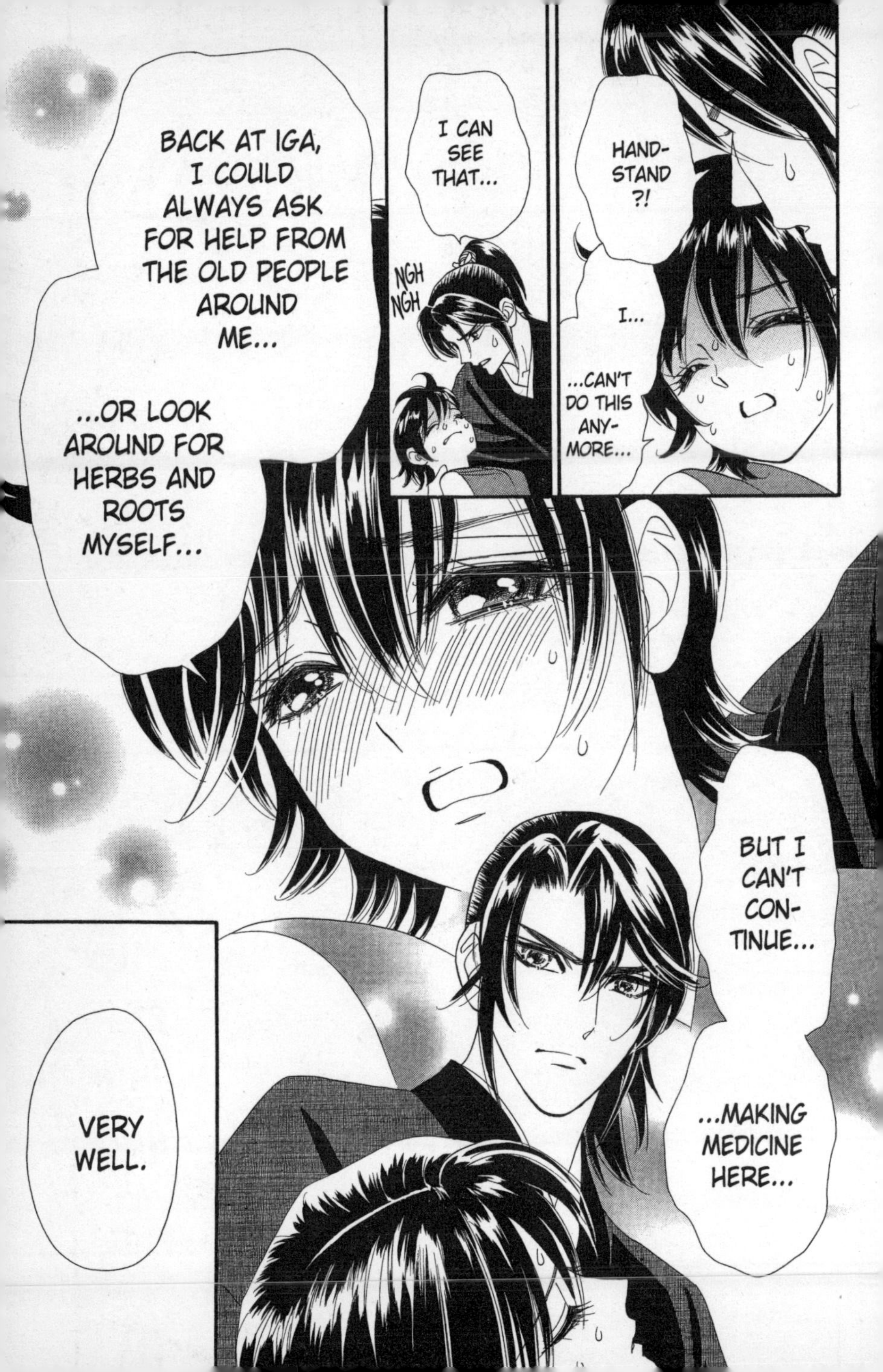
HAND-STAND?!
I...
...CAN'T DO THIS ANY-MORE...
I CAN SEE THAT...
NGH NGH
BACK AT IGA, I COULD ALWAYS ASK FOR HELP FROM THE OLD PEOPLE AROUND ME...
...OR LOOK AROUND FOR HERBS AND ROOTS MYSELF...
BUT I CAN'T CON-TINUE...
...MAKING MEDICINE HERE...
VERY WELL.

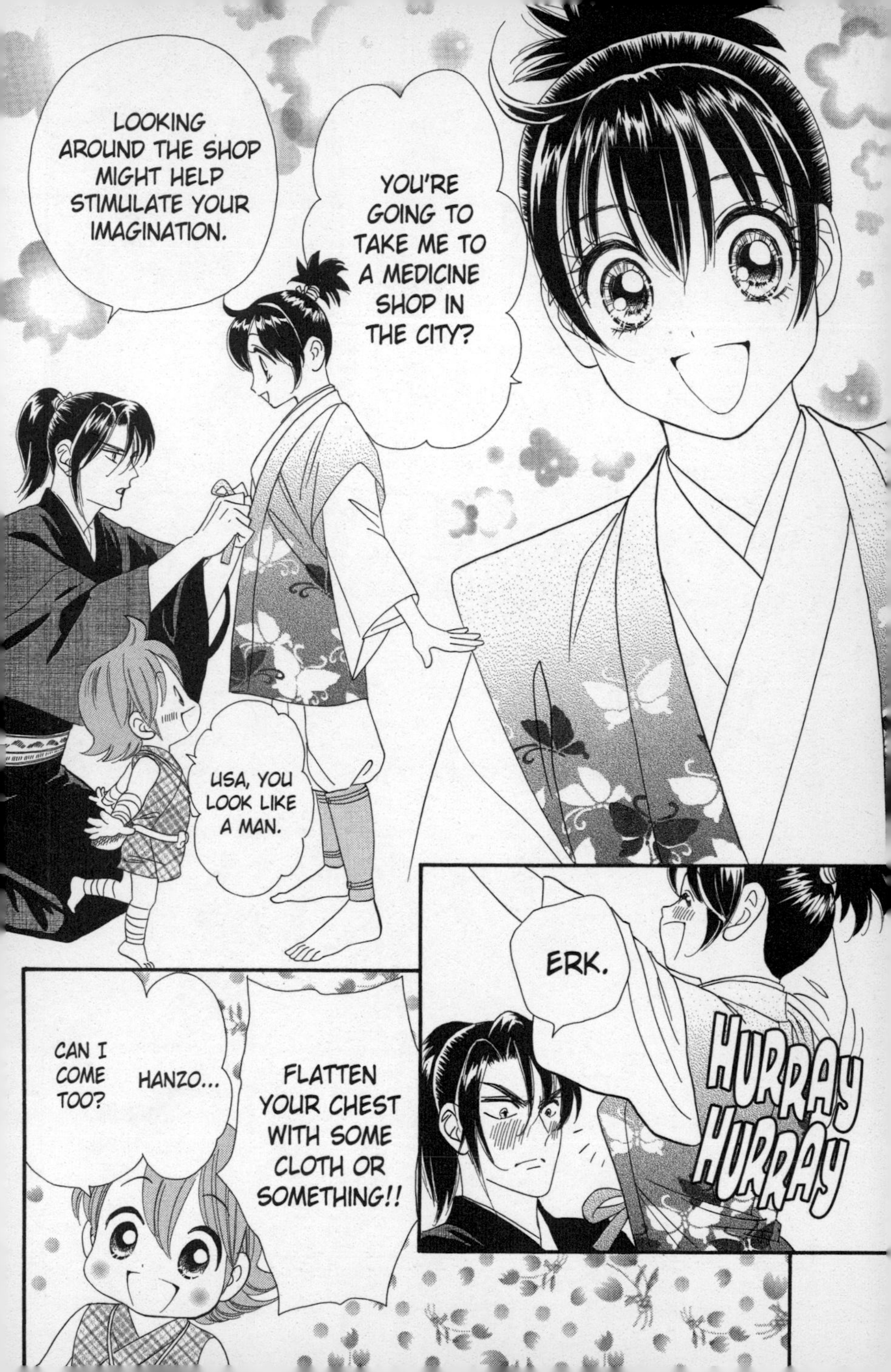
YOU'RE GOING TO TAKE ME TO A MEDICINE SHOP IN THE CITY?
LOOKING AROUND THE SHOP MIGHT HELP STIMULATE YOUR IMAGINATION.
USA, YOU LOOK LIKE A MAN.
ERK.
HURRAY HURRAY
FLATTEN YOUR CHEST WITH SOME CLOTH OR SOMETHING!!
HANZO...
CAN I COME TOO?

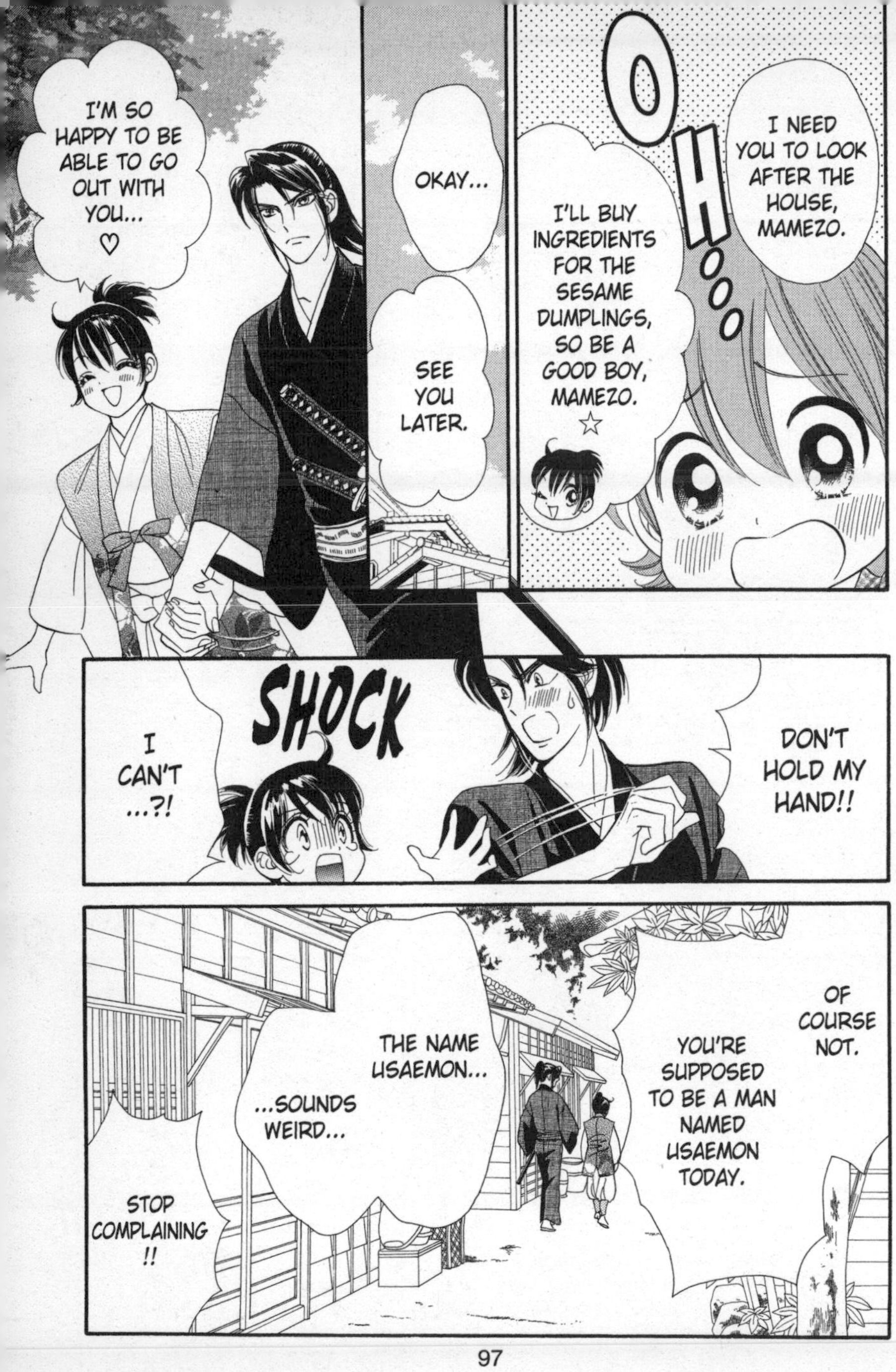
I NEED YOU TO LOOK AFTER THE HOUSE, MAMEZO.
OHOOO
I'LL BUY INGREDIENTS FOR THE SESAME DUMPLINGS, SO BE A GOOD BOY, MAMEZO. ☆
OKAY...
SEE YOU LATER.
I'M SO HAPPY TO BE ABLE TO GO OUT WITH YOU... ♡
DON'T HOLD MY HAND!!
SHOCK
I CAN'T ...?!
OF COURSE NOT.
YOU'RE SUPPOSED TO BE A MAN NAMED USAEMON TODAY.
THE NAME USAEMON...
...SOUNDS WEIRD...
STOP COMPLAINING!!

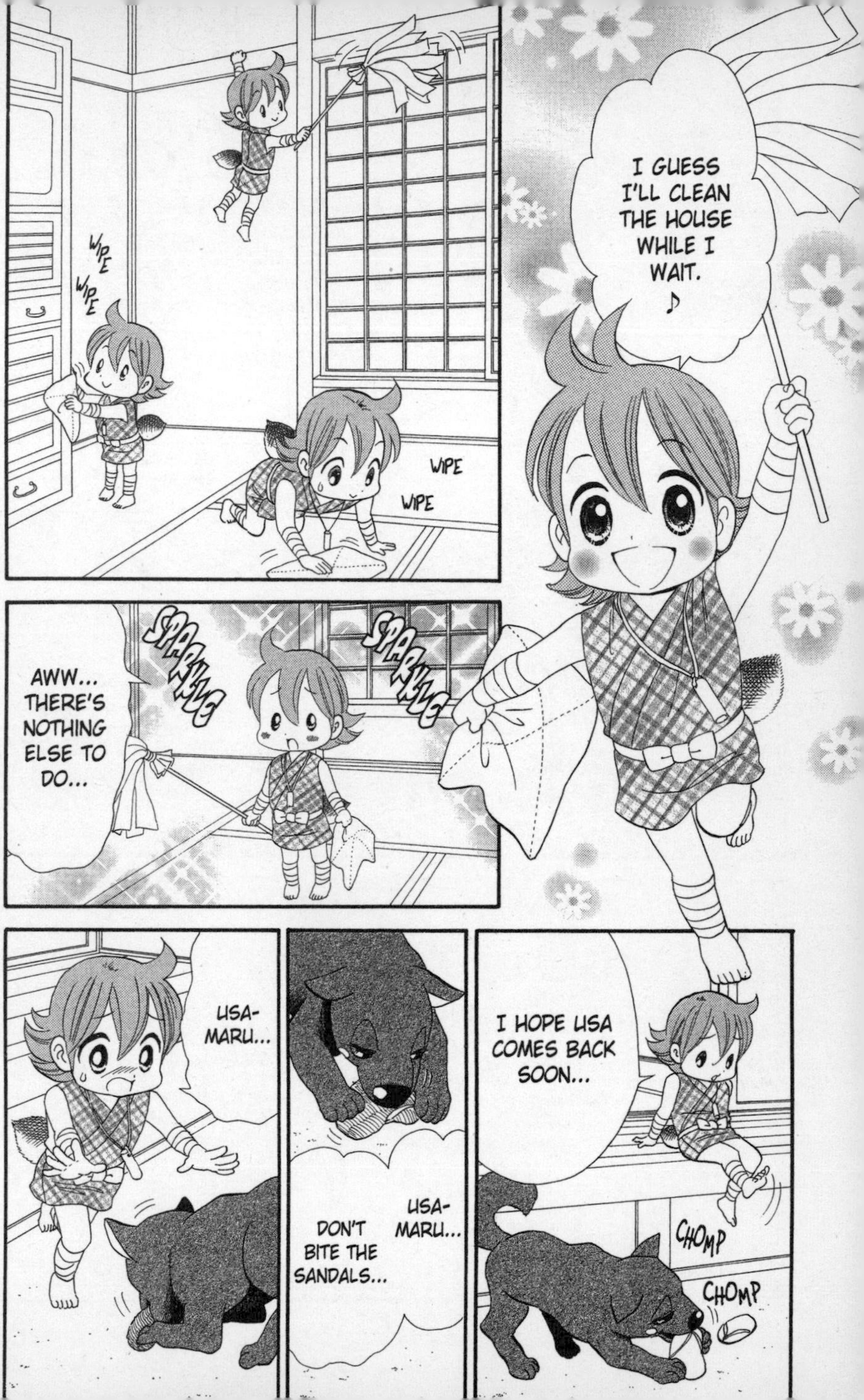
I GUESS I'LL CLEAN THE HOUSE WHILE I WAIT. ♪
WIPE
WIPE
WIPE
WIPE
SPARKLING
SPARKLING
AWW... THERE'S NOTHING ELSE TO DO...
I HOPE USA COMES BACK SOON...
CHOMP
CHOMP
USA-MARU...
DON'T BITE THE SANDALS...
USA-MARU...

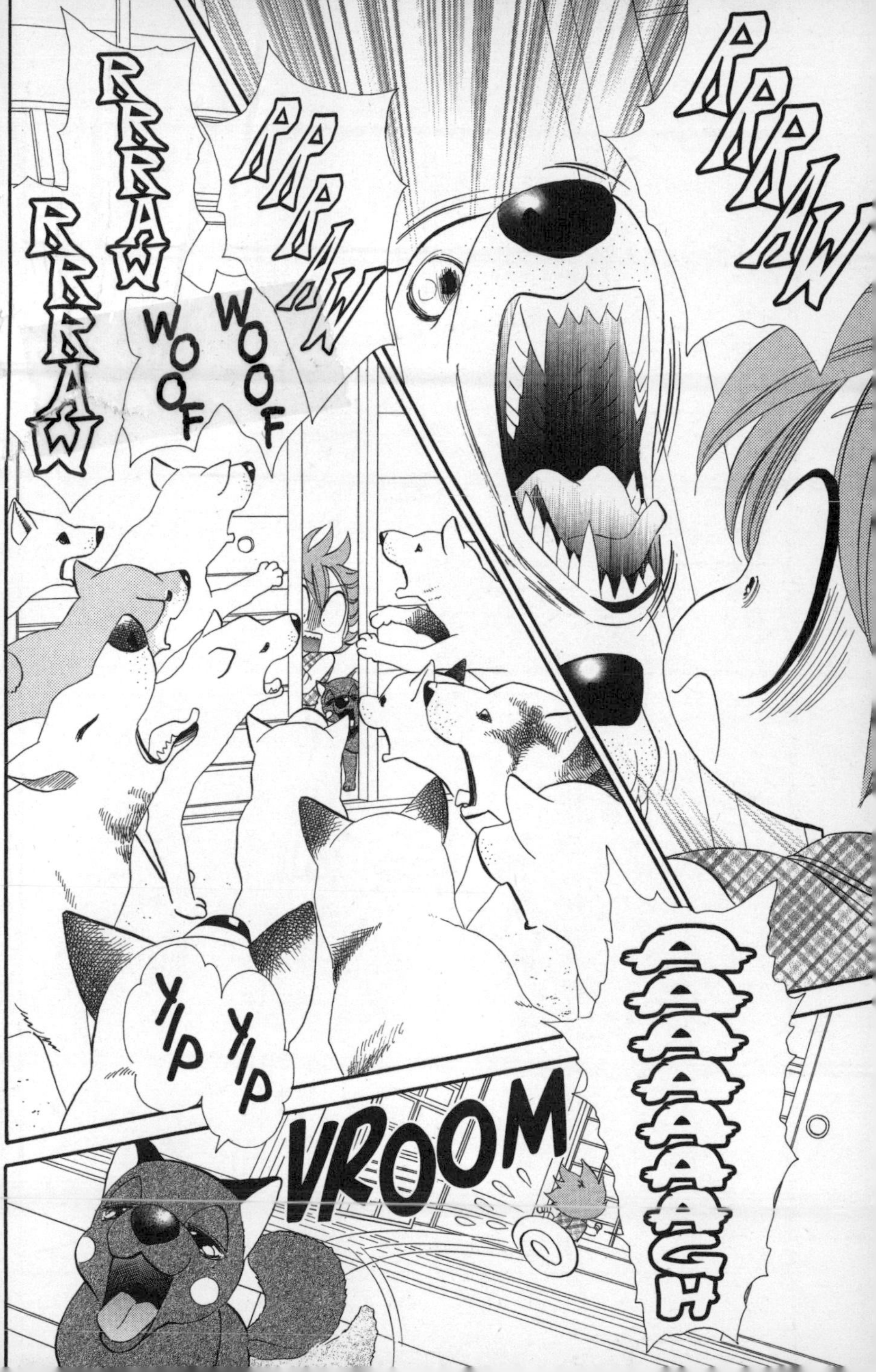
RRRRAW
RRRRAW
WOOF
WOOF
RRRAW
RRRRAW
YIP YIP
AAAAAAAAGH
VROOM

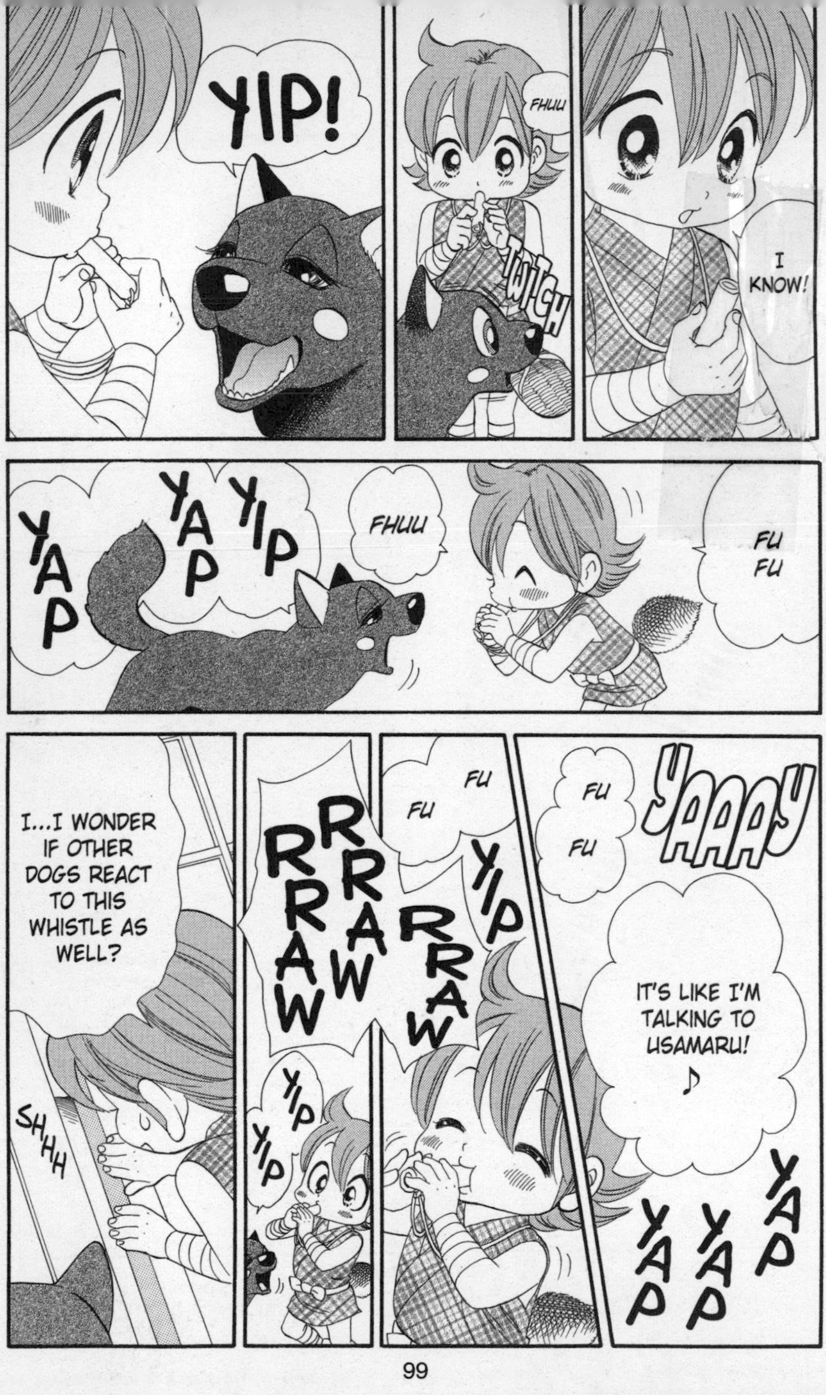

I KNOW!
FHUU
TWITCH
YIP!
FU FU
FHUU
YIP
YAP
YAP
YAAAY
FU FU
IT'S LIKE I'M TALKING TO USAMARU! ♪
YAP YAP YAP
FU FU
YIP
RRAW
RRAW RRAW
YIP YIP
I...I WONDER IF OTHER DOGS REACT TO THIS WHISTLE AS WELL?
SHHH

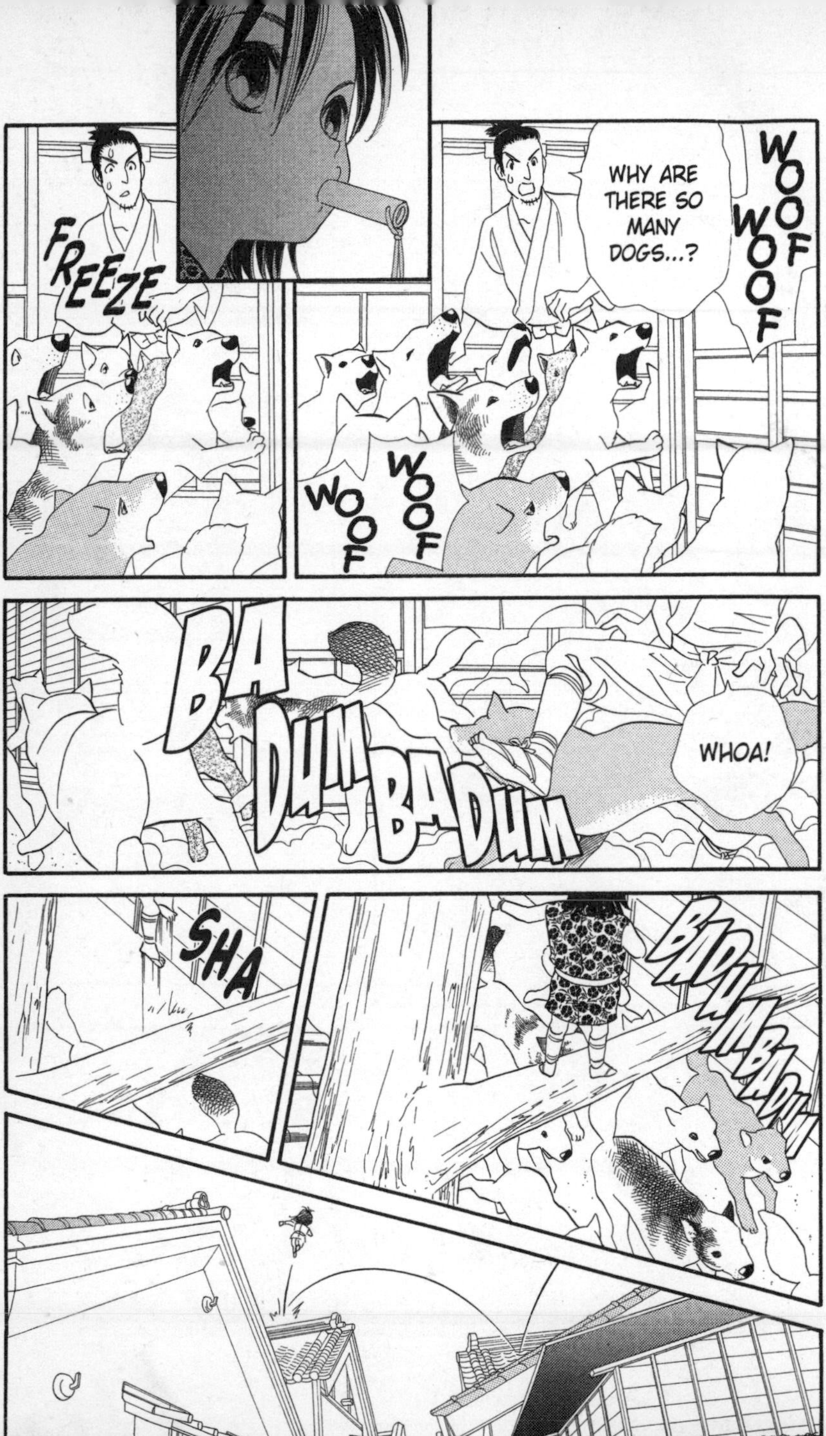
WHY ARE THERE SO MANY DOGS...?
WOOF WOOF
WOOF WOOF
FREEZE
WHOA!
BA DUM BA DUM
BADUM BADUM
SHA

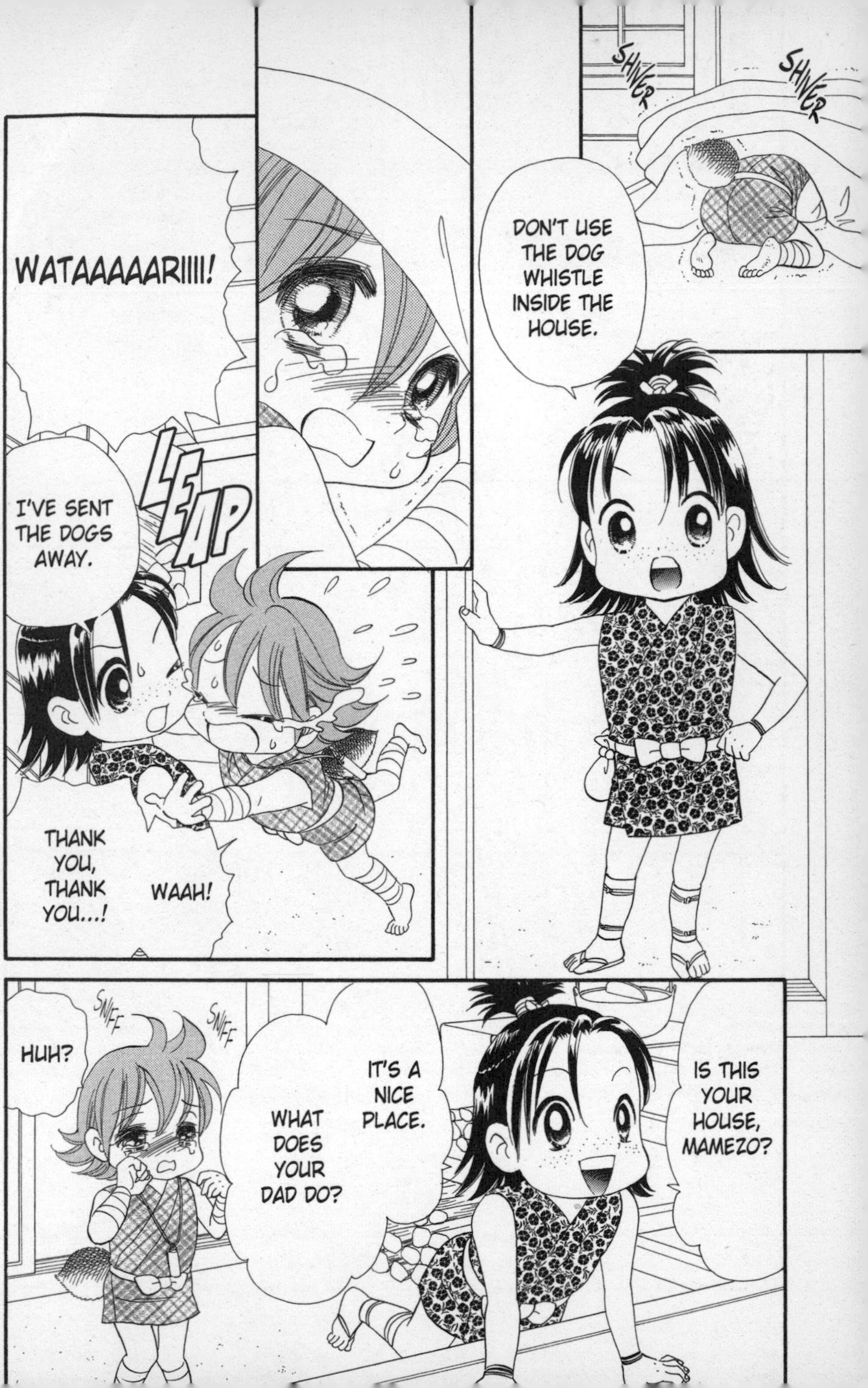
SHIVER
SHIVER
DON'T USE THE DOG WHISTLE INSIDE THE HOUSE.
WATAAAAARIIII!
LEAP
I'VE SENT THE DOGS AWAY.
WAAH!
THANK YOU, THANK YOU...!
IS THIS YOUR HOUSE, MAMEZO?
IT'S A NICE PLACE.
WHAT DOES YOUR DAD DO?
SNIFF
SNIFF
HUH?

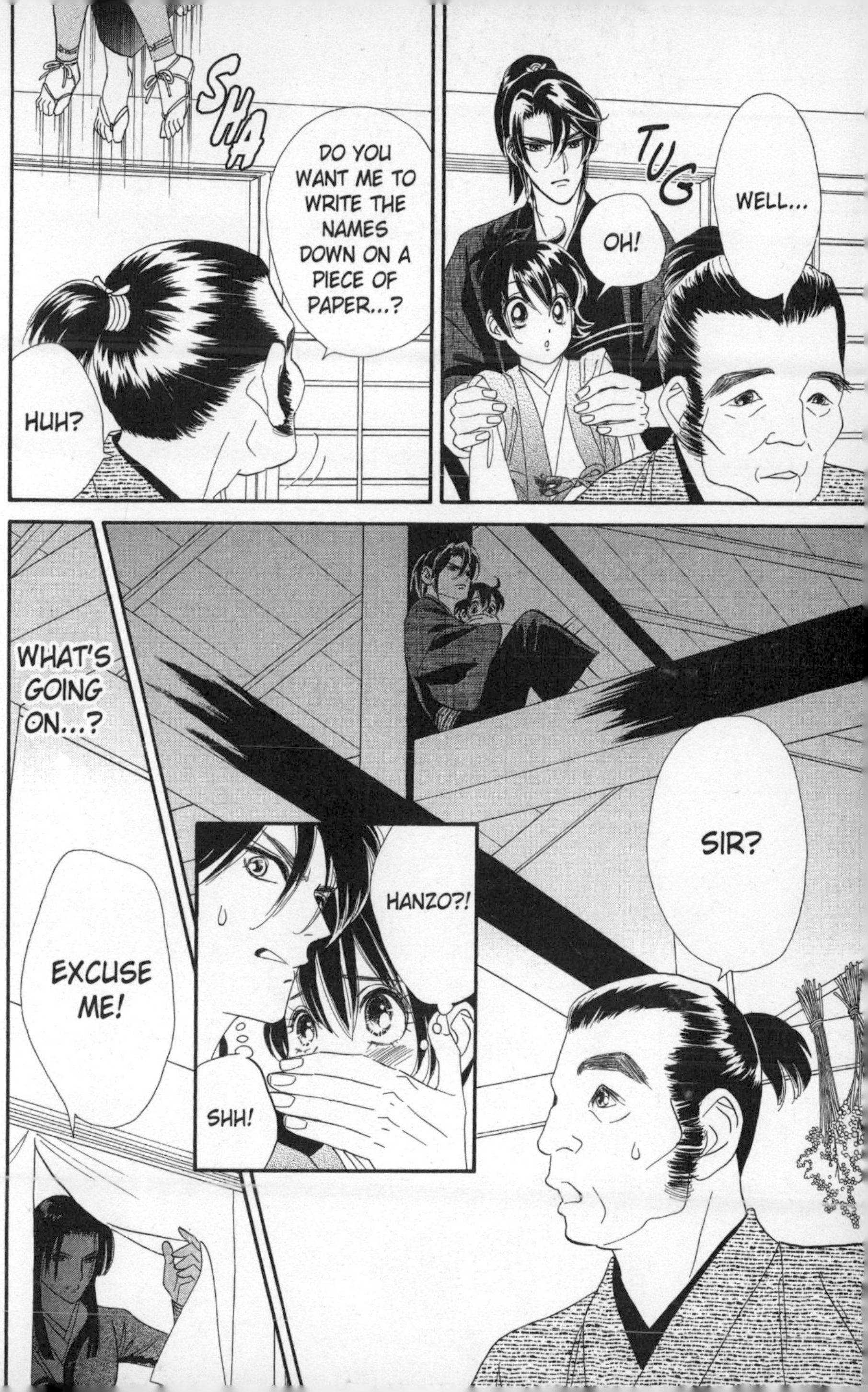

WELL...
TUG
OH!
SHA
DO YOU WANT ME TO WRITE THE NAMES DOWN ON A PIECE OF PAPER...?
HUH?
SIR?
WHAT'S GOING ON...?
HANZO?!
SHH!
EXCUSE ME!

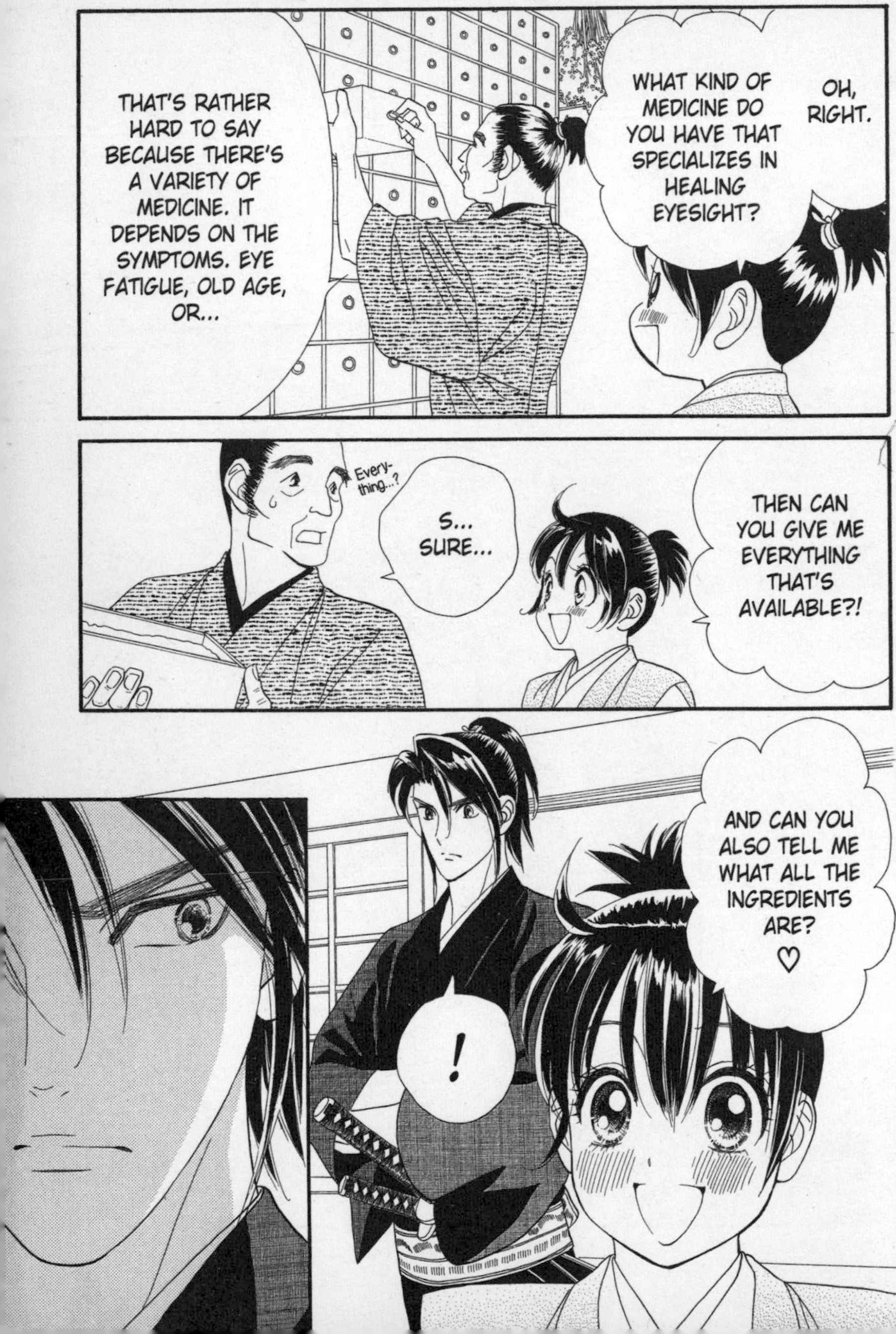
OH, RIGHT.
WHAT KIND OF MEDICINE DO YOU HAVE THAT SPECIALIZES IN HEALING EYESIGHT?
THAT'S RATHER HARD TO SAY BECAUSE THERE'S A VARIETY OF MEDICINE. IT DEPENDS ON THE SYMPTOMS. EYE FATIGUE, OLD AGE, OR...
THEN CAN YOU GIVE ME EVERYTHING THAT'S AVAILABLE?!
S... SURE...
Every-thing...?
AND CAN YOU ALSO TELL ME WHAT ALL THE INGREDIENTS ARE? ♡
!

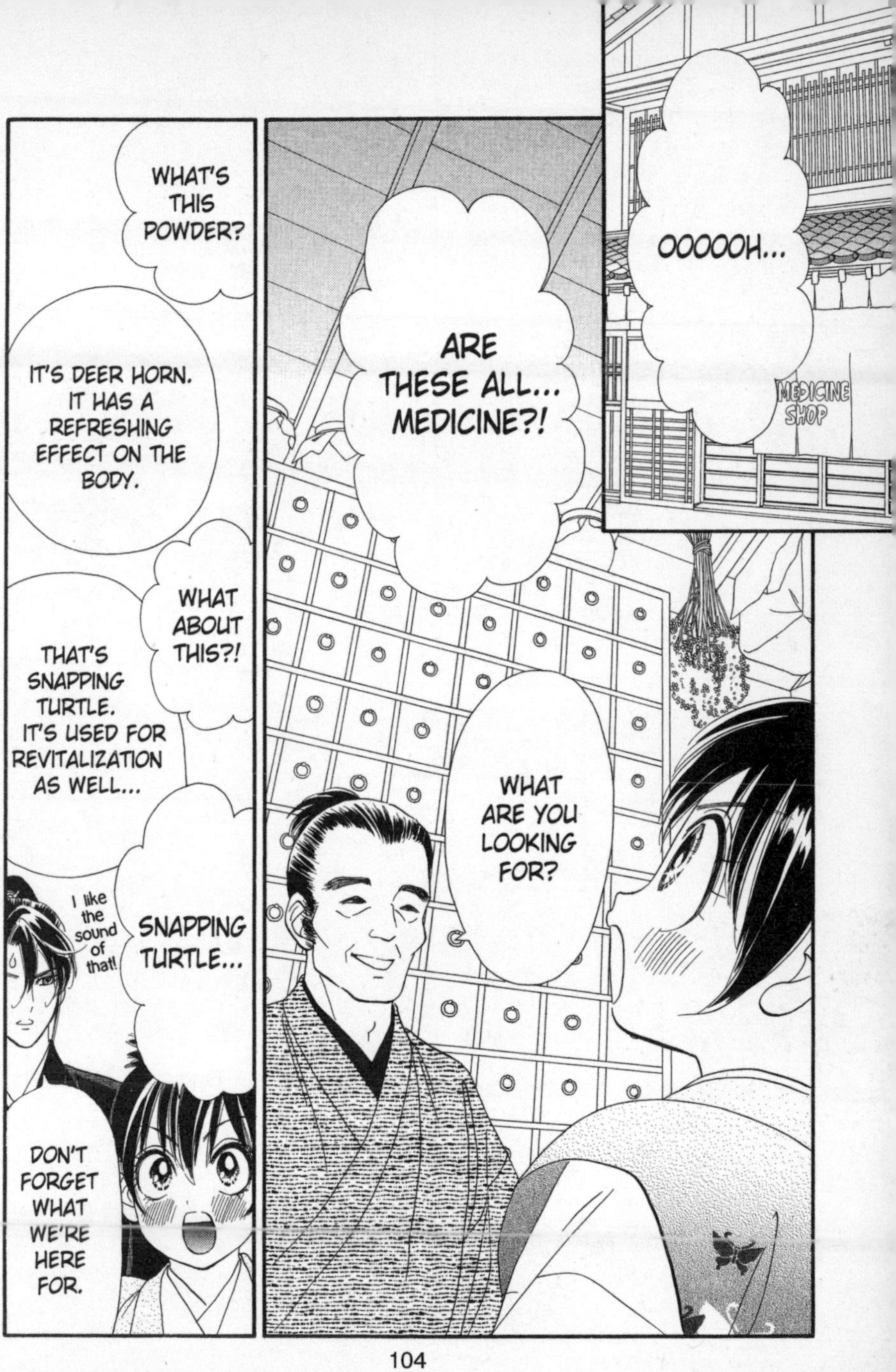
OOOOOH...
MEDICINE SHOP
ARE THESE ALL... MEDICINE?!
WHAT ARE YOU LOOKING FOR?
WHAT'S THIS POWDER?
IT'S DEER HORN. IT HAS A REFRESHING EFFECT ON THE BODY.
WHAT ABOUT THIS?!
THAT'S SNAPPING TURTLE. IT'S USED FOR REVITALIZATION AS WELL...
SNAPPING TURTLE...
I like the sound of that!
DON'T FORGET WHAT WE'RE HERE FOR.

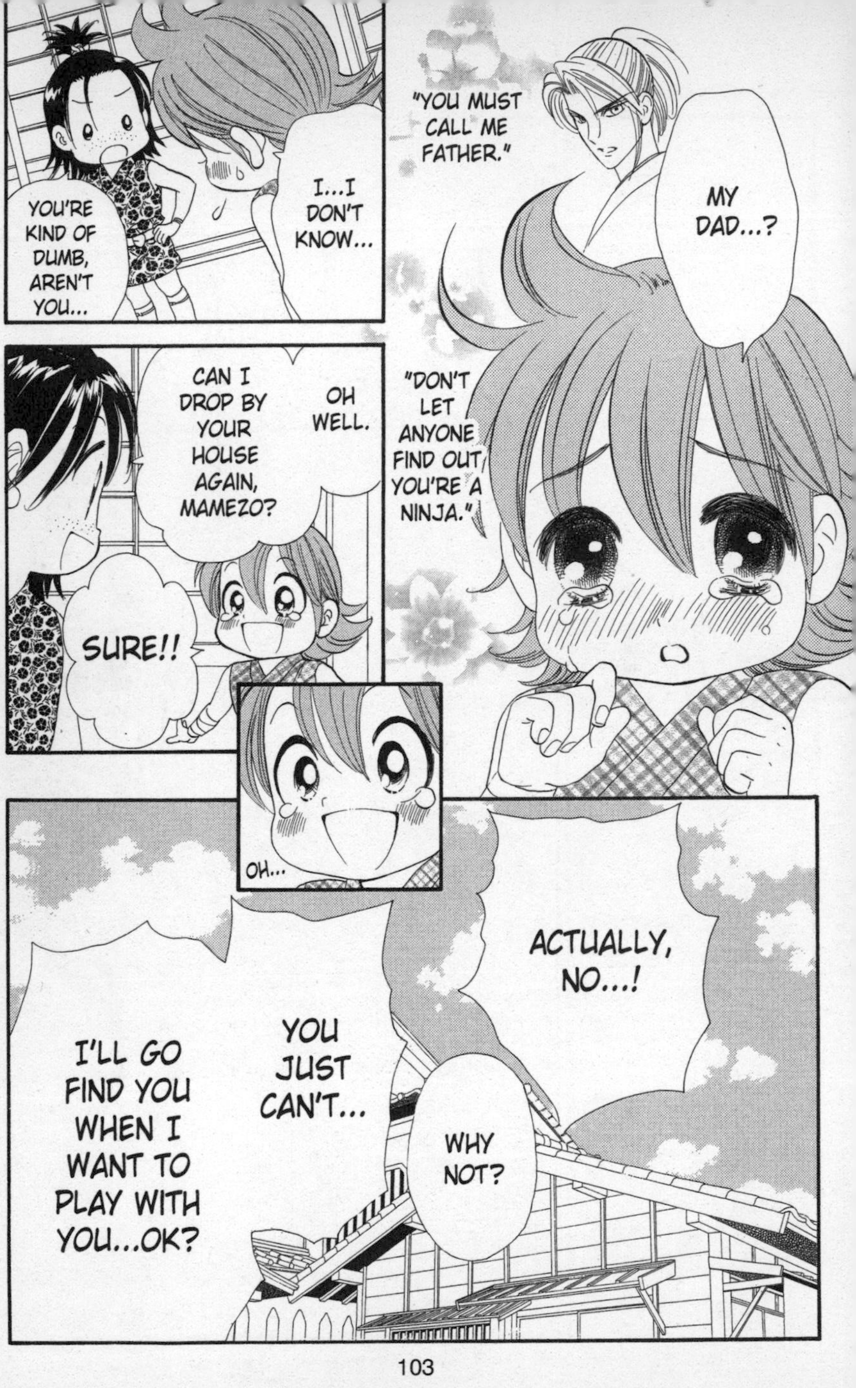
MY DAD...?
"YOU MUST CALL ME FATHER."
"DON'T LET ANYONE FIND OUT YOU'RE A NINJA."
I...I DON'T KNOW...
YOU'RE KIND OF DUMB, AREN'T YOU...
OH WELL.
CAN I DROP BY YOUR HOUSE AGAIN, MAMEZO?
SURE!!
OH...
ACTUALLY, NO...!
YOU JUST CAN'T...
WHY NOT?
I'LL GO FIND YOU WHEN I WANT TO PLAY WITH YOU...OK?

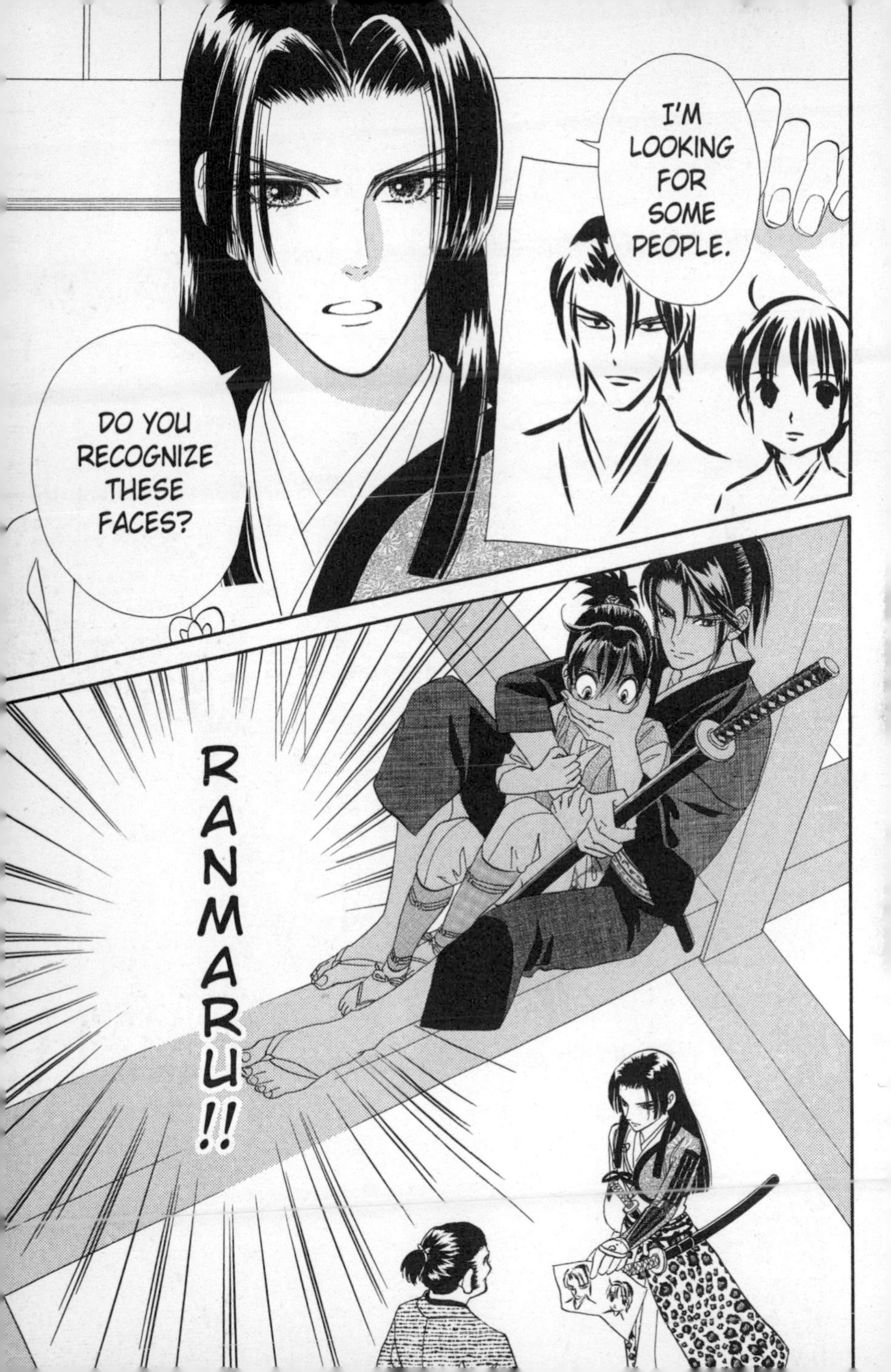
I'M LOOKING FOR SOME PEOPLE.
DO YOU RECOGNIZE THESE FACES?
RANMARU!!

TAIL OF THE MOON EXTRA: TODAY'S MISSION

"I WANT TO SEE HANZO AS A FATHER!!"

☆POOH☆, FUKUOKA PREFECTURE

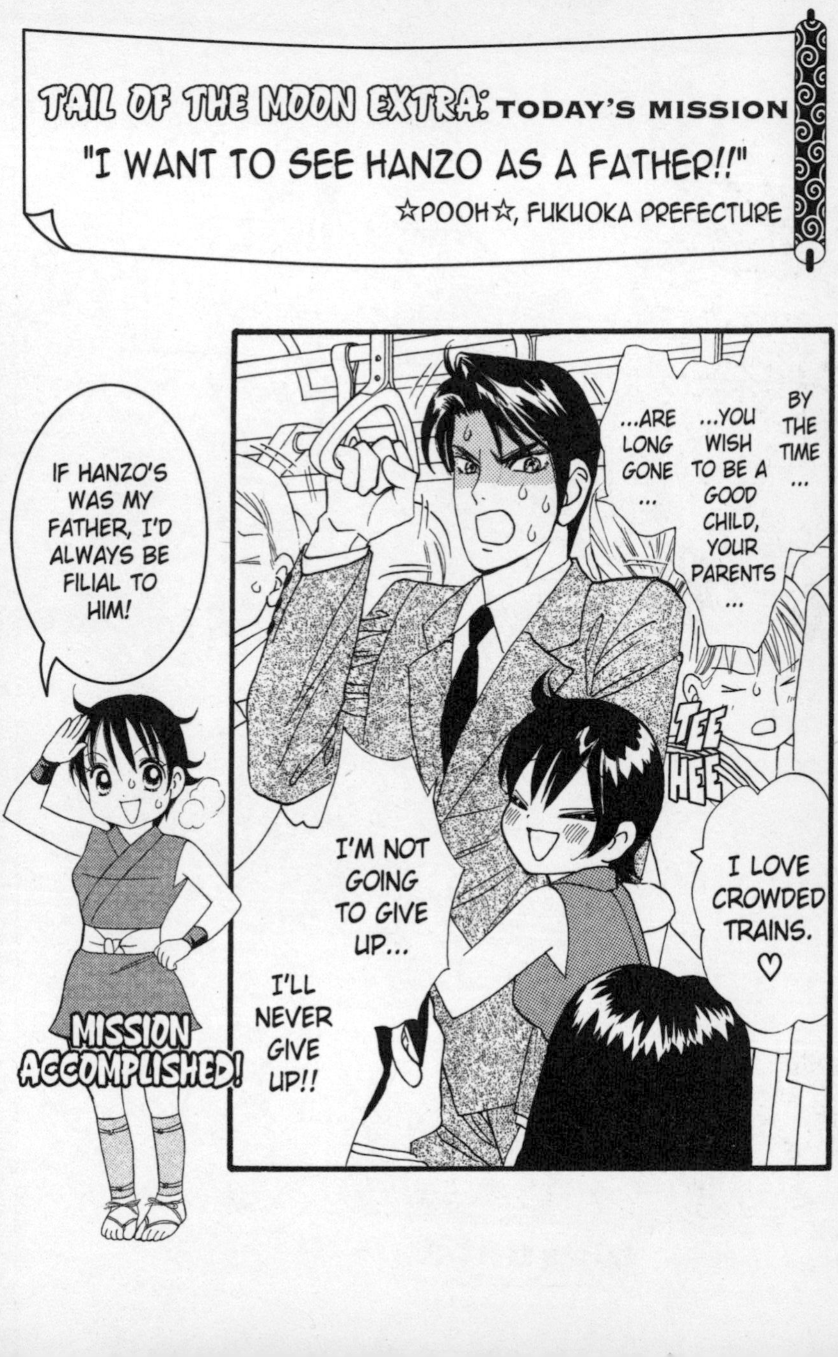
BY THE TIME ...
...YOU WISH TO BE A GOOD CHILD, YOUR PARENTS ...
...ARE LONG GONE ...
TEE HEE
I LOVE CROWDED TRAINS. ♡
I'M NOT GOING TO GIVE UP...
I'LL NEVER GIVE UP!!
IF HANZO'S WAS MY FATHER, I'D ALWAYS BE FILIAL TO HIM!
MISSION ACCOMPLISHED!

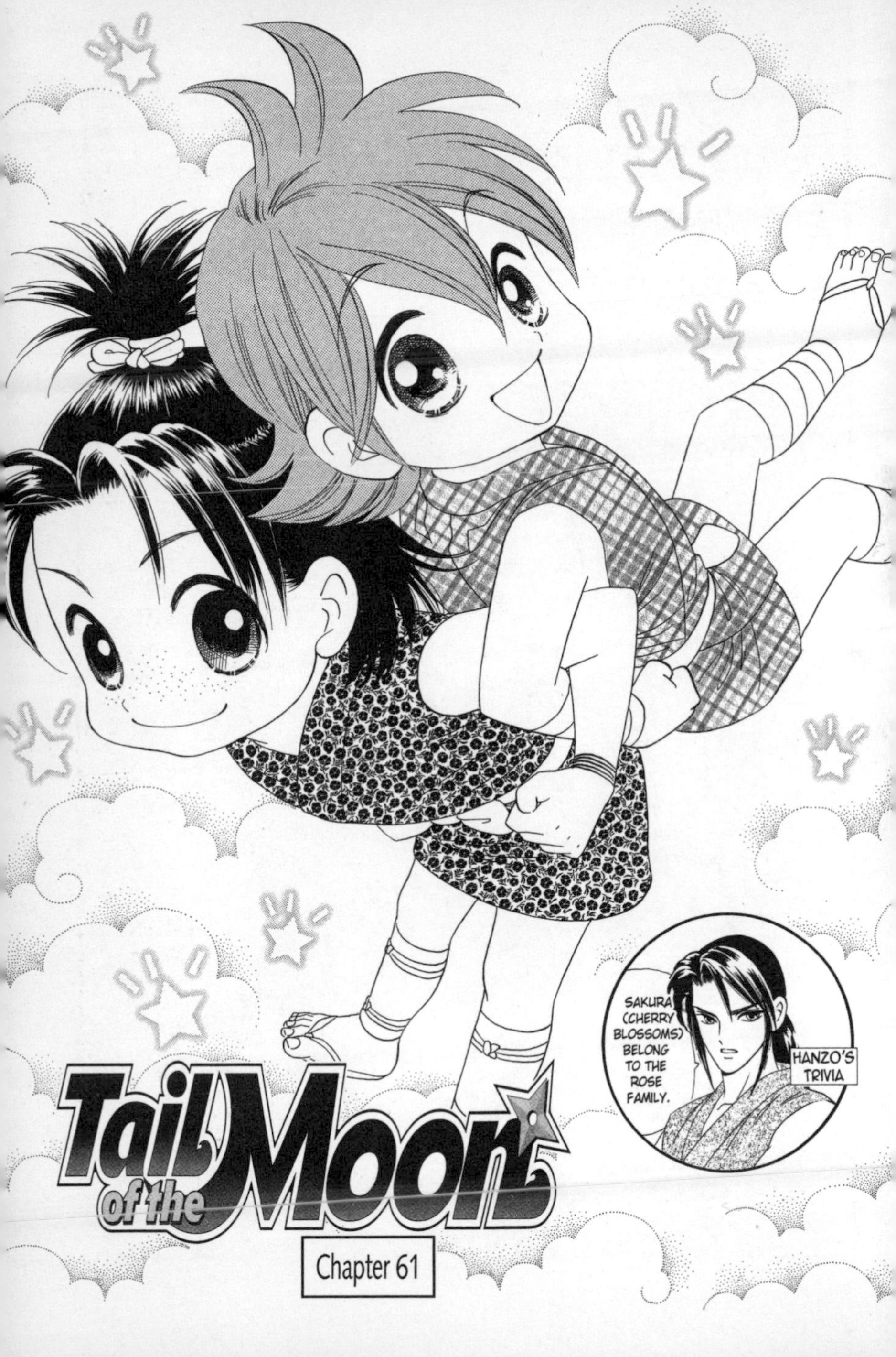
SAKURA (CHERRY BLOSSOMS) BELONG TO THE ROSE FAMILY.
HANZO'S TRIVIA
Tail of the Moon
Chapter 61

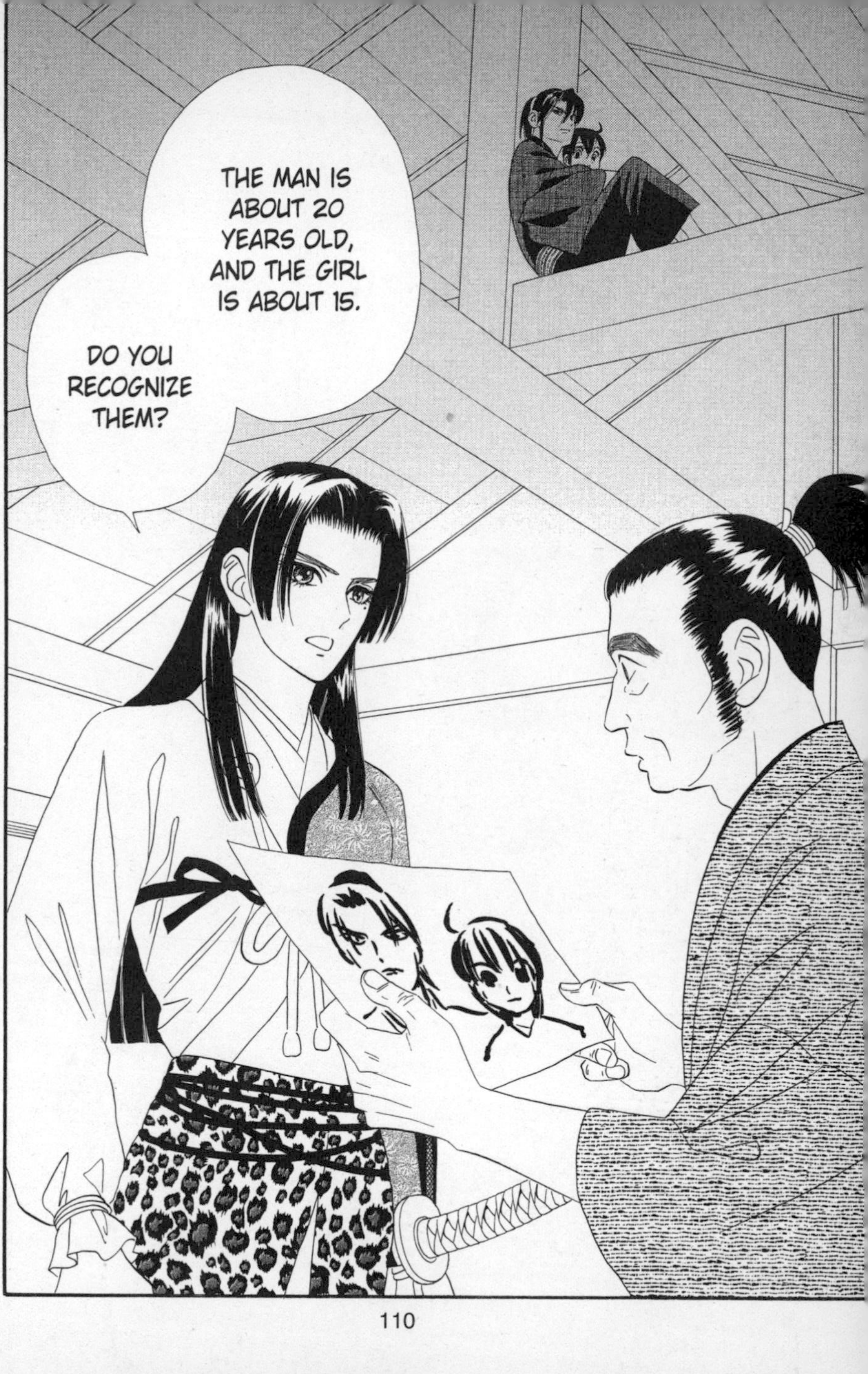
THE MAN IS ABOUT 20 YEARS OLD, AND THE GIRL IS ABOUT 15.
DO YOU RECOGNIZE THEM?

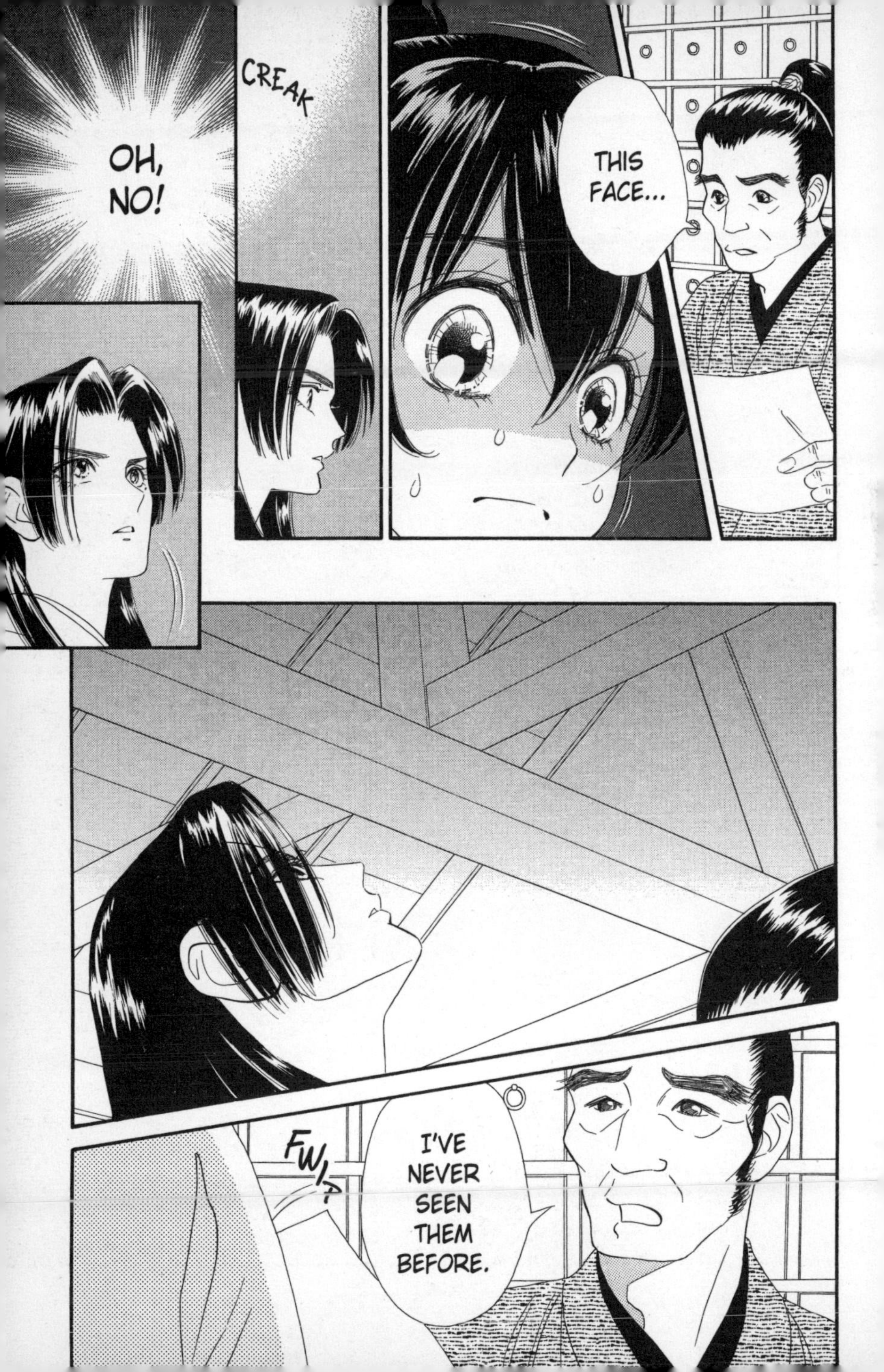
THIS FACE...
CREAK
OH, NO!
I'VE NEVER SEEN THEM BEFORE.
FWIP

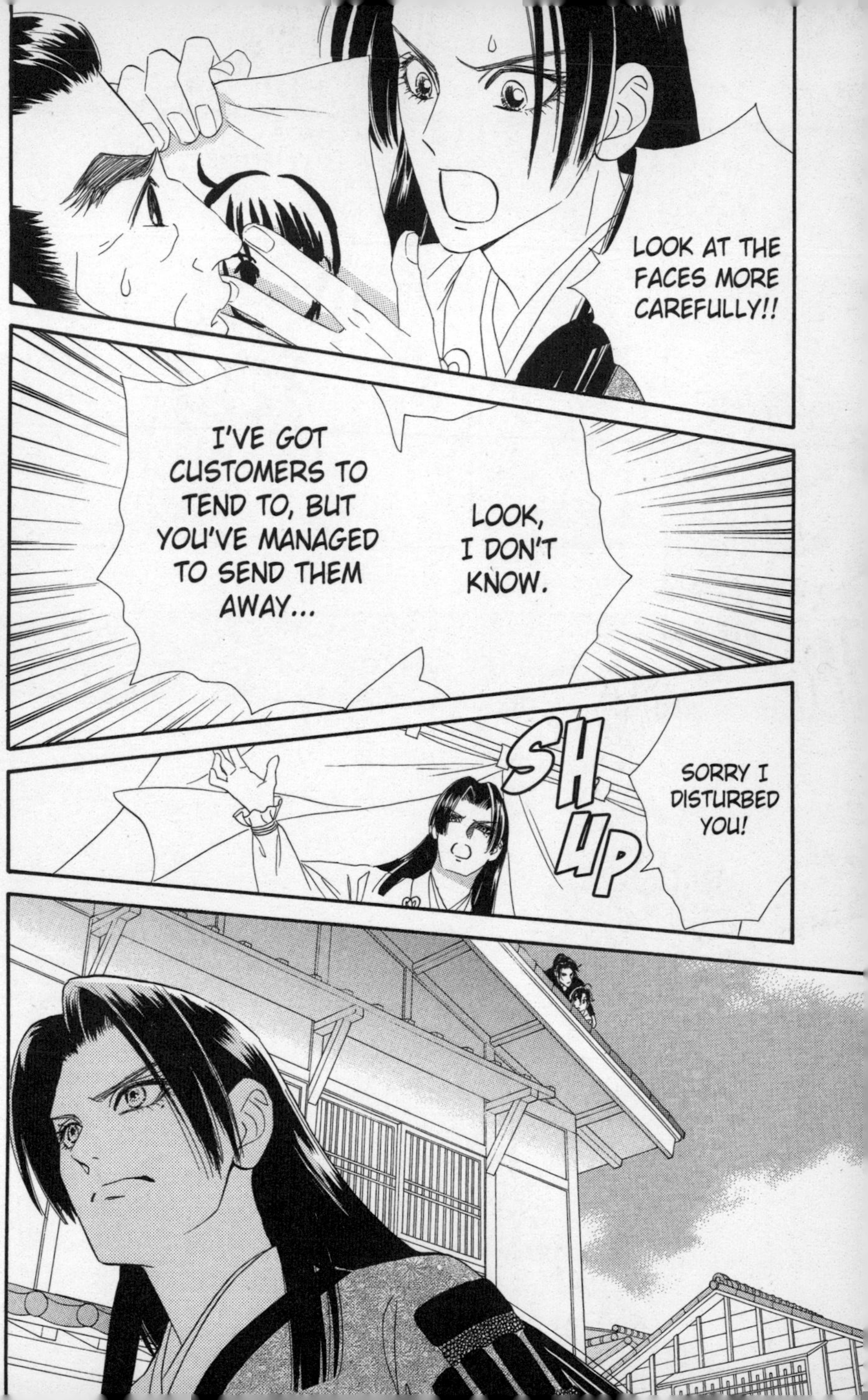
LOOK AT THE FACES MORE CAREFULLY!!
LOOK, I DON'T KNOW.
I'VE GOT CUSTOMERS TO TEND TO, BUT YOU'VE MANAGED TO SEND THEM AWAY...
SORRY I DISTURBED YOU!
SHUP

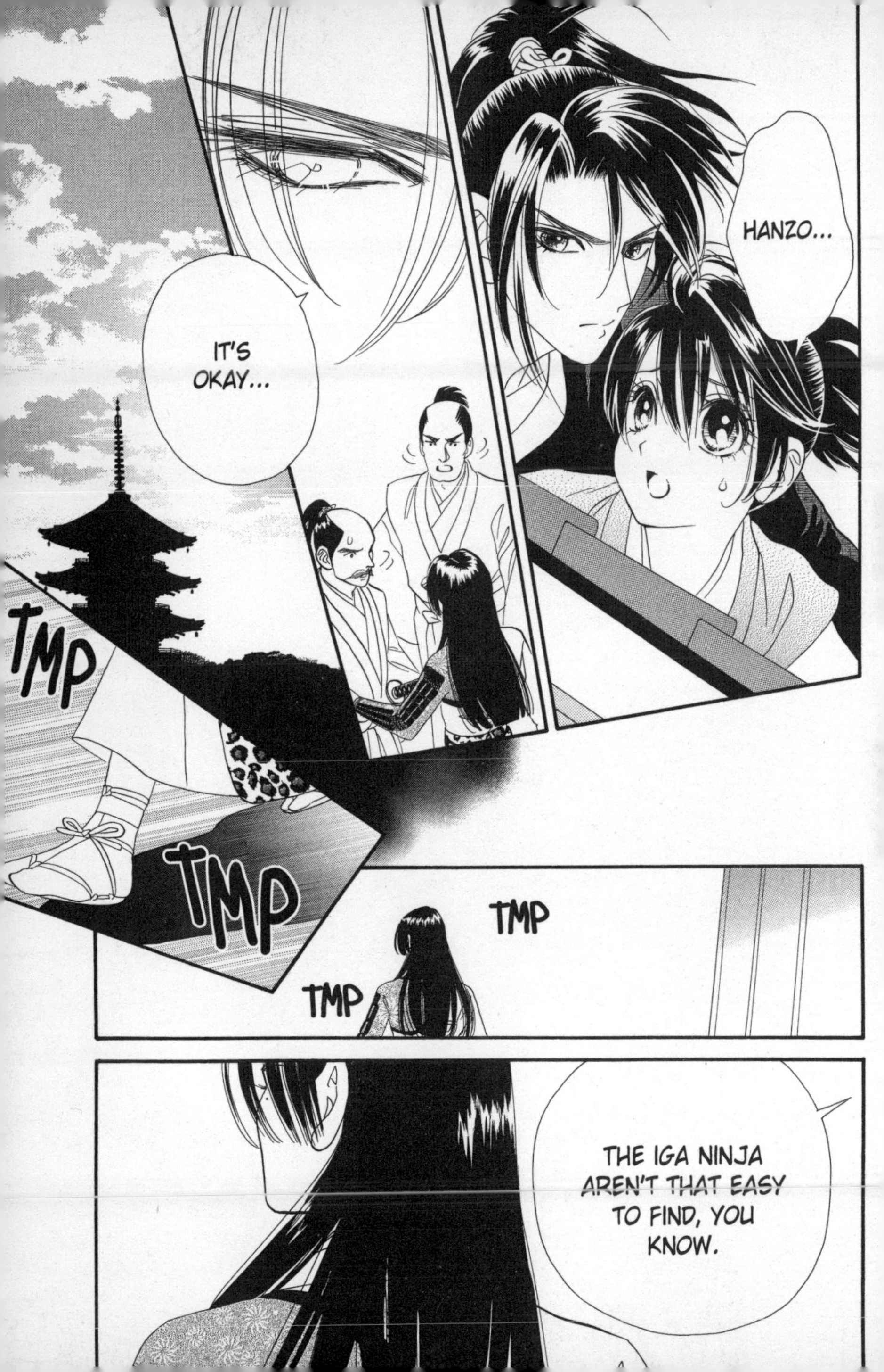
HANZO...
IT'S OKAY...
TMP
TMP
TMP
TMP
THE IGA NINJA AREN'T THAT EASY TO FIND, YOU KNOW.

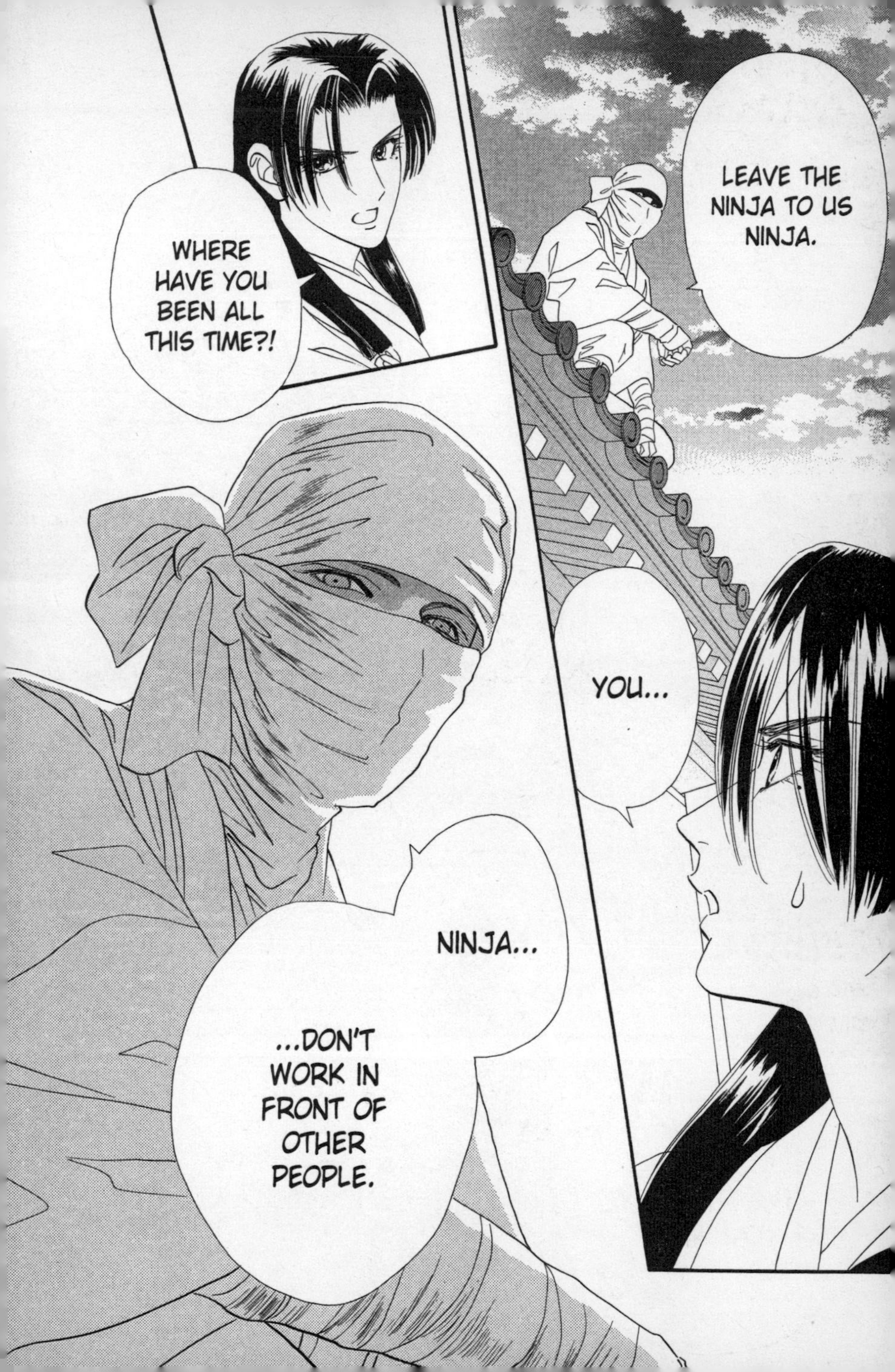
LEAVE THE NINJA TO US NINJA.
WHERE HAVE YOU BEEN ALL THIS TIME?!
YOU...
NINJA...
...DON'T WORK IN FRONT OF OTHER PEOPLE.

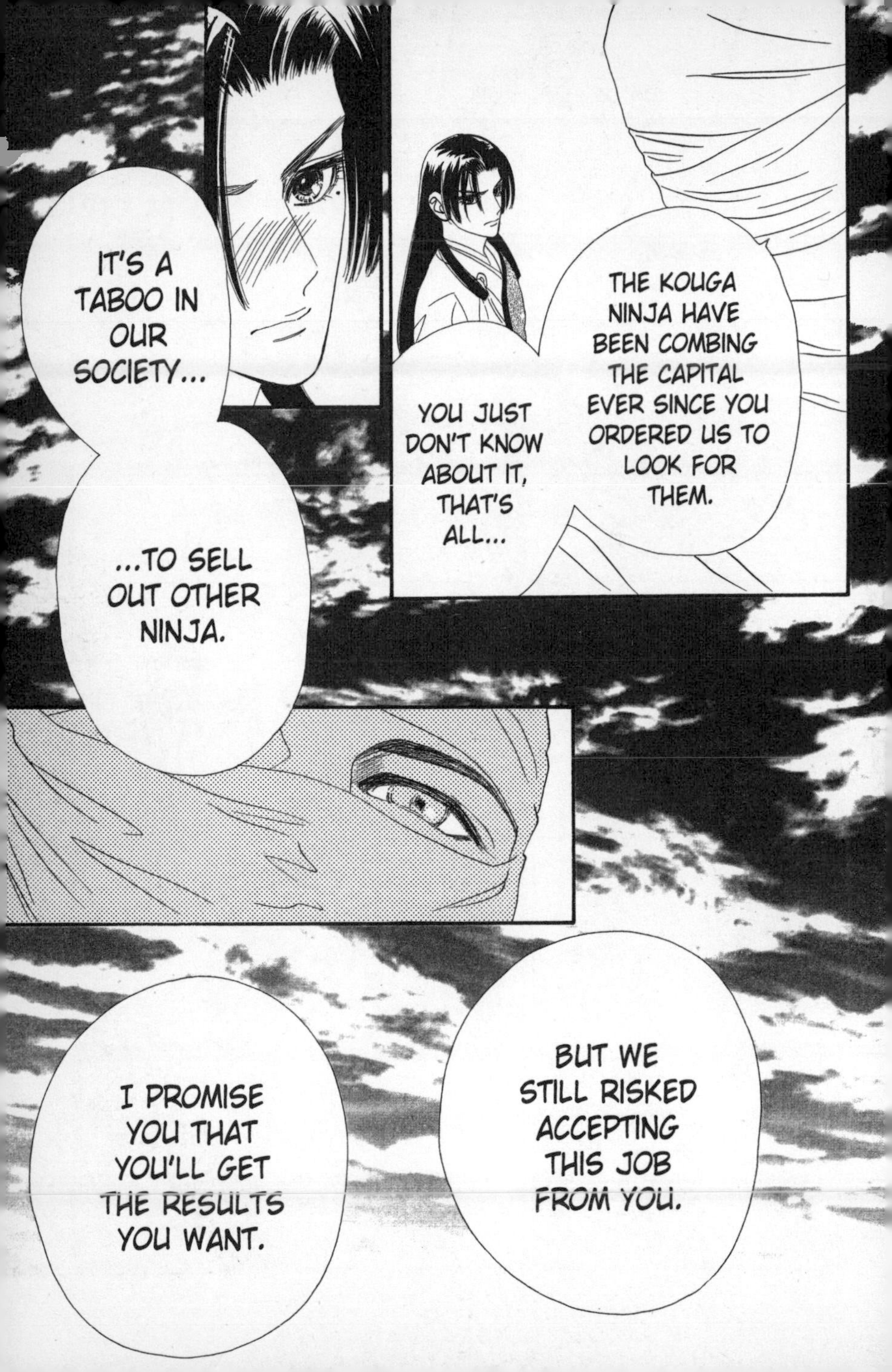
THE KOUGA NINJA HAVE BEEN COMBING THE CAPITAL EVER SINCE YOU ORDERED US TO LOOK FOR THEM.
YOU JUST DON'T KNOW ABOUT IT, THAT'S ALL...
IT'S A TABOO IN OUR SOCIETY...
...TO SELL OUT OTHER NINJA.
BUT WE STILL RISKED ACCEPTING THIS JOB FROM YOU.
I PROMISE YOU THAT YOU'LL GET THE RESULTS YOU WANT.

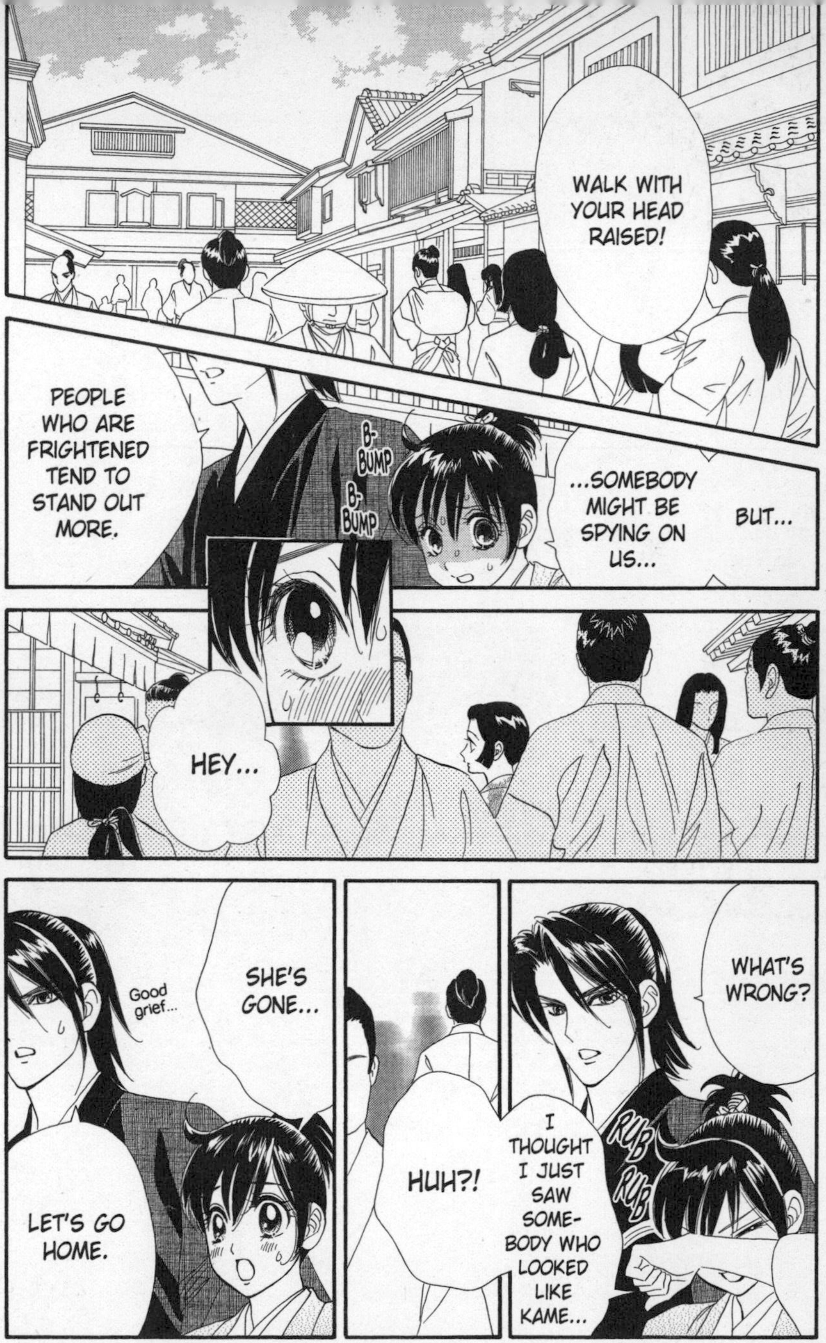
WALK WITH YOUR HEAD RAISED!
BUT...
...SOMEBODY MIGHT BE SPYING ON US...
B-BUMP B-BUMP
PEOPLE WHO ARE FRIGHTENED TEND TO STAND OUT MORE.
HEY...
WHAT'S WRONG?
RUB RUB
I THOUGHT I JUST SAW SOME-BODY WHO LOOKED LIKE KAME...
HUH?!
SHE'S GONE...
Good grief...
LET'S GO HOME.

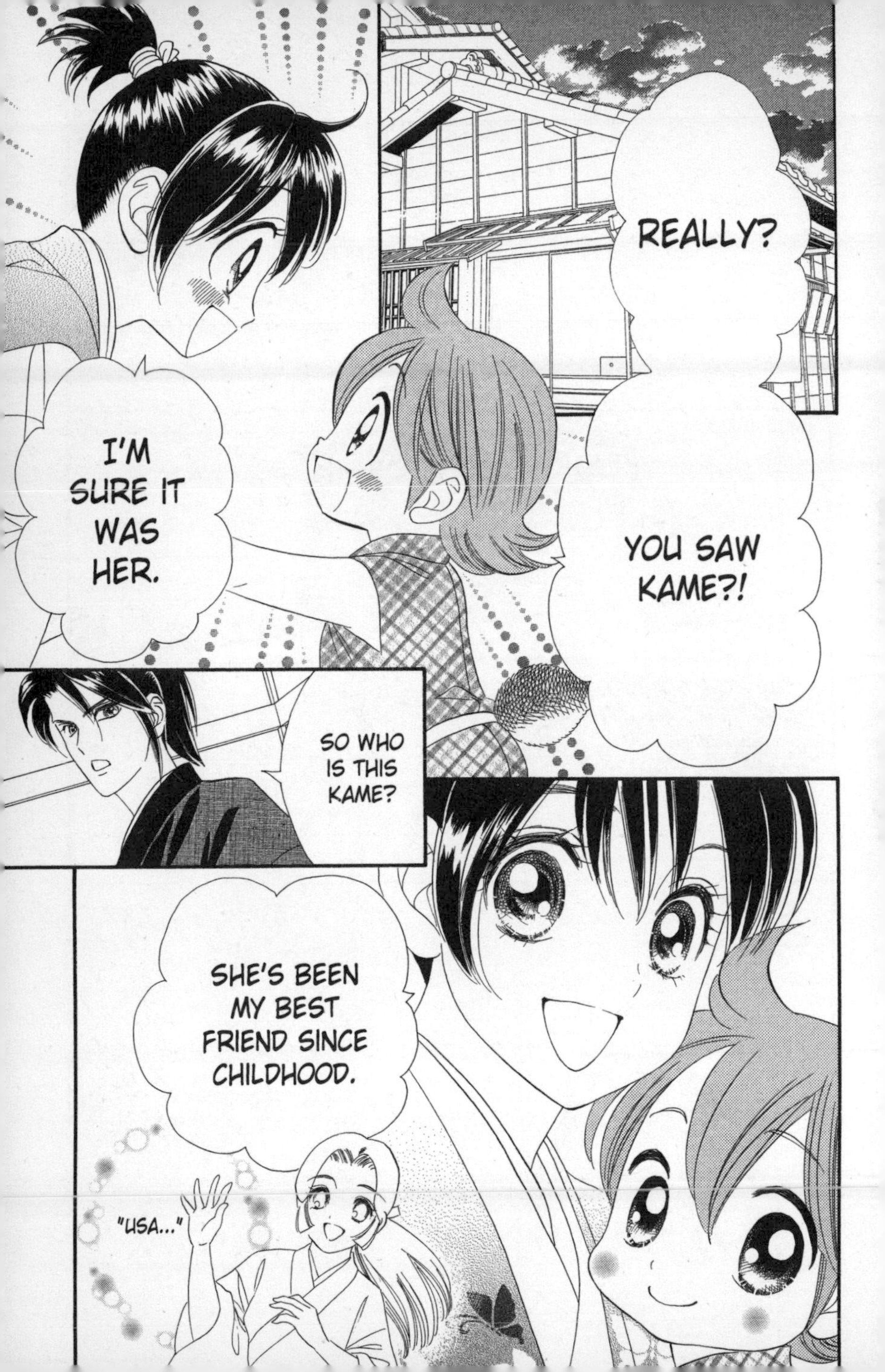
REALLY?
YOU SAW KAME?!
I'M SURE IT WAS HER.
SO WHO IS THIS KAME?
SHE'S BEEN MY BEST FRIEND SINCE CHILDHOOD.
"USA..."

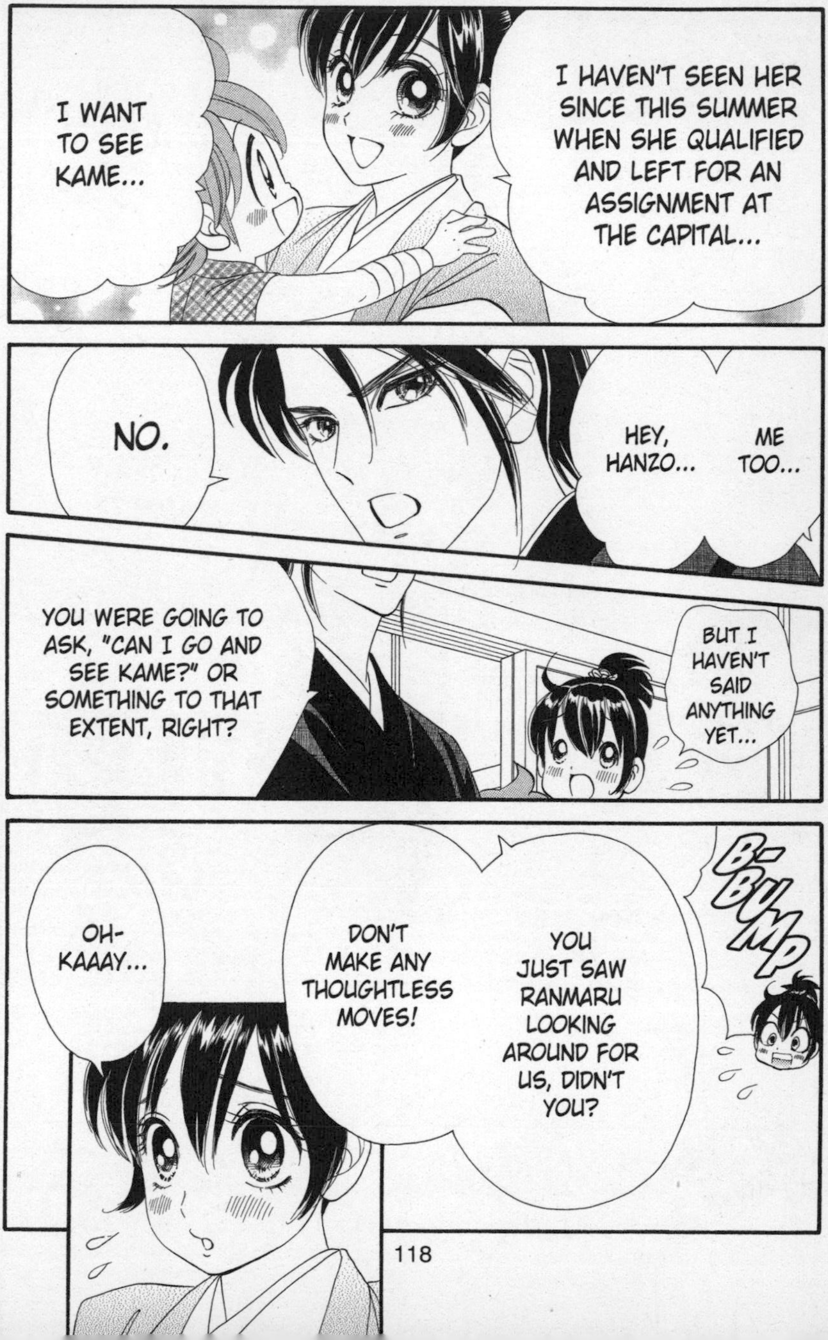
I HAVEN'T SEEN HER SINCE THIS SUMMER WHEN SHE QUALIFIED AND LEFT FOR AN ASSIGNMENT AT THE CAPITAL...
I WANT TO SEE KAME...
HEY, HANZO... ME TOO...
NO.
BUT I HAVEN'T SAID ANYTHING YET...
YOU WERE GOING TO ASK, "CAN I GO AND SEE KAME?" OR SOMETHING TO THAT EXTENT, RIGHT?
B-BUMP
YOU JUST SAW RANMARU LOOKING AROUND FOR US, DIDN'T YOU?
DON'T MAKE ANY THOUGHTLESS MOVES!
OH-KAAAY...

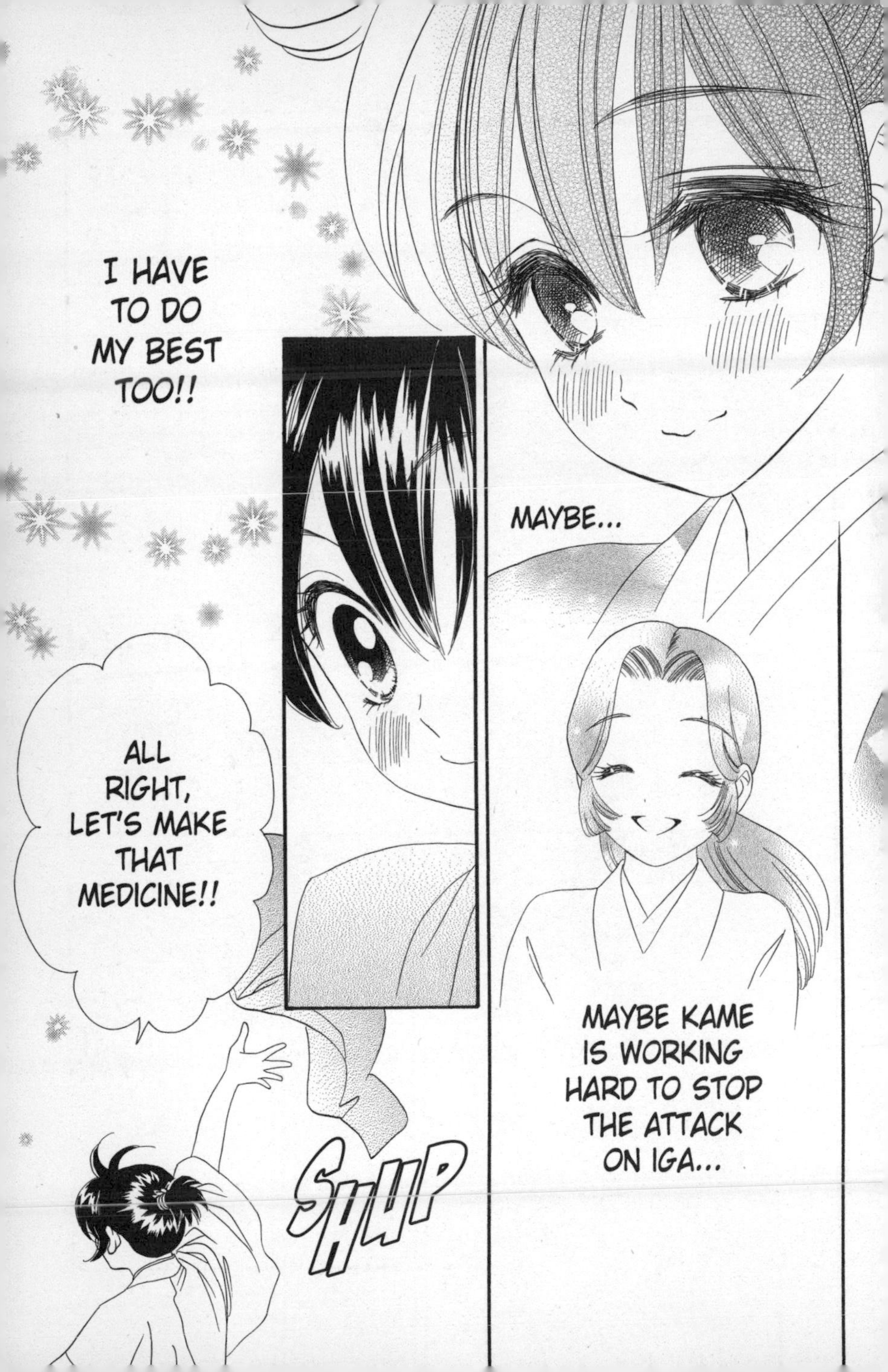
MAYBE...
MAYBE KAME IS WORKING HARD TO STOP THE ATTACK ON IGA...
I HAVE TO DO MY BEST TOO!!
ALL RIGHT, LET'S MAKE THAT MEDICINE!!
SHUP

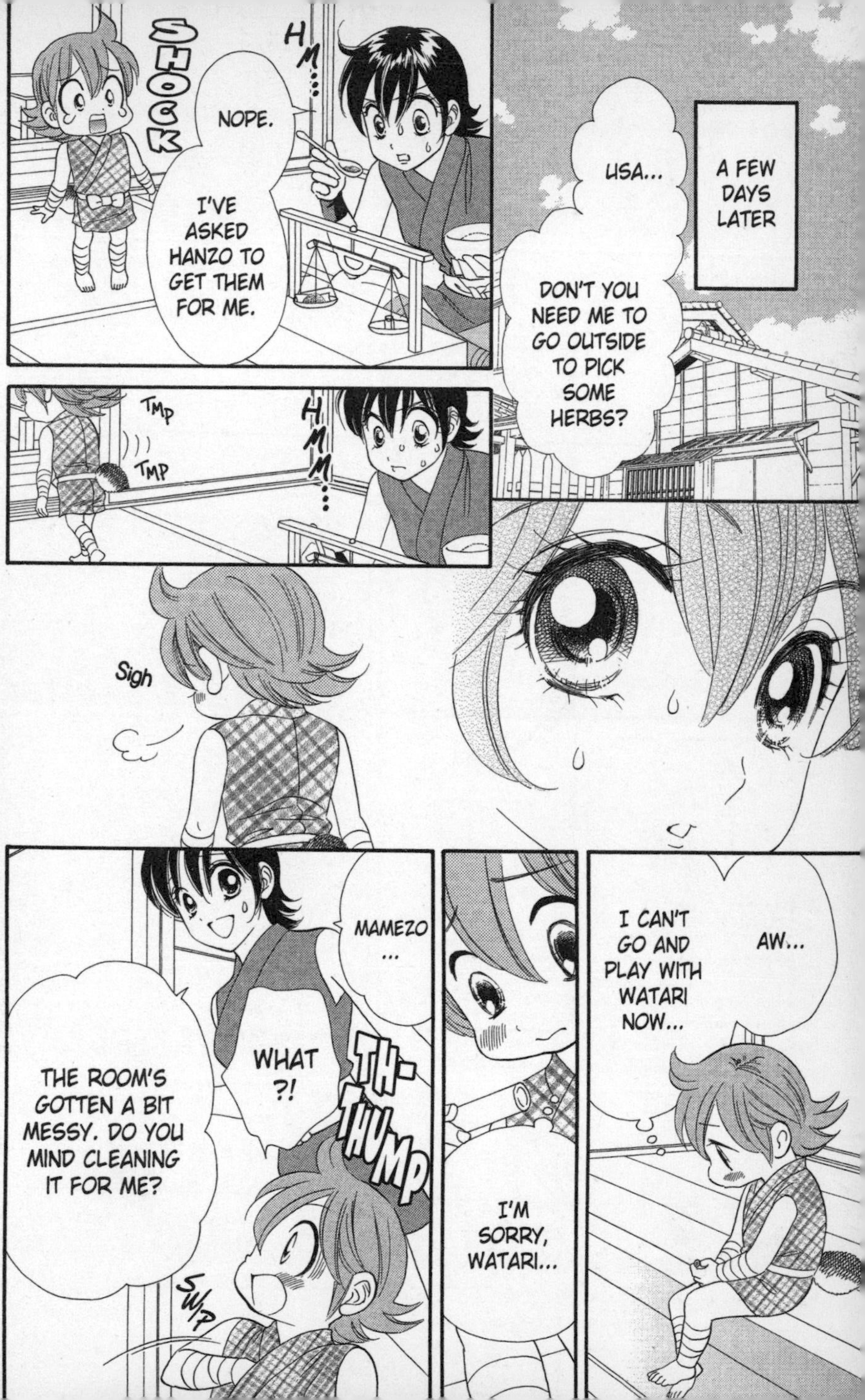
A FEW DAYS LATER
USA...
DON'T YOU NEED ME TO GO OUTSIDE TO PICK SOME HERBS?
HM...
NOPE.
I'VE ASKED HANZO TO GET THEM FOR ME.
SHOCK
HMMM...
TMP
TMP
Sigh
AW...
I CAN'T GO AND PLAY WITH WATARI NOW...
I'M SORRY, WATARI...
MAMEZO...
WHAT?!
TH-THUMP
THE ROOM'S GOTTEN A BIT MESSY. DO YOU MIND CLEANING IT FOR ME?
SWP

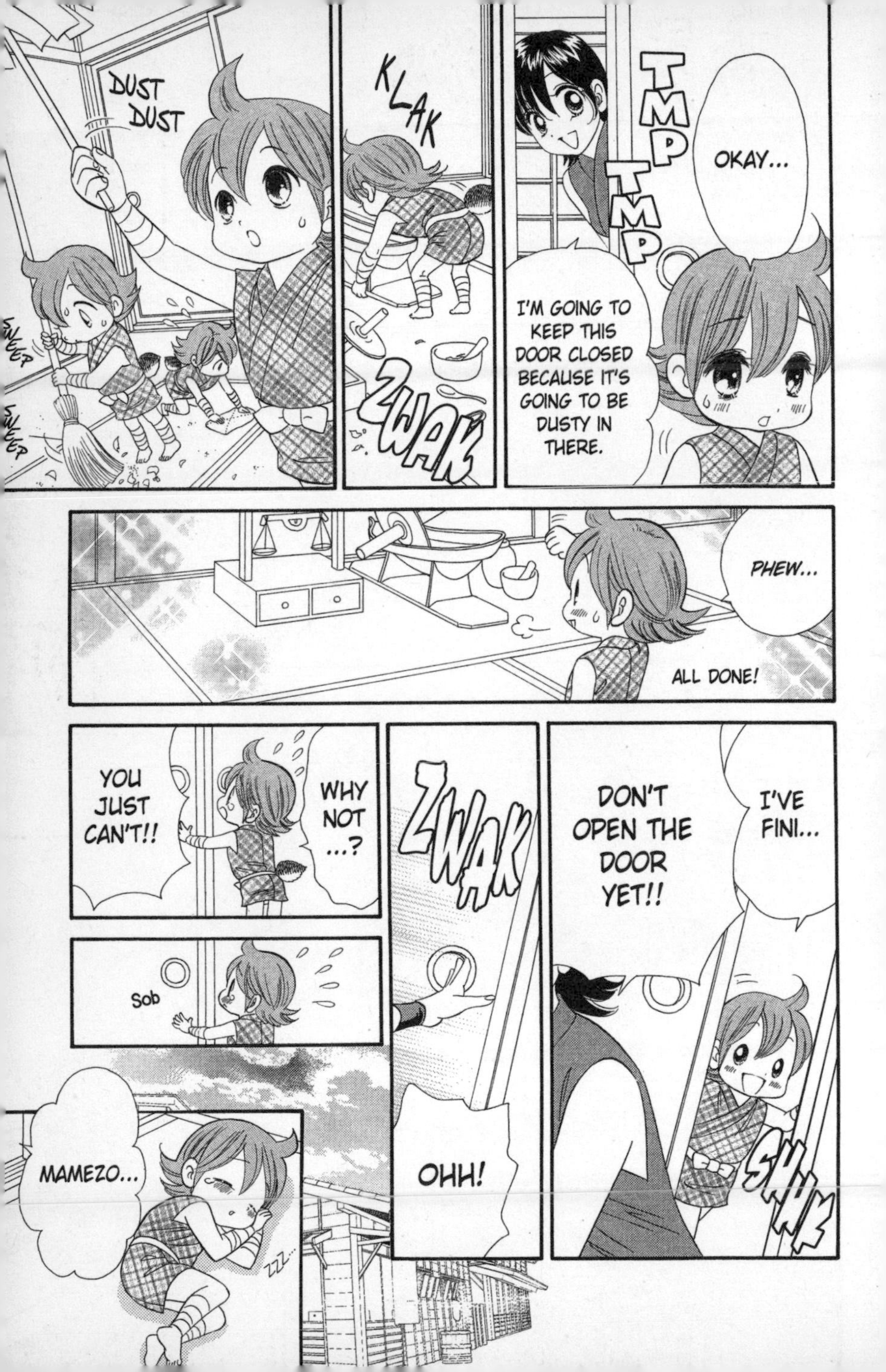
OKAY...
TMP TMP
I'M GOING TO KEEP THIS DOOR CLOSED BECAUSE IT'S GOING TO BE DUSTY IN THERE.
KLAK
ZWAK
DUST DUST
SWEEP SWEEP
PHEW...
ALL DONE!
I'VE FINI...
DON'T OPEN THE DOOR YET!!
ZWAK
OHH!
WHY NOT ...?
YOU JUST CAN'T!!
Sob
MAMEZO...
ZZZ...

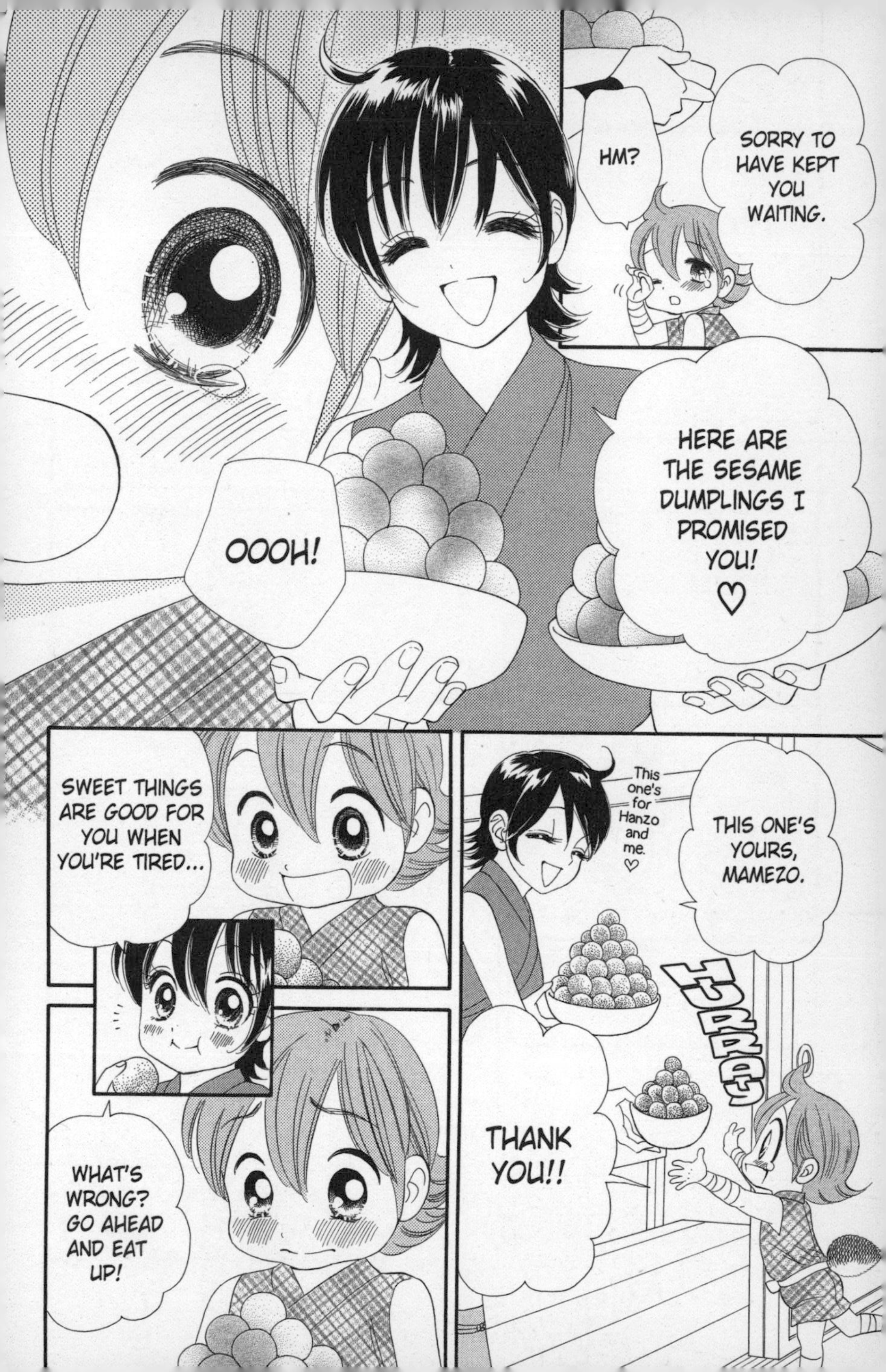
SORRY TO HAVE KEPT YOU WAITING.
HM?
HERE ARE THE SESAME DUMPLINGS I PROMISED YOU! ♡
OOOH!
THIS ONE'S YOURS, MAMEZO.
This one's for Hanzo and me. ♡
THANK YOU!!
SWEET THINGS ARE GOOD FOR YOU WHEN YOU'RE TIRED...
WHAT'S WRONG? GO AHEAD AND EAT UP!

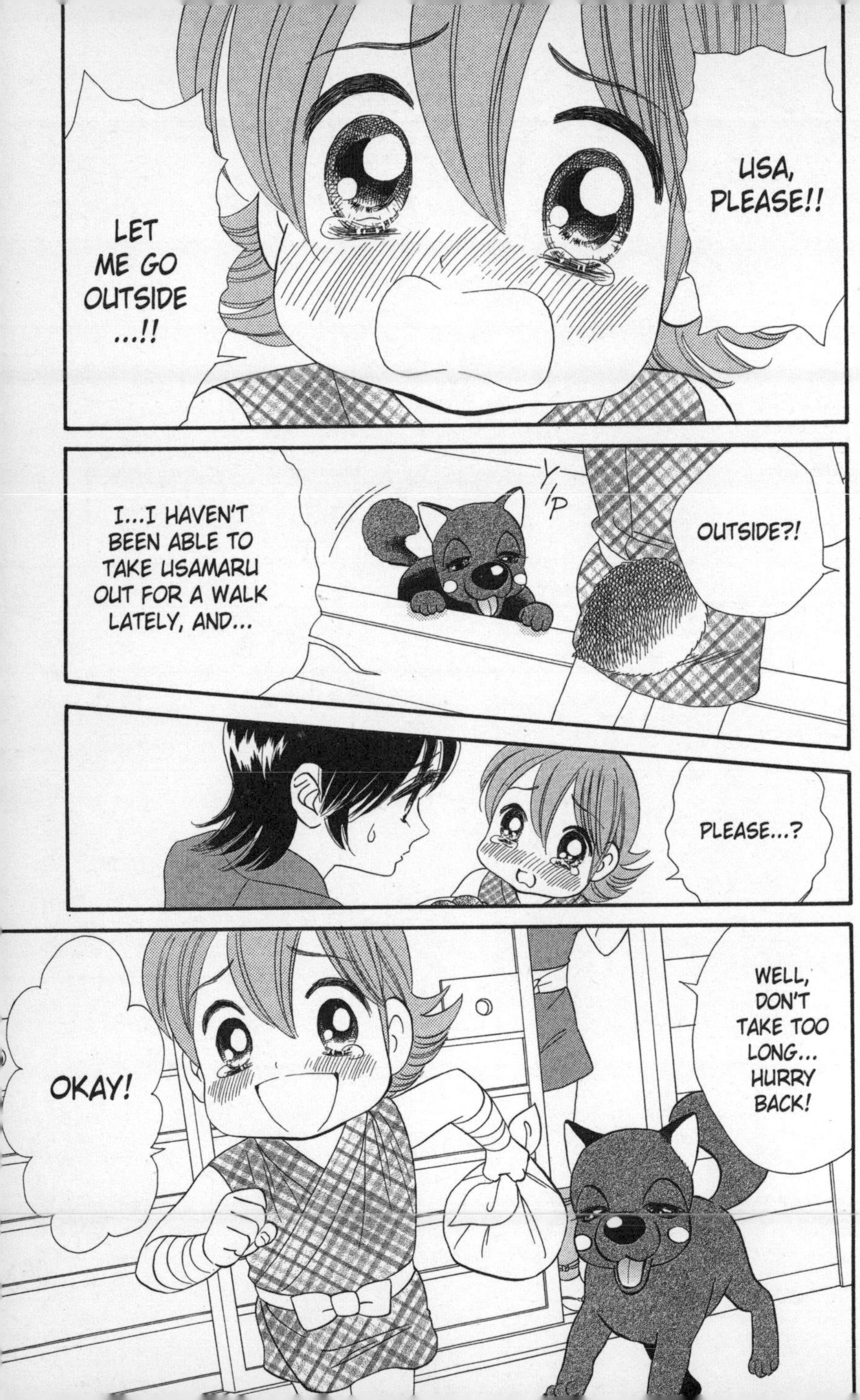
USA, PLEASE!!
LET ME GO OUTSIDE ...!!
OUTSIDE?!
YIP
I...I HAVEN'T BEEN ABLE TO TAKE USAMARU OUT FOR A WALK LATELY, AND...
PLEASE...?
WELL, DON'T TAKE TOO LONG... HURRY BACK!
OKAY!

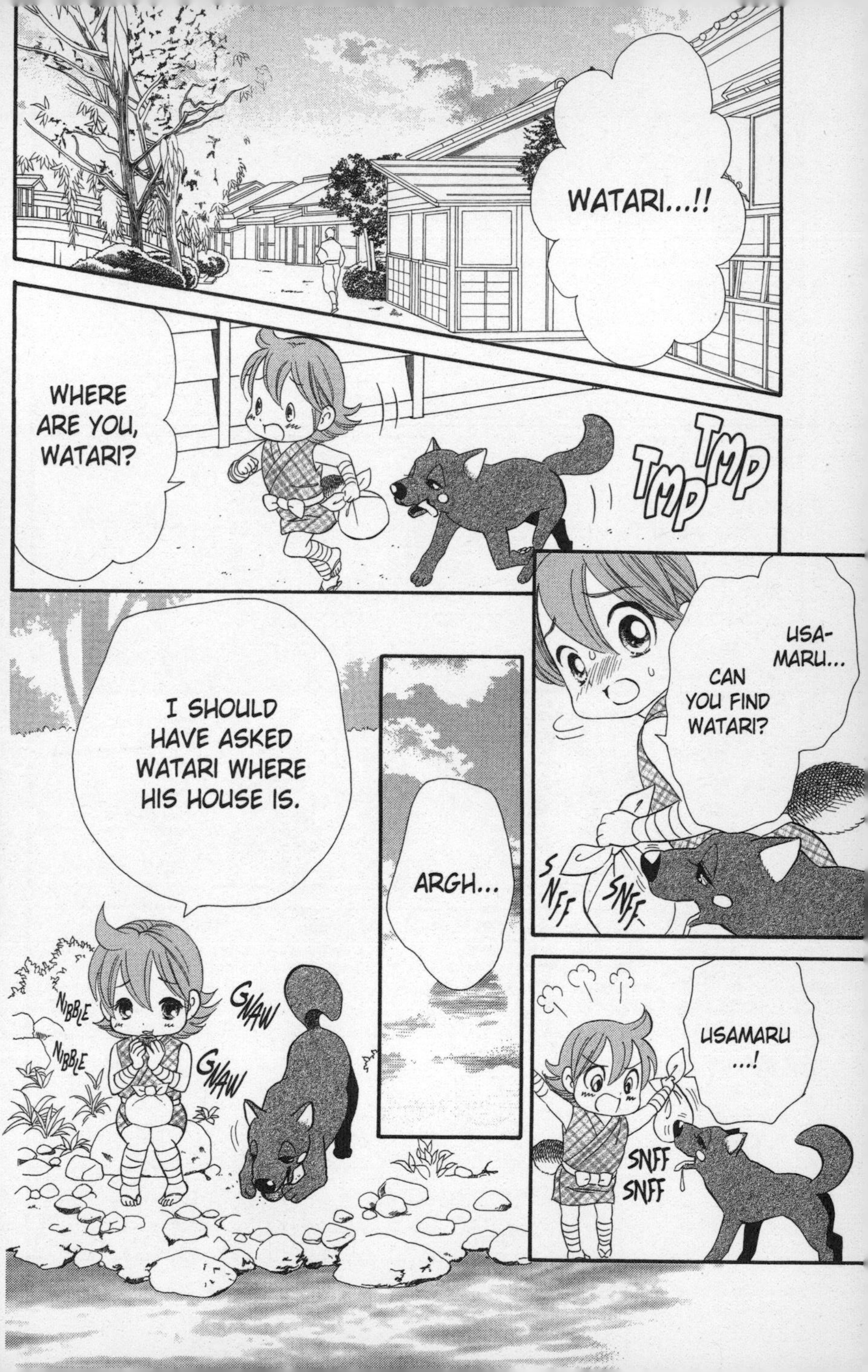
WATARI...!!
TMP TMP
WHERE ARE YOU, WATARI?
USA-MARU...
CAN YOU FIND WATARI?
SNFF
SNFF
USAMARU ...!
SNFF SNFF
ARGH...
I SHOULD HAVE ASKED WATARI WHERE HIS HOUSE IS.
GNAW
GNAW
NIBBLE
NIBBLE

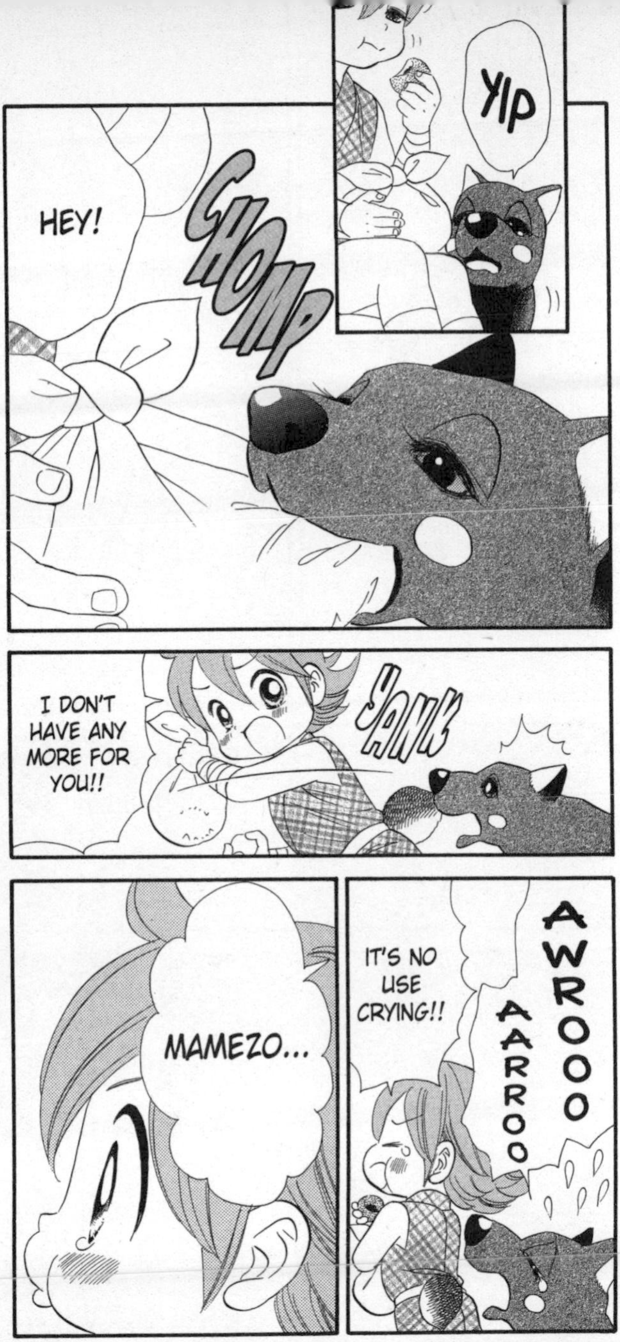
YIP
CHOMP
HEY!
YANK
I DON'T HAVE ANY MORE FOR YOU!!
AWROOO
AARROO
IT'S NO USE CRYING!!
MAMEZO...

UE-RIN'S WAY OF THE MANGA ⑲

During the wintertime when I was getting close to my school application deadline, I got a phone call from the editorial office telling me that I was finally going to make my debut.

Even though I was happy, it didn't seem real. I just stood there in a daze.

But in my mind, I secretly raised my arms up in triumph, thinking, "Maybe now I have a reason for applying to a school with an art department!"

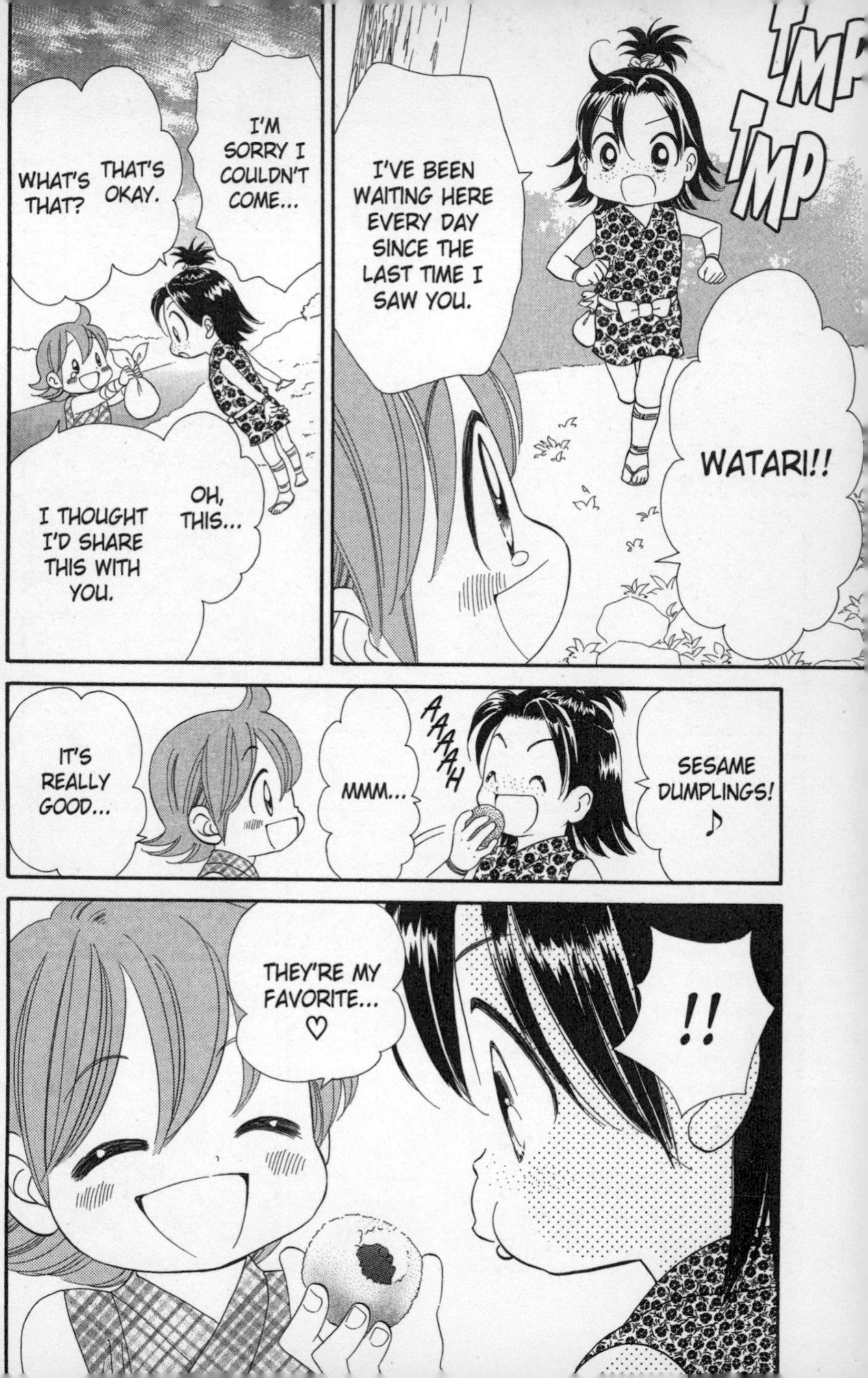
TMP TMP
WATARI!!
I'VE BEEN WAITING HERE EVERY DAY SINCE THE LAST TIME I SAW YOU.
I'M SORRY I COULDN'T COME...
THAT'S OKAY.
WHAT'S THAT?
OH, THIS...
I THOUGHT I'D SHARE THIS WITH YOU.
SESAME DUMPLINGS! ♪
AAAAH
MMM...
IT'S REALLY GOOD...
!!
THEY'RE MY FAVORITE... ♡

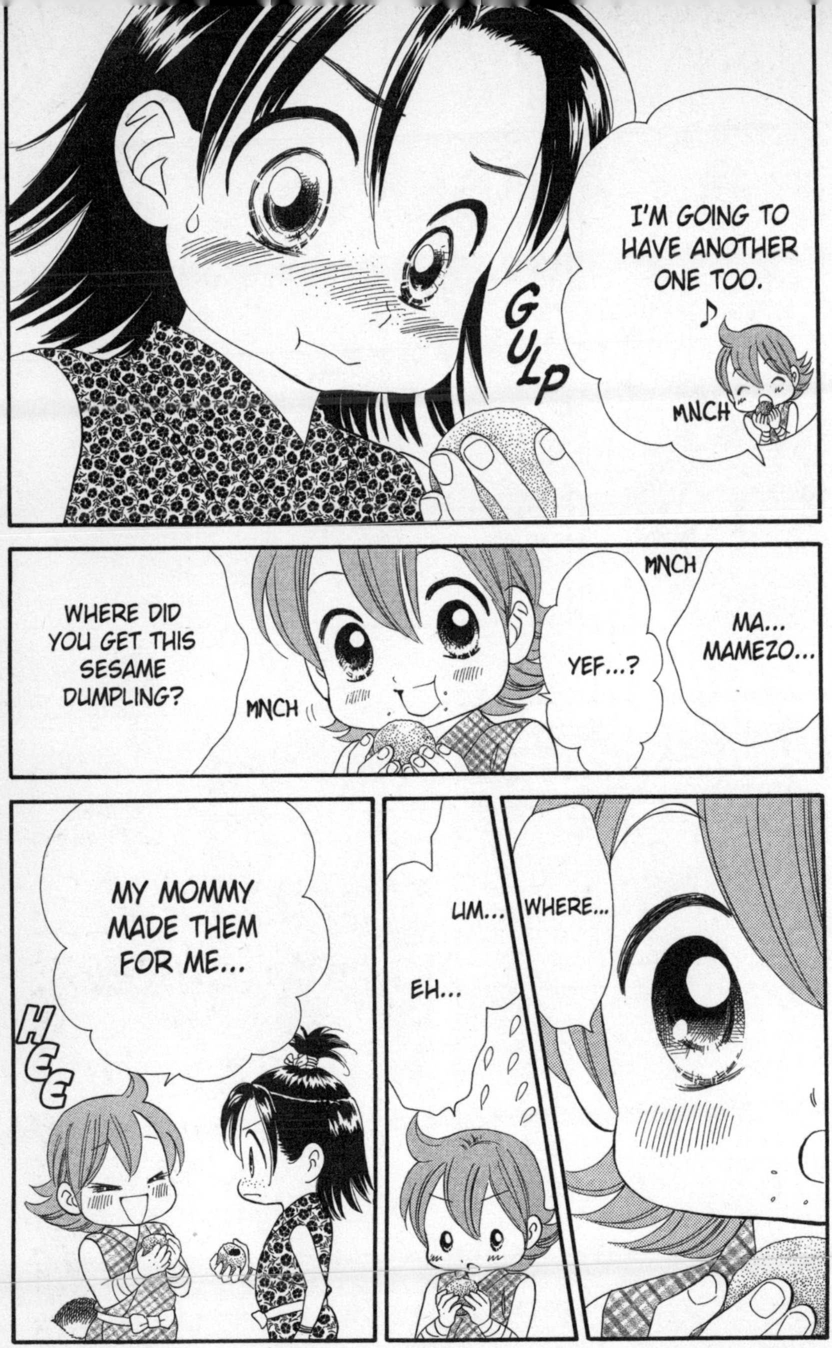
I'M GOING TO HAVE ANOTHER ONE TOO. ♪
MNCH
GULP
MA... MAMEZO...
MNCH
YEF...?
MNCH
WHERE DID YOU GET THIS SESAME DUMPLING?
WHERE...
UM...
EH...
MY MOMMY MADE THEM FOR ME...
HEE

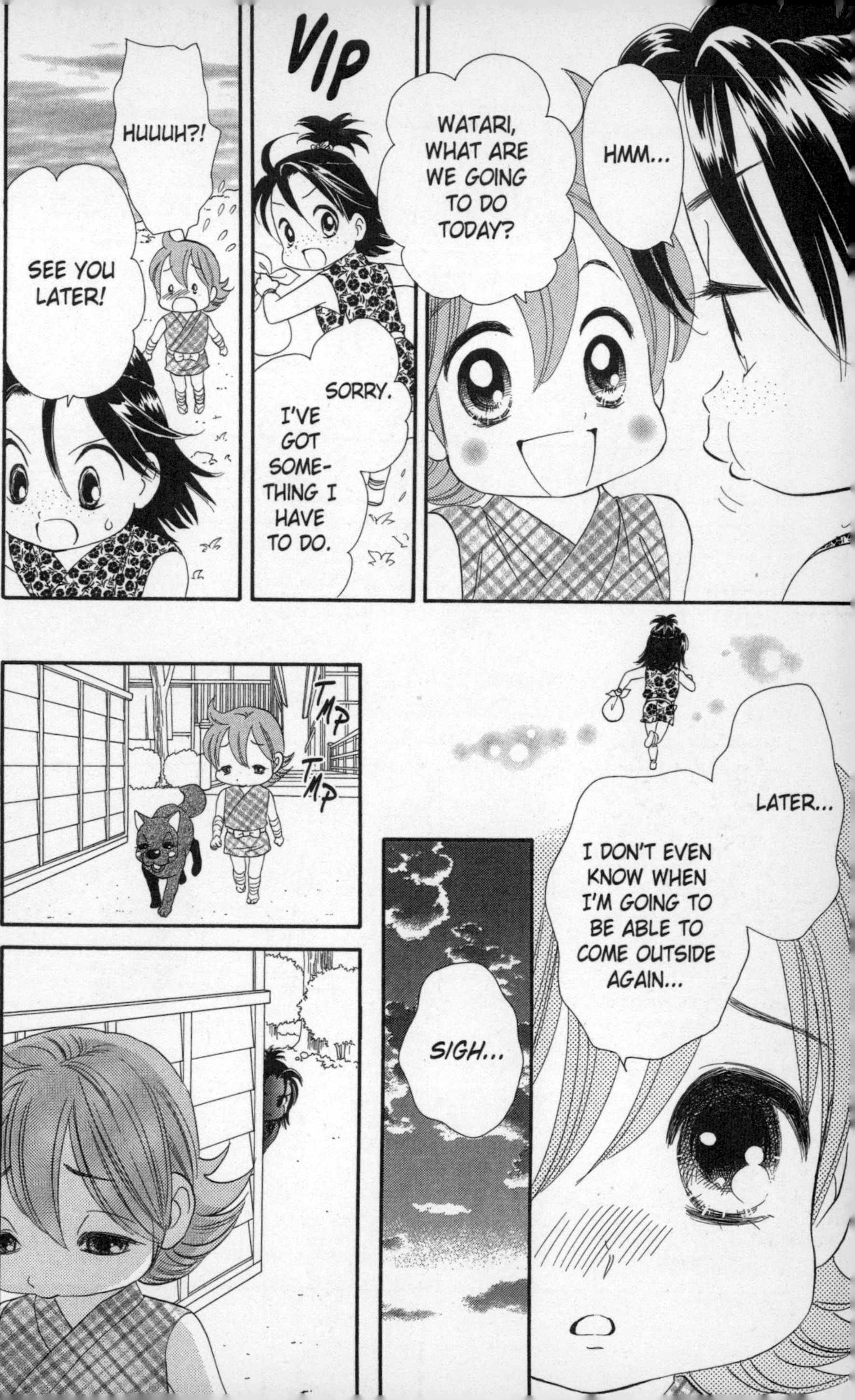

WATARI, WHAT ARE WE GOING TO DO TODAY?
HMM...
VIP
SORRY. I'VE GOT SOME-THING I HAVE TO DO.
HUUUH?!
SEE YOU LATER!
LATER...
I DON'T EVEN KNOW WHEN I'M GOING TO BE ABLE TO COME OUTSIDE AGAIN...
SIGH...
TMP TMP

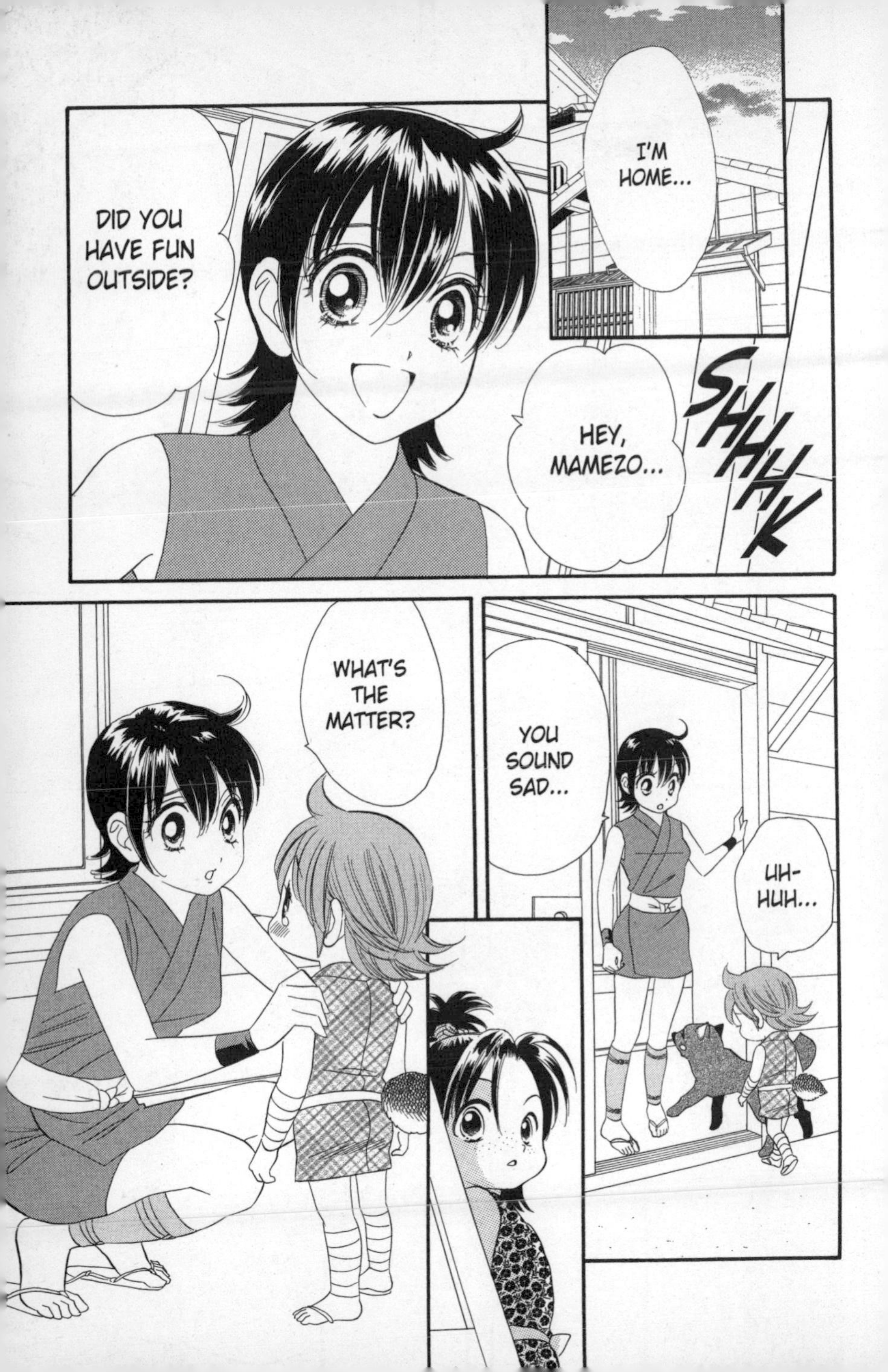
I'M HOME...
SHHHK
HEY, MAMEZO...
DID YOU HAVE FUN OUTSIDE?
YOU SOUND SAD...
UH-HUH...
WHAT'S THE MATTER?

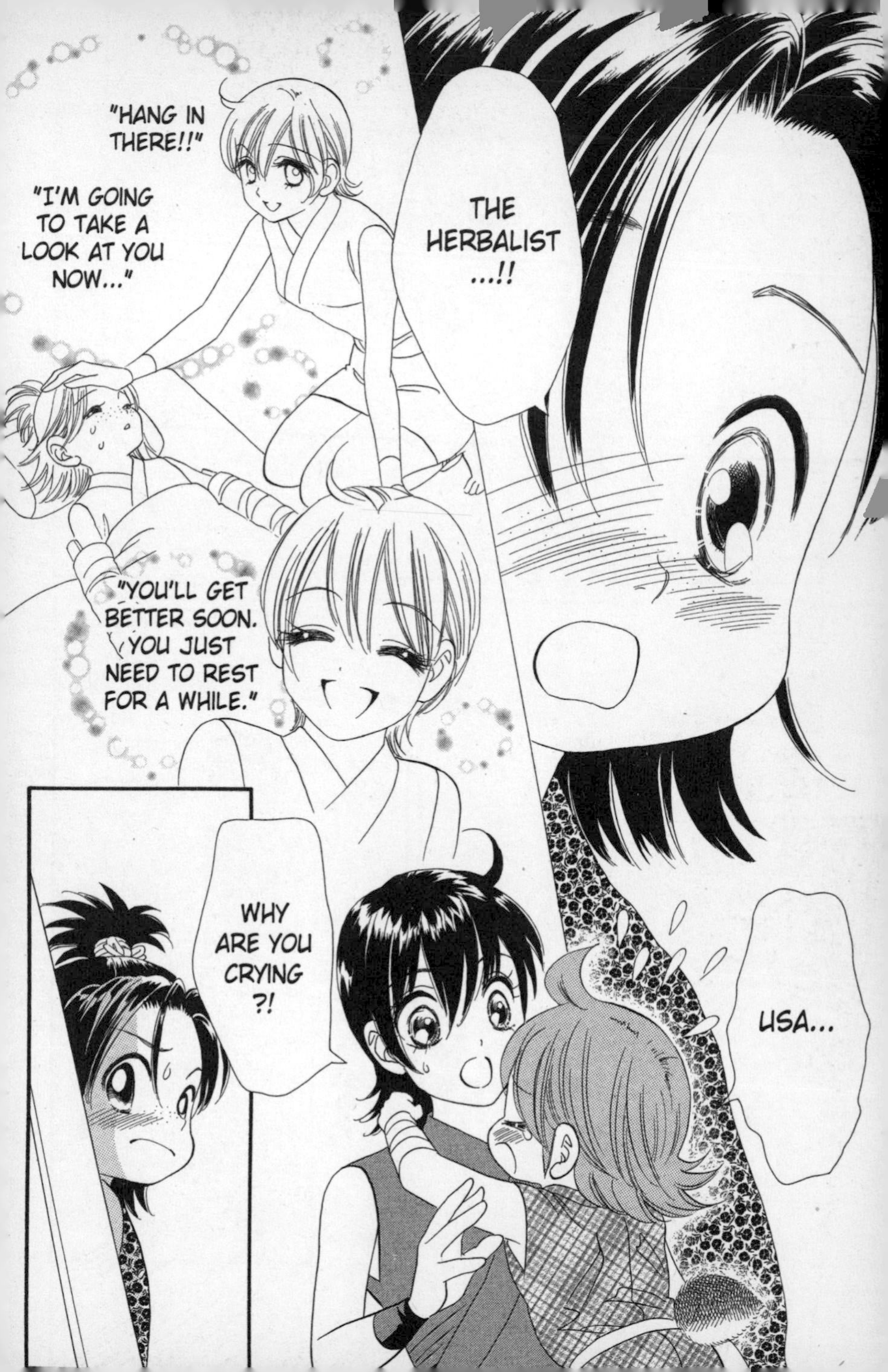
THE HERBALIST ...!!
"HANG IN THERE!!"
"I'M GOING TO TAKE A LOOK AT YOU NOW..."
"YOU'LL GET BETTER SOON. YOU JUST NEED TO REST FOR A WHILE."
USA...
WHY ARE YOU CRYING ?!

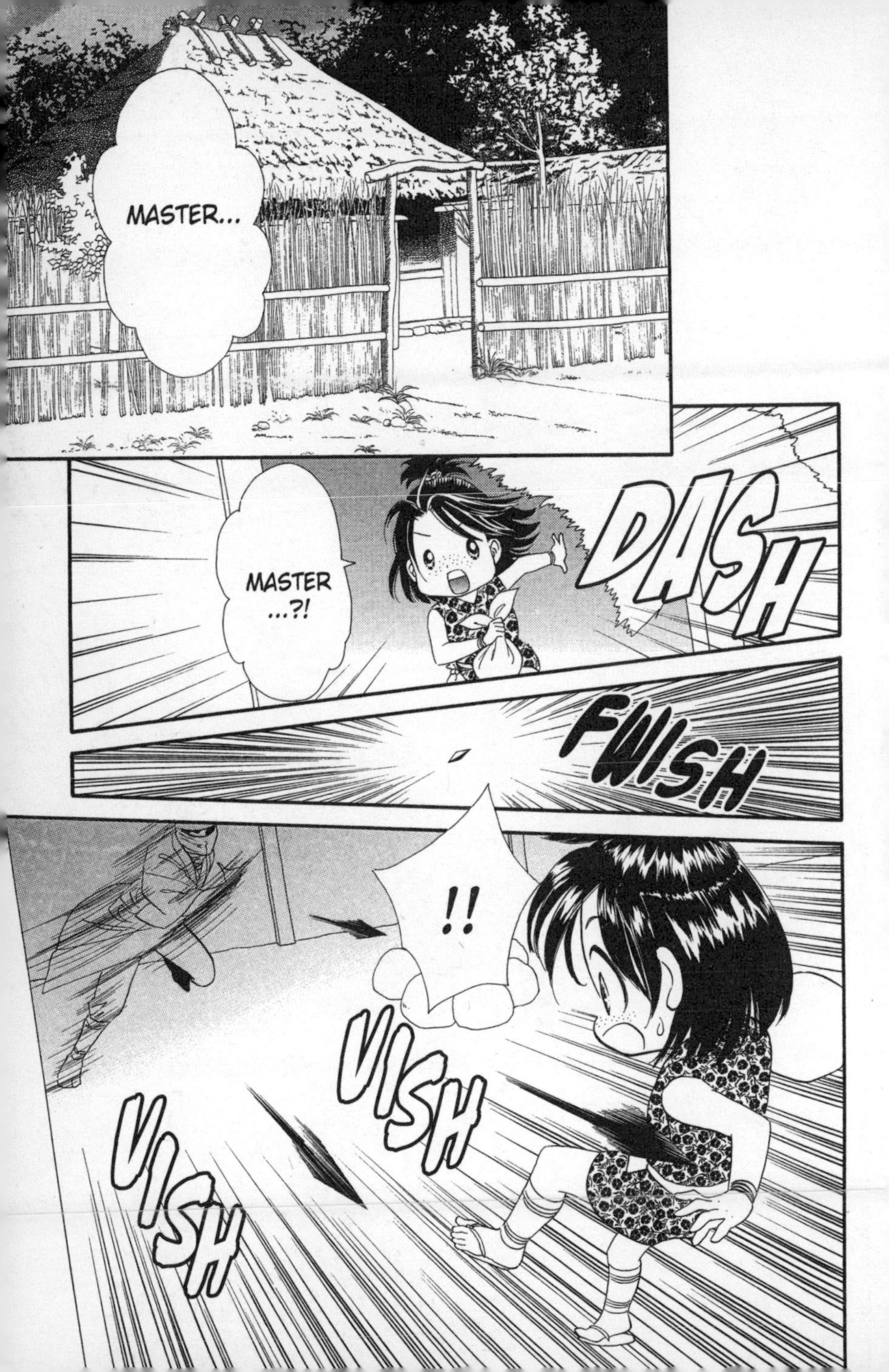
MASTER...
DASH
MASTER ...?!
FWISH
!!
VISH
VISH

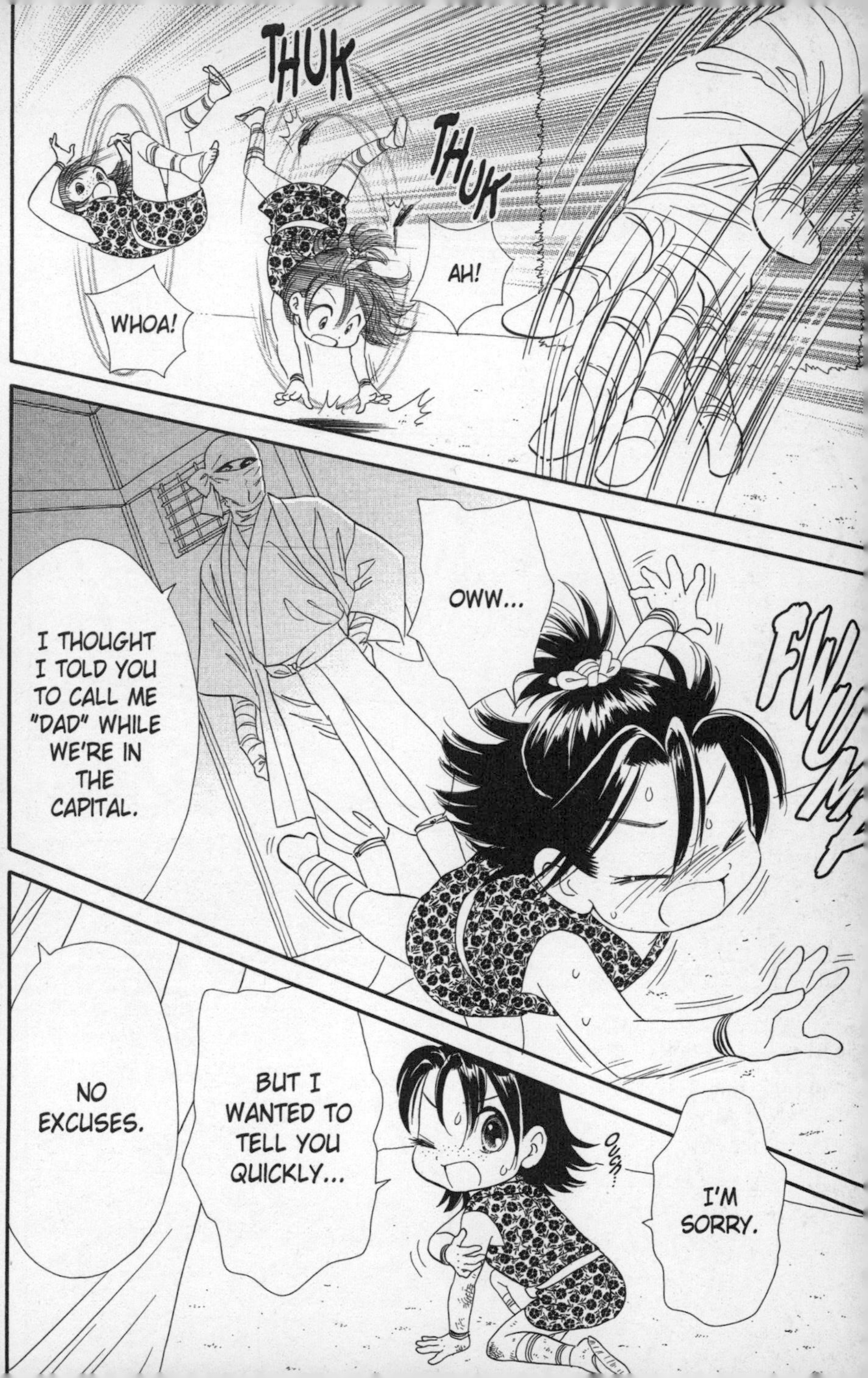
THUK
THUK
AH!
WHOA!
FWUMP
OWW...
I THOUGHT I TOLD YOU TO CALL ME "DAD" WHILE WE'RE IN THE CAPITAL.
I'M SORRY.
OUCH...
BUT I WANTED TO TELL YOU QUICKLY...
NO EXCUSES.

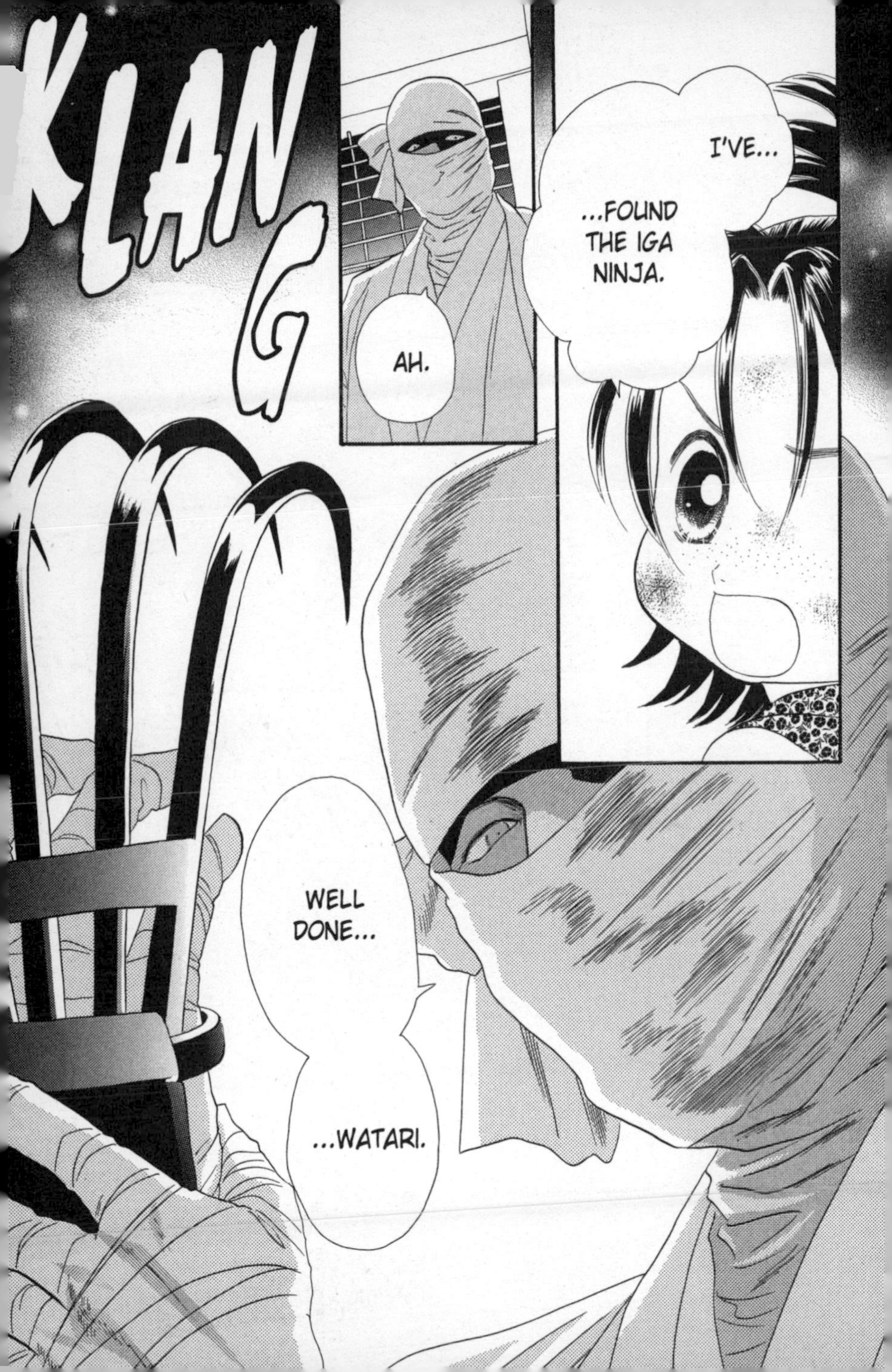
I'VE...
...FOUND THE IGA NINJA.
AH.
KLANG
WELL DONE...
...WATARI.

TAIL OF THE MOON EXTRA: TODAY'S MISSION

"I WANT TO SEE HANZO IN A RABBIT COSTUME!"

-KAOTAMU, IBARAKI PREFECTURE

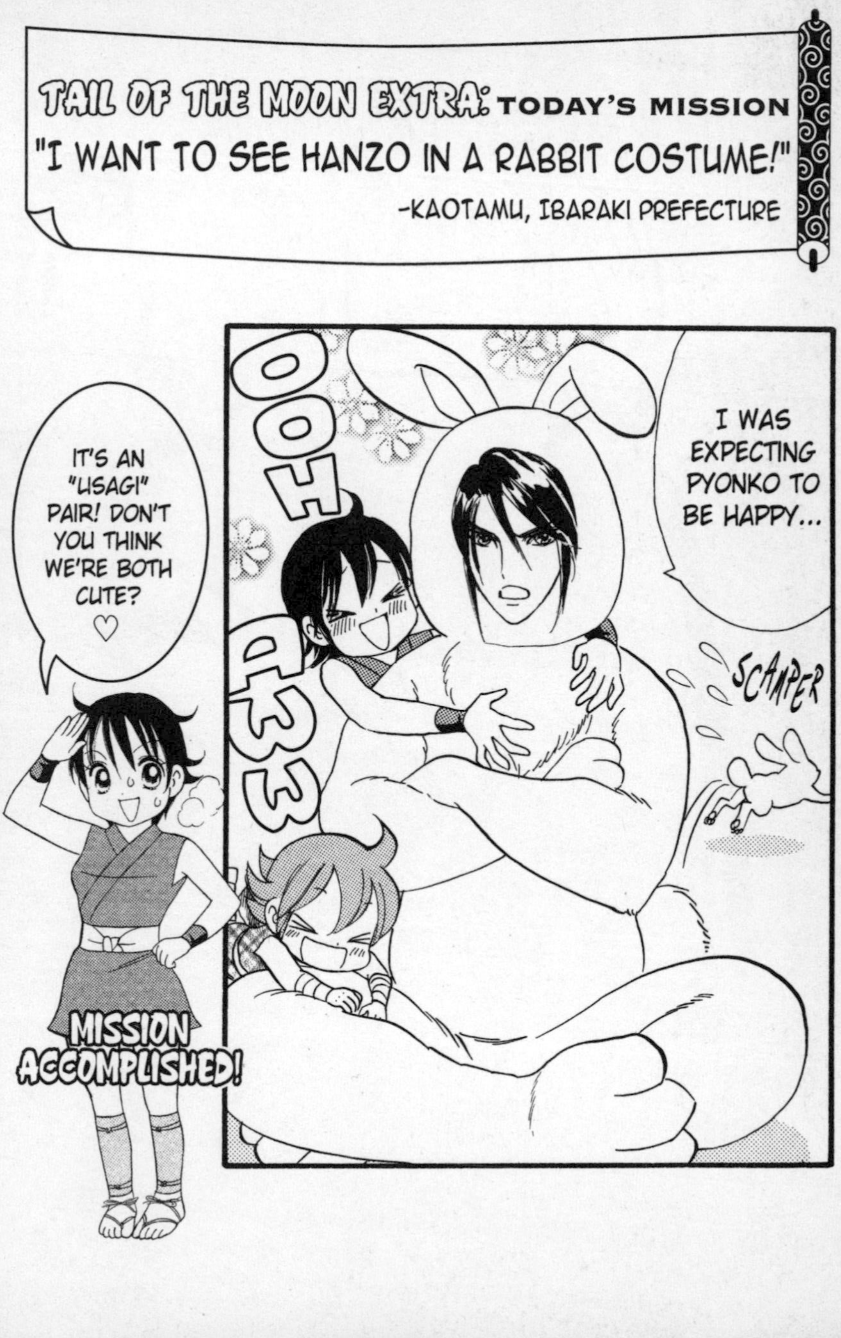
I WAS EXPECTING PYONKO TO BE HAPPY...
SCAMPER
IT'S AN "USAGI" PAIR! DON'T YOU THINK WE'RE BOTH CUTE? ♡
MISSION ACCOMPLISHED!

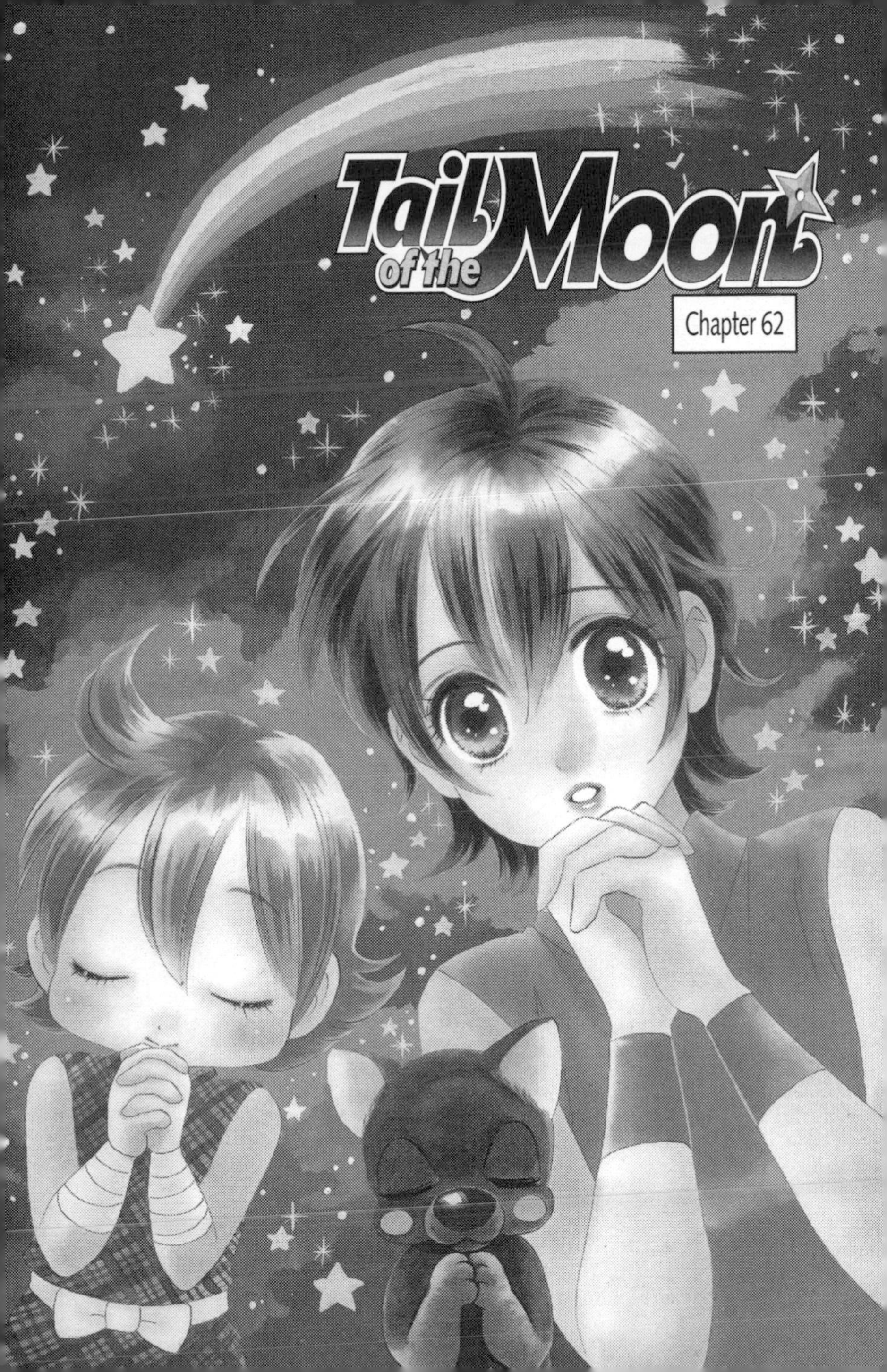
Tail of the Moon
Chapter 62

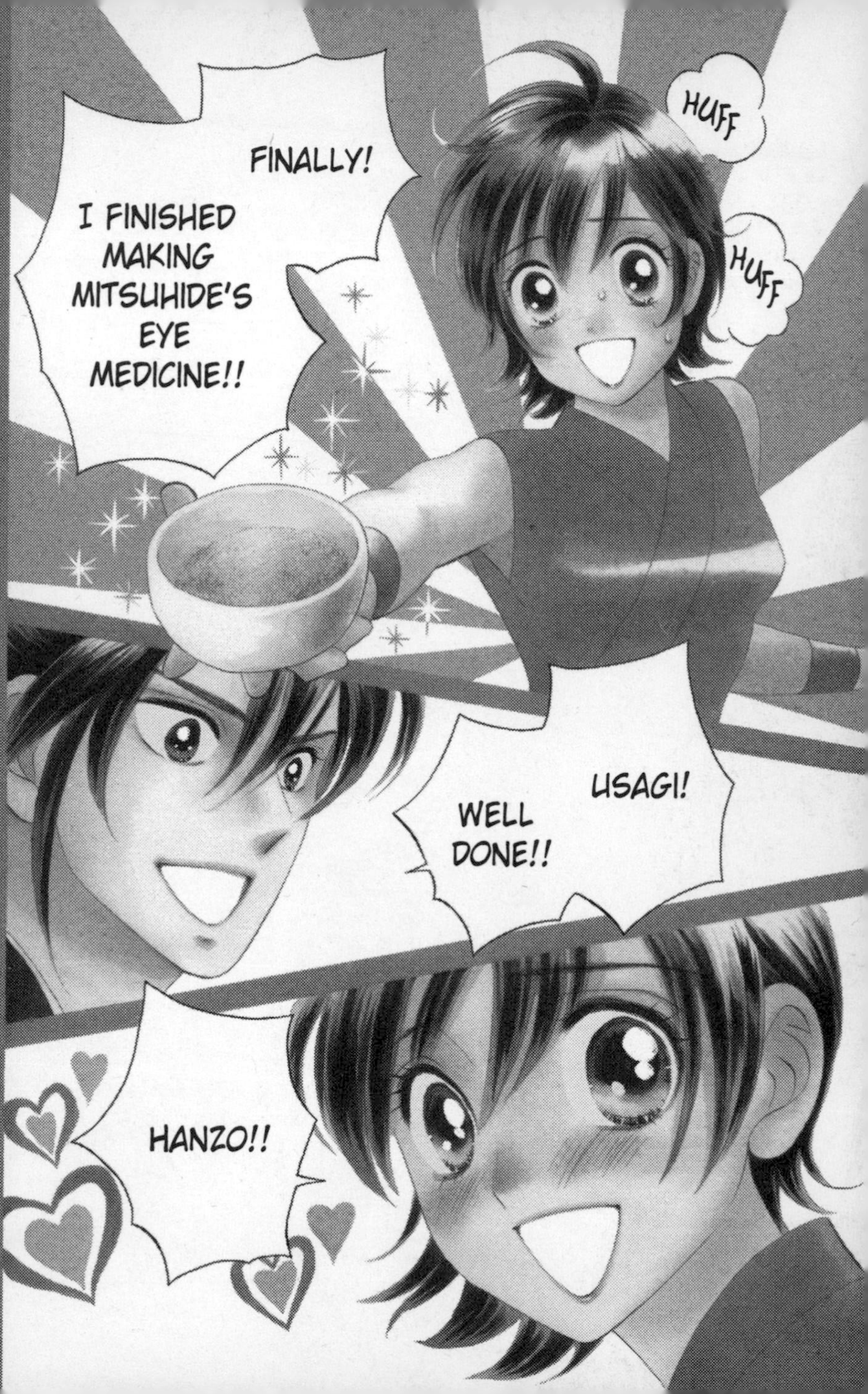
HUFF
HUFF
FINALLY!
I FINISHED MAKING MITSUHIDE'S EYE MEDICINE!!
USAGI!
WELL DONE!!
HANZO!!

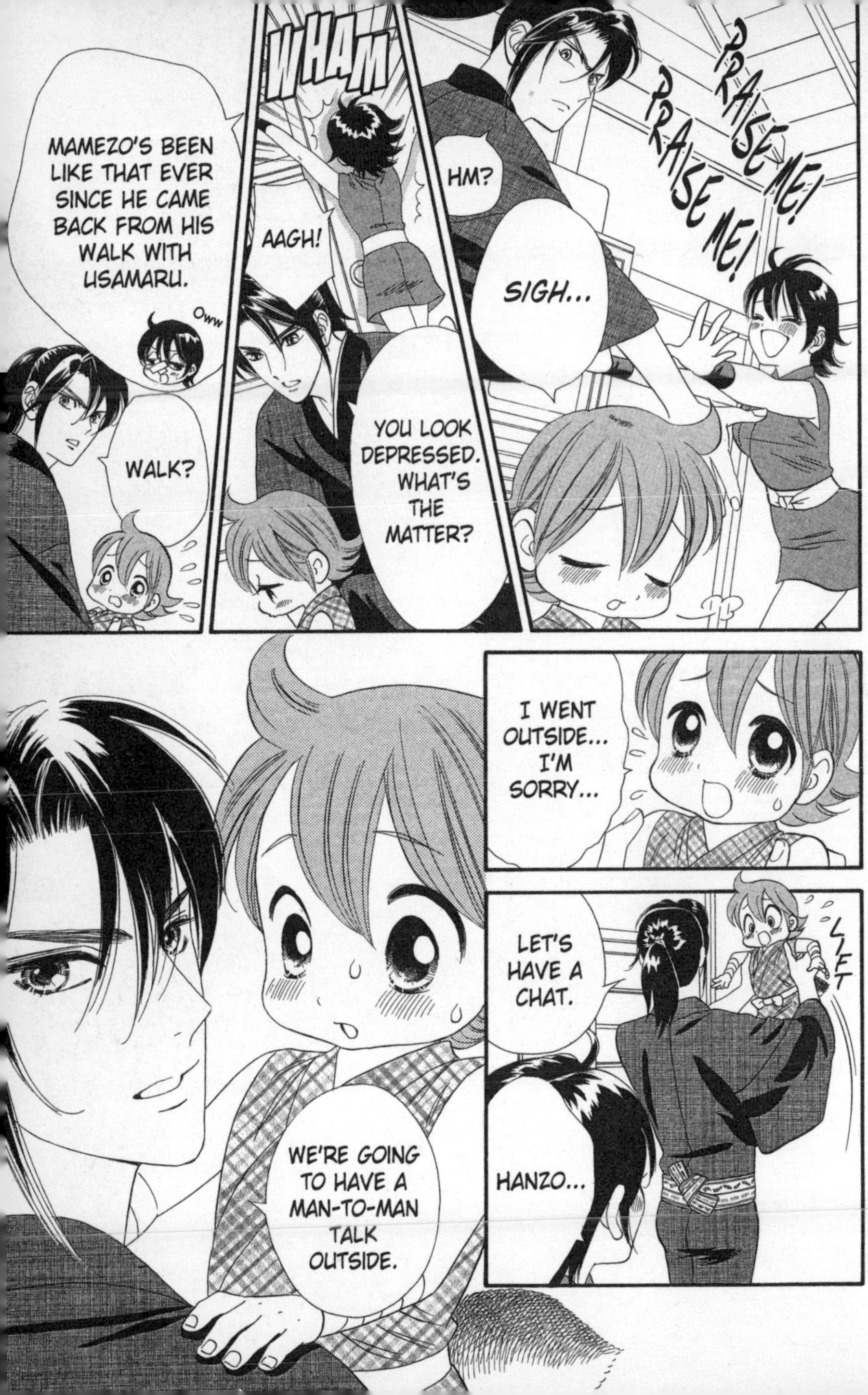
PRAISE ME! PRAISE ME!
HM?
SIGH...
YOU LOOK DEPRESSED. WHAT'S THE MATTER?
WHAM
AAGH!
MAMEZO'S BEEN LIKE THAT EVER SINCE HE CAME BACK FROM HIS WALK WITH USAMARU.
Oww
WALK?
I WENT OUTSIDE... I'M SORRY...
LET'S HAVE A CHAT.
LIFT
HANZO...
WE'RE GOING TO HAVE A MAN-TO-MAN TALK OUTSIDE.

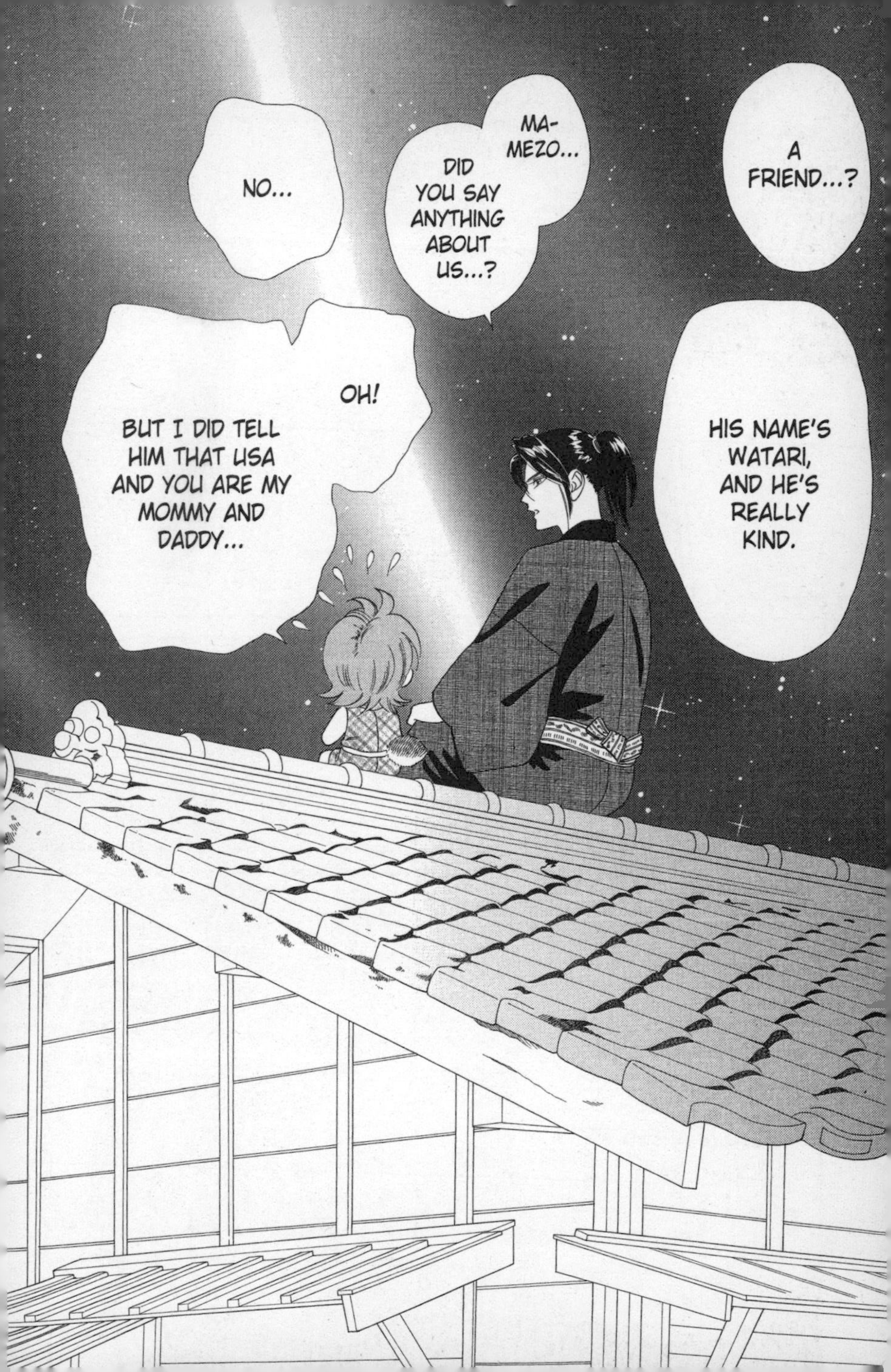
A FRIEND...?
HIS NAME'S WATARI, AND HE'S REALLY KIND.
MA-MEZO...
DID YOU SAY ANYTHING ABOUT US...?
NO...
OH!
BUT I DID TELL HIM THAT USA AND YOU ARE MY MOMMY AND DADDY...

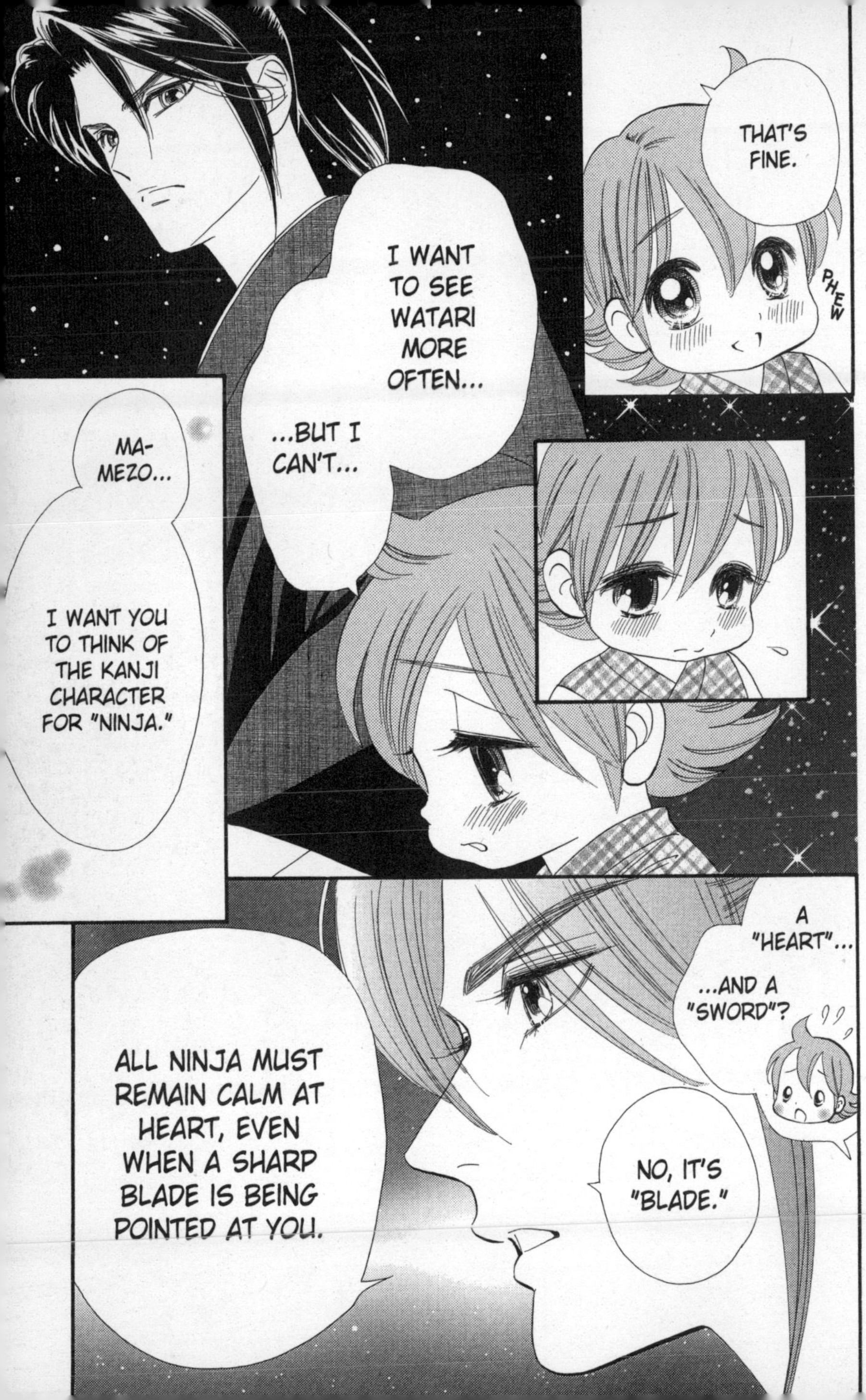
THAT'S FINE.
PHEW
I WANT TO SEE WATARI MORE OFTEN...
...BUT I CAN'T...
MA-MEZO...
I WANT YOU TO THINK OF THE KANJI CHARACTER FOR "NINJA."
A "HEART"...
...AND A "SWORD"?
NO, IT'S "BLADE."
ALL NINJA MUST REMAIN CALM AT HEART, EVEN WHEN A SHARP BLADE IS BEING POINTED AT YOU.

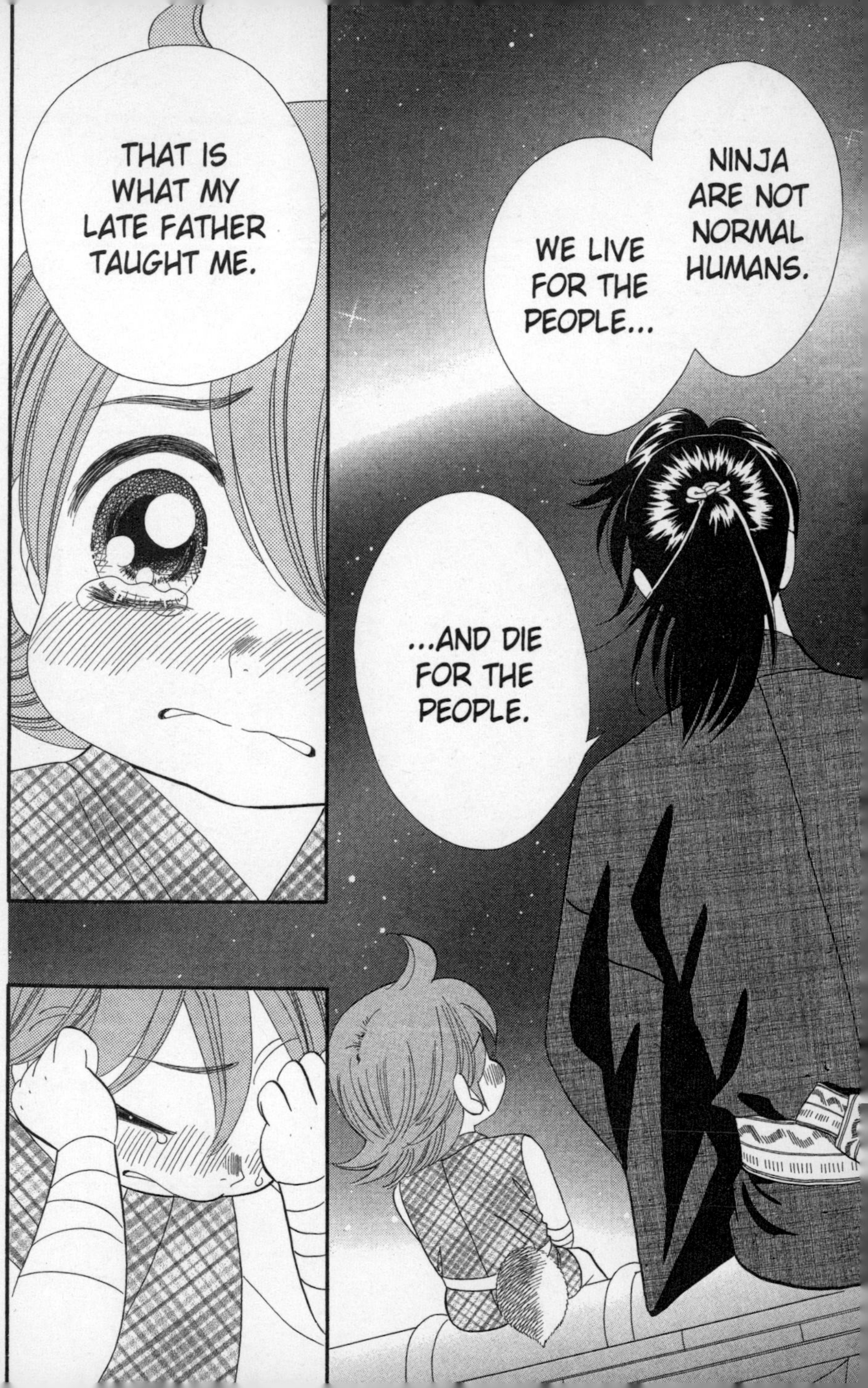
NINJA ARE NOT NORMAL HUMANS.
WE LIVE FOR THE PEOPLE...
...AND DIE FOR THE PEOPLE.
THAT IS WHAT MY LATE FATHER TAUGHT ME.

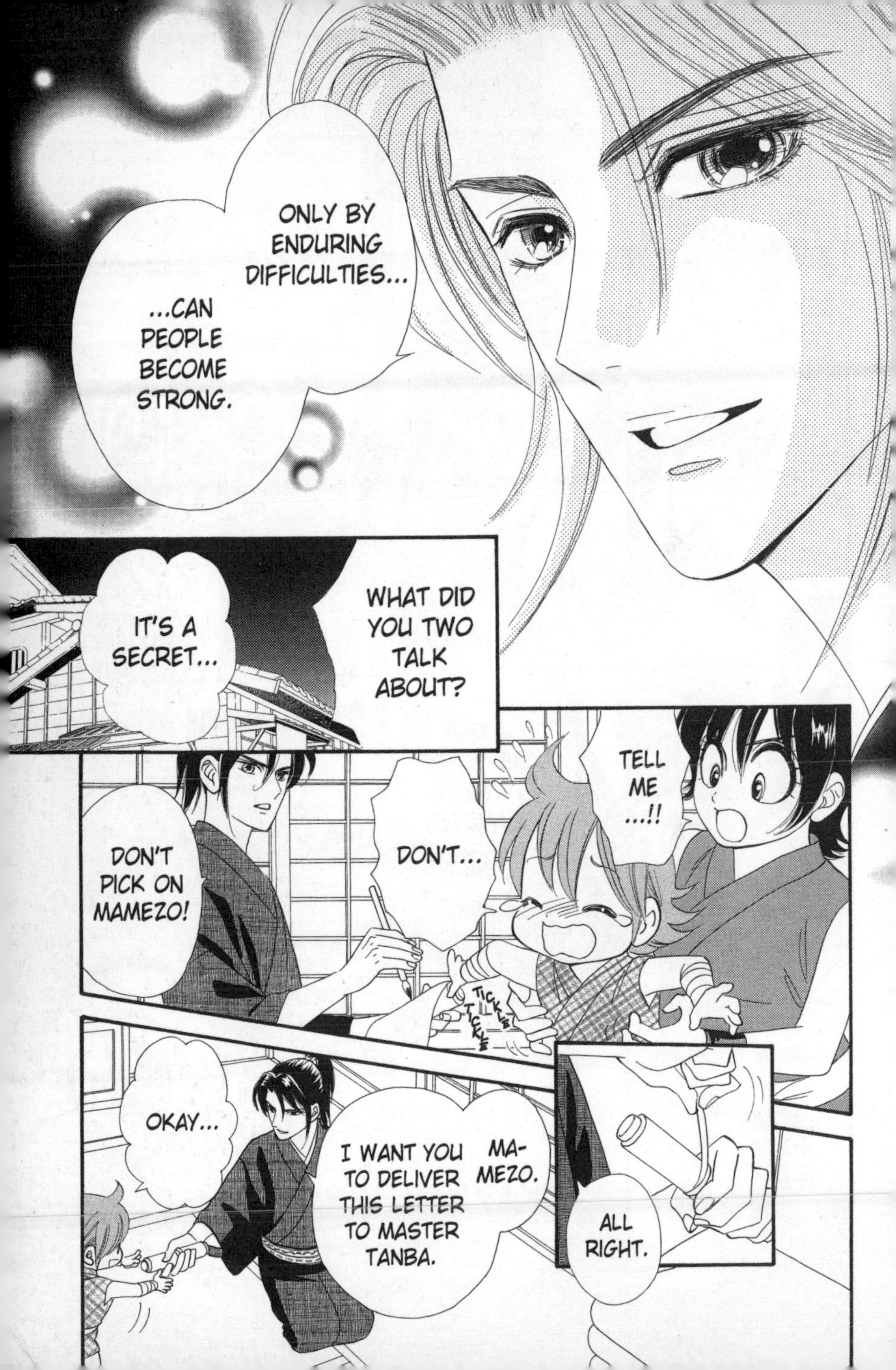
ONLY BY ENDURING DIFFICULTIES...
...CAN PEOPLE BECOME STRONG.
WHAT DID YOU TWO TALK ABOUT?
IT'S A SECRET...
TELL ME ...!!
DON'T...
DON'T PICK ON MAMEZO!
TICKLE TICKLE
ALL RIGHT.
MA-MEZO.
I WANT YOU TO DELIVER THIS LETTER TO MASTER TANBA.
OKAY...

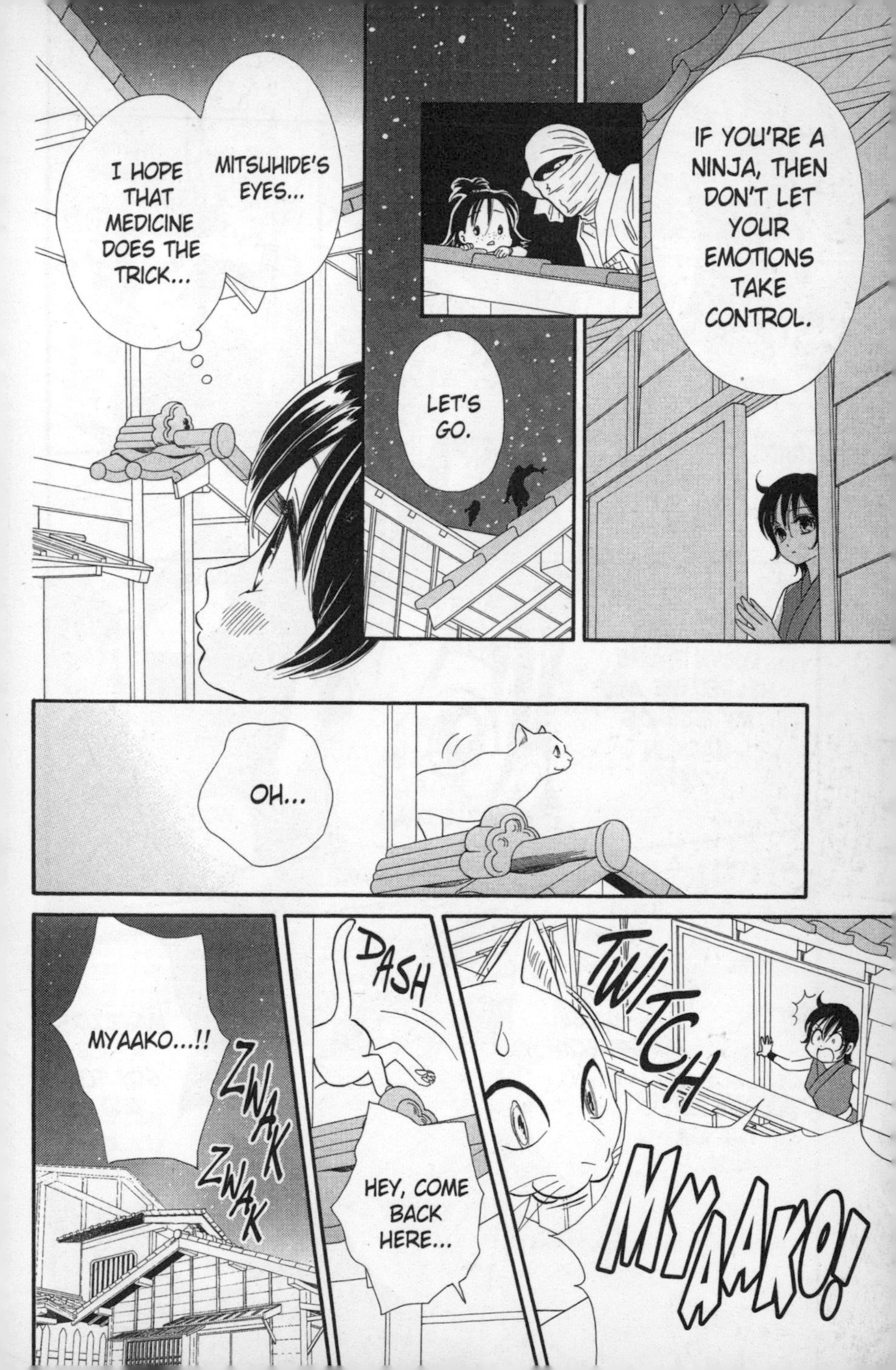
IF YOU'RE A NINJA, THEN DON'T LET YOUR EMOTIONS TAKE CONTROL.
LET'S GO.
MITSUHIDE'S EYES...
I HOPE THAT MEDICINE DOES THE TRICK...
OH...
TWITCH
MYAAKO!
DASH
HEY, COME BACK HERE...
MYAAKO...!!
ZWAK
ZWAK

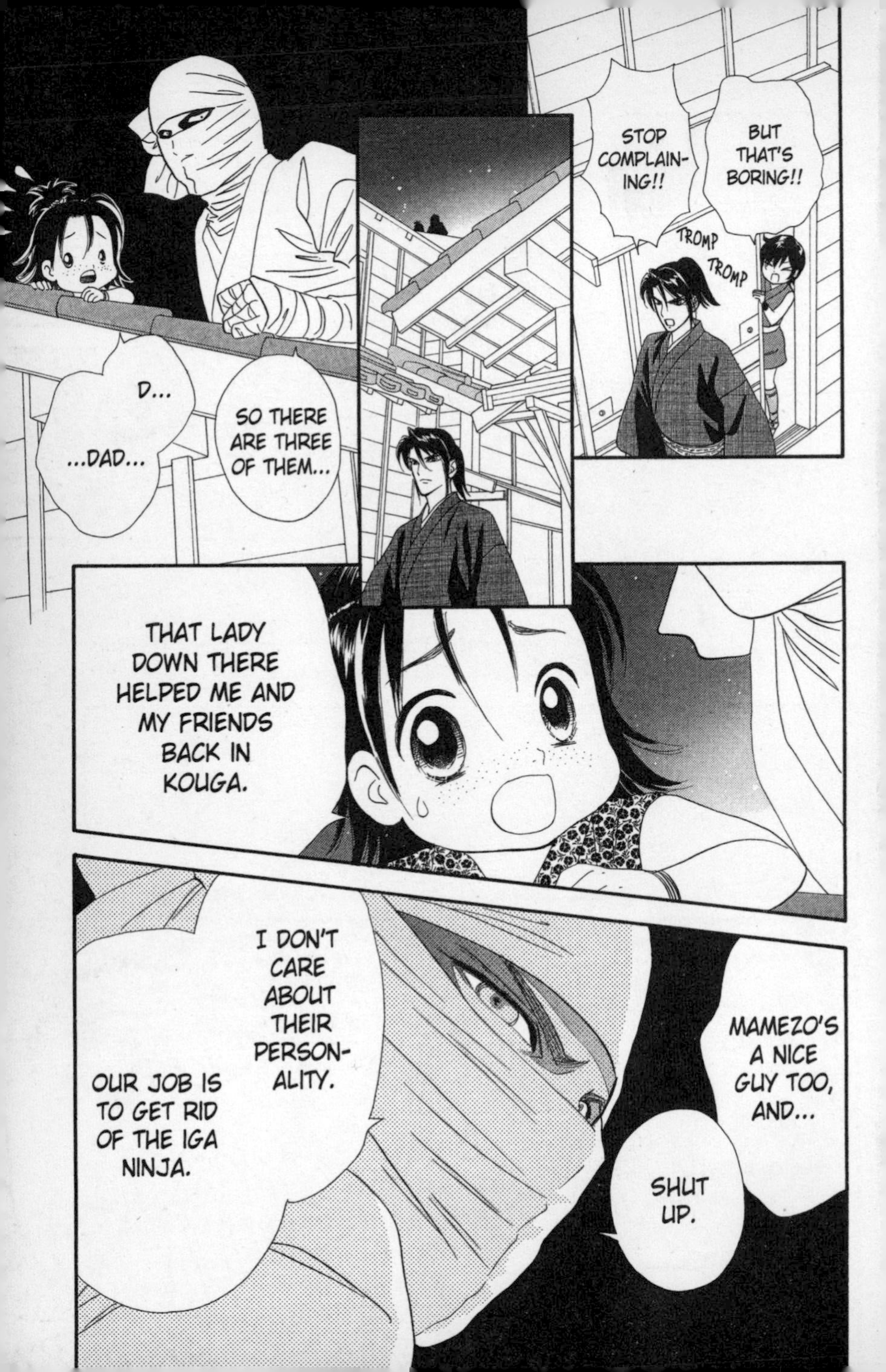
BUT THAT'S BORING!!
STOP COMPLAIN-ING!!
TROMP TROMP
SO THERE ARE THREE OF THEM...
D... ...DAD...
THAT LADY DOWN THERE HELPED ME AND MY FRIENDS BACK IN KOUGA.
MAMEZO'S A NICE GUY TOO, AND...
SHUT UP.
I DON'T CARE ABOUT THEIR PERSON-ALITY.
OUR JOB IS TO GET RID OF THE IGA NINJA.

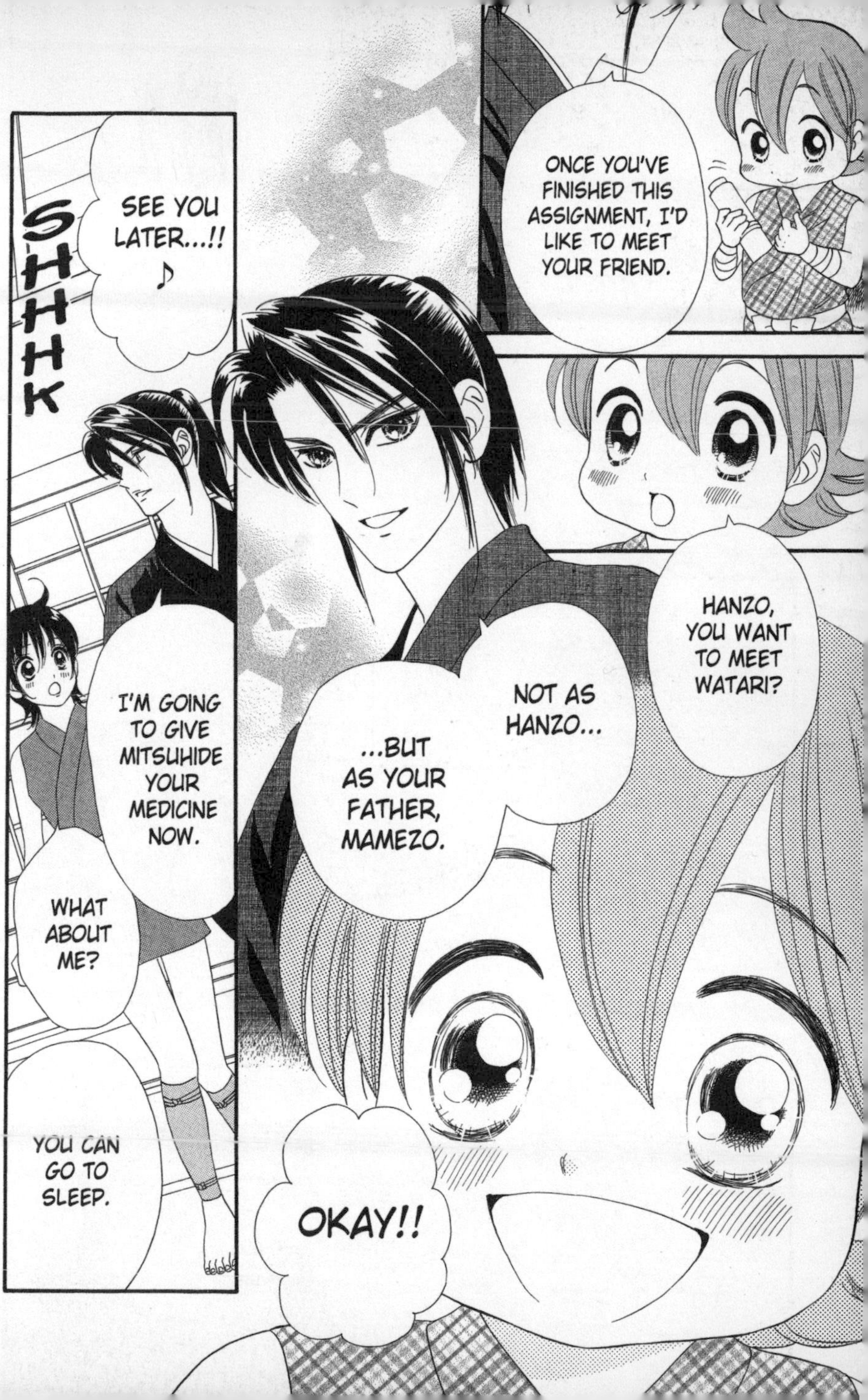
ONCE YOU'VE FINISHED THIS ASSIGNMENT, I'D LIKE TO MEET YOUR FRIEND.
HANZO, YOU WANT TO MEET WATARI?
NOT AS HANZO...
...BUT AS YOUR FATHER, MAMEZO.
OKAY!!
SEE YOU LATER...!! ♪
SHHHK
I'M GOING TO GIVE MITSUHIDE YOUR MEDICINE NOW.
WHAT ABOUT ME?
YOU CAN GO TO SLEEP.

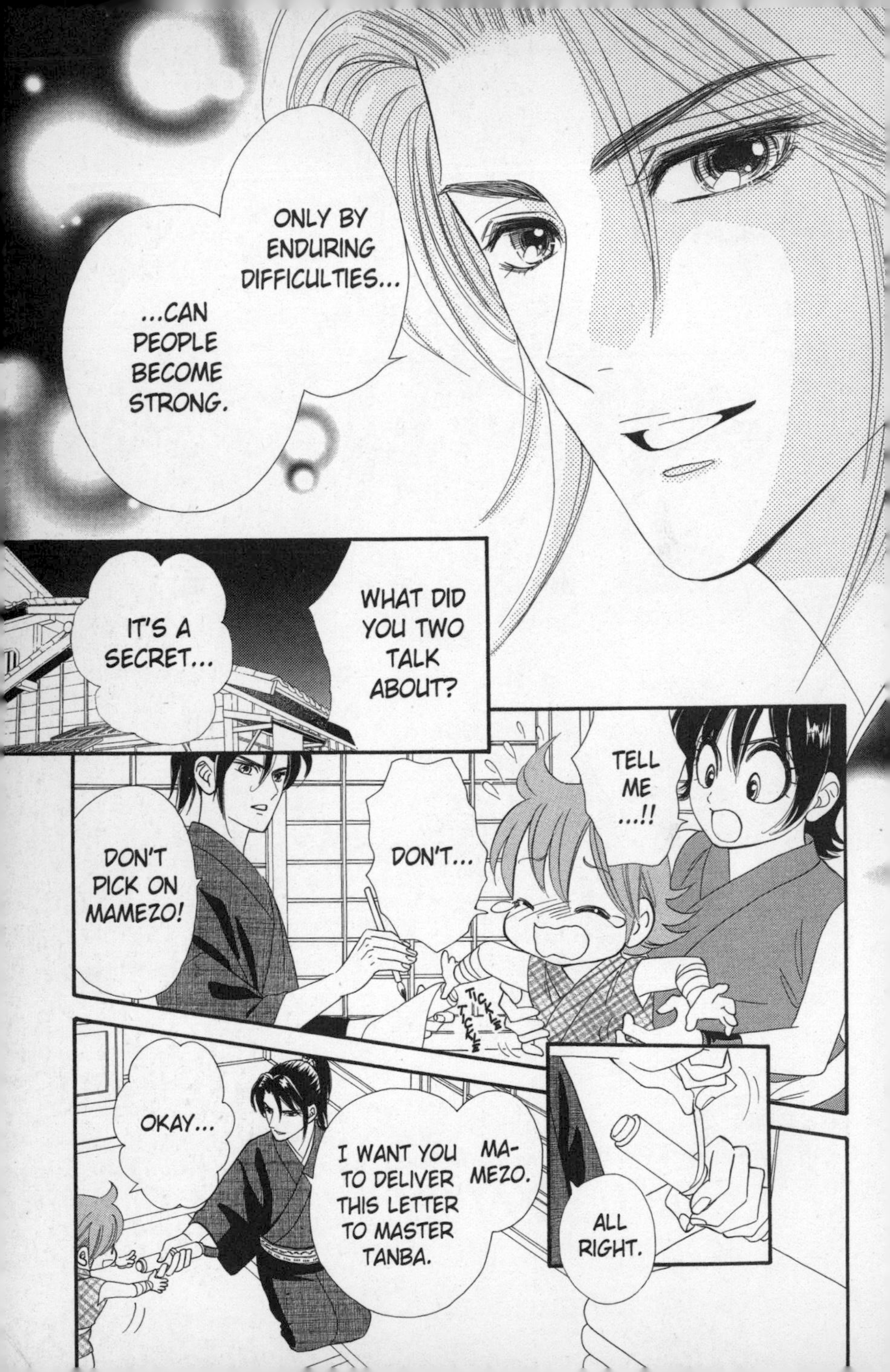
ONLY BY ENDURING DIFFICULTIES...
...CAN PEOPLE BECOME STRONG.
WHAT DID YOU TWO TALK ABOUT?
IT'S A SECRET...
TELL ME ...!!
DON'T...
TICKLE TICKLE TICKLE
DON'T PICK ON MAMEZO!
ALL RIGHT.
MAMEZO.
I WANT YOU TO DELIVER THIS LETTER TO MASTER TANBA.
OKAY...

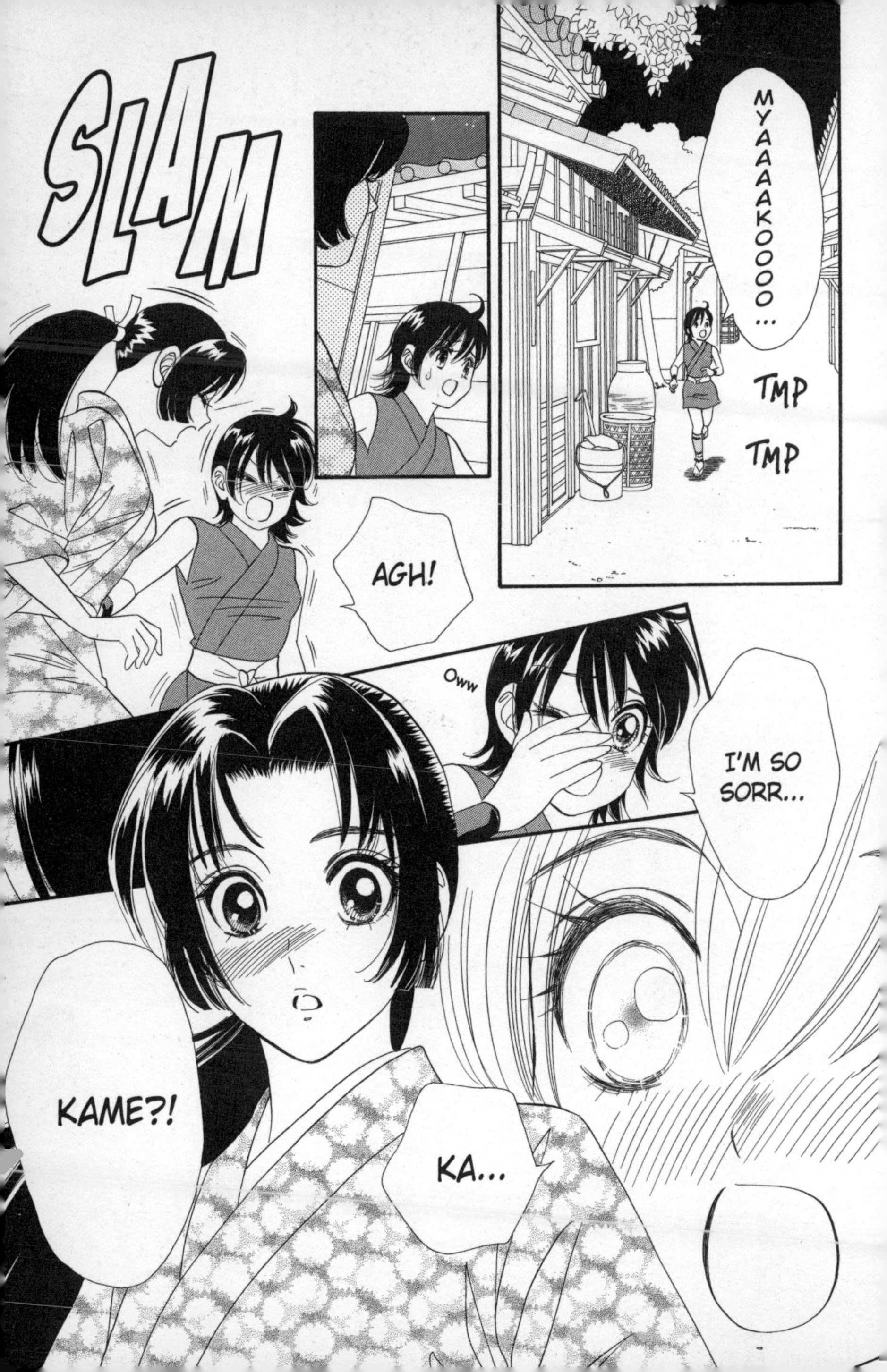
MYAAAAKOOOO...
TMP
TMP
SLAM
AGH!
I'M SO SORR...
Oww
KA...
KAME?!

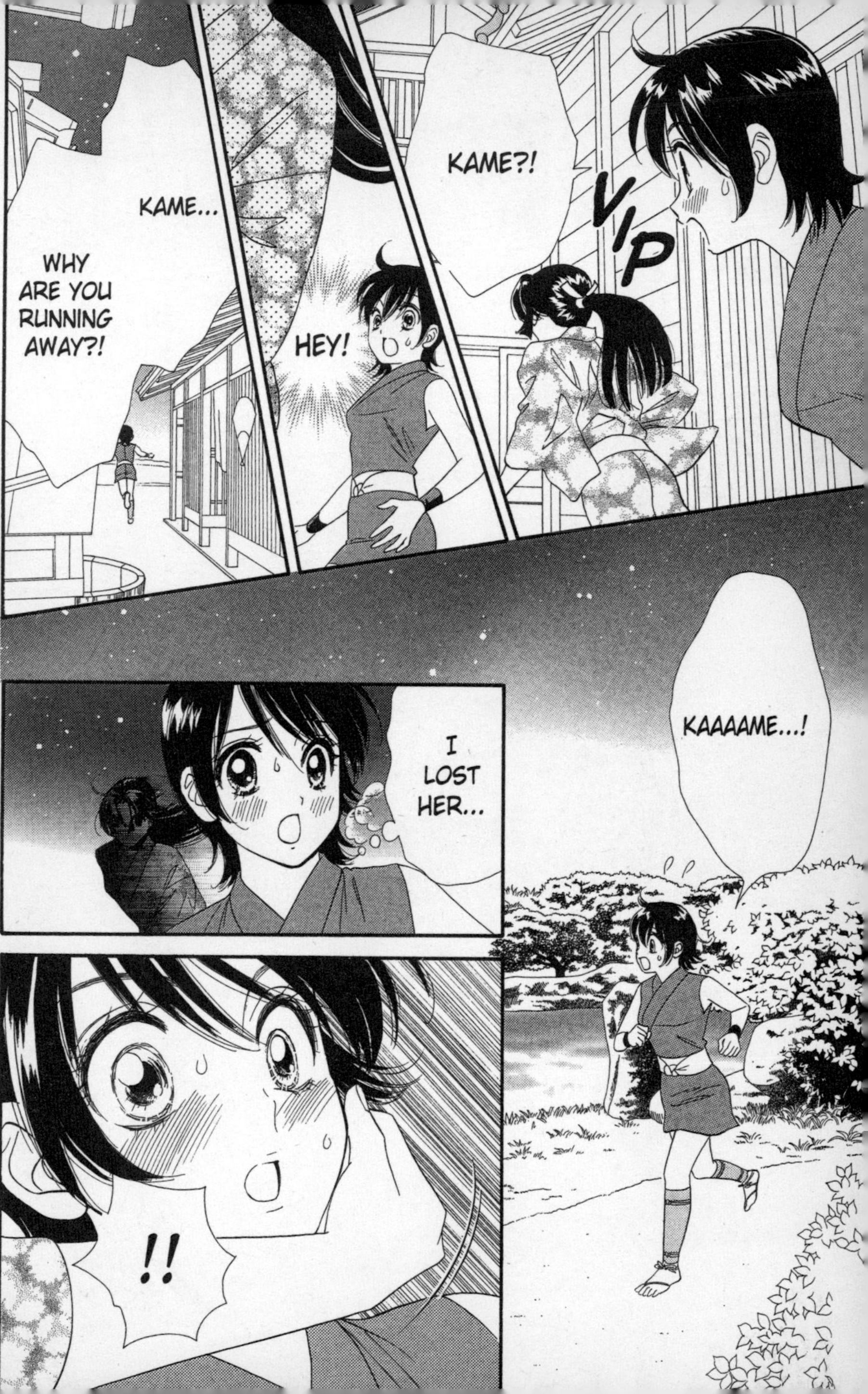
VIP
KAME?!
HEY!
KAME...
WHY ARE YOU RUNNING AWAY?!
KAAAAME...!
I LOST HER...
!!

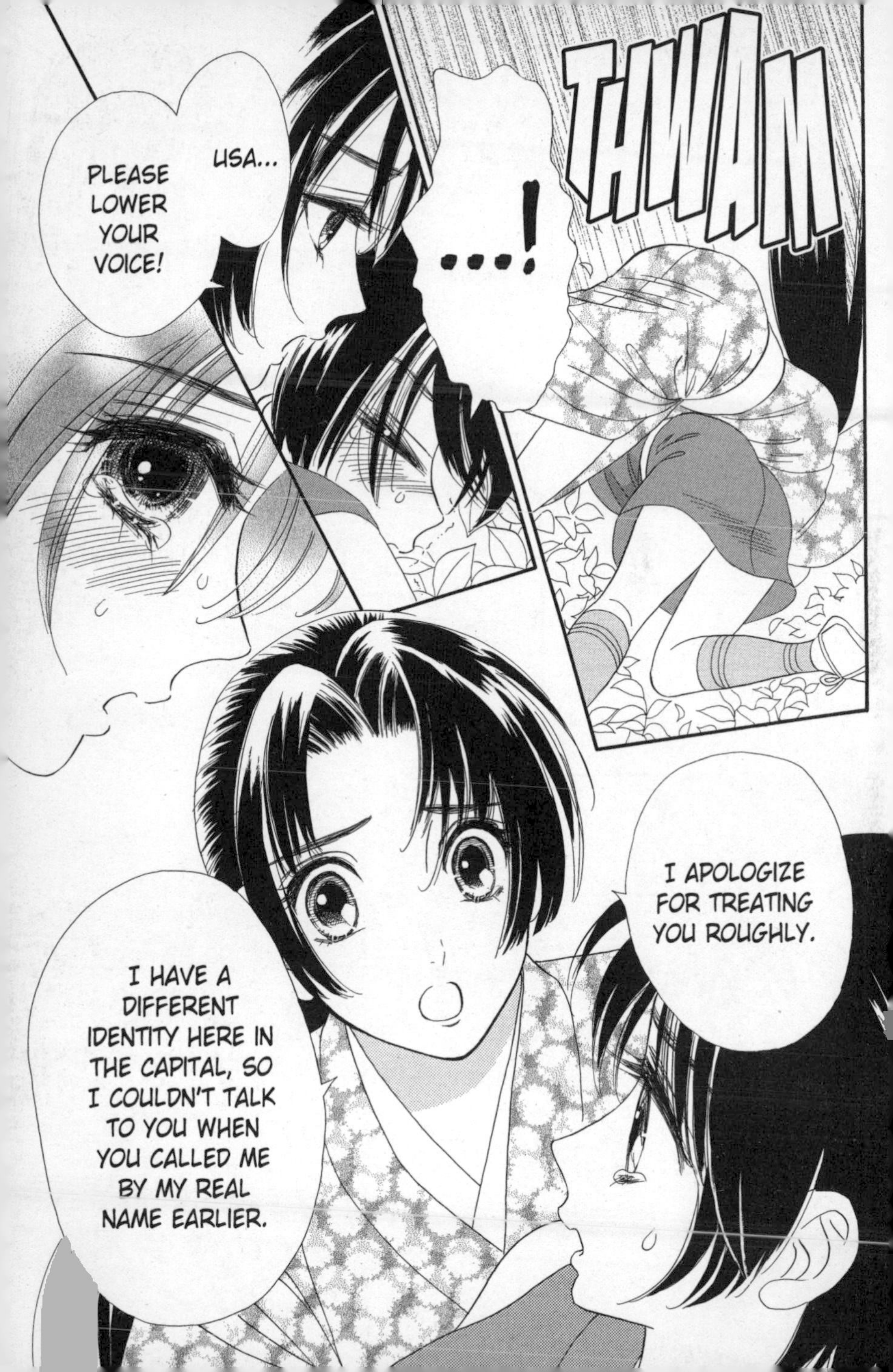
THWAM
...!
USA...
PLEASE LOWER YOUR VOICE!
I APOLOGIZE FOR TREATING YOU ROUGHLY.
I HAVE A DIFFERENT IDENTITY HERE IN THE CAPITAL, SO I COULDN'T TALK TO YOU WHEN YOU CALLED ME BY MY REAL NAME EARLIER.

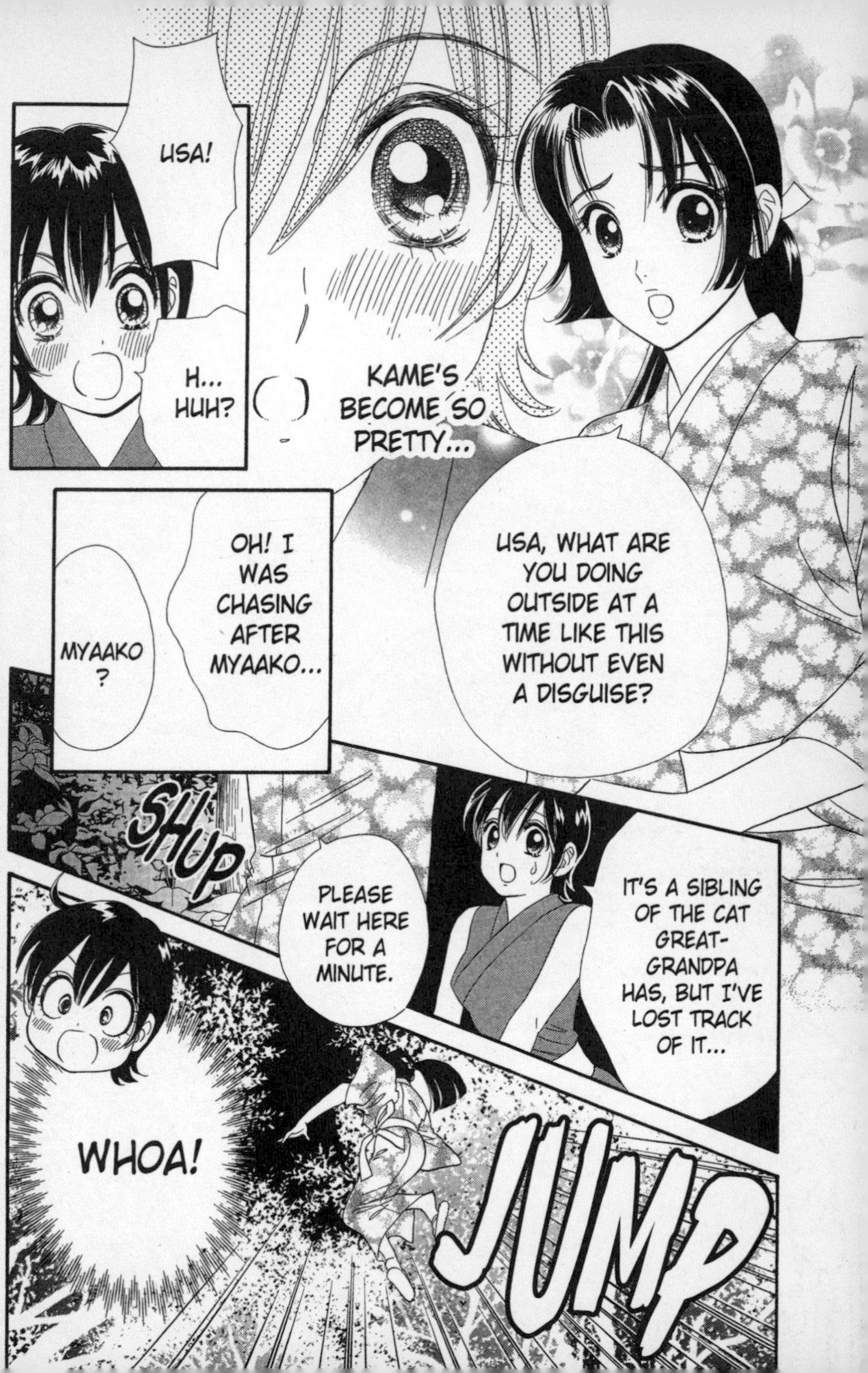
USA!
H... HUH?
KAME'S BECOME SO PRETTY...
USA, WHAT ARE YOU DOING OUTSIDE AT A TIME LIKE THIS WITHOUT EVEN A DISGUISE?
OH! I WAS CHASING AFTER MYAAKO...
MYAAKO?
IT'S A SIBLING OF THE CAT GREAT-GRANDPA HAS, BUT I'VE LOST TRACK OF IT...
PLEASE WAIT HERE FOR A MINUTE.
SHUP
JUMP
WHOA!

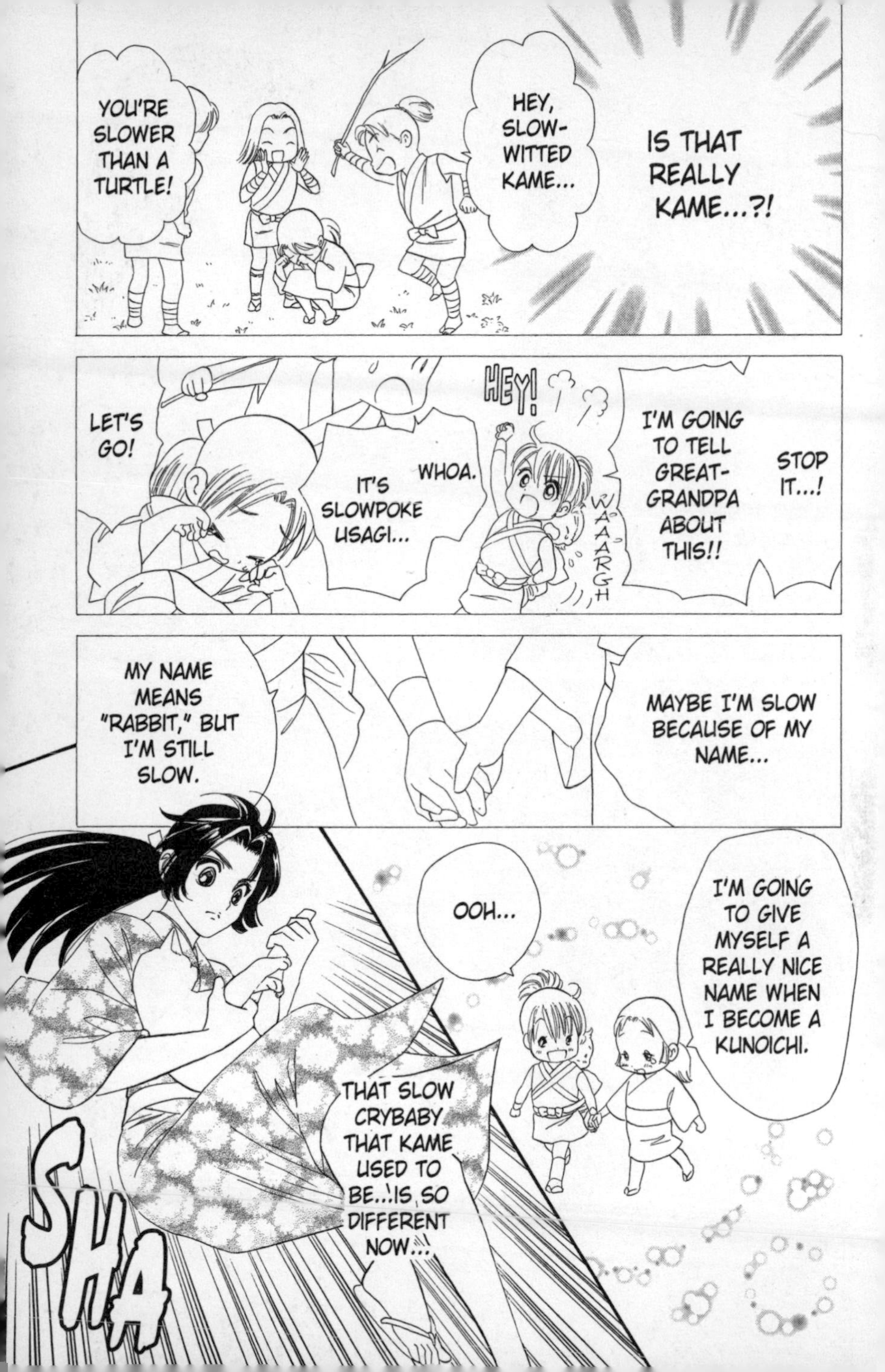
IS THAT REALLY KAME...?!
HEY, SLOW-WITTED KAME...
YOU'RE SLOWER THAN A TURTLE!
STOP IT...!
I'M GOING TO TELL GREAT-GRANDPA ABOUT THIS!!
HEY!
WAAARGH
WHOA.
IT'S SLOWPOKE USAGI...
LET'S GO!
MAYBE I'M SLOW BECAUSE OF MY NAME...
MY NAME MEANS "RABBIT," BUT I'M STILL SLOW.
I'M GOING TO GIVE MYSELF A REALLY NICE NAME WHEN I BECOME A KUNOICHI.
OOH...
THAT SLOW CRYBABY THAT KAME USED TO BE... IS SO DIFFERENT NOW...
SHA

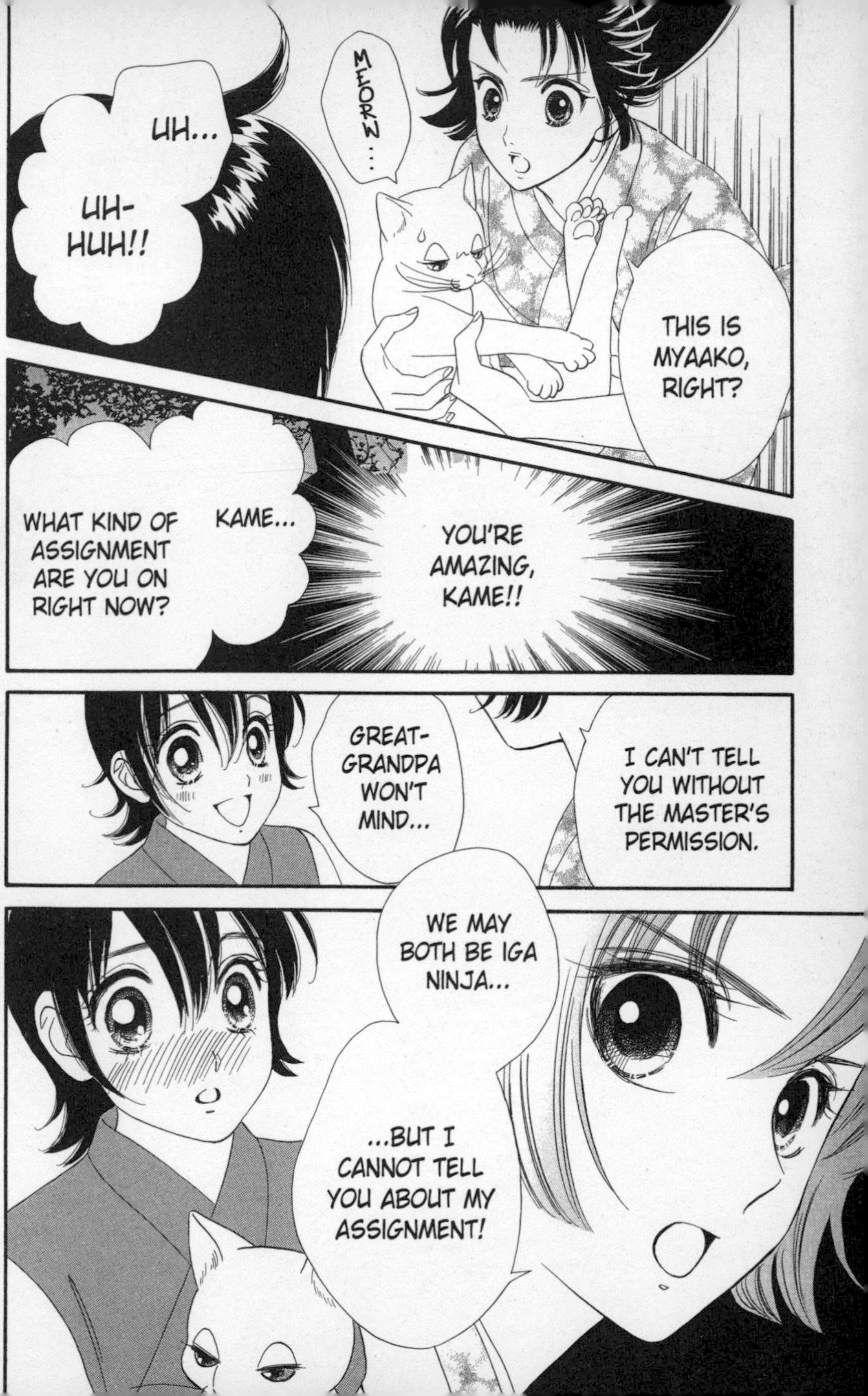
THIS IS MYAAKO, RIGHT?
MEORW...
UH...
UH-HUH!!
YOU'RE AMAZING, KAME!!
KAME...
WHAT KIND OF ASSIGNMENT ARE YOU ON RIGHT NOW?
I CAN'T TELL YOU WITHOUT THE MASTER'S PERMISSION.
GREAT-GRANDPA WON'T MIND...
WE MAY BOTH BE IGA NINJA...
...BUT I CANNOT TELL YOU ABOUT MY ASSIGNMENT!

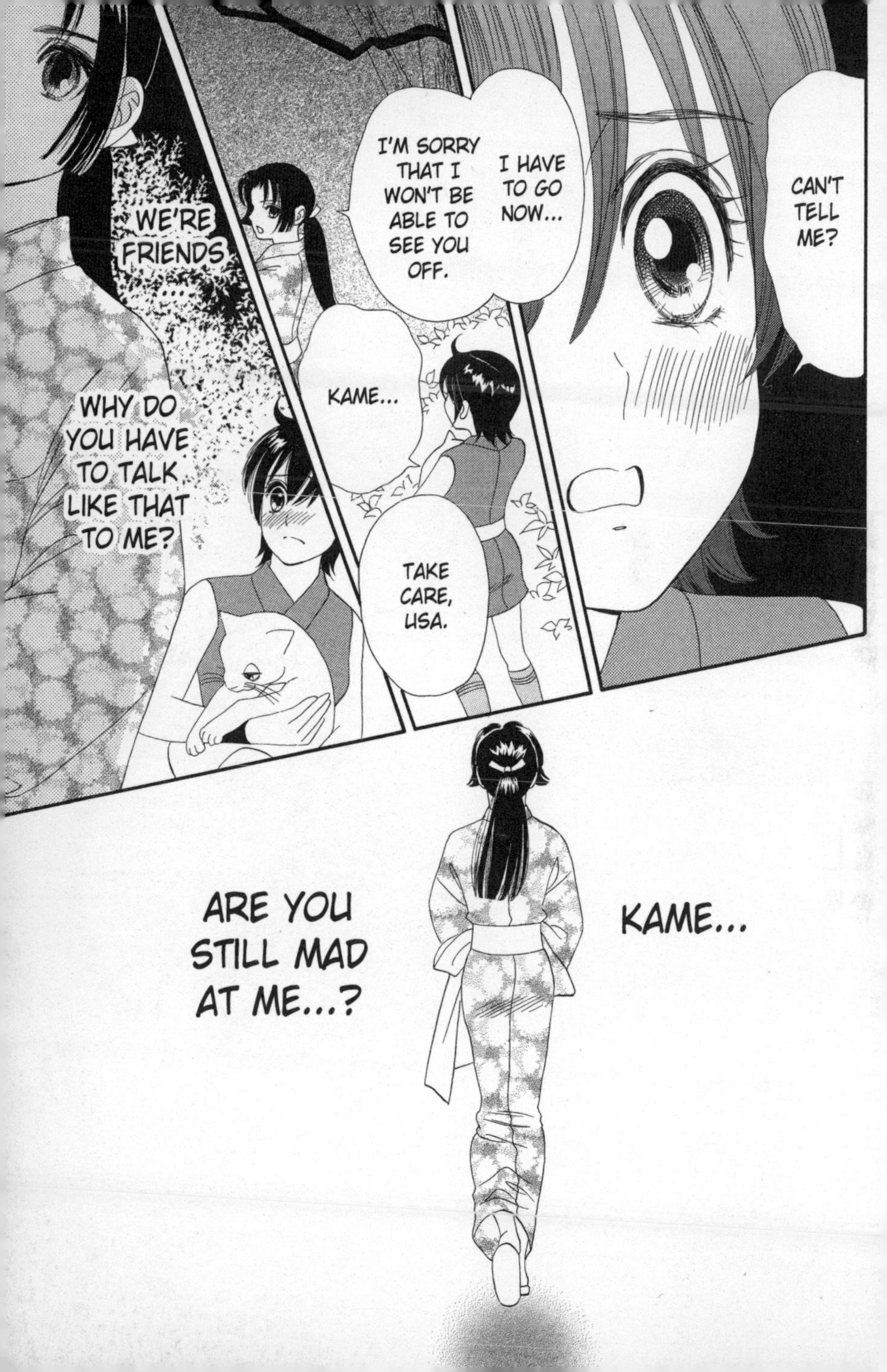
CAN'T TELL ME?
I HAVE TO GO NOW...
I'M SORRY THAT I WON'T BE ABLE TO SEE YOU OFF.
KAME...
TAKE CARE, USA.
WE'RE FRIENDS ...
WHY DO YOU HAVE TO TALK LIKE THAT TO ME?
KAME...
ARE YOU STILL MAD AT ME...?

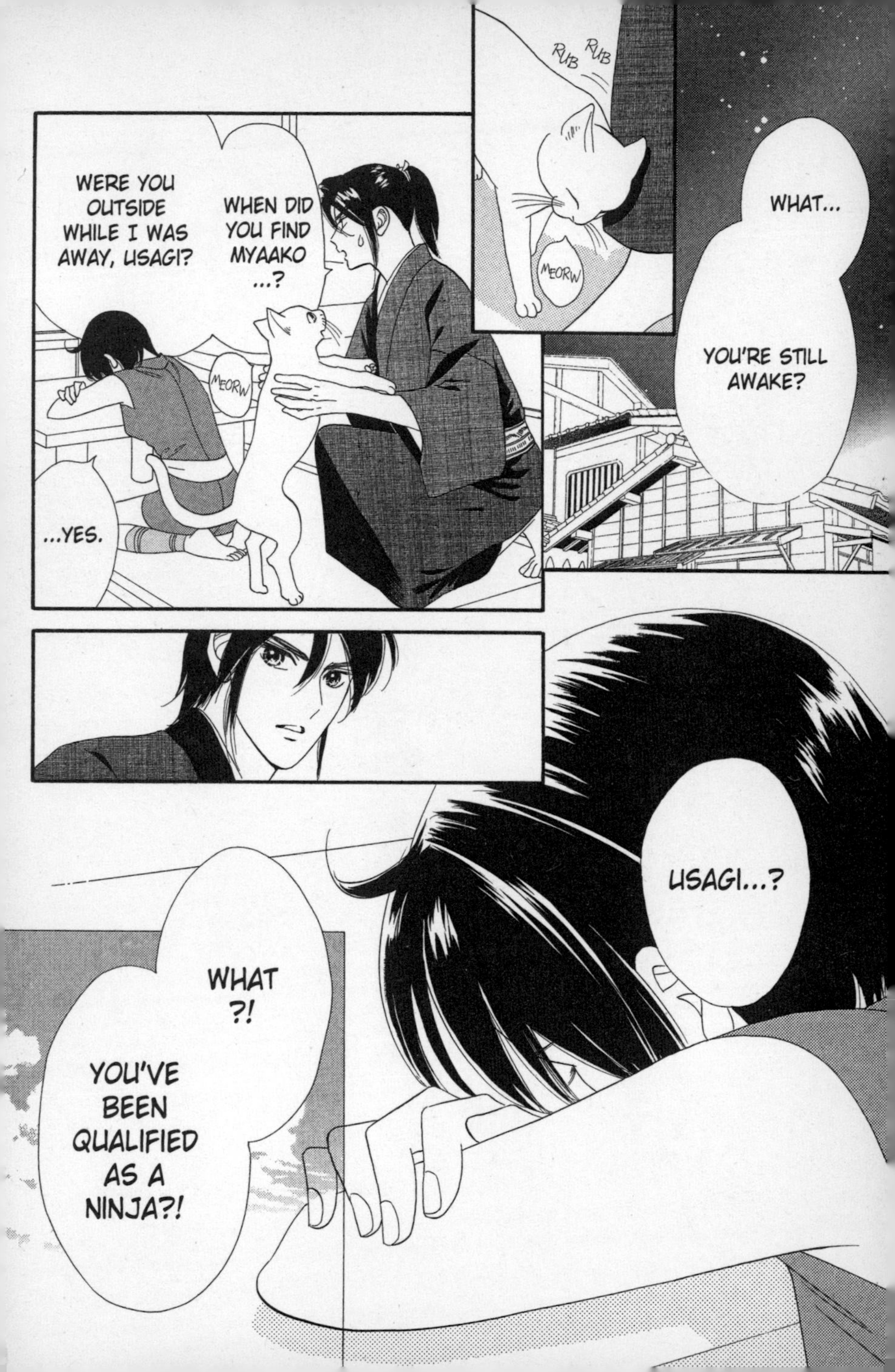
WHAT...
YOU'RE STILL AWAKE?
RUB RUB
MEORW
WHEN DID YOU FIND MYAAKO ...?
MEORW
WERE YOU OUTSIDE WHILE I WAS AWAY, USAGI?
...YES.
USAGI...?
WHAT ?!
YOU'VE BEEN QUALIFIED AS A NINJA?!

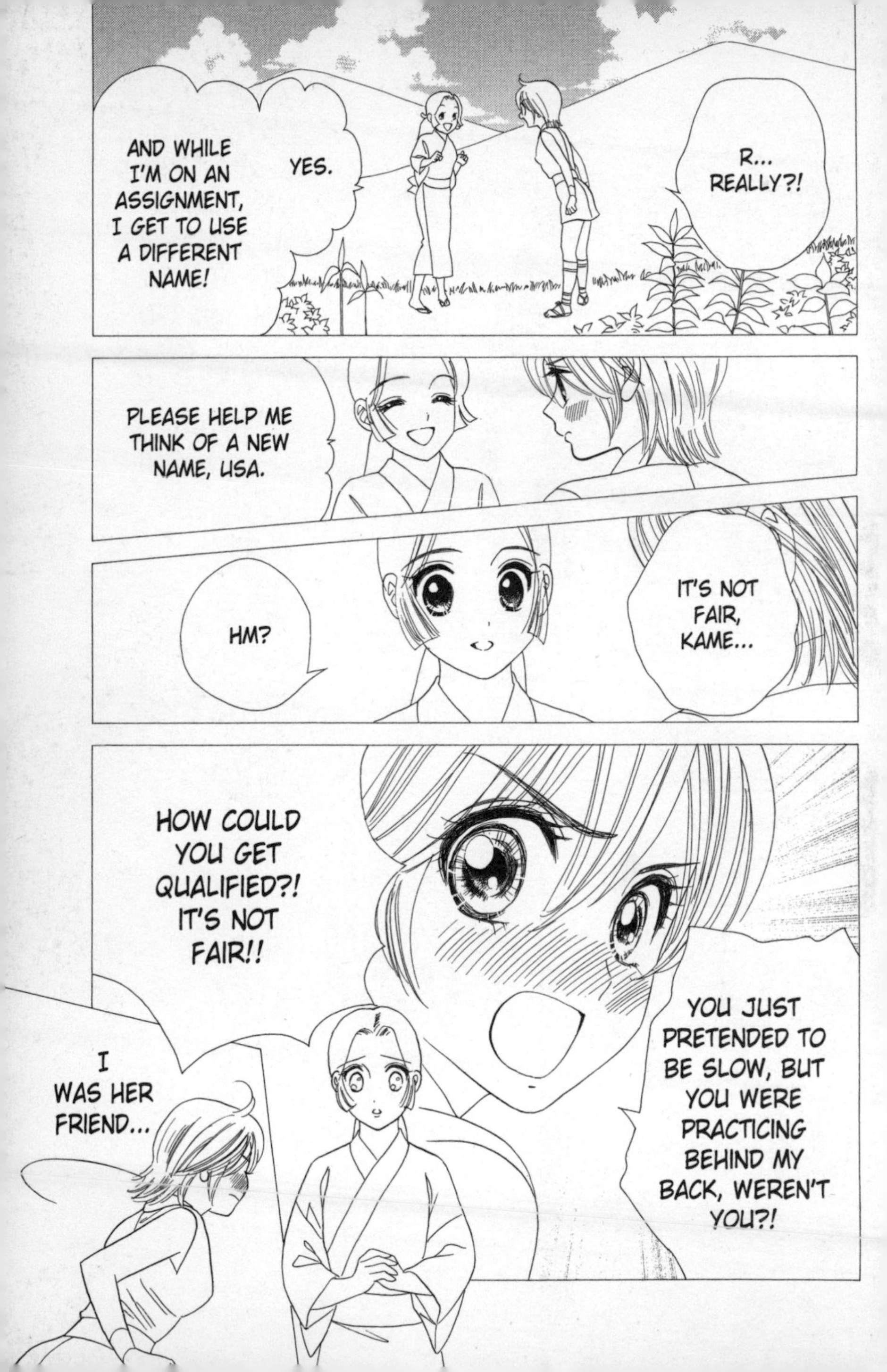
R... REALLY?!
YES.
AND WHILE I'M ON AN ASSIGNMENT, I GET TO USE A DIFFERENT NAME!
PLEASE HELP ME THINK OF A NEW NAME, USA.
IT'S NOT FAIR, KAME...
HM?
HOW COULD YOU GET QUALIFIED?! IT'S NOT FAIR!!
YOU JUST PRETENDED TO BE SLOW, BUT YOU WERE PRACTICING BEHIND MY BACK, WEREN'T YOU?!
I WAS HER FRIEND...

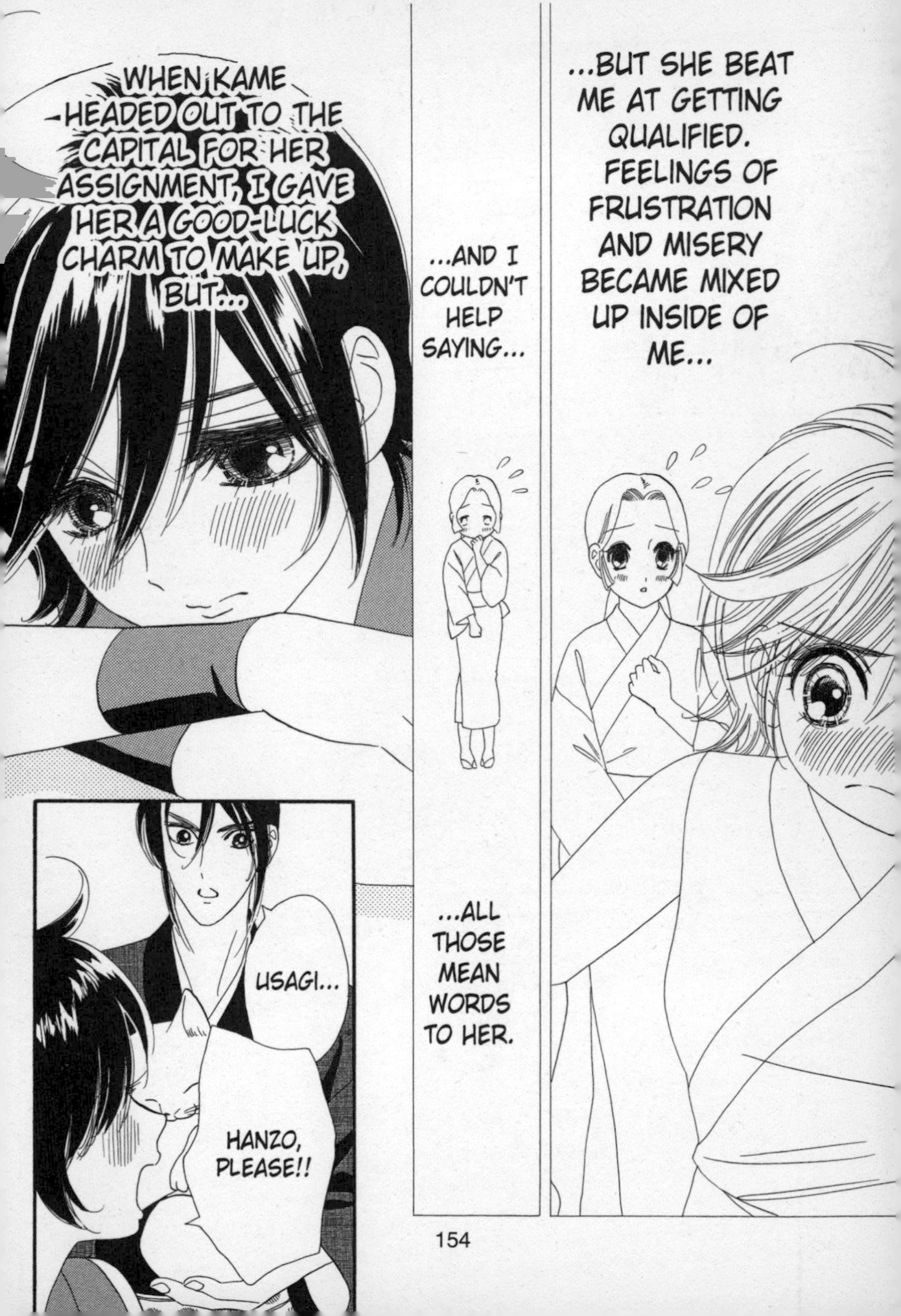
...BUT SHE BEAT ME AT GETTING QUALIFIED. FEELINGS OF FRUSTRATION AND MISERY BECAME MIXED UP INSIDE OF ME...
...AND I COULDN'T HELP SAYING...
...ALL THOSE MEAN WORDS TO HER.
WHEN KAME HEADED OUT TO THE CAPITAL FOR HER ASSIGNMENT, I GAVE HER A GOOD-LUCK CHARM TO MAKE UP, BUT...
USAGI...
HANZO, PLEASE!!

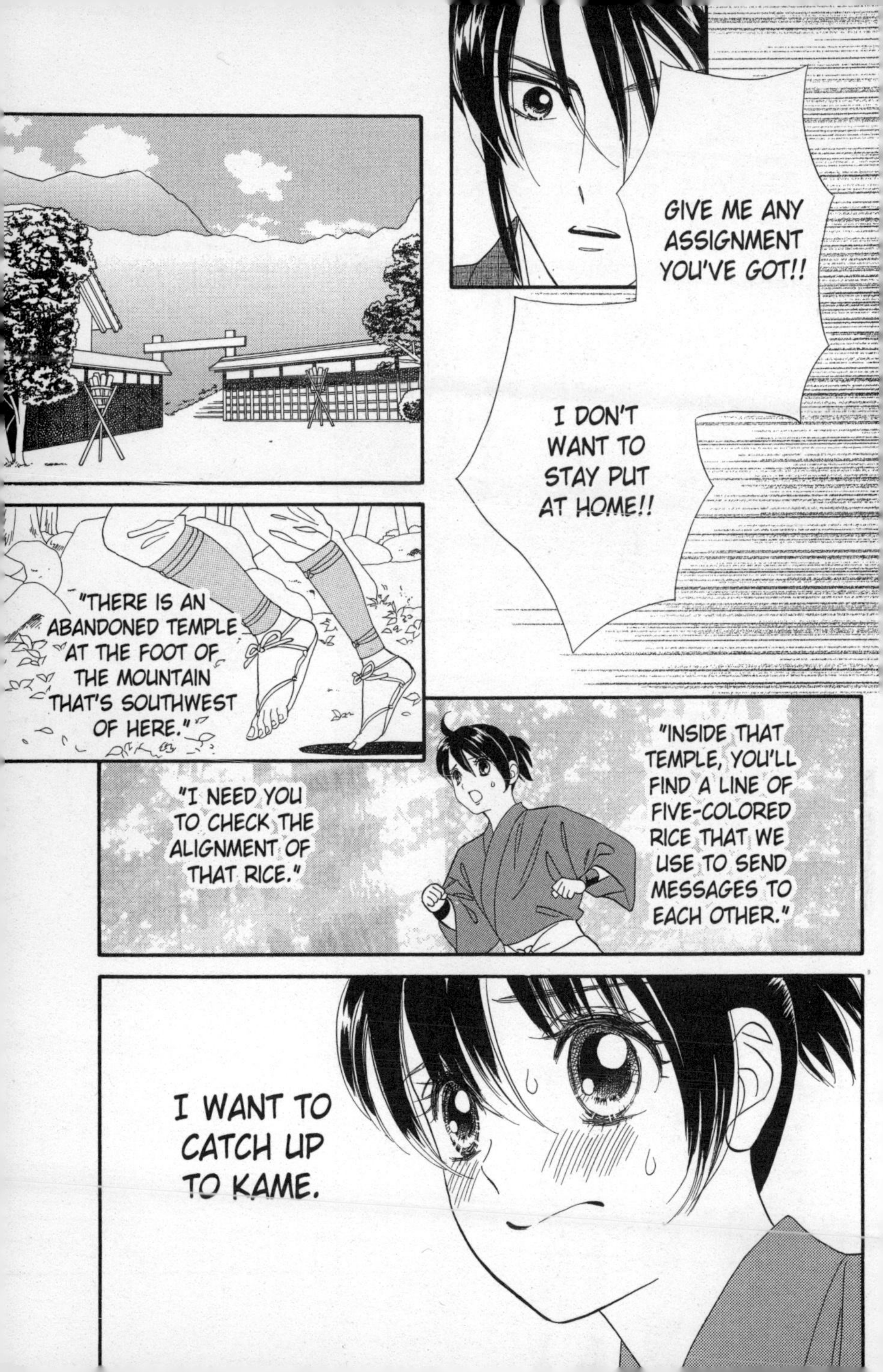
GIVE ME ANY ASSIGNMENT YOU'VE GOT!!
I DON'T WANT TO STAY PUT AT HOME!!
"THERE IS AN ABANDONED TEMPLE AT THE FOOT OF THE MOUNTAIN THAT'S SOUTHWEST OF HERE."
"INSIDE THAT TEMPLE, YOU'LL FIND A LINE OF FIVE-COLORED RICE THAT WE USE TO SEND MESSAGES TO EACH OTHER."
"I NEED YOU TO CHECK THE ALIGNMENT OF THAT RICE."
I WANT TO CATCH UP TO KAME.

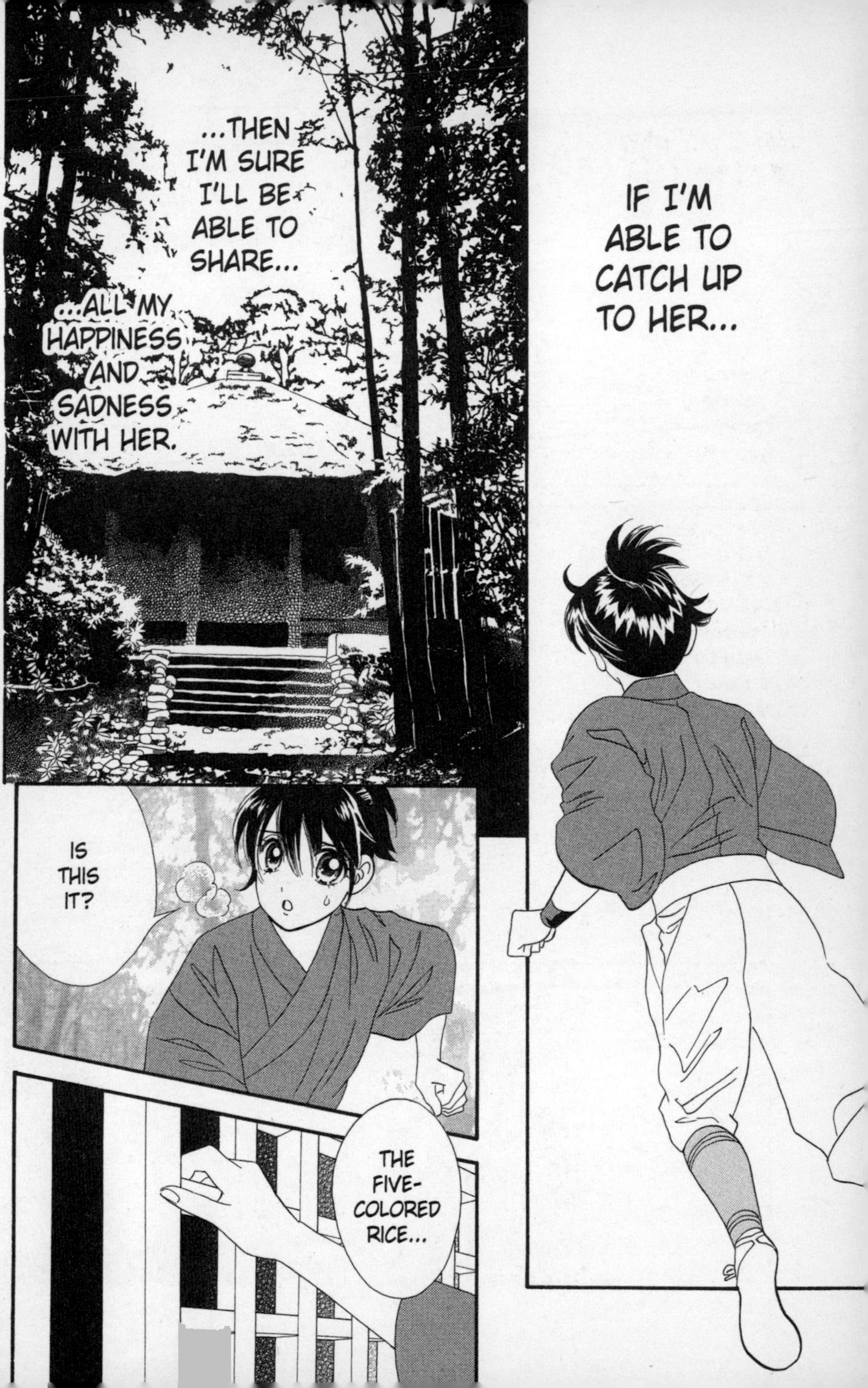
IF I'M ABLE TO CATCH UP TO HER...
...THEN I'M SURE I'LL BE ABLE TO SHARE...
...ALL MY HAPPINESS AND SADNESS WITH HER.
IS THIS IT?
THE FIVE-COLORED RICE...

UE-RIN'S WAY OF THE MANGA 20

All the award money I won from manga submissions as well as the pay I received for my debut manga went straight to my mother's bank account. I persuaded my mom to use that money for my private school tuition, so I finally succeeded in getting permission to apply to the art department.

Around that time, I got another phone call from the editorial office telling me that although I was going to make my debut, the one-shot that had won the debut award was too amateurish. They wanted me to redraw it, which really surprised me.

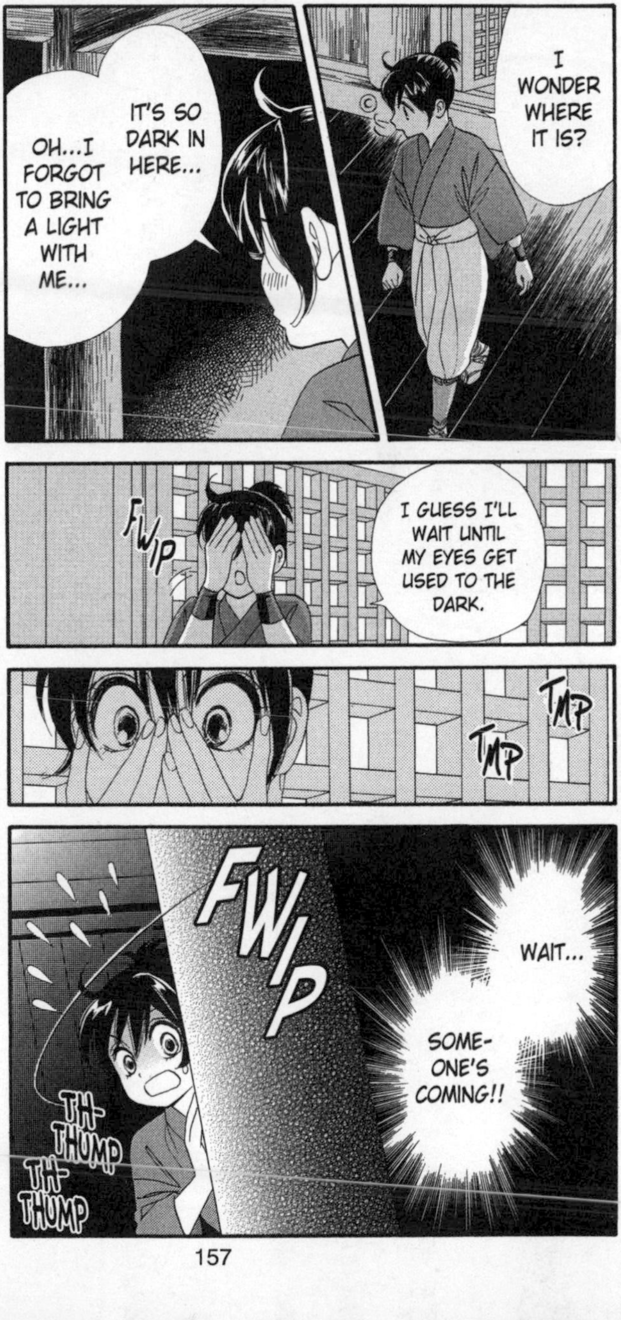
I WONDER WHERE IT IS?
IT'S SO DARK IN HERE...
OH...I FORGOT TO BRING A LIGHT WITH ME...
FWIP
I GUESS I'LL WAIT UNTIL MY EYES GET USED TO THE DARK.
TMP
TMP
FWIP
WAIT...
SOME-ONE'S COMING!!
TH-THUMP
TH-THUMP

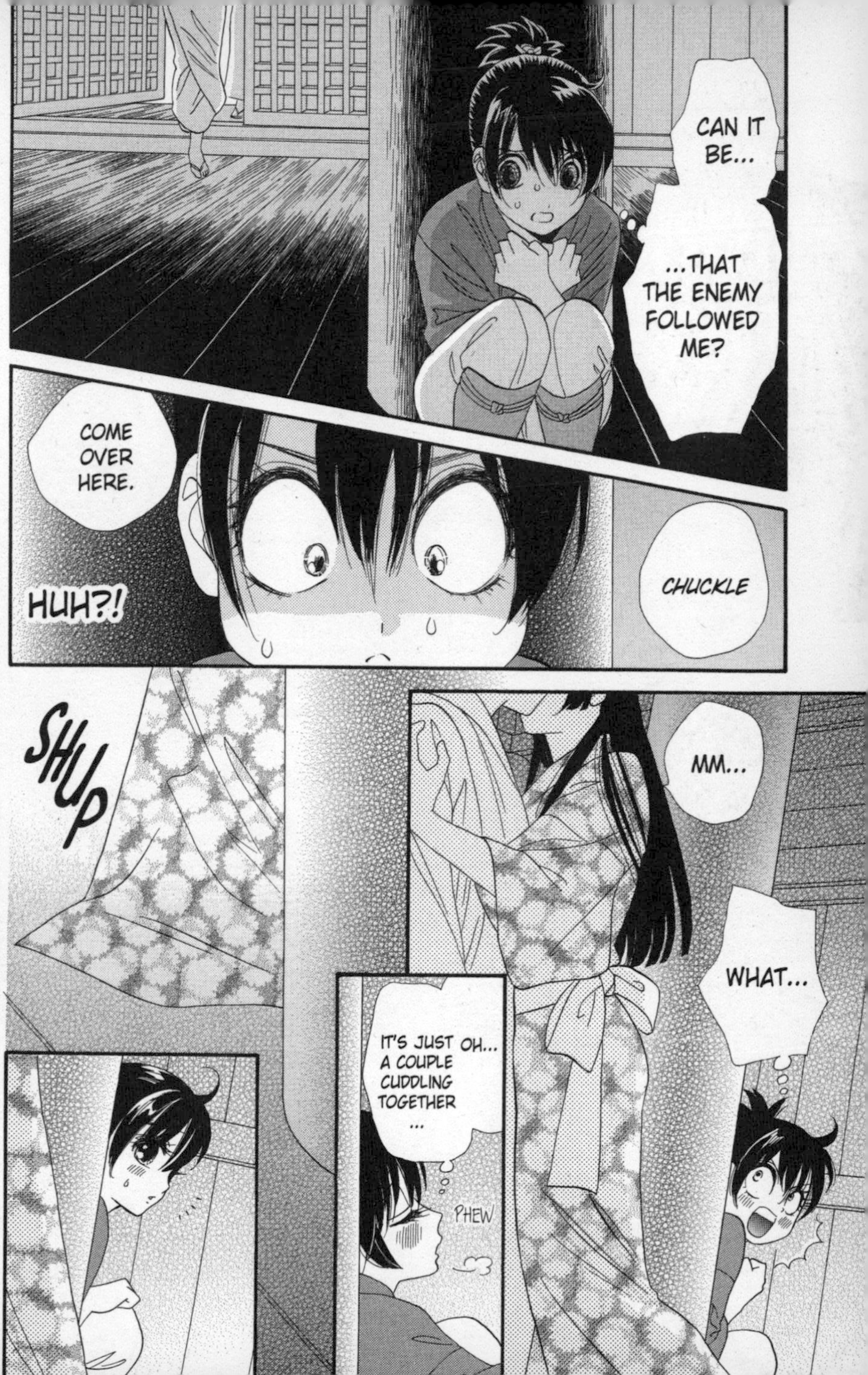
CAN IT BE...
...THAT THE ENEMY FOLLOWED ME?
CHUCKLE
COME OVER HERE.
HUH?!
MM...
WHAT...
SHUP
OH...
IT'S JUST A COUPLE CUDDLING TOGETHER ...
PHEW

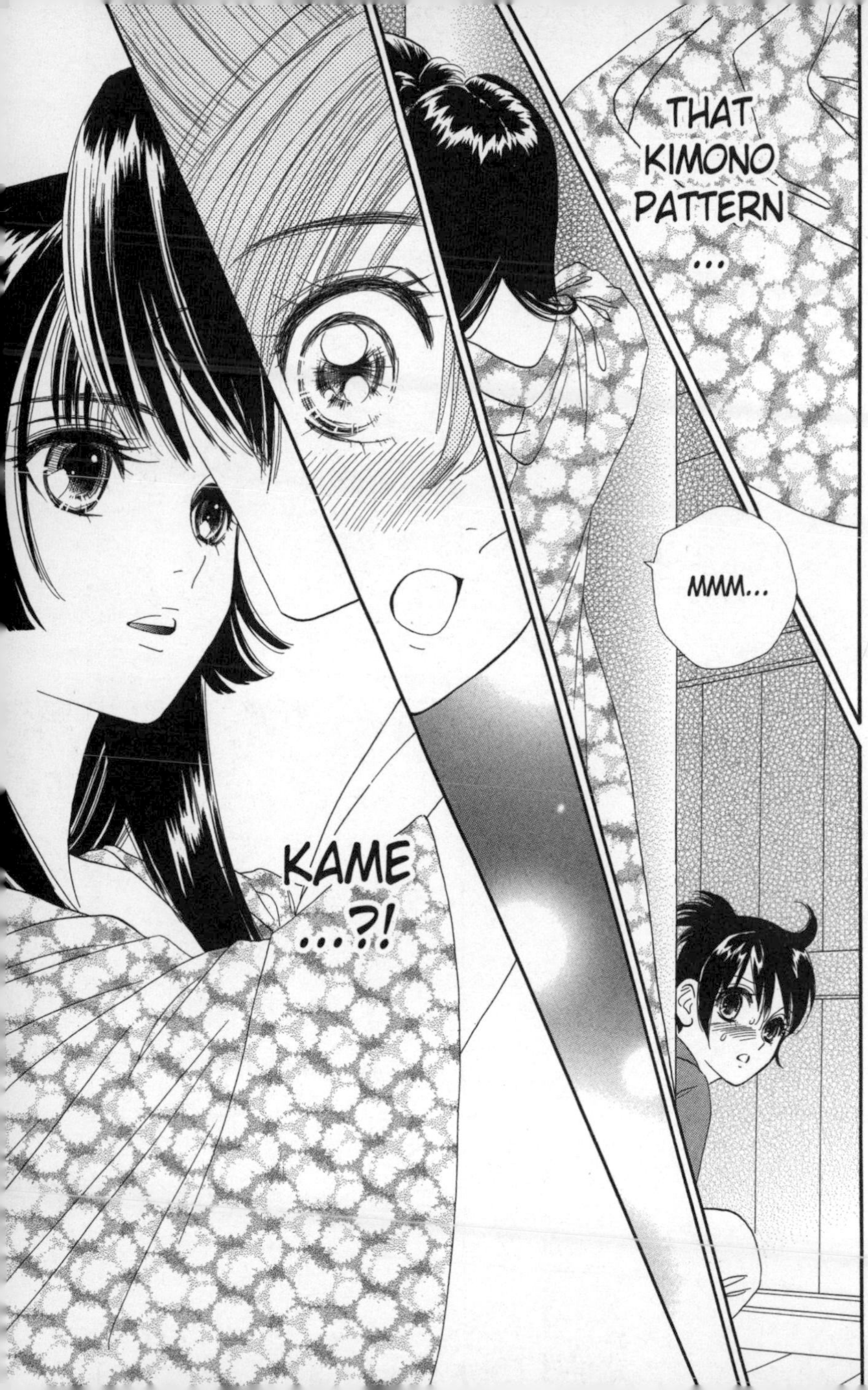
THAT KIMONO PATTERN ...
MMM...
KAME ...?!

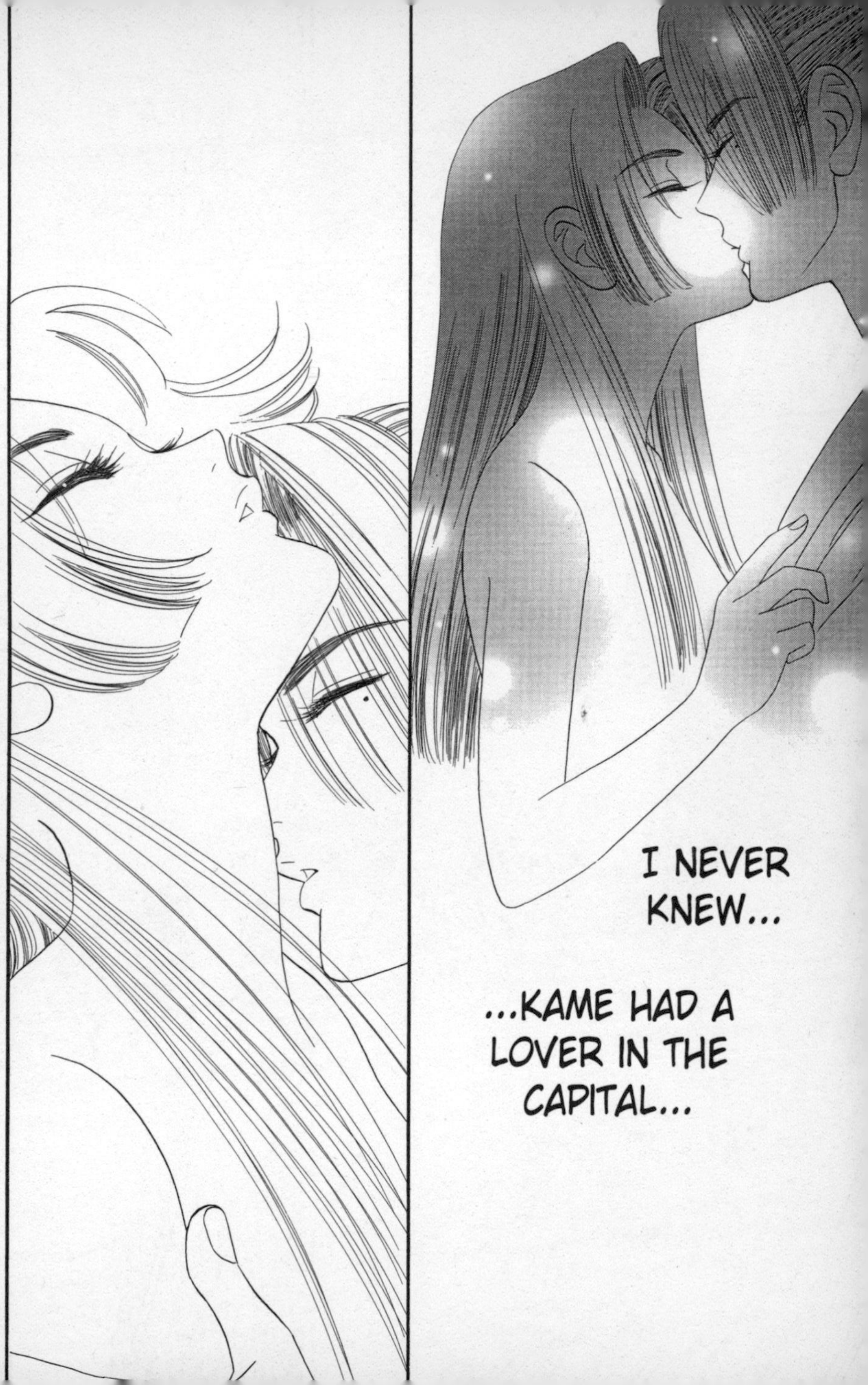
I NEVER KNEW...
...KAME HAD A LOVER IN THE CAPITAL...

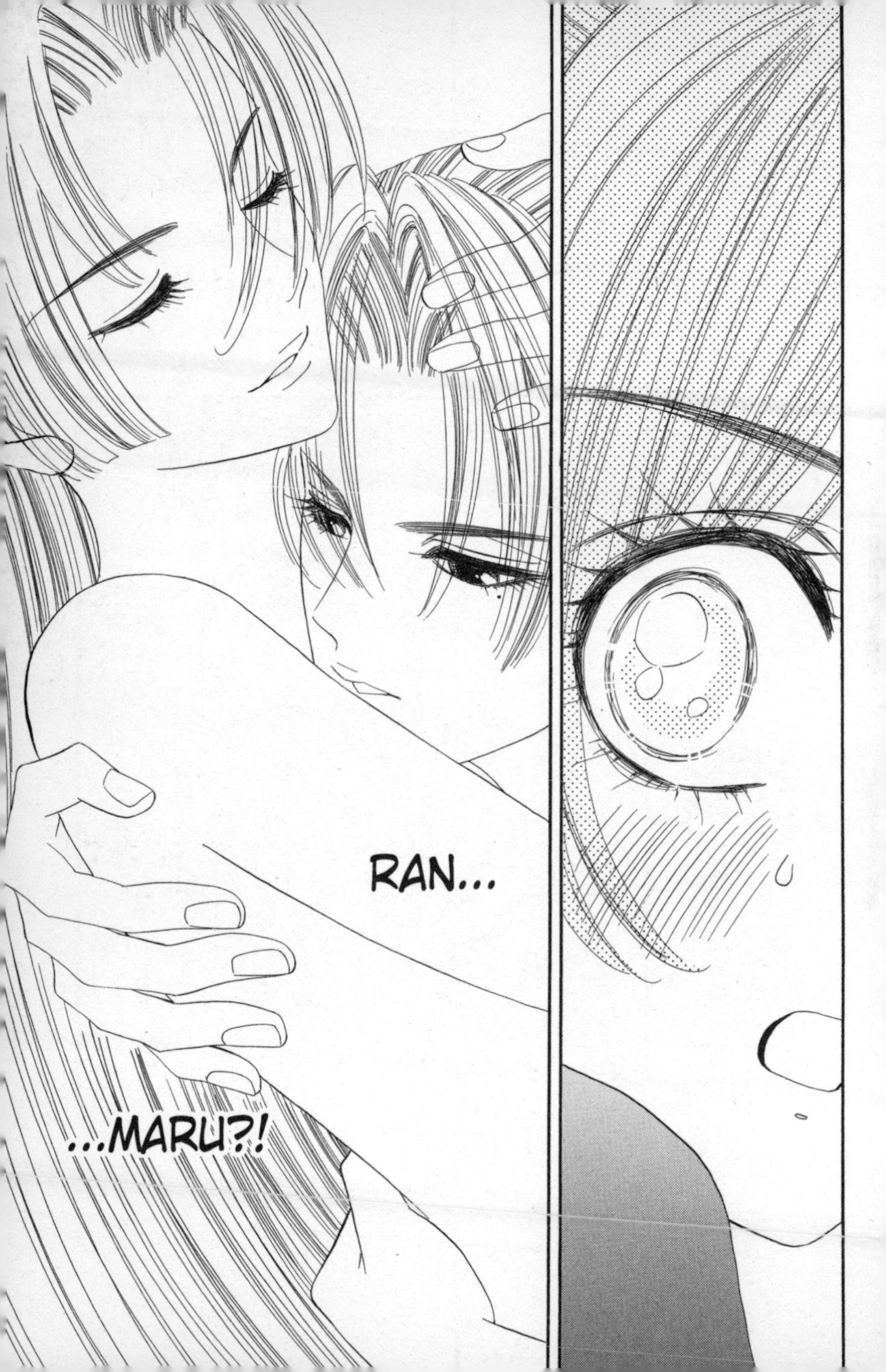
RAN...
...MARU?!

TAIL OF THE MOON EXTRA: TODAY'S MISSION

"I WANT TO SEE HANZO AND HANZOU IN SHINSENGUMI CLOTHES!"

-MAIKO KOTAKEMORI, OKAYAMA PREFECTURE

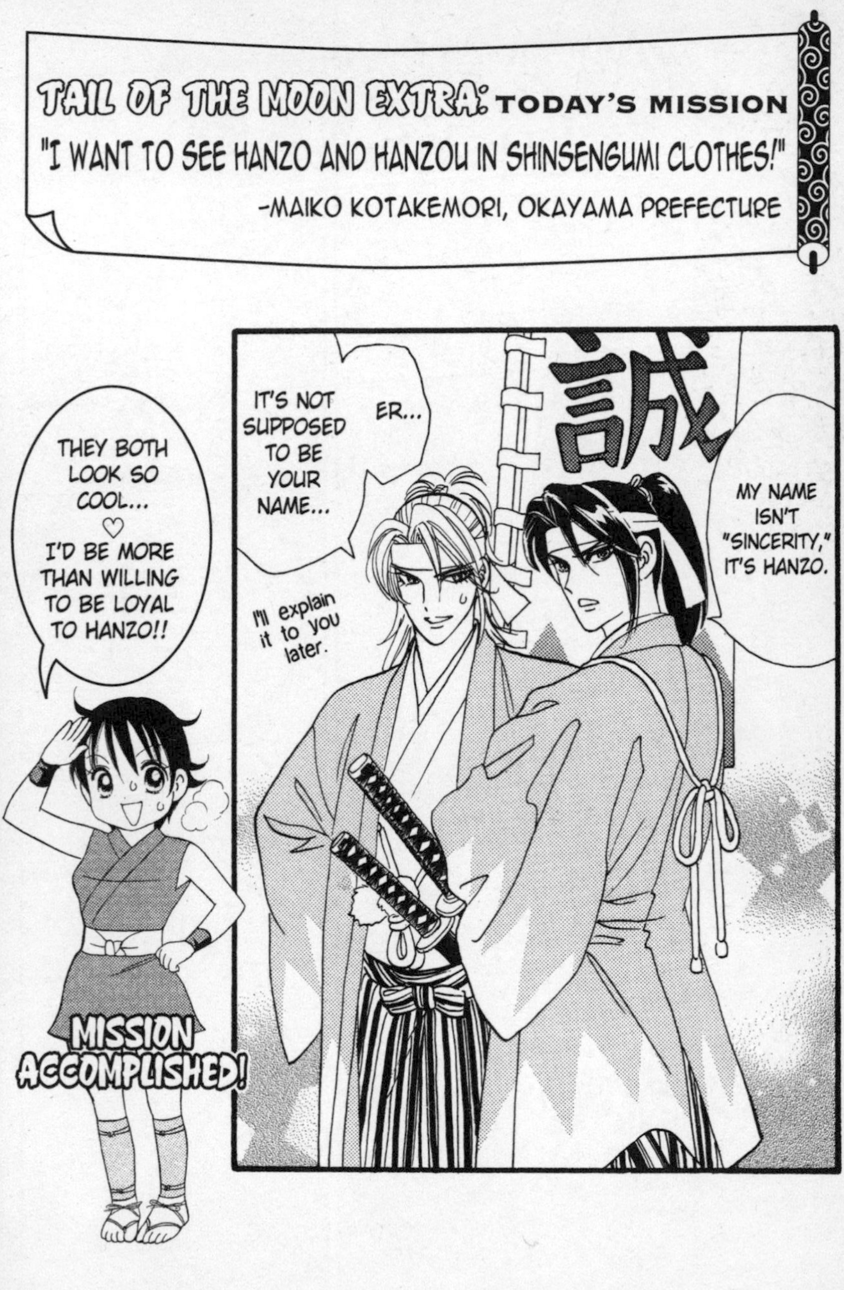

誠
MY NAME ISN'T "SINCERITY," IT'S HANZO.
ER...
IT'S NOT SUPPOSED TO BE YOUR NAME...
I'll explain it to you later.
THEY BOTH LOOK SO COOL... ♡ I'D BE MORE THAN WILLING TO BE LOYAL TO HANZO!!
MISSION ACCOMPLISHED!

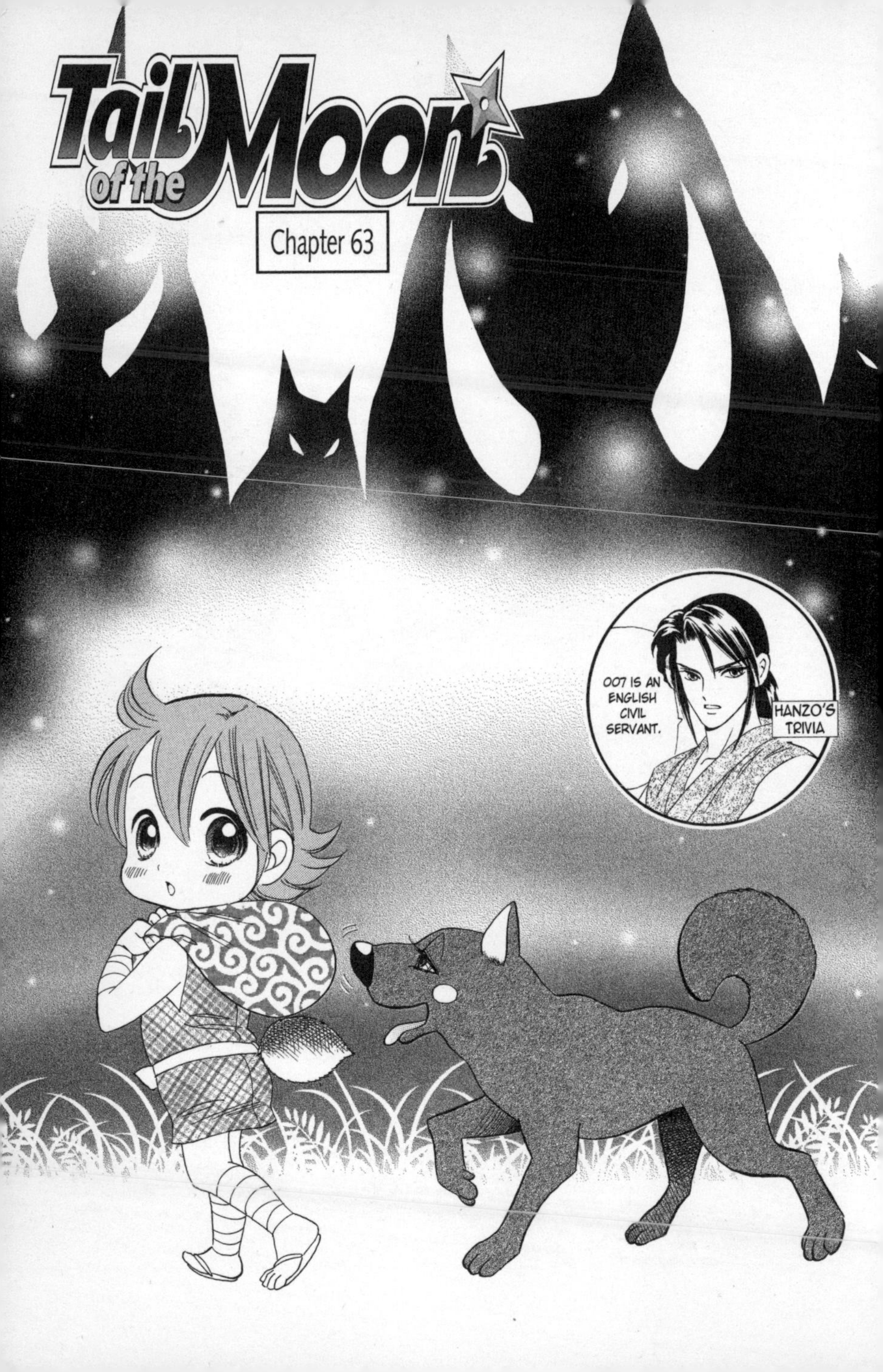
Tail of the Moon 5
Chapter 63
007 IS AN ENGLISH CIVIL SERVANT.
HANZO'S TRIVIA

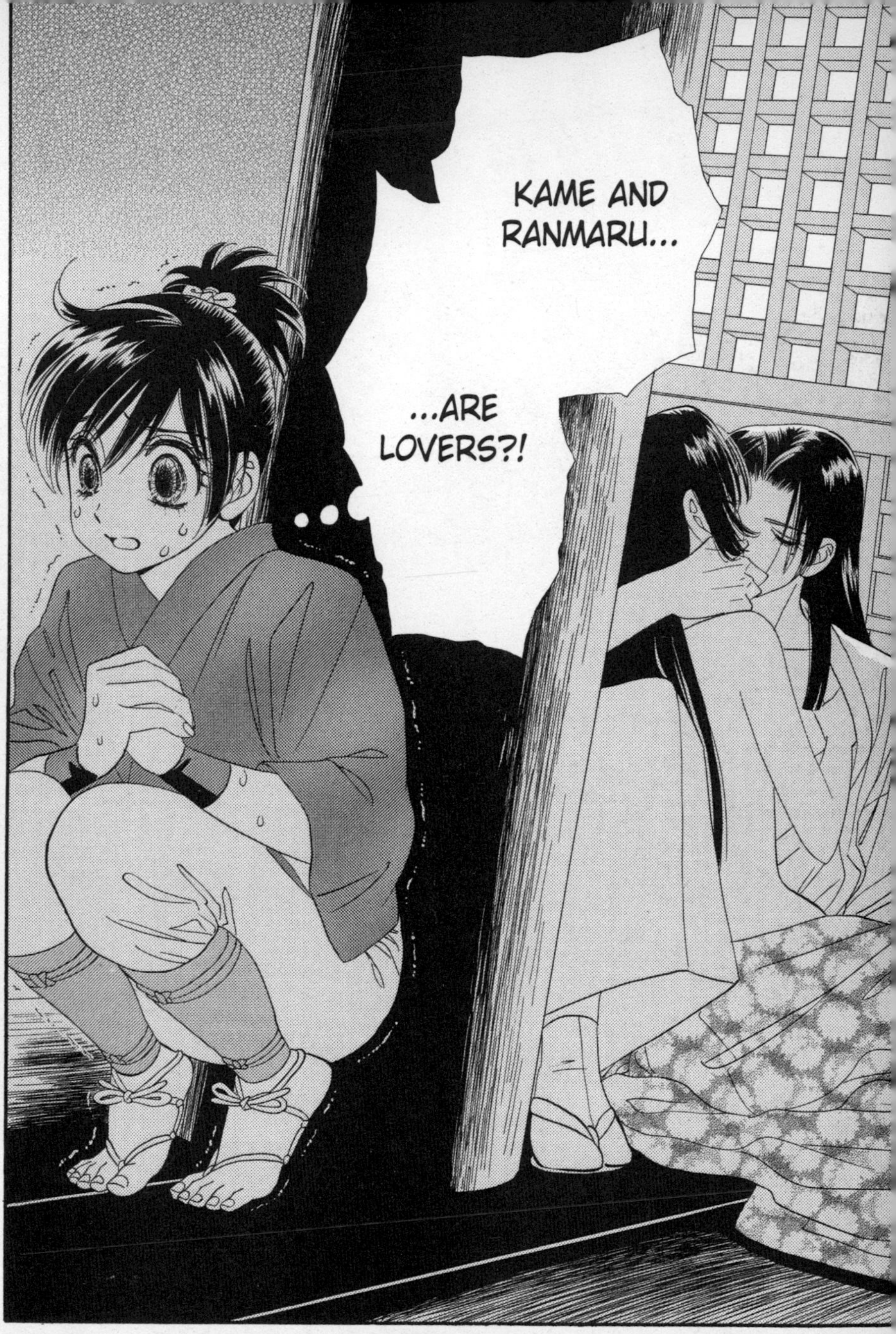
KAME AND RANMARU...
...ARE LOVERS?!
...

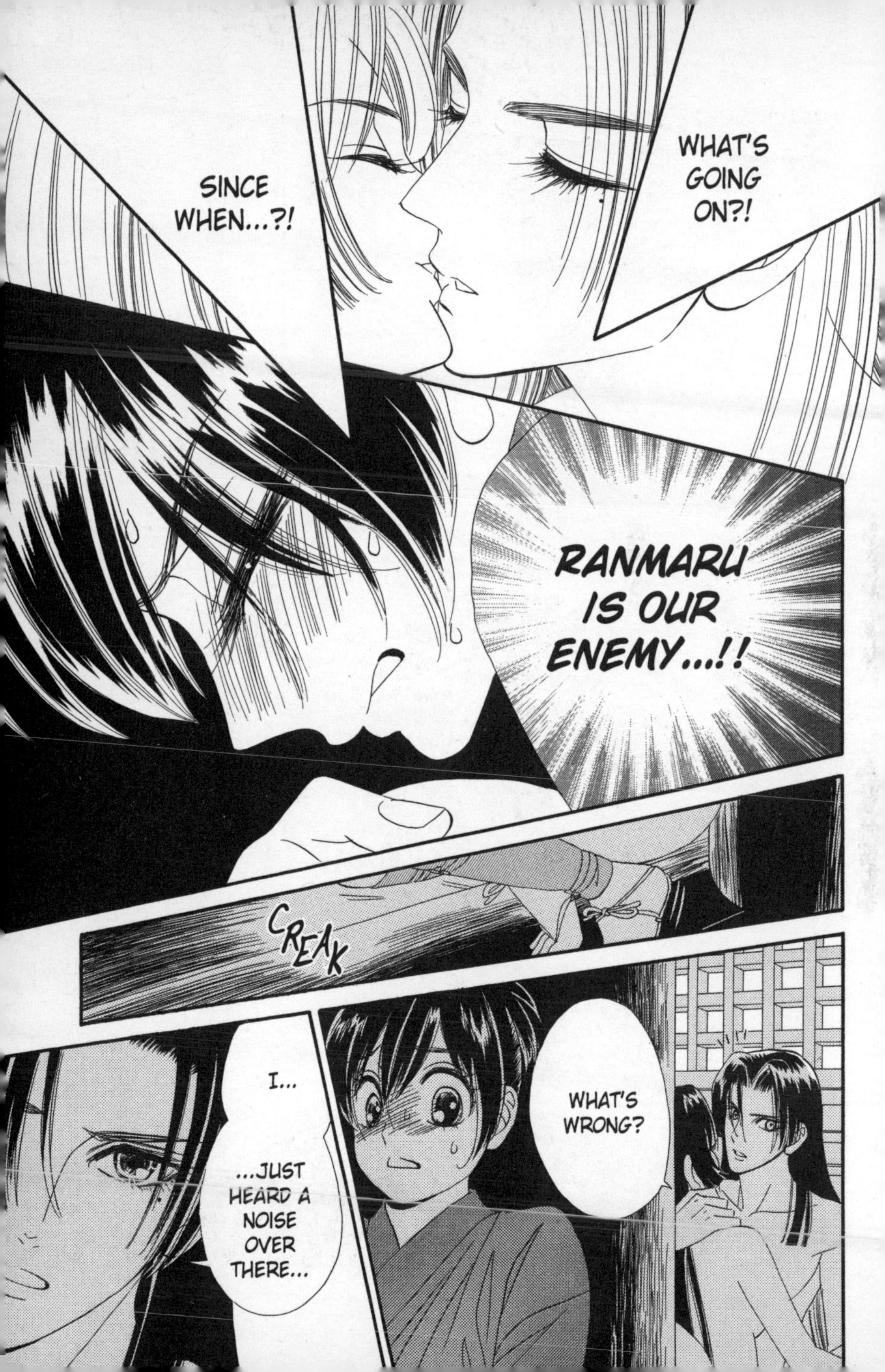
WHAT'S GOING ON?!
SINCE WHEN...?!
RANMARU IS OUR ENEMY...!!
CREAK
WHAT'S WRONG?
I...
...JUST HEARD A NOISE OVER THERE...

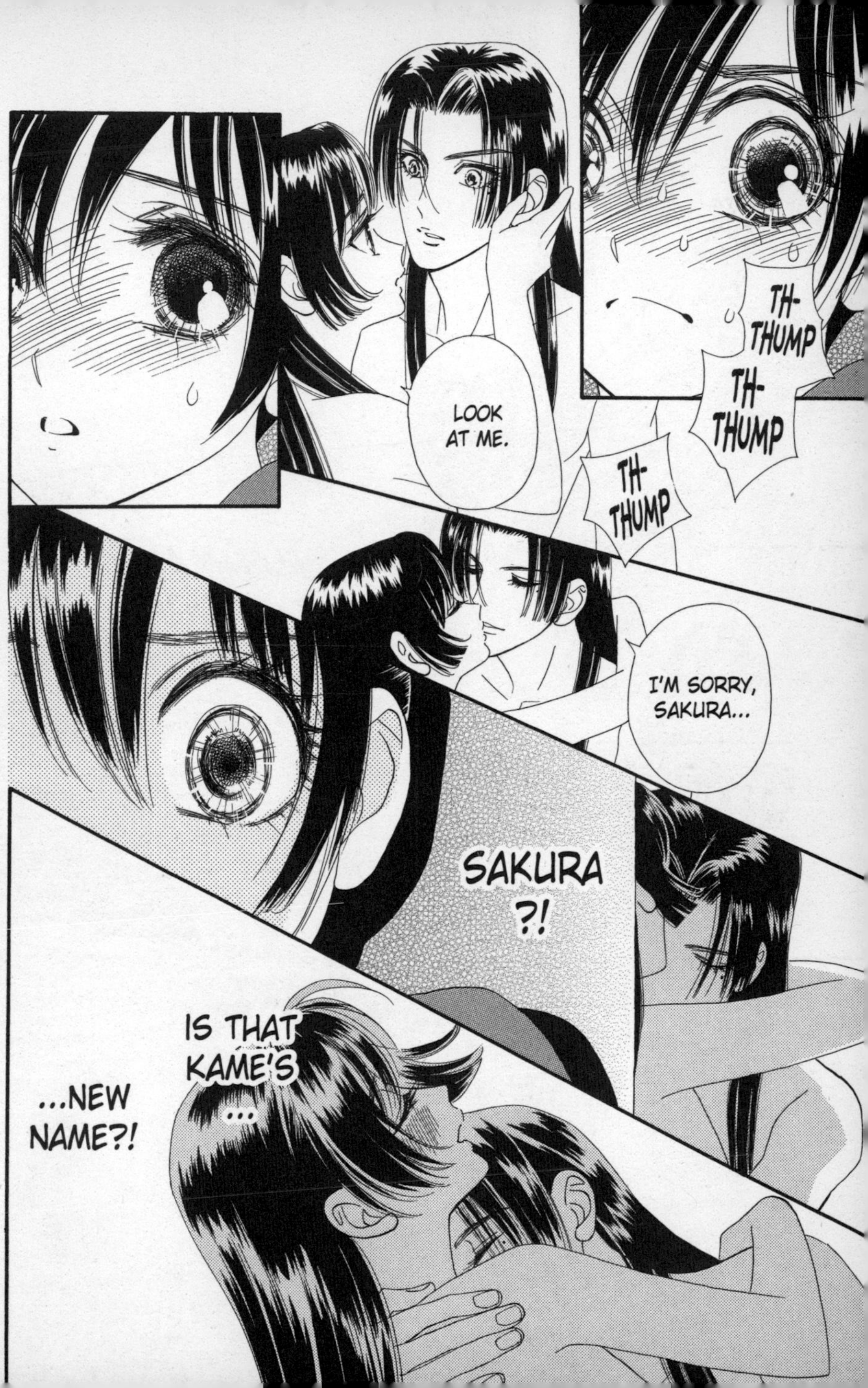
TH-THUMP
TH-THUMP
TH-THUMP
LOOK AT ME.
I'M SORRY, SAKURA...
SAKURA?!
IS THAT KAME'S...
...NEW NAME?!

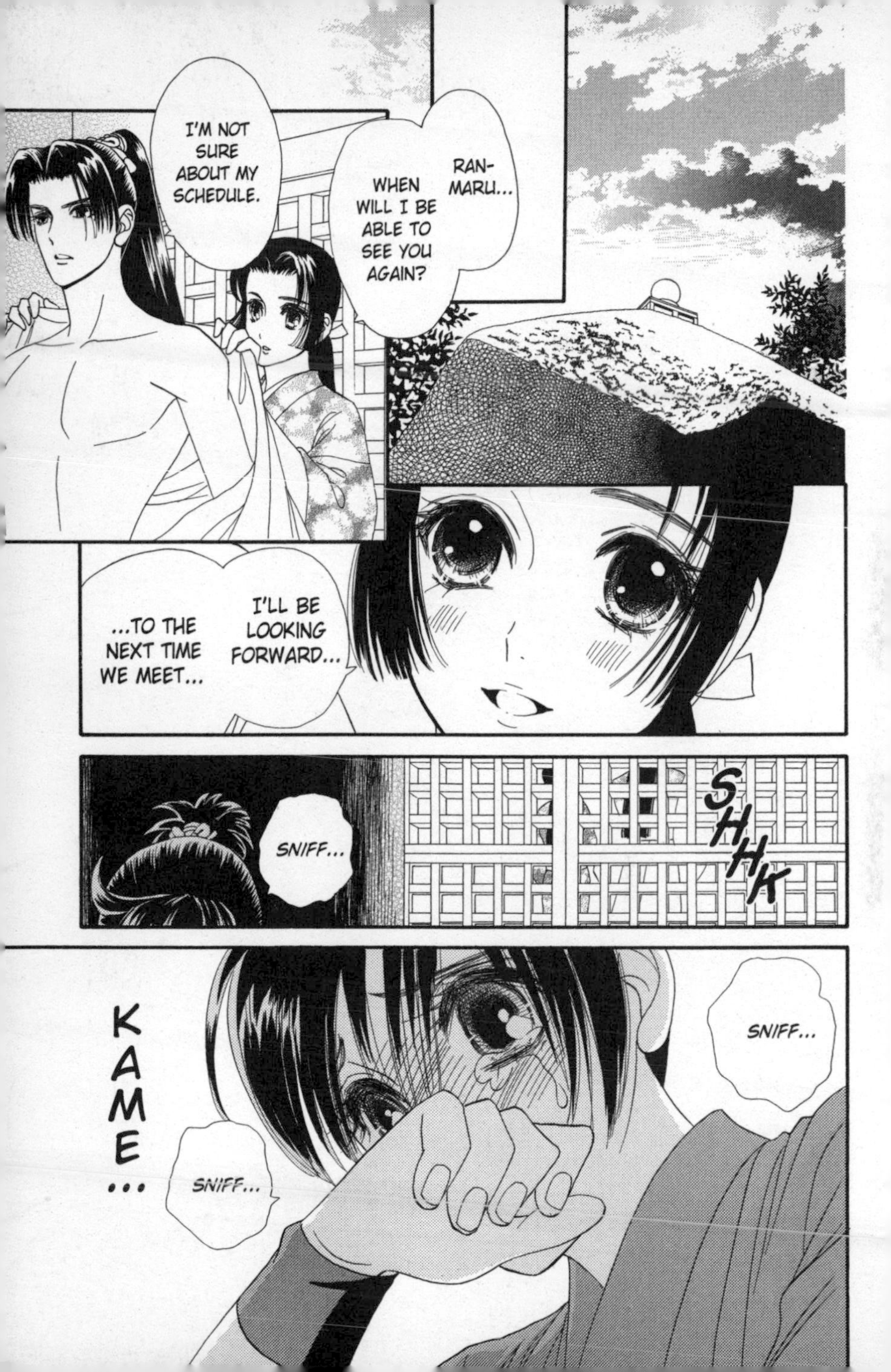

RAN-MARU... WHEN WILL I BE ABLE TO SEE YOU AGAIN?
I'M NOT SURE ABOUT MY SCHEDULE.
I'LL BE LOOKING FORWARD...
...TO THE NEXT TIME WE MEET...
SHHK
SNIFF...
SNIFF...
KAME...
SNIFF...

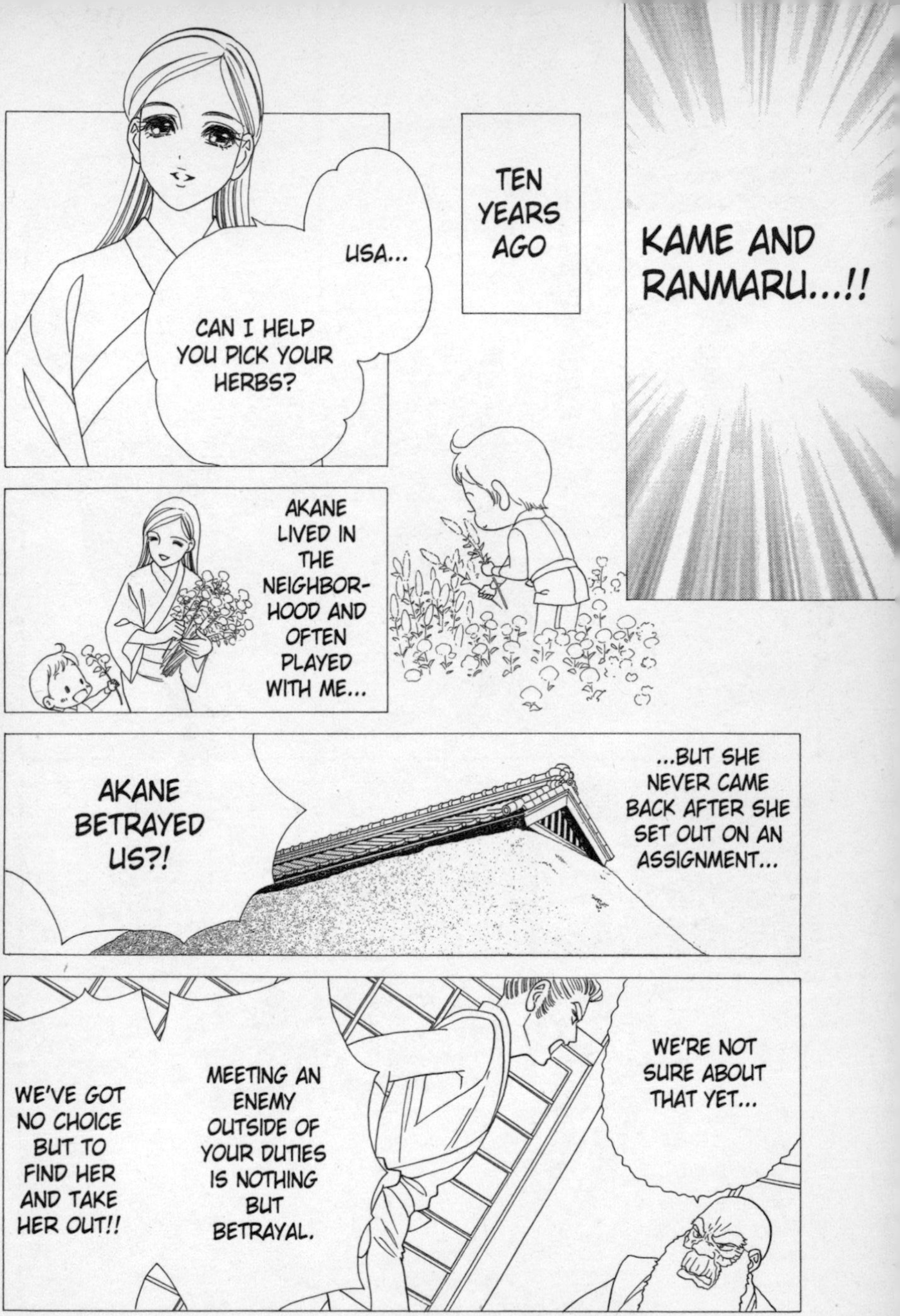
KAME AND RANMARU...!!
TEN YEARS AGO
USA...
CAN I HELP YOU PICK YOUR HERBS?
AKANE LIVED IN THE NEIGHBOR-HOOD AND OFTEN PLAYED WITH ME...
...BUT SHE NEVER CAME BACK AFTER SHE SET OUT ON AN ASSIGNMENT...
AKANE BETRAYED US?!
WE'RE NOT SURE ABOUT THAT YET...
MEETING AN ENEMY OUTSIDE OF YOUR DUTIES IS NOTHING BUT BETRAYAL.
WE'VE GOT NO CHOICE BUT TO FIND HER AND TAKE HER OUT!!

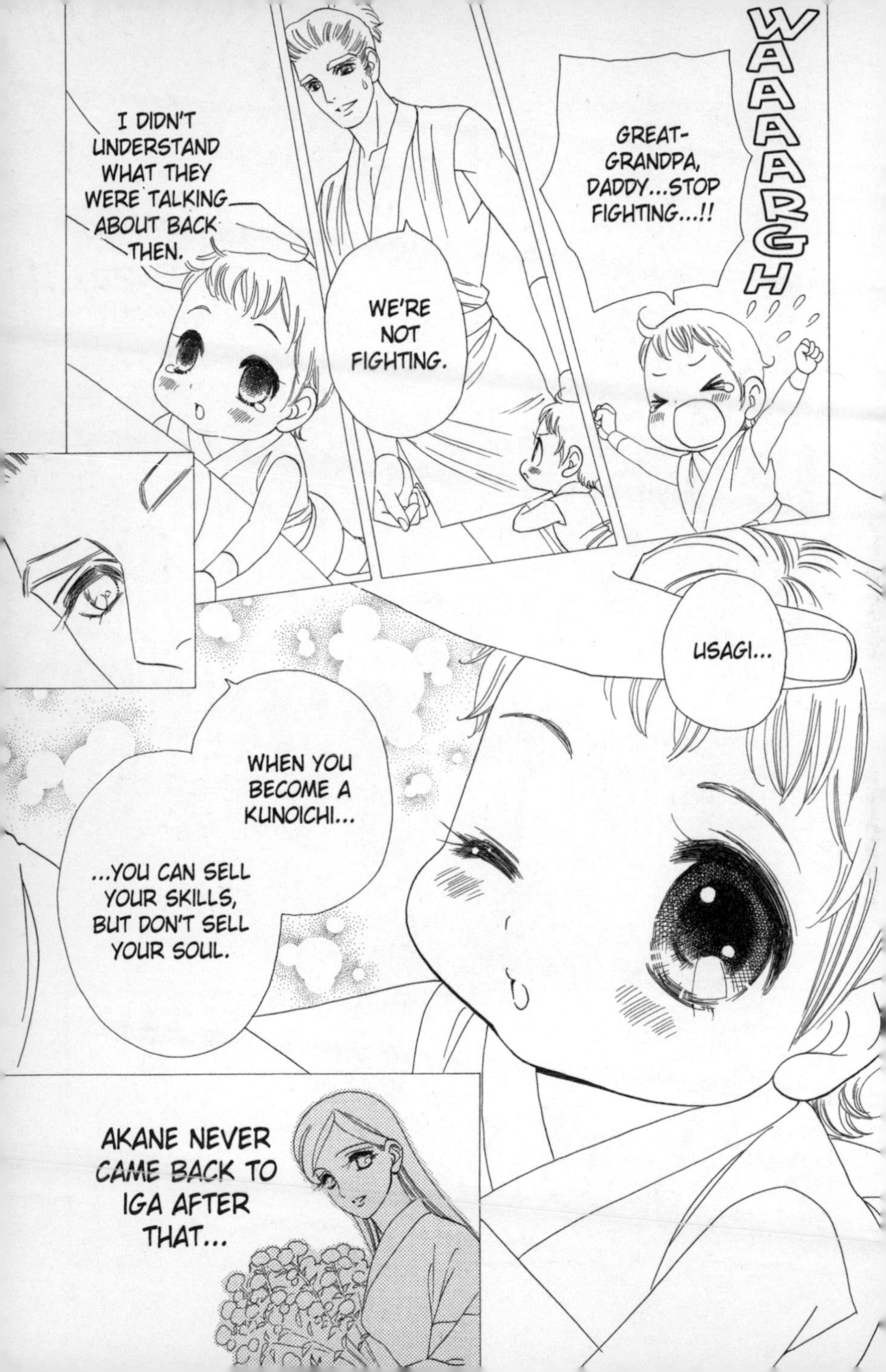
WAAAARGH
GREAT-GRANDPA, DADDY...STOP FIGHTING...!!
WE'RE NOT FIGHTING.
I DIDN'T UNDERSTAND WHAT THEY WERE TALKING ABOUT BACK THEN.
USAGI...
WHEN YOU BECOME A KUNOICHI...
...YOU CAN SELL YOUR SKILLS, BUT DON'T SELL YOUR SOUL.
AKANE NEVER CAME BACK TO IGA AFTER THAT...

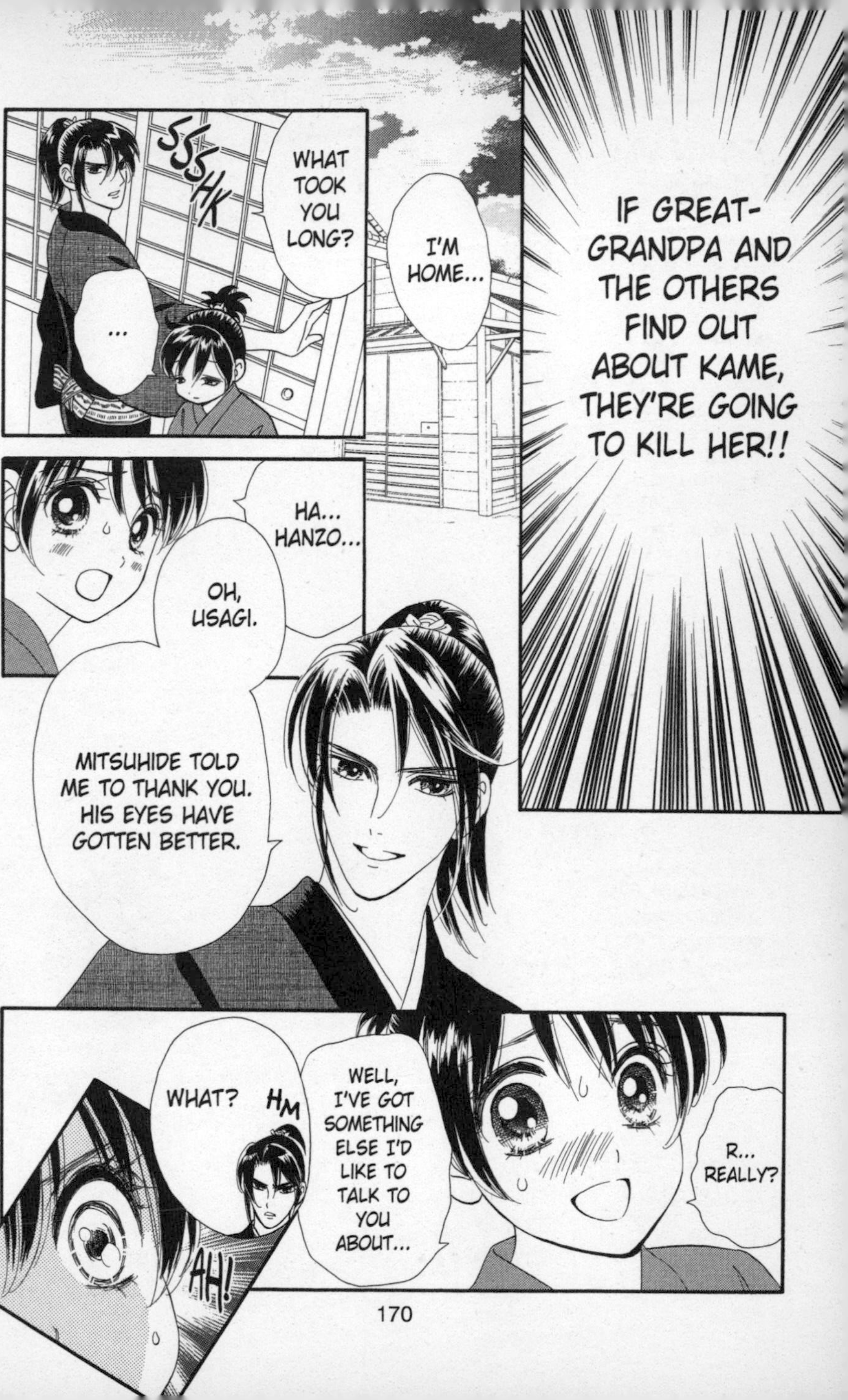
IF GREAT-GRANDPA AND THE OTHERS FIND OUT ABOUT KAME, THEY'RE GOING TO KILL HER!!
I'M HOME...
WHAT TOOK YOU LONG?
SSSHK
...
HA... HANZO...
OH, USAGI.
MITSUHIDE TOLD ME TO THANK YOU. HIS EYES HAVE GOTTEN BETTER.
R... REALLY?
WELL, I'VE GOT SOMETHING ELSE I'D LIKE TO TALK TO YOU ABOUT...
HM
WHAT?
AH!

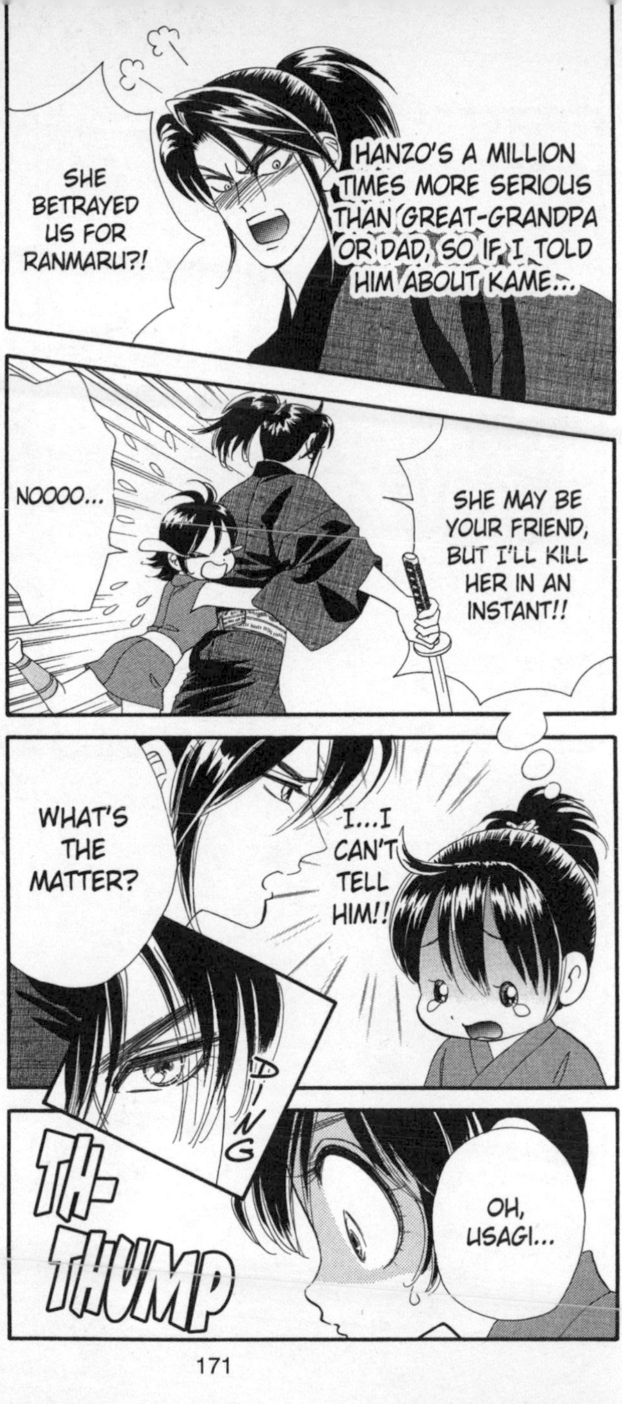
HANZO'S A MILLION TIMES MORE SERIOUS THAN GREAT-GRANDPA OR DAD, SO IF I TOLD HIM ABOUT KAME...
SHE BETRAYED US FOR RANMARU?!
SHE MAY BE YOUR FRIEND, BUT I'LL KILL HER IN AN INSTANT!!
NOOOO...
I...I CAN'T TELL HIM!!
WHAT'S THE MATTER?
OH, USAGI...
DING
TH-THUMP

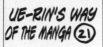

UE-RIN'S WAY OF THE MANGA 21

So in the end, the original manga for my debut became history, and the one-shot I had to redraw from scratch was introduced to the world as my debut piece. It wasn't until a few years later that I realized that making my debut wasn't "the end goal of the way of the manga," but "the beginning of the true way of the manga."

To be continued...!!

Send your messages and letters to the following address. We're looking forward to your requests for the Extra Missions as well!

Rinko Ueda
C/O Shojo Beat
Viz Media
P.O. Box 77010
San Francisco, CA
94107

Rinko Ueda

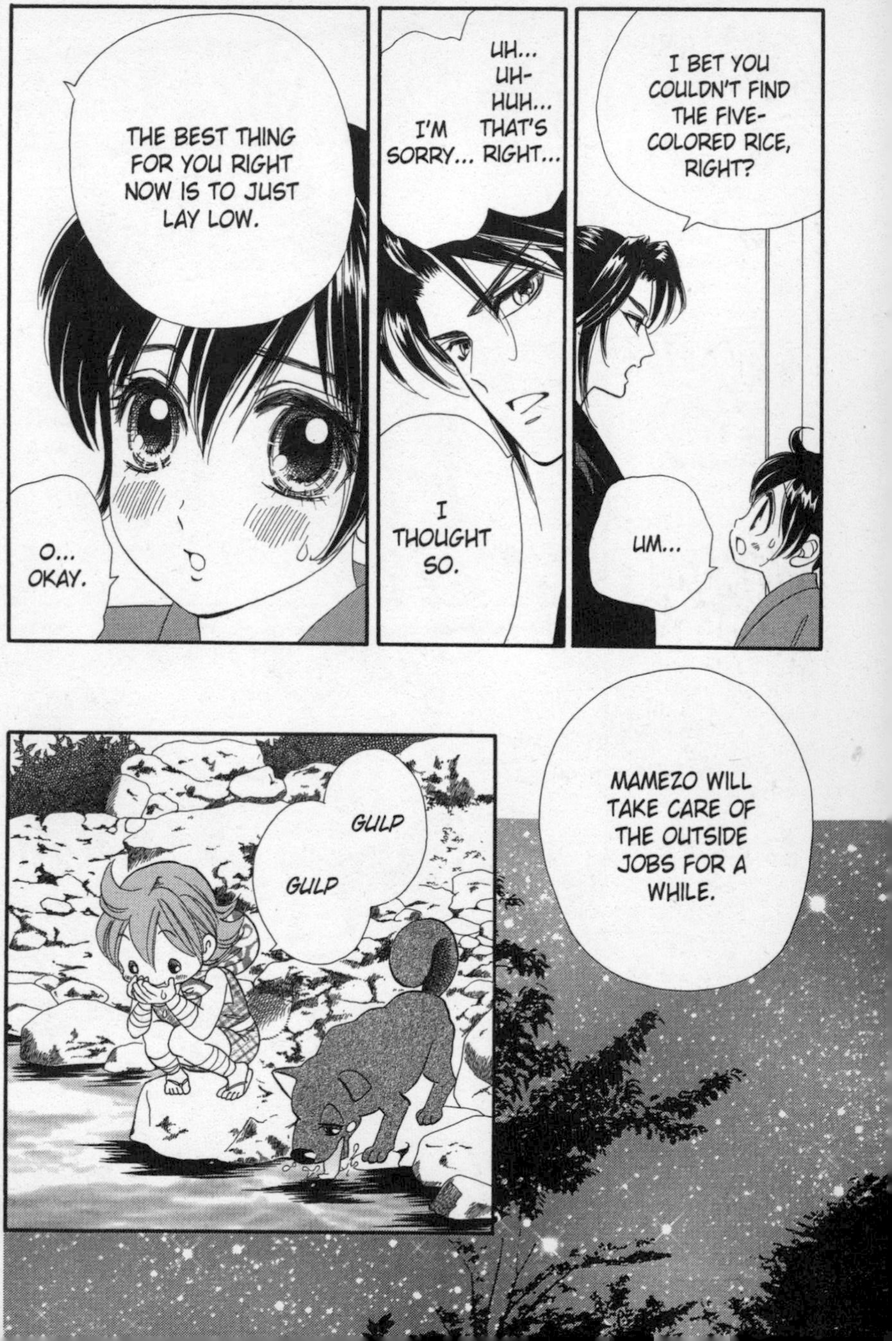
I BET YOU COULDN'T FIND THE FIVE-COLORED RICE, RIGHT?
UM...
UH... UH-HUH... THAT'S RIGHT...
I'M SORRY...
I THOUGHT SO.
THE BEST THING FOR YOU RIGHT NOW IS TO JUST LAY LOW.
O... OKAY.
MAMEZO WILL TAKE CARE OF THE OUTSIDE JOBS FOR A WHILE.
GULP
GULP

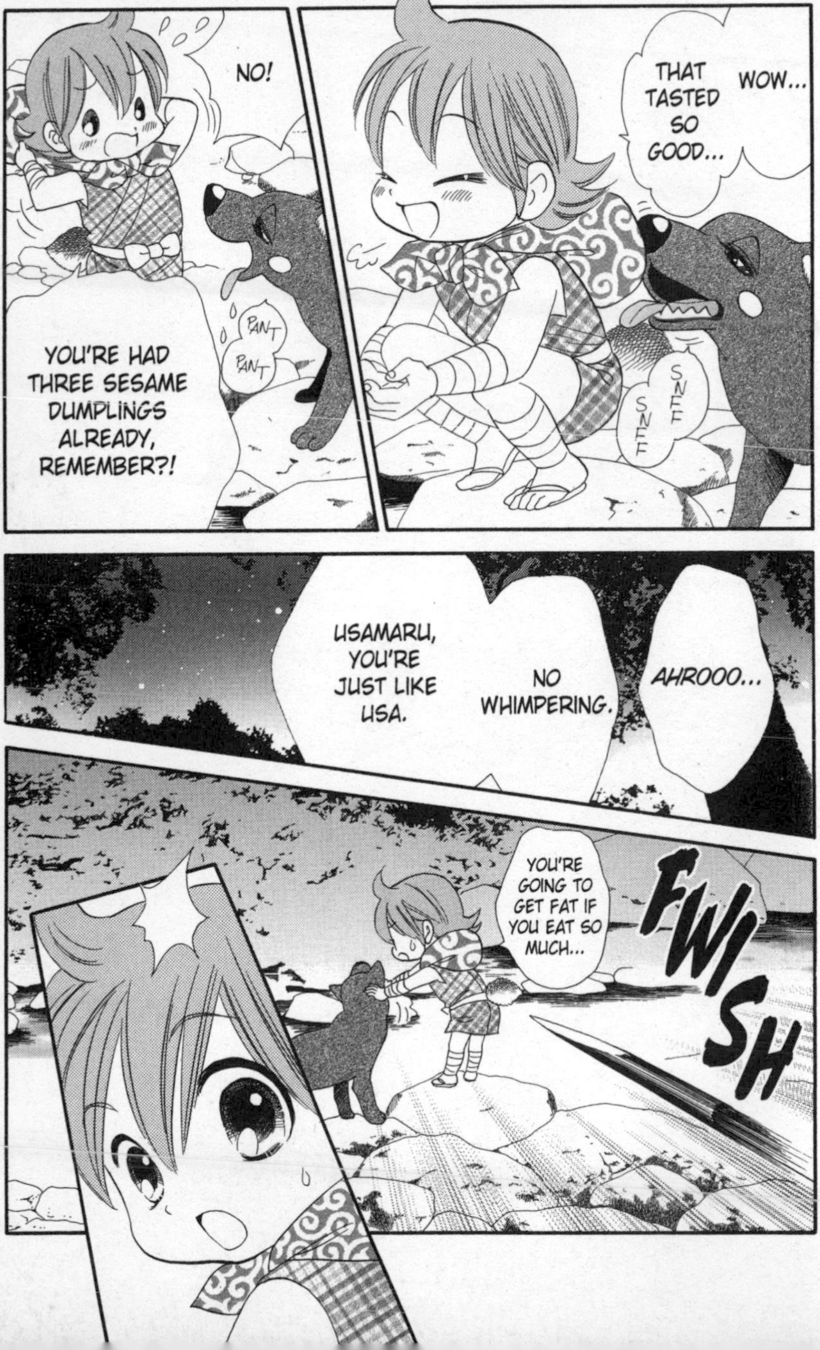
WOW...
THAT TASTED SO GOOD...
SNFF SNFF
NO!
PANT PANT
YOU'RE HAD THREE SESAME DUMPLINGS ALREADY, REMEMBER?!
AHROOO...
NO WHIMPERING.
USAMARU, YOU'RE JUST LIKE USA.
FWISH
YOU'RE GOING TO GET FAT IF YOU EAT SO MUCH...

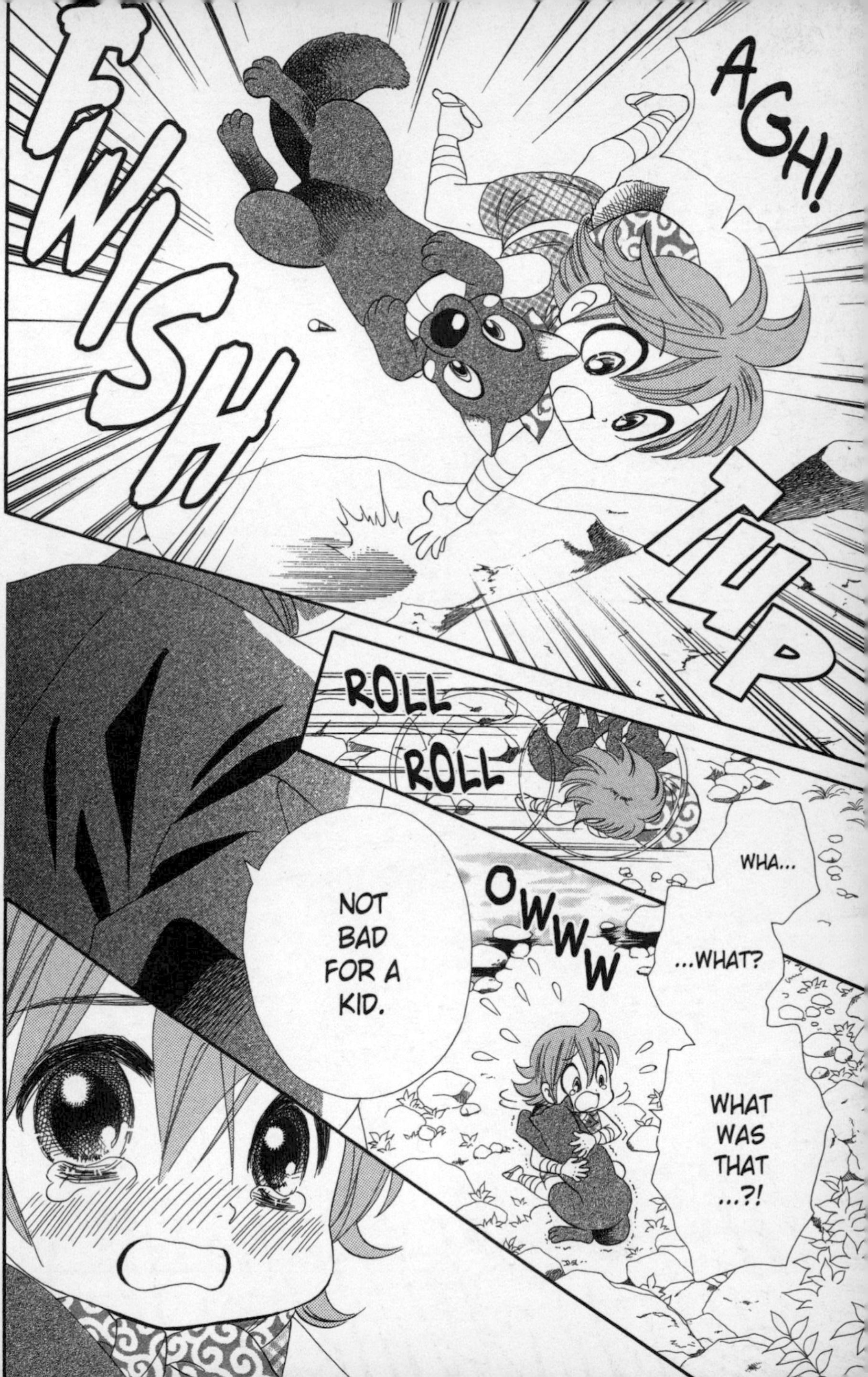
AGH!
FWISH
THUP
ROLL
ROLL
OWWW
WHA...
...WHAT?
WHAT WAS THAT ...?!
NOT BAD FOR A KID.

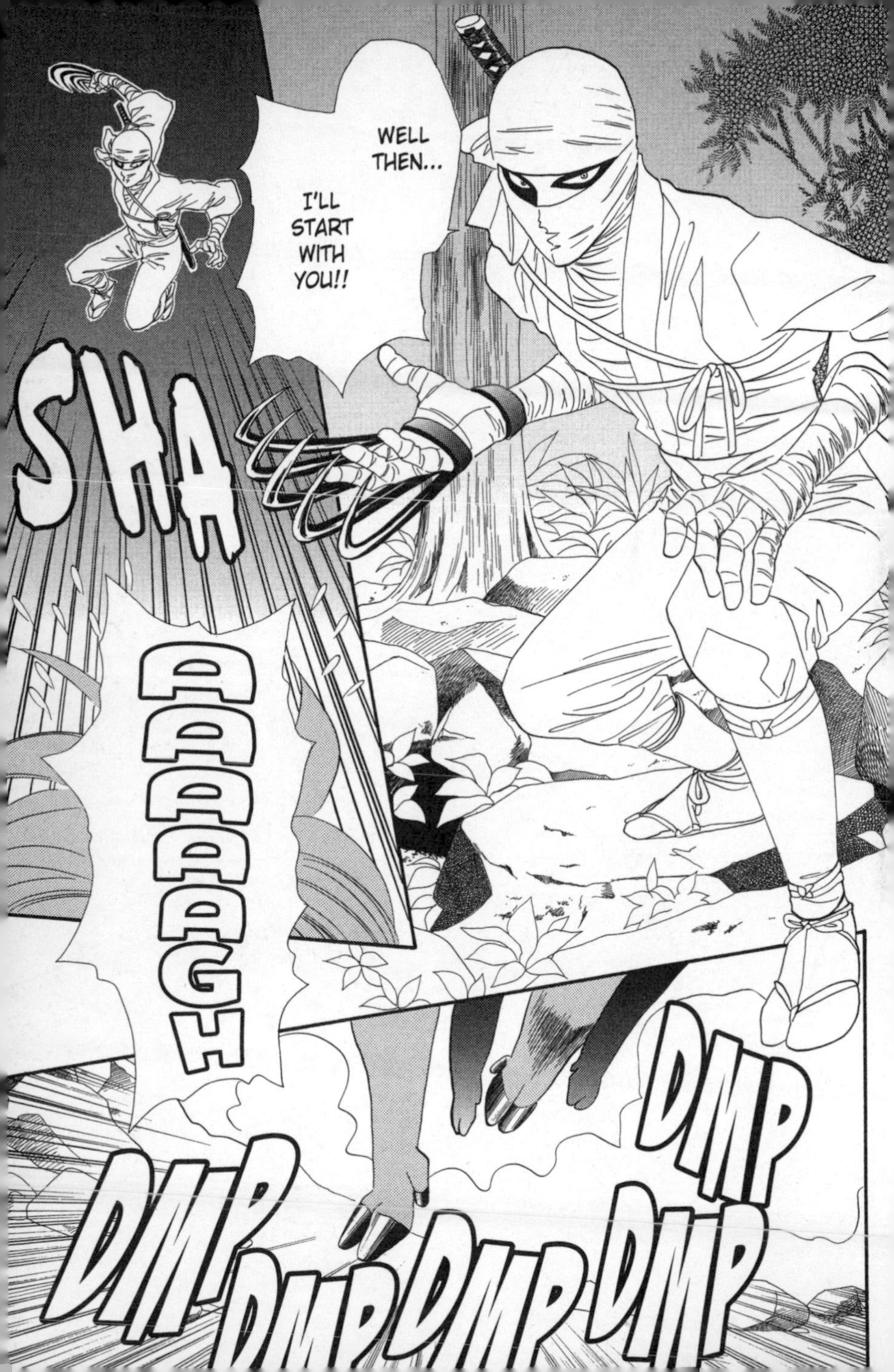
WELL THEN...
I'LL START WITH YOU!!
SHA
AAAAAAAGH
DMP
DMP
DMP DMP DMP DMP

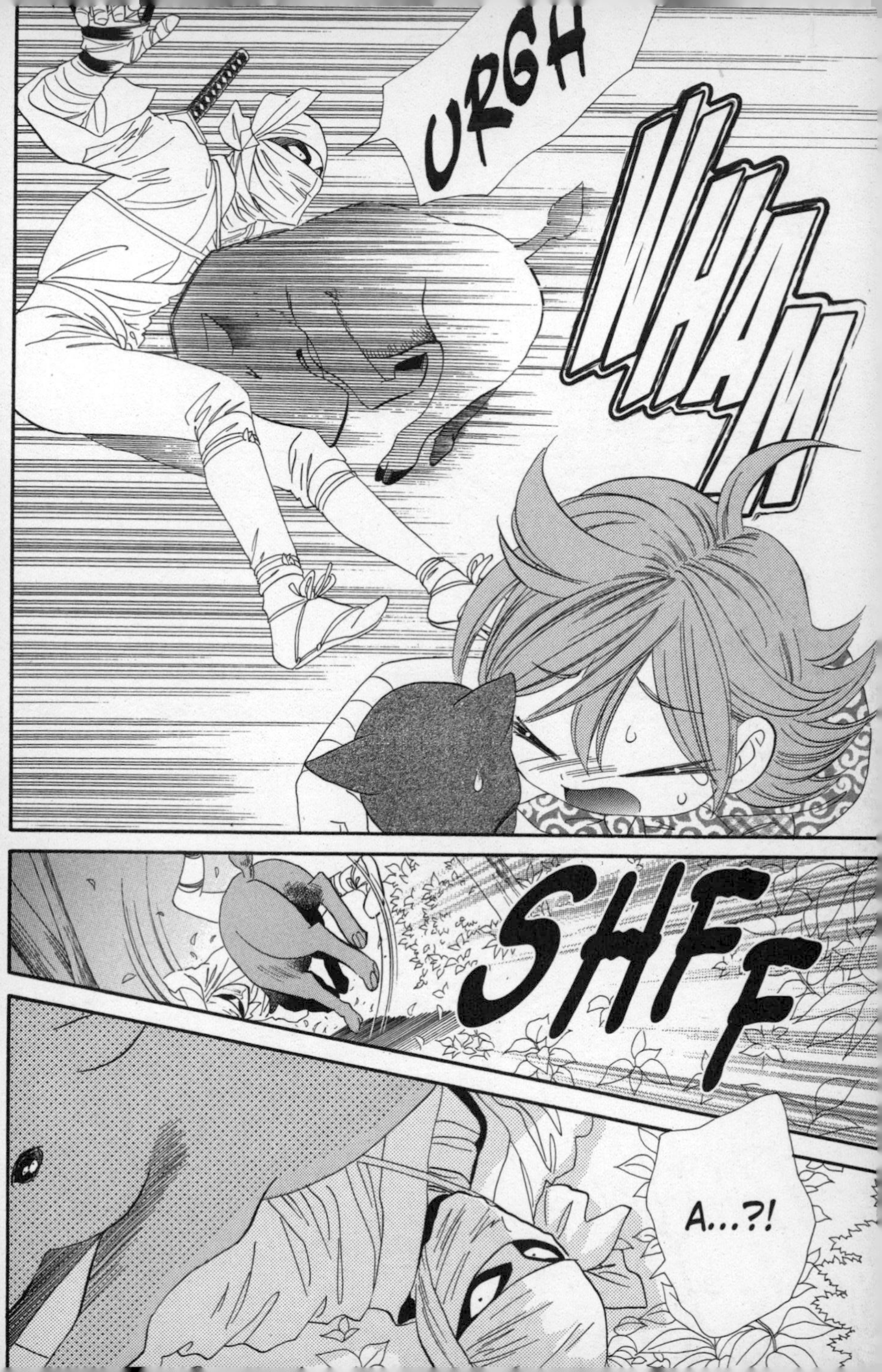
WHAM
URGH
SHFF
A...?!

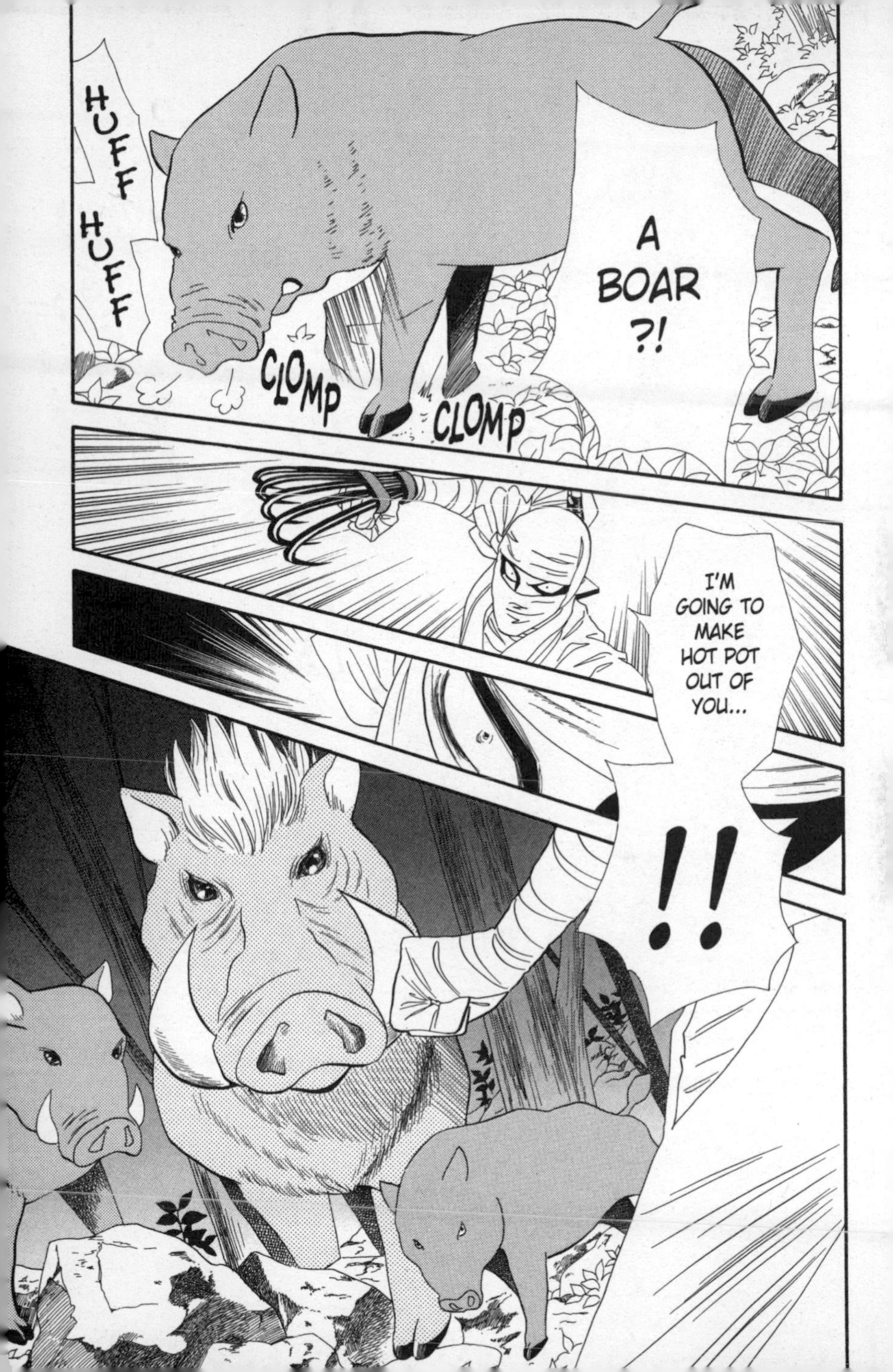
A BOAR ?!
HUFF HUFF
CLOMP CLOMP
I'M GOING TO MAKE HOT POT OUT OF YOU...
!!

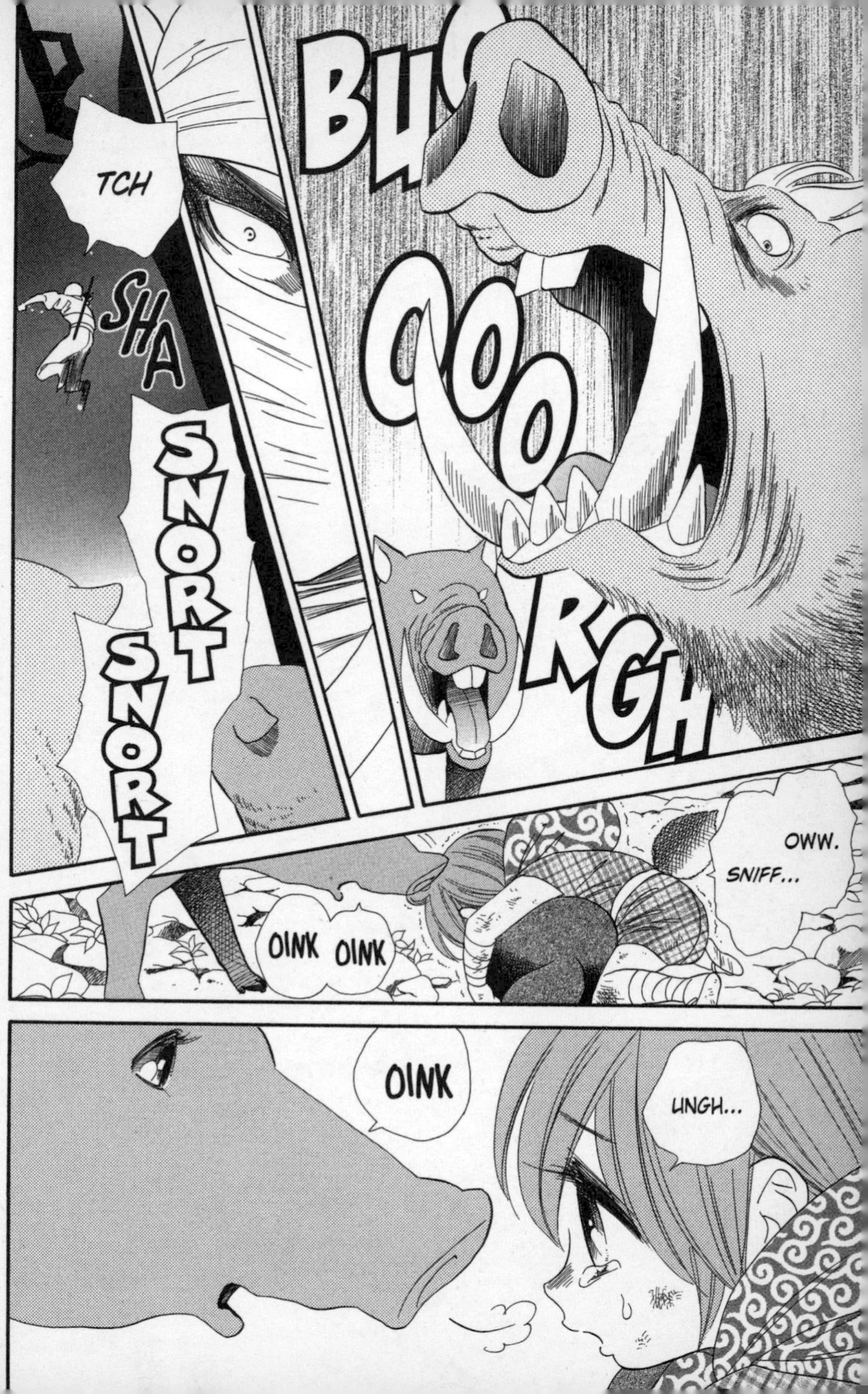
BUOOOORGH
SNORT
SNORT
TCH
SHA
OWW.
SNIFF...
OINK OINK
UNGH...
OINK

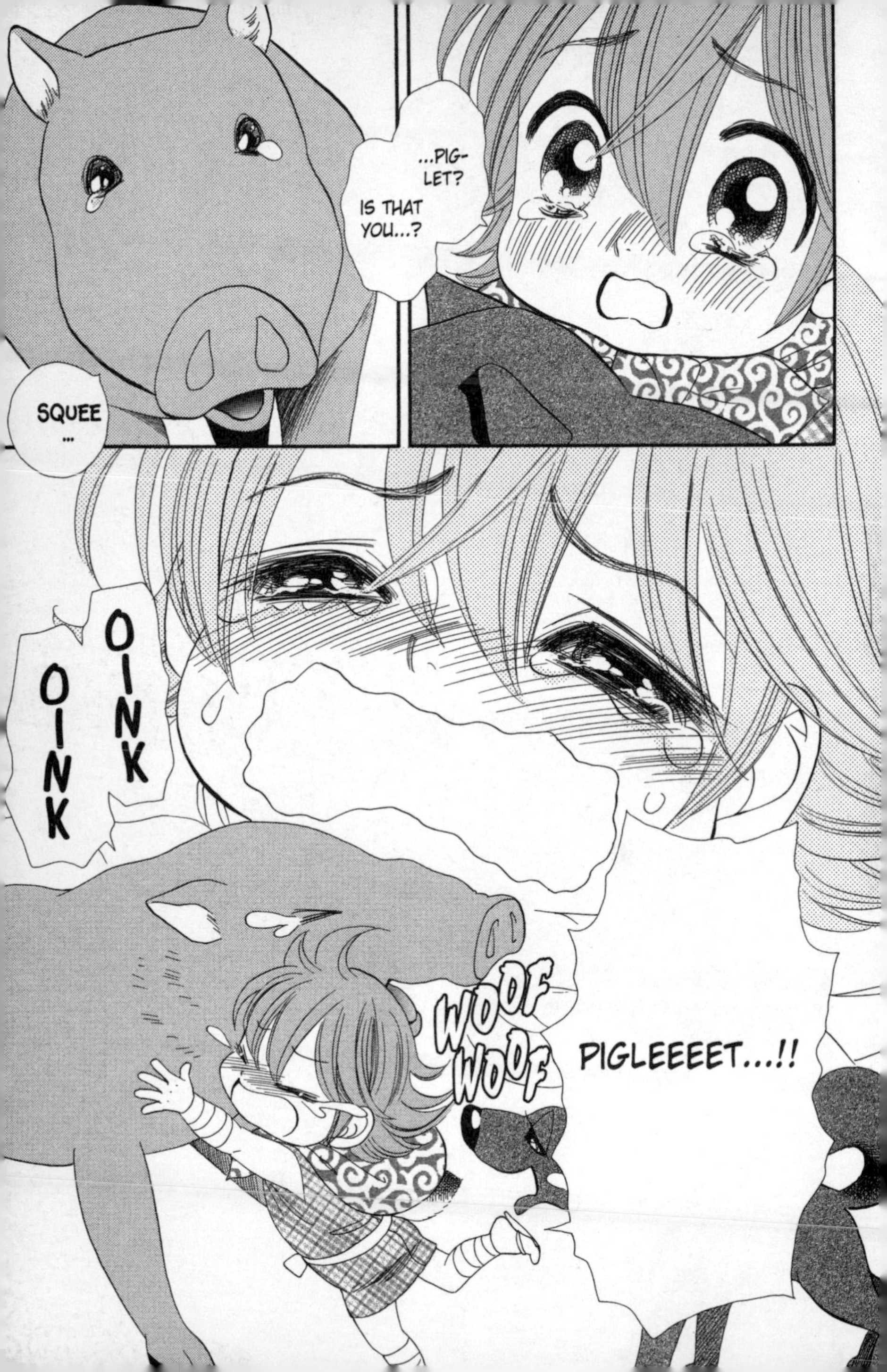
...PIG- LET? IS THAT YOU...?
SQUEE ...
OINK OINK
PIGLEEEET...!!
WOOF WOOF

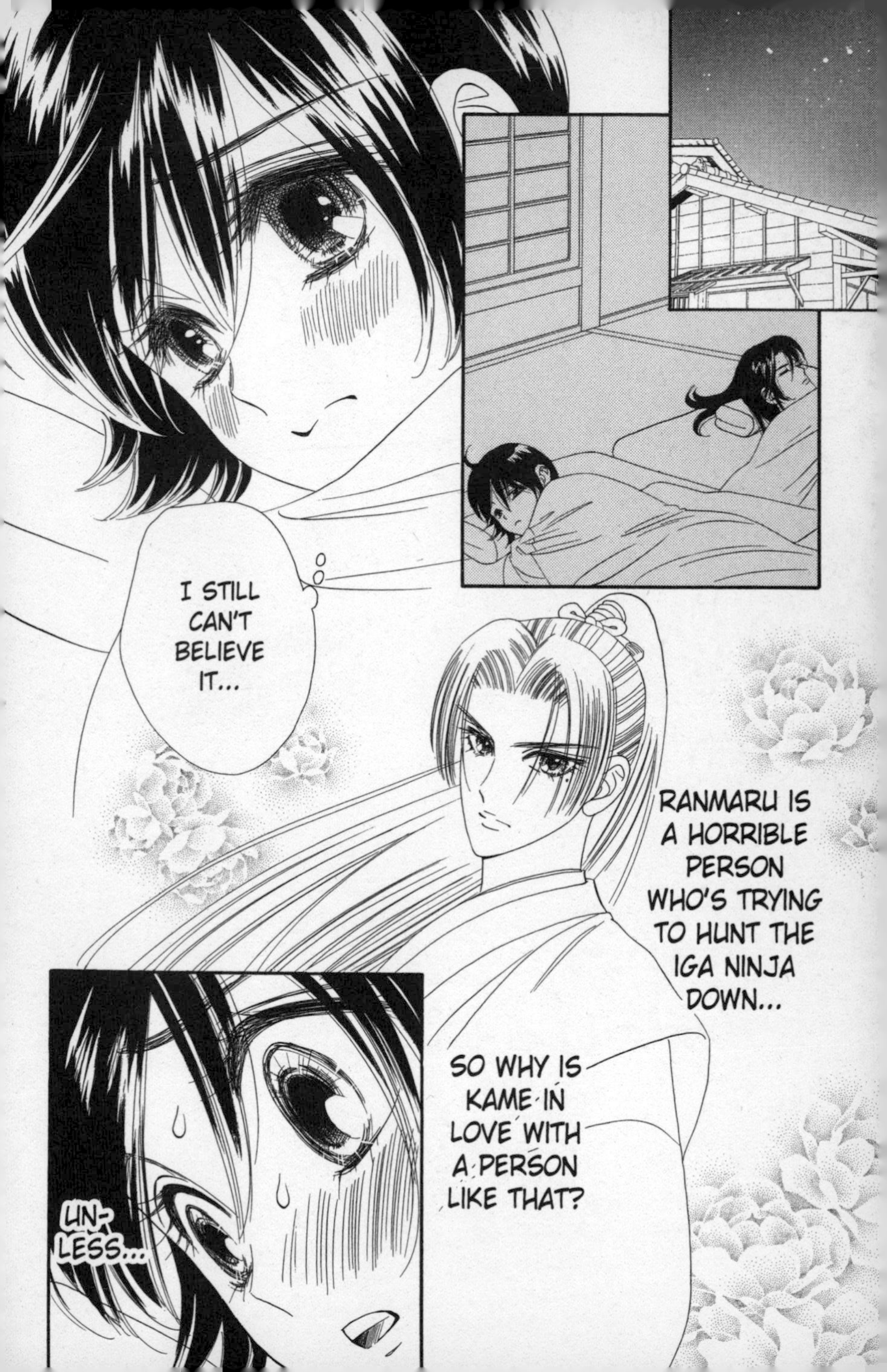
I STILL CAN'T BELIEVE IT...
RANMARU IS A HORRIBLE PERSON WHO'S TRYING TO HUNT THE IGA NINJA DOWN...
SO WHY IS KAME IN LOVE WITH A PERSON LIKE THAT?
UN-LESS...

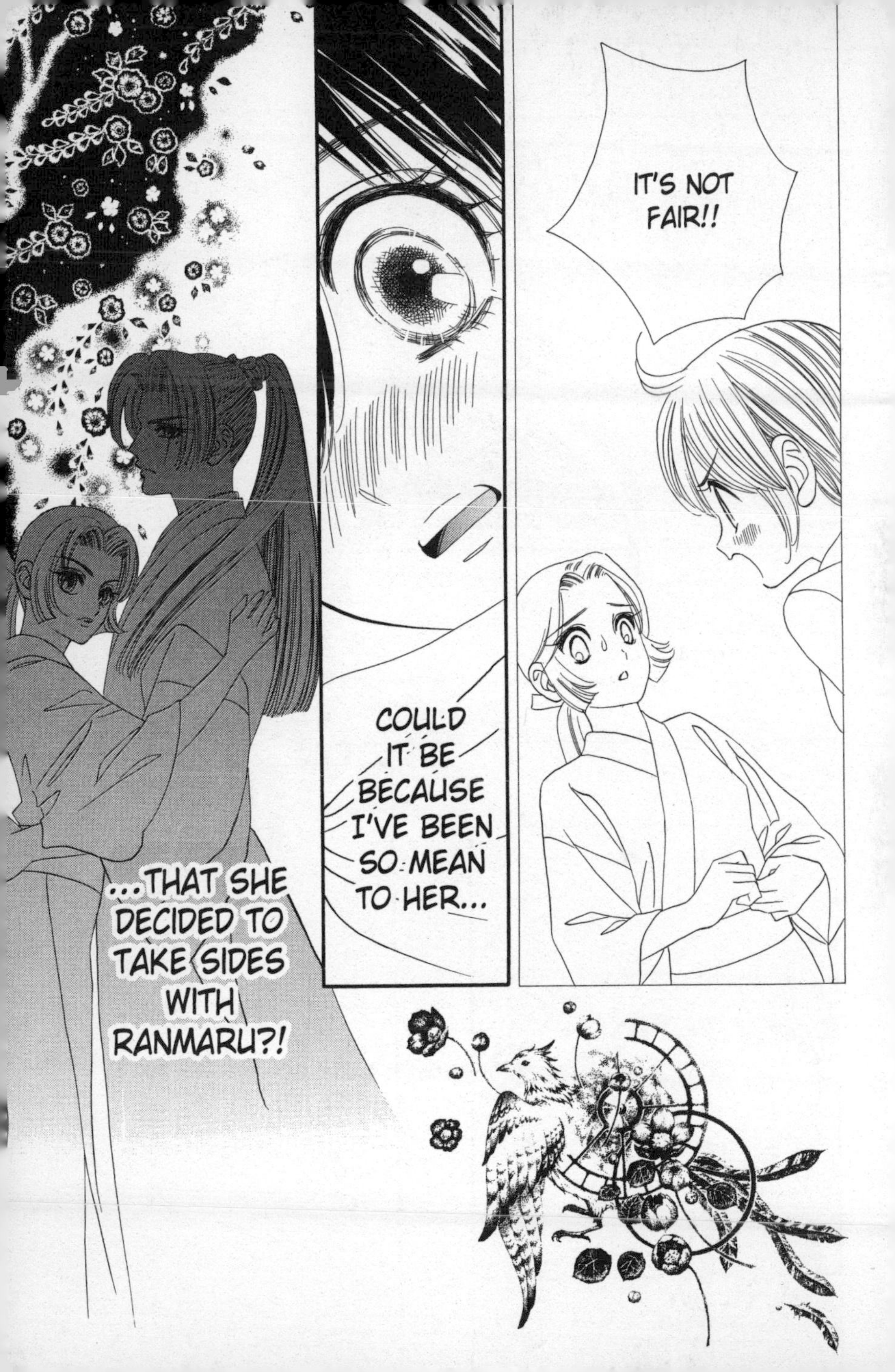
IT'S NOT FAIR!!
COULD IT BE BECAUSE I'VE BEEN SO MEAN TO HER...
...THAT SHE DECIDED TO TAKE SIDES WITH RANMARU?!

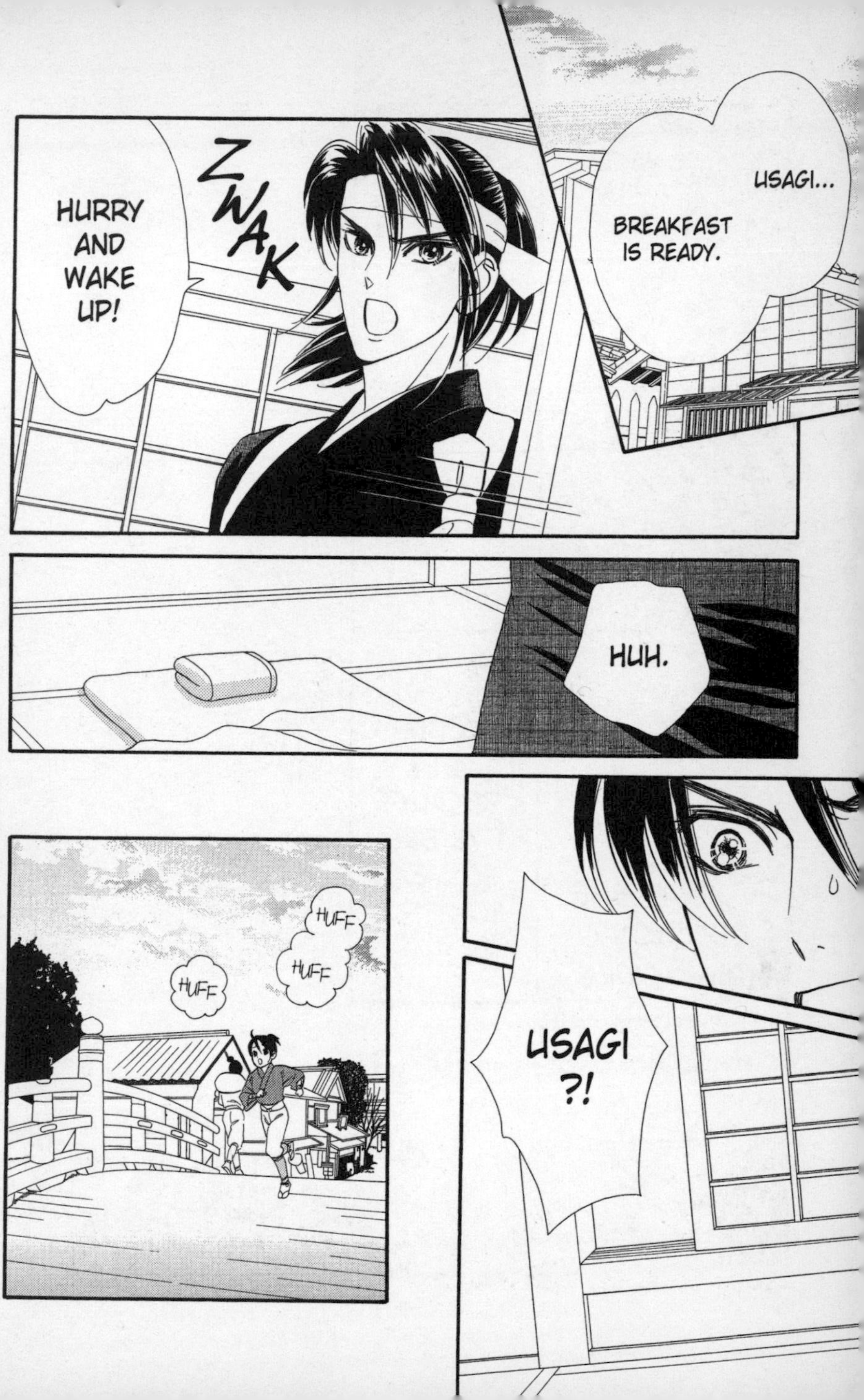
USAGI...
BREAKFAST IS READY.
ZWAK
HURRY AND WAKE UP!
HUH.
USAGI ?!
HUFF
HUFF
HUFF

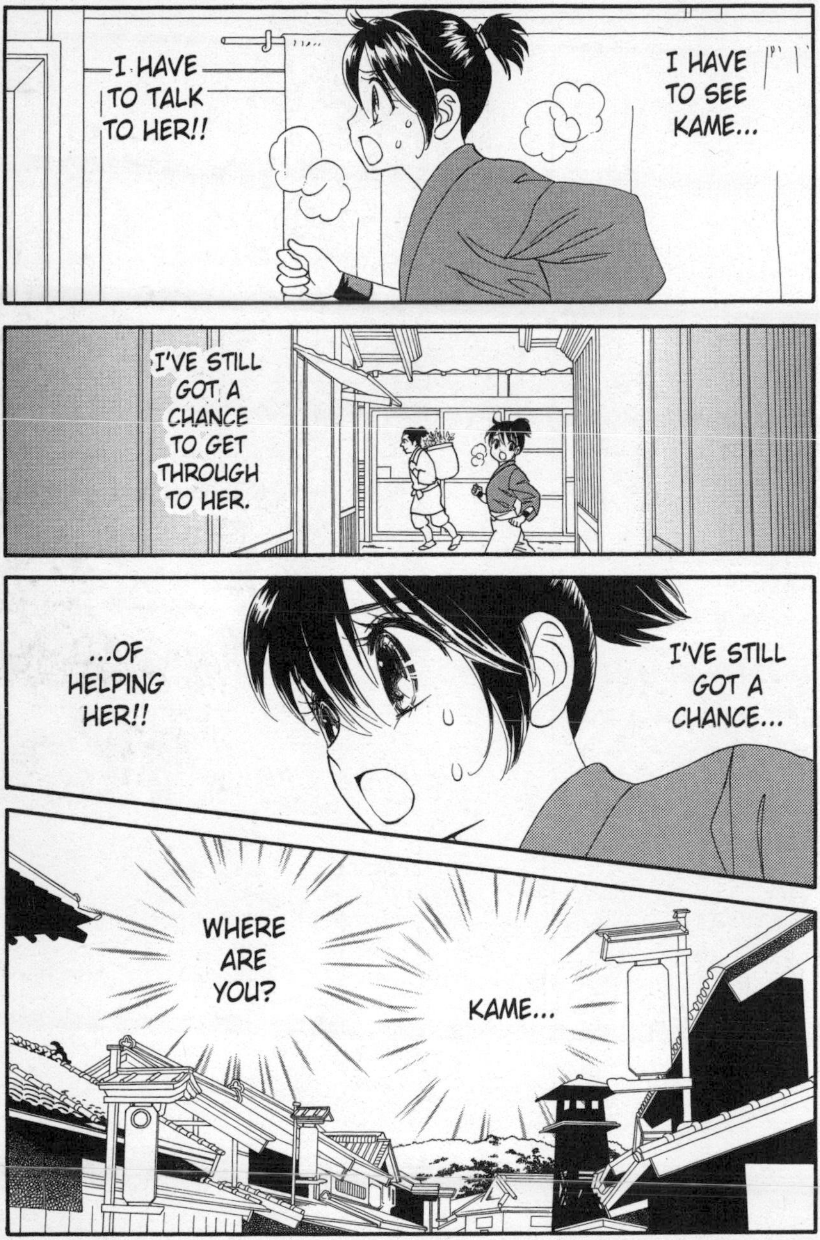
I HAVE TO SEE KAME...
I HAVE TO TALK TO HER!!
I'VE STILL GOT A CHANCE TO GET THROUGH TO HER.
I'VE STILL GOT A CHANCE...
...OF HELPING HER!!
KAME...
WHERE ARE YOU?

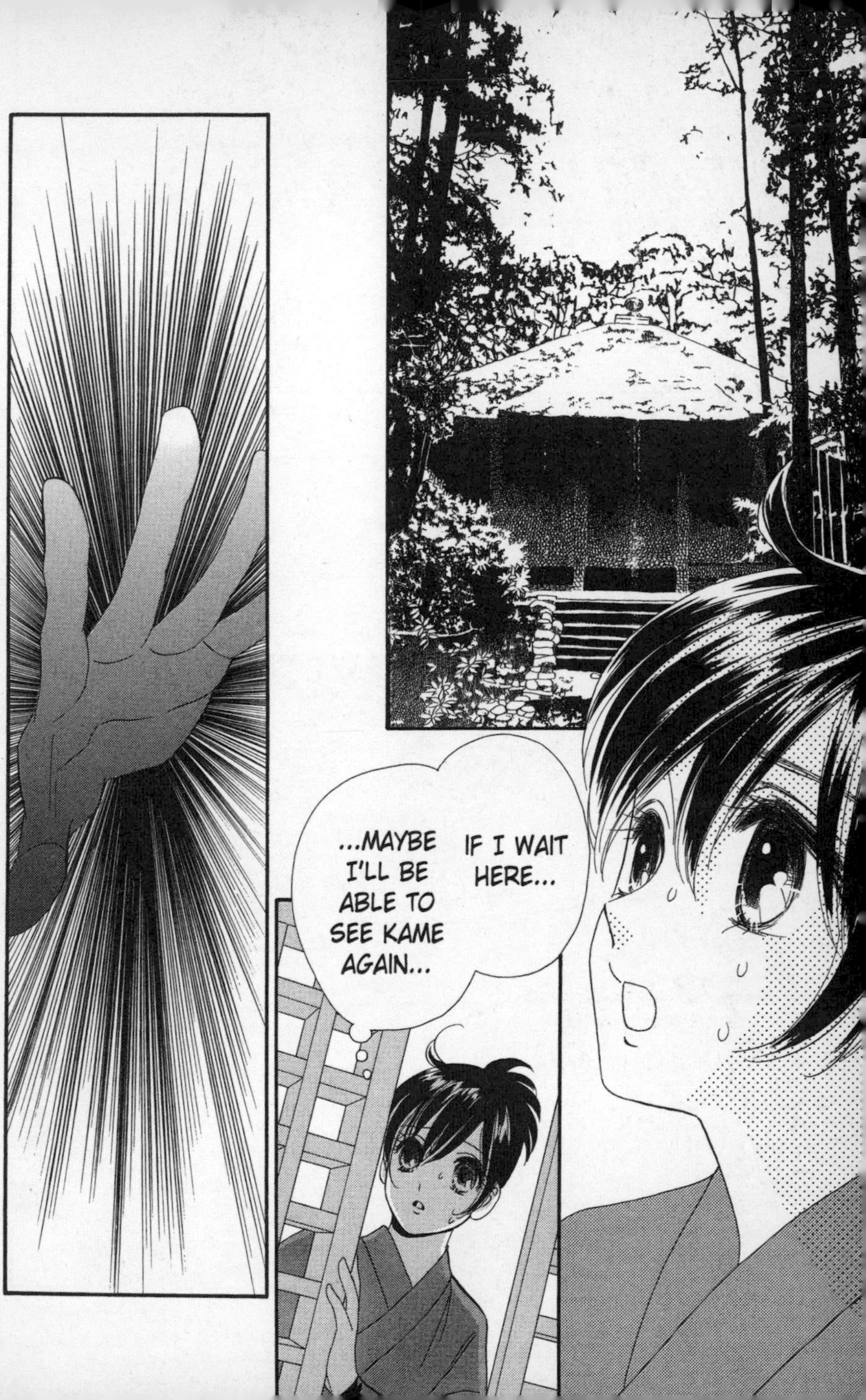
IF I WAIT HERE...
...MAYBE I'LL BE ABLE TO SEE KAME AGAIN...

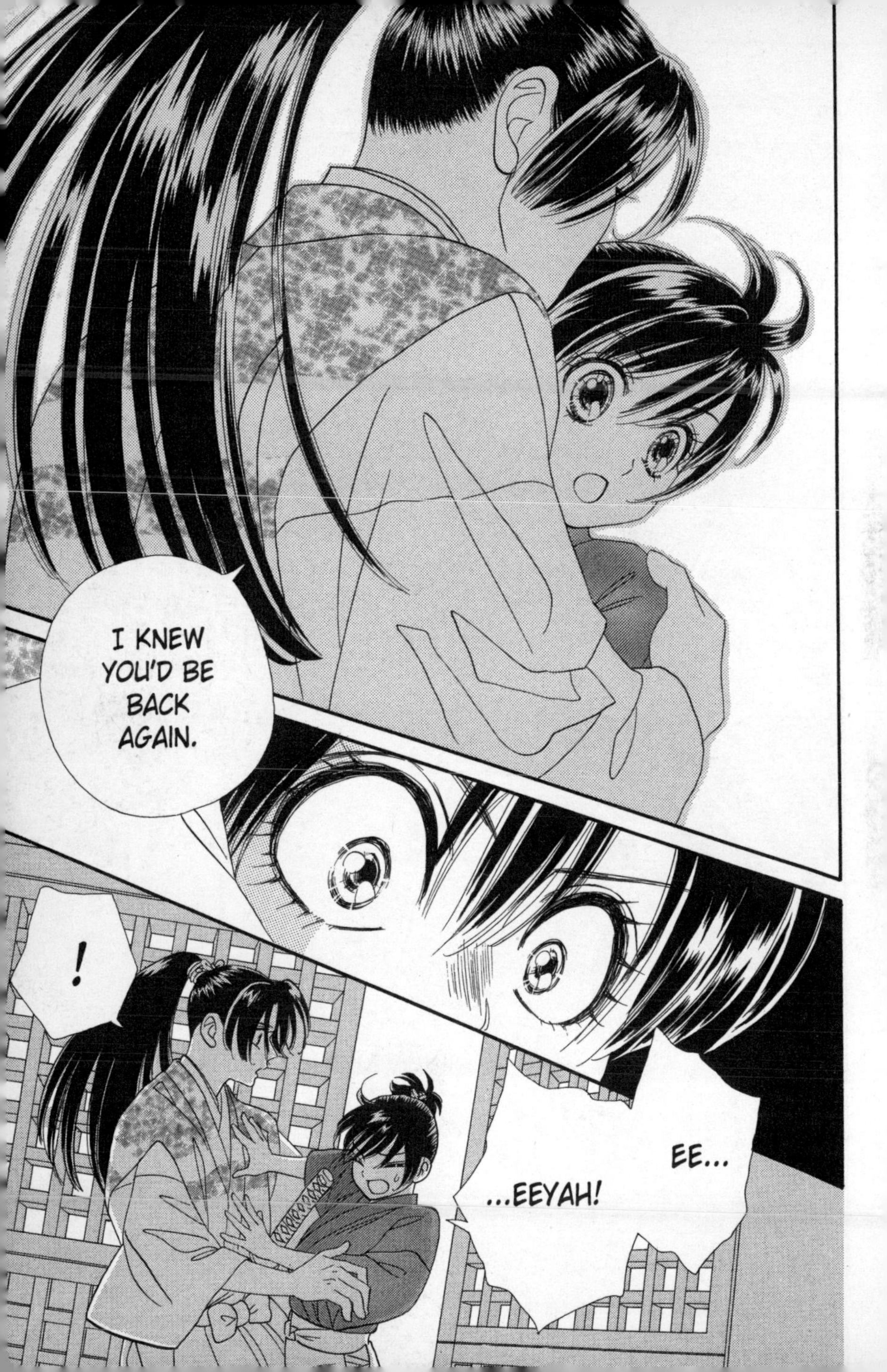
I KNEW YOU'D BE BACK AGAIN.
EE...
...EEYAH!
!

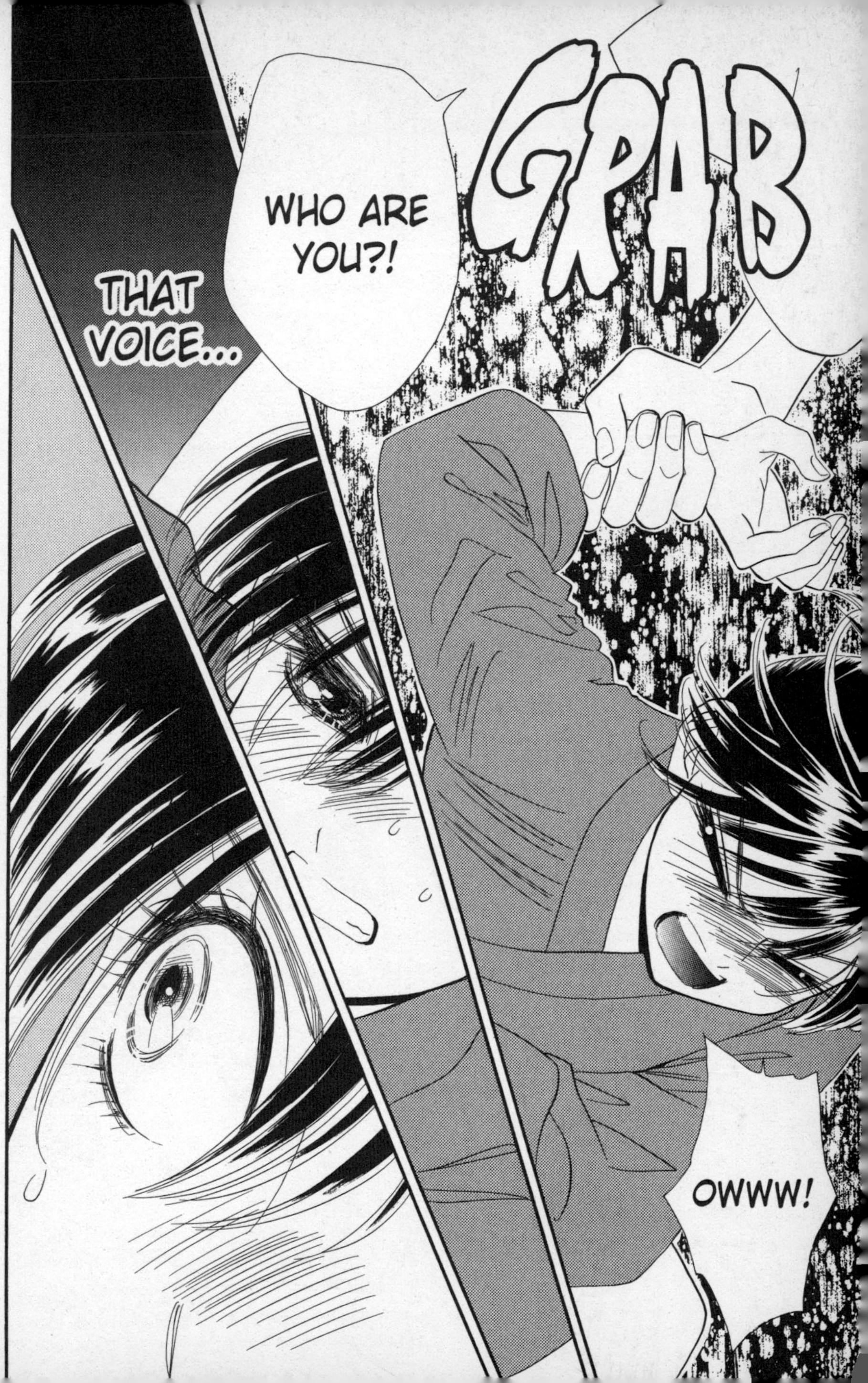
GRAB
WHO ARE YOU?!
OWWW!
THAT VOICE...

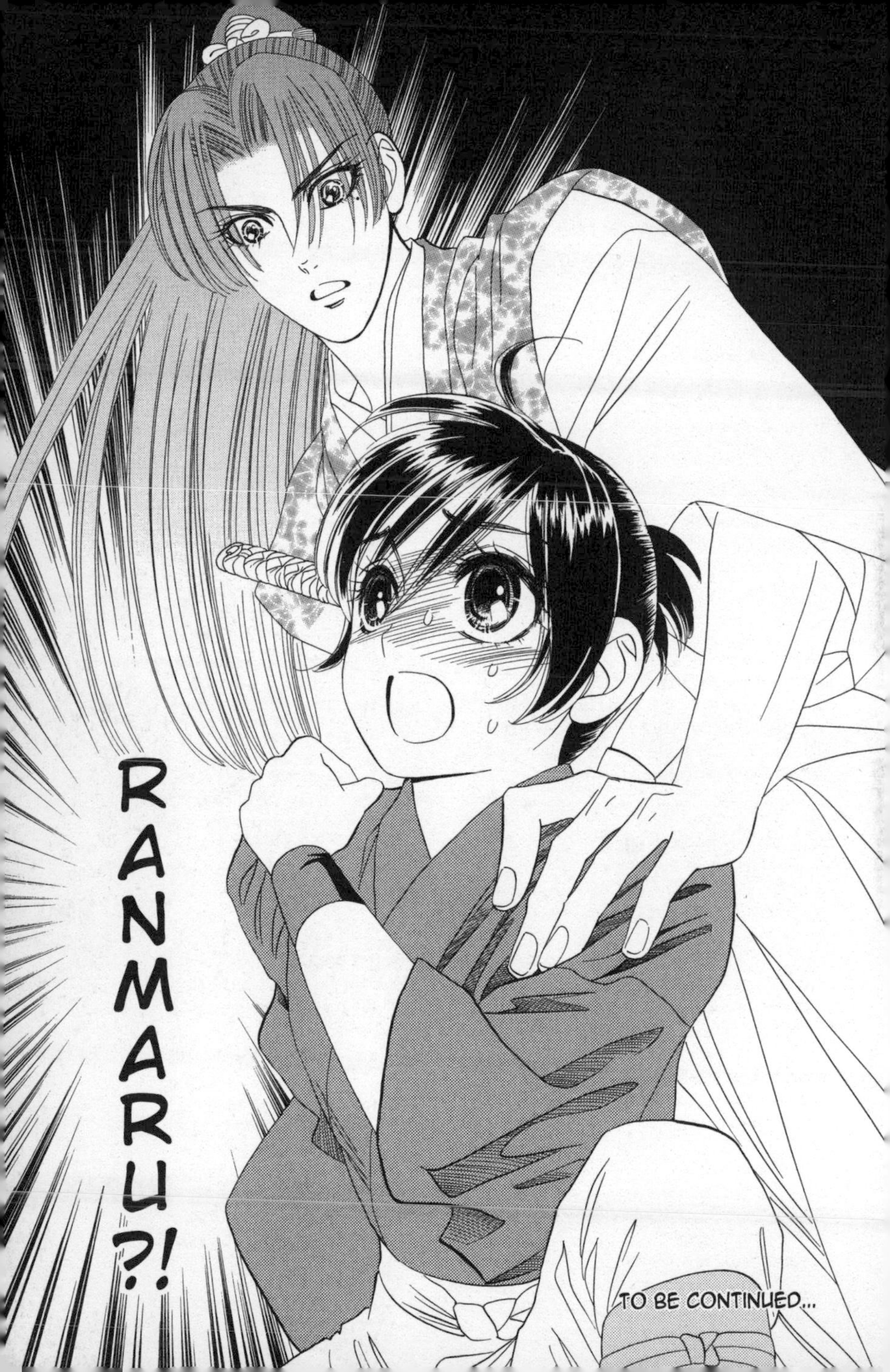
RANMARU?!
TO BE CONTINUED...

> *The ways of the ninja are mysterious indeed, so here is a glossary of terms to help you navigate the intricacies of their world.*

Page 2: Azuchi
Azuchi is on Lake Biwa in Shiga Prefecture, where Oda Nobunaga built his castle and the town that were the center of his operations.

Page 2: Honnoji
Honnoji is a temple in Kyoto. Oda Nobunaga often stayed here when he traveled to the capital.

Page 10, panel 3: Sakai
Sakai is a city in Osaka prefecture that is one of the largest and most important seaports in Japan. Once known for samurai swords, Sakai is now famous for quality kitchen knives and other cutlery.

Page 21, panel 4: Kunoichi
A term often used for female ninja. The word is spelled く ノ 一, and when combined, the letters form the kanji for woman, 女。

Page 35, panel 2: Mitsuhide Akechi
Mitsuhide Akechi became one of Oda Nobunaga's retainers after Nobunaga's conquest of Mino province (now Gifu prefecture) in 1566. Akechi is known to have been more of an intellectual and a pacifier than a warrior.

Page 56: Yatagarasu
The Yatagarasu is a three-legged raven that appears in Japanese mythology. It is the bird of the sun goddess Amaterasu.

Page 2: Shimo no Hanzo
Shimo no means "the Lower," and in this case refers to Hanzo's geographic location rather than social status.

Page 2: Iga
Iga is a region on the island of Honshu and also the name of the famous ninja clan that originated there. Another area famous for its ninja is Kouga, in the Shiga prefecture on Honshu. Many books claim that these two ninja clans were mortal enemies, but in reality inter-ninja relations were not as bad as stories might suggest.

Page 2: Ranmaru Mori
Ranmaru Mori is one of Nobunaga's most famous vassals. He became Oda Nobunaga's attendant at a young age and was recognized for his talent and loyalty.

Page 2: Okazaki
Okazaki is in Aichi Prefecture on the main island of Honshu, about 22 miles from Nagoya.

Page 2: Oda Nobunaga
Nobunaga lived from 1534 to 1582, and came close to unifying Japan. He is probably one of the most famous Japanese warlords. He was the first warlord to successfully incorporate the gun in battle, and was notorious for his ruthlessness.

Page 82: **Rakugo**

Rakugo is a type of traditional Japanese comedy where a storyteller sits on a large pillow called *zabuton*, uses a paper fan as a prop, and proceeds to tell a long and complicated comical story.

Page 134: **Usagi**

Usagi means "rabbit" in Japanese. In this case, Usagi is referring to herself and Hanzo in the rabbit costume as the pair.

Page 149, panel 1: **Kame**

Kame means "turtle" in Japanese.

Page 162: **Shinsengumi**

The Shinsengumi were a group of masterless samurai created as a special police force in the Kyoto area during the Tokugawa shogunate period. Their flag is famous for having the single kanji for "sincerity" on it.

Many types of animals appear in this manga. I had a puppy and a pet bird when I was young, but aside from that, I haven't had much to do with animals. Whenever an animal appears in the story, I need to flip through books and photos in order to draw them. Just when I finally get the hang of drawing animals, however, they tend to cease appearing in the manga. *Wry smile* Out of all the animals, I have the greatest difficulty drawing cats.

–Rinko Ueda

Rinko Ueda is from Nara prefecture. She enjoys listening to the radio, drama CDs, and Rakugo comedy performances. Her works include *Ryo*, a series based on the legend of Gojo Bridge, *Home*, a story about love crossing national boundaries, and *Tail of the Moon (Tsuki no Shippo)*, a romantic ninja comedy.

TAIL OF THE MOON
Vol. 9
The Shojo Beat Manga Edition

STORY & ART BY
RINKO UEDA

Translation & Adaptation/Tetsuichiro Miyaki
Touch-up Art & Lettering/Mark McMurray
Design/Izumi Hirayama
Editor/Amy Yu

Editor in Chief, Books/Alvin Lu
Editor in Chief, Magazines/Marc Weidenbaum
Sr. Director of Acquisitions/Rika Inouye
VP of Sales/Gonzalo Ferreyra
Sr. VP of Marketing/Liza Coppola
Publisher/Hyoe Narita

Printed in Canada

Published by VIZ Media, LLC
P.O. Box 77064
San Francisco, CA 94107

Shojo Beat Manga Edition
10 9 8 7 6 5 4 3 2 1
First printing, February 2008

www.viz.com store.viz.com

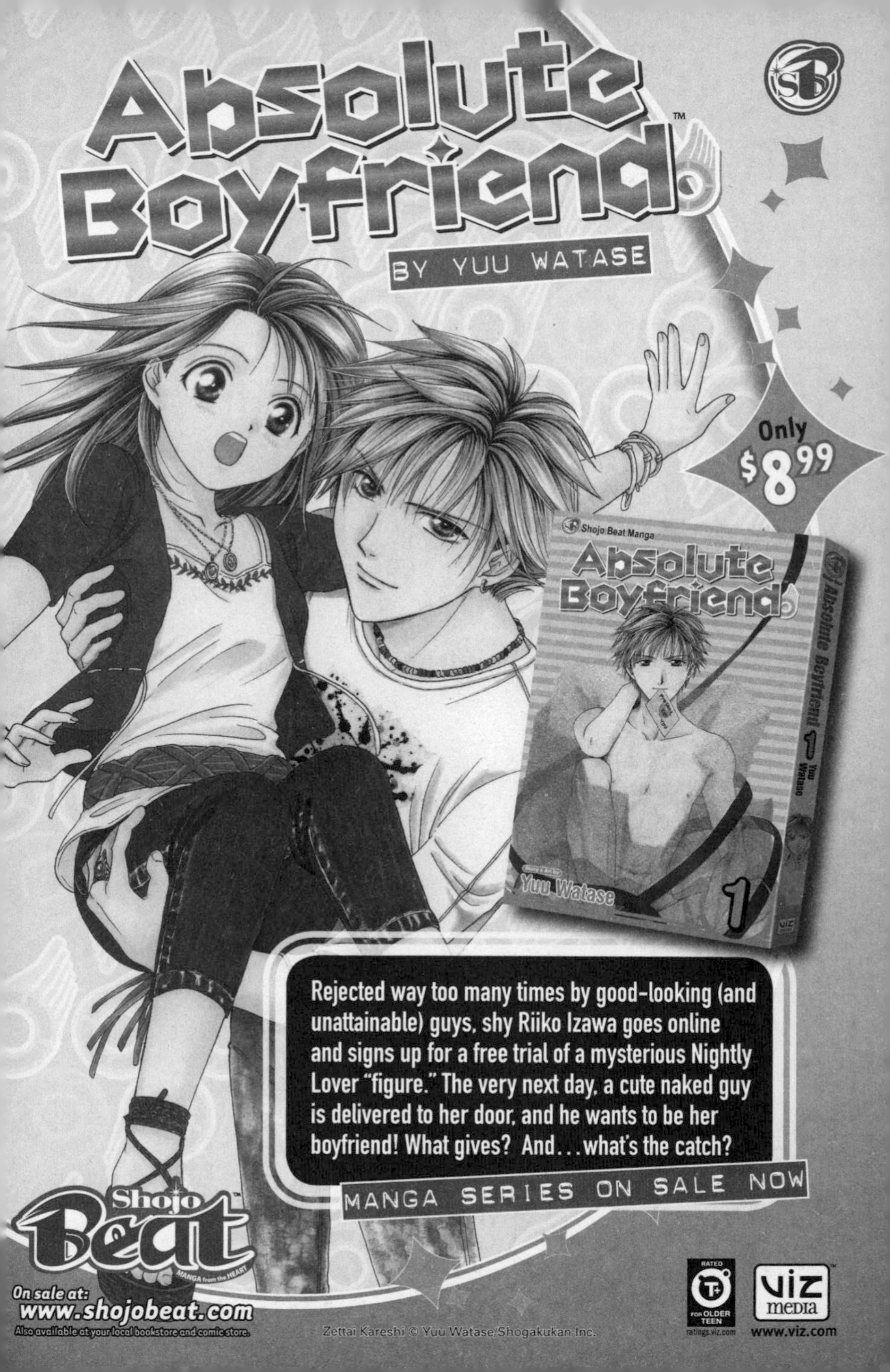
Absolute Boyfriend™
BY YUU WATASE
Only $8.99
Shojo Beat Manga
Absolute Boyfriend
Absolute Boyfriend 1 Yuu Watase
Yuu Watase
1
Rejected way too many times by good-looking (and unattainable) guys, shy Riiko Izawa goes online and signs up for a free trial of a mysterious Nightly Lover "figure." The very next day, a cute naked guy is delivered to her door, and he wants to be her boyfriend! What gives? And…what's the catch?
MANGA SERIES ON SALE NOW
Shojo Beat™
MANGA from the HEART
On sale at:
www.shojobeat.com
Also available at your local bookstore and comic store.
Zettai Kareshi © Yuu Watase/Shogakukan Inc.
RATED T+ FOR OLDER TEEN
ratings.viz.com
VIZ MEDIA
www.viz.com

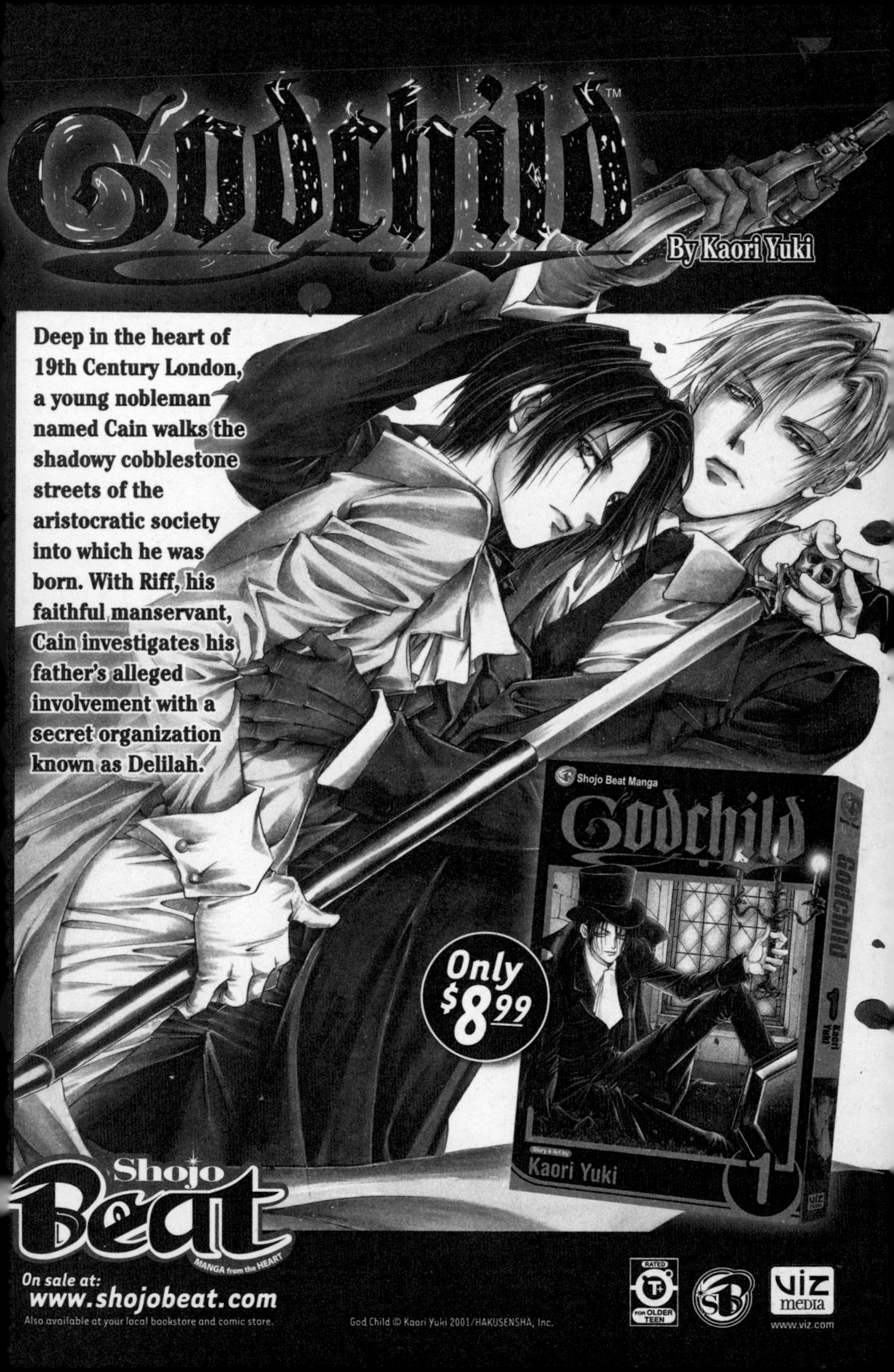

Godchild™
By Kaori Yuki
Deep in the heart of 19th Century London, a young nobleman named Cain walks the shadowy cobblestone streets of the aristocratic society into which he was born. With Riff, his faithful manservant, Cain investigates his father's alleged involvement with a secret organization known as Delilah.
Shojo Beat Manga
Godchild
Story & Art by
Kaori Yuki
1
Only $8.99
Shojo Beat™
MANGA from the HEART
On sale at:
www.shojobeat.com
Also available at your local bookstore and comic store.
God Child © Kaori Yuki 2001/HAKUSENSHA, Inc.
RATED T+ FOR OLDER TEEN
viz media
www.viz.com

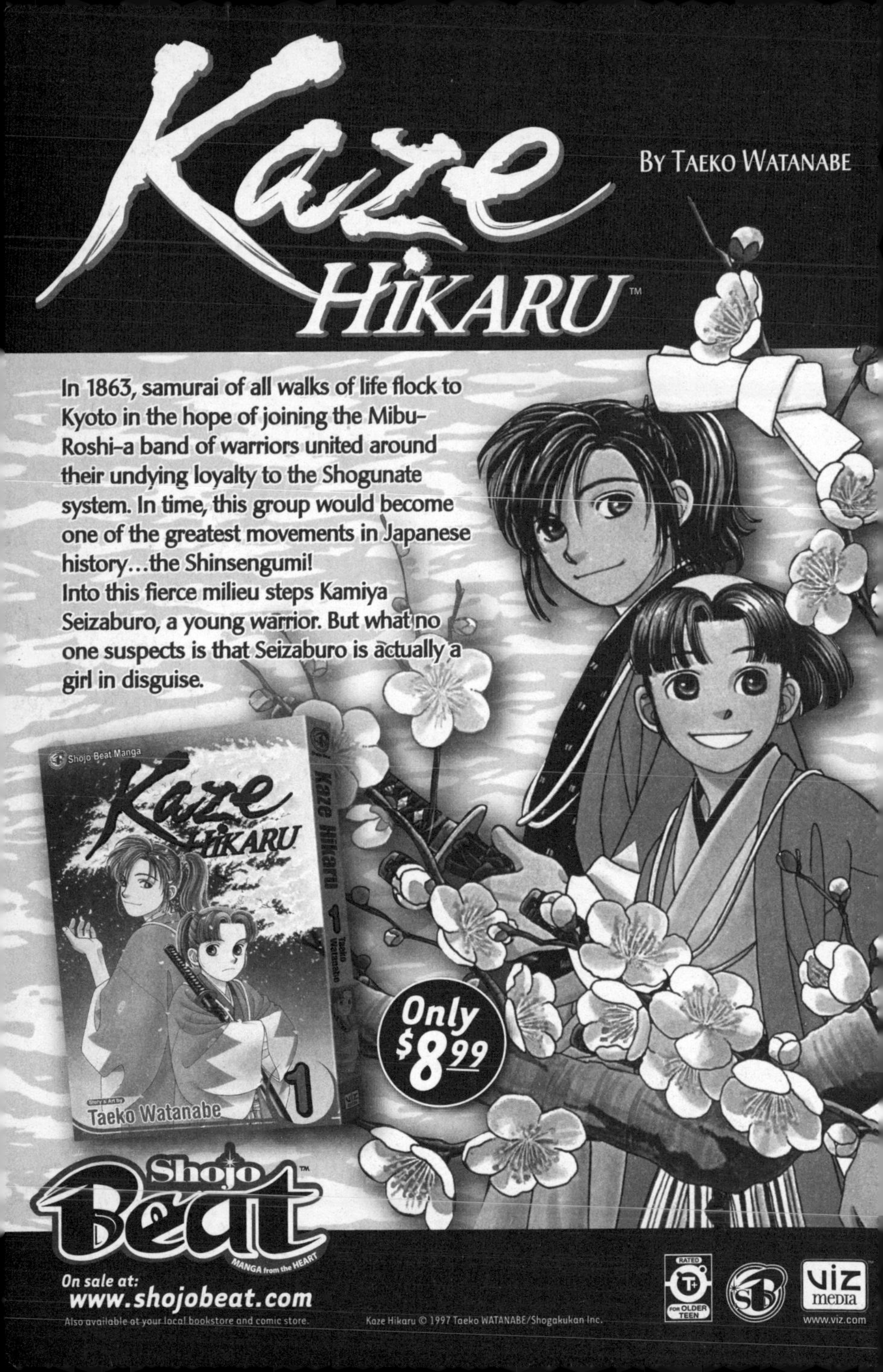
Kaze Hikaru™
By Taeko Watanabe
In 1863, samurai of all walks of life flock to Kyoto in the hope of joining the Mibu-Roshi–a band of warriors united around their undying loyalty to the Shogunate system. In time, this group would become one of the greatest movements in Japanese history…the Shinsengumi!
Into this fierce milieu steps Kamiya Seizaburo, a young warrior. But what no one suspects is that Seizaburo is actually a girl in disguise.
Shojo Beat Manga
Kaze Hikaru
Kaze Hikaru 1 Taeko Watanabe
Story & Art by
Taeko Watanabe
1
Only $8.99
Shojo Beat™
MANGA from the HEART
On sale at:
www.shojobeat.com
Also available at your local bookstore and comic store.
Kaze Hikaru © 1997 Taeko WATANABE/Shogakukan Inc.
RATED T+ FOR OLDER TEEN
viz media
www.viz.com

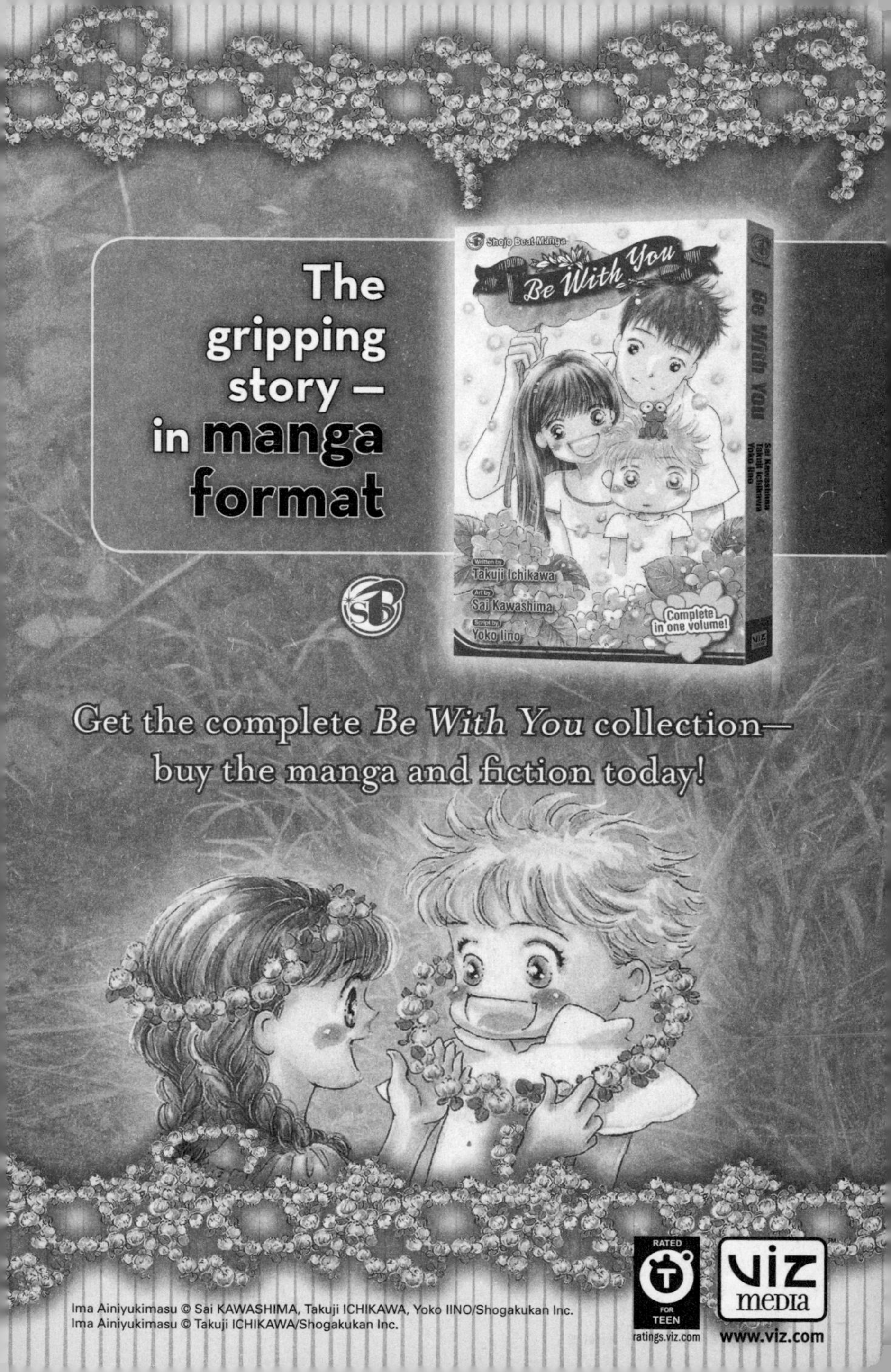

The gripping story — in manga format
Shojo Beat Manga
Be With You
Written by Takuji Ichikawa
Art by Sai Kawashima
Script by Yoko Iino
Complete in one volume!
Get the complete *Be With You* collection— buy the manga and fiction today!
Ima Ainiyukimasu © Sai KAWASHIMA, Takuji ICHIKAWA, Yoko IINO/Shogakukan Inc.
Ima Ainiyukimasu © Takuji ICHIKAWA/Shogakukan Inc.
RATED T FOR TEEN
ratings.viz.com
VIZ MEDIA
www.viz.com

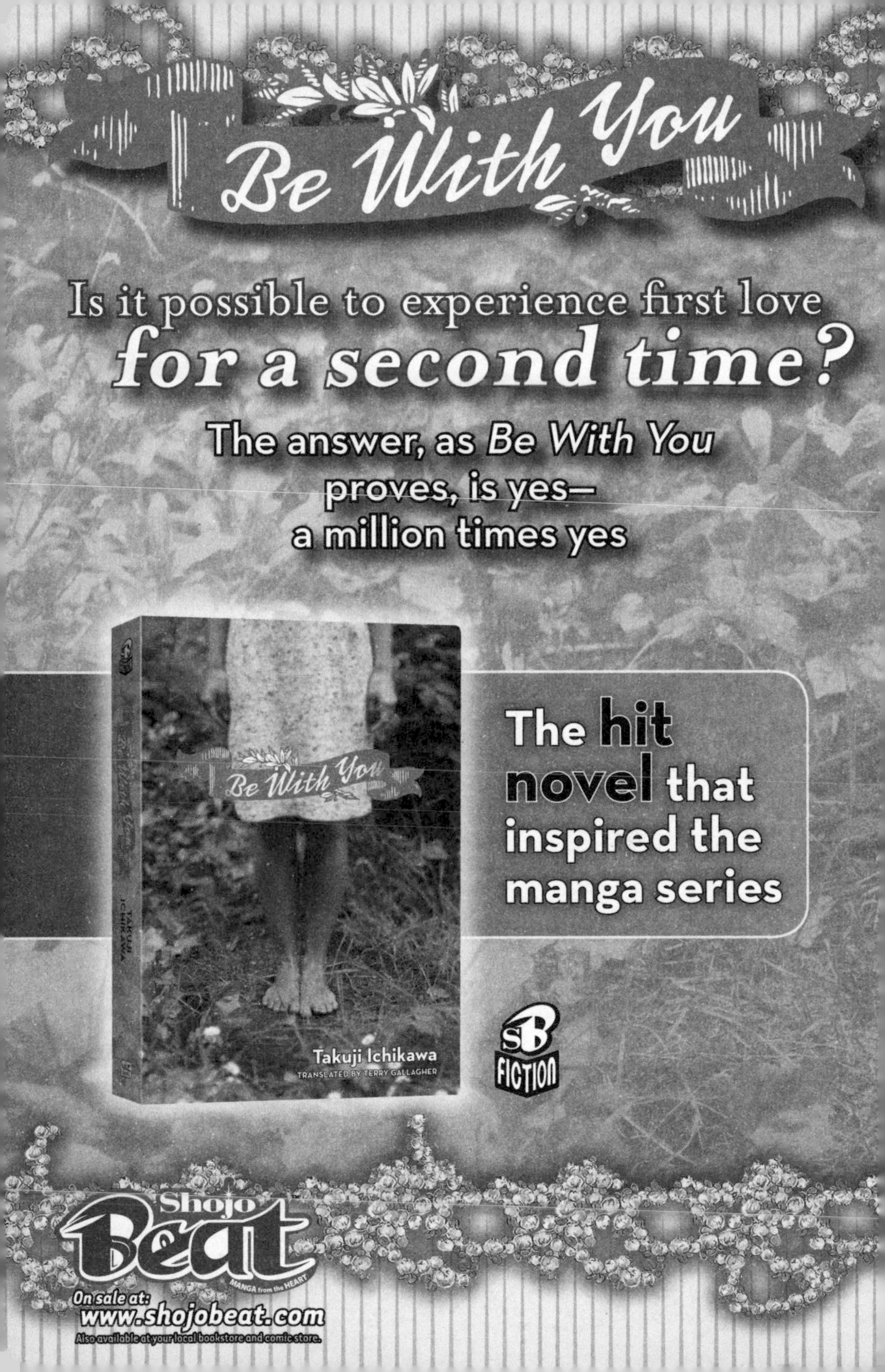
Be With You
Is it possible to experience first love
for a second time?
The answer, as Be With You
proves, is yes—
a million times yes
Be With You
Takuji Ichikawa
TRANSLATED BY TERRY GALLAGHER
The hit novel that inspired the manga series
SB FICTION
Shojo Beat
MANGA from the HEART
On sale at:
www.shojobeat.com
Also available at your local bookstore and comic store.

Tell us what you think about Shojo Beat Manga!

Our survey is now available online. Go to:

shojobeat.com/mangasurvey

Help us make our product offerings better!

Shojo Beat™

MANGA from the HEART

The Shojo Manga Authority

12 GIANT issues for ONLY $34.99*

That's **51% OFF** the cover price!

The most **ADDICTIVE** shojo manga stories from Japan **PLUS** unique editorial coverage on the arts, music, culture, fashion, and much more!

Subscribe NOW and become a member of the 🅱 Sub Club!

- **SAVE** 51% OFF the cover price
- **ALWAYS** get every issue
- **ACCESS** exclusive areas of www.shojobeat.com
- **FREE** members-only gifts several times a year

Strictly VIP!

3 EASY WAYS TO SUBSCRIBE!

1) Send in the subscription order form from this book **OR**
2) Log on to: www.shojobeat.com **OR**
3) Call 1-800-541-7876

VIZ media
www.viz.com